EVERY DAY
—A NEW—
BEGINNING

ALBERTO R. TIMM

 Pacific Press®
Publishing Association
Nampa, Idaho | www.pacificpress.com

EVERY DAY
—A NEW—
BEGINNING

ALBERTO R. TIMM

Pacific Press®
Publishing Association
Nampa, Idaho | www.pacificpress.com

Cover design: Daniel Añez
Cover design resources: GettyImages.com | amenic181, GettyImages.com | Jasmina007,
  GettyImages.com | EXTREME-PHOTOGRAPHER
Interior design: Aaron Troia

The author assumes full responsibility for the accuracy of all facts and quotations as cited in this book.

Purchase additional copies of this book by calling toll-free 1-800-765-6955 or by visiting Adventist BookCenter.com.

ISBN 978-0-8163-6827-3

July 2022

$\mathcal{D}$EDICATION

Dedicated
to my beloved wife,
Marly Lopes Timm,
whose unconditional support
was crucial during the whole process
of researching and writing
this book.

A Word to the Reader

New daily devotionals always generate expectations, and I am sure you have yours. So before we start our journey together this year, let me explain the overall approach I followed. When I was asked to write this book, I received the suggestion of combining, whenever possible, three basic elements: the theological, the historical, and the devotional. I liked the idea and tried to follow it as closely as possible in each of these short readings.

Each reading is related to a specific event or fact that occurred on that date in world history, within Christianity, the Seventh-day Adventist Church, the life of Ellen G. White, or other individuals. The historic date is always highlighted in bold. Your greatest temptation will be to question why I chose some less meaningful events, leaving out some far more important ones. My goal was to combine well-known happenings with not-so-obvious ones, providing room for at least some element of surprise. This approach is intended to help us draw spiritual lessons not only from religious events but also from everyday matters.

Why should we be concerned about the distant past? What is done is done. Fullness of life implies a harmonious balance between the past from which we came, the present in which we live, and the future toward which we are moving. But how should we relate to these three stages of life? One of the best answers is provided in the threefold counsel often attributed to Albert Einstein, "Learn from Yesterday. Live for Today. Hope for Tomorrow." According to Spanish philosopher George Santayana, "Those who cannot remember the past are condemned to repeat it."[1]

It is worthwhile to reflect on the following statement by Ellen White:

Live the life of faith day by day. Do not become anxious and distressed about the time of trouble, and thus have a time of trouble beforehand. Do not keep thinking, "I am afraid I shall not stand in the great testing day." You are to live for the present, for this day only. Tomorrow is not yours. Today you are to maintain the victory over self. Today you are to live a life of prayer. Today you are to fight the good fight of faith. Today you are to believe that God blesses you. And as you gain the victory over darkness and unbelief, you will meet the requirements of the Master, and will become a blessing to those around you.[2]

May every day of this new year bring you a deeper experience with our wonderful Lord and Savior, Jesus Christ!

—Alberto R. Timm

An Open Door

"I know your works. See, I have set before you an open door, and no one can shut it; for you have a little strength, have kept My word, and have not denied My name."

—Revelation 3:8

Every New Year brings about new expectations and new challenges. But when was **January 1** chosen as New Year's Day? We are indebted to ancient Romans for this. For political and military reasons, in 153 BC, the Roman Senate set January 1 as the beginning of the new year. Despite some disagreement, the day was kept in both the Julian calendar, adopted in 46 BC, and the Gregorian calendar, adopted first in 1582 by most Catholic countries and later by others.

Some historians argue that the name January (Latin *Ianuarius*) derives from the Latin term *ianua* (door) because January is the door to the year. But most historians associate January with Janus, the Roman god of doors and gates, of beginnings and transitions. As a two-faced god, he could look back to the past and forward to the future. At any rate, both possible interpretations express the notion of an open door to the future.

In contrast to the ancient Roman god Janus, Jesus Christ presents Himself to us as the "way" (John 14:6), "the Alpha and the Omega, the Beginning and the End, the First and the Last" (Revelation 22:13), and the One who has set before us "an open door, and no one can shut it" (Revelation 3:8). He has graciously opened for us the door of access to a new set of 365 time segments that we call days.

We are just starting our journey into this new year, and every single day is a new beginning. And we are not alone in our journey. In Matthew 28:20, Christ promised us, "I am with you always, even to the end of the age"; or, as stated in *The Message* paraphrase, "I'll be with you . . . day after day after day, right up to the end of the age." This means that He will be with us on our cloudy and rainy days as well as our sunny ones.

Keep in mind that your life is a succession of days, and each day is your life in miniature. Without change, you will remain just what you are. If change is needed, why not begin today? Make the best of your life for God's sake and for the sake of lost humanity, in need of salvation. With God by your side every day, this can be the best year of your life. Happy New Year!

A Dim View

For now we see in a mirror, dimly, but then face to face. Now I know in part, but then I shall know just as I also am known.

—1 Corinthians 13:12

Photographs perpetuate our most precious memories. They bring our past to life again, giving wings to our imagination and touching our deepest feelings. Indeed, as Edward Steichen supposedly noted, "a portrait is not made in the camera but on either side of it." And "a true photograph need not be explained, nor can it be contained in words."[1] Today almost everyone is an amateur photographer, sharing pictures through social media. But it has not always been this way.

In 1826 or 1827, the French inventor Nicéphore Niépce took the earliest known photograph of a real-world scene. On **January 2, 1839**, another Frenchman, Louis Daguerre, took the first reported picture of the moon. Unfortunately, two months later, a fire destroyed his laboratory, including that picture. Those early pictures were black-and-white, presenting only a dim view of reality. They could not reproduce all the beauty of the people and scenes photographed. From those early days, photography has passed through many stages of development, using metallic plates, glass plates, plastic films, and Polaroid papers, and photographers have used different chemical substances to capture the light's effects.

Even so, your best modern digital photographs cannot portray the full panorama and majesty of your favorite places. Having no feelings in themselves, they are only images evoking memories. A photo of a sunset is the image of the actual sunset and not vice versa, for there is much more in the real sunset than in its picture. Likewise, the book of Revelation provides only a dim and vague picture of the heavenly realm; its description of heaven is far from representing its full glory and majesty (1 Corinthians 13:12).

While we are still in this world, we should keep in mind the insightful words attributed to Ziad K. Abdelnour: "Life is like a camera. Focus on what's important. Capture the good times. And if things don't work out, just take another shot." But when God takes us from this world into heaven, from time into eternity, then all our best pictures of this life will lose their significance. Then we "will see his face," and He will be our light (Revelation 22:4, 5). In the very presence of God, we will find the fullest expression of our existence!

$\mathcal{A}$UTUMN $\mathcal{L}$EAVES

"But you shall receive power when the Holy Spirit has come upon you; and you shall be witnesses to Me in Jerusalem, and in all Judea and Samaria, and to the end of the earth."

—Acts 1:8

Forests can be classified in different ways and from different perspectives. For example, by latitude, the three main types of forests are tropical, temperate, and boreal. From the perspective of how their foliage reacts to seasonal changes, we have evergreen forests and deciduous forests. While the former consist entirely or mainly of trees that retain green foliage throughout the whole year, the latter are dominated by broad-leaved trees that lose their leaves each year.

Ellen White drew helpful spiritual lessons from trees. The evergreens exemplify the commitment we should have to God and His Word. She stated, "In summer there is no noticeable difference between *evergreens* and other trees; but when the blasts of winter come, the *evergreens* remain unchanged, while other trees are stripped of their foliage. So the falsehearted professor may not now be distinguished from the real Christian, but the time [of religious intolerance] is just upon us when the difference will be apparent."[2]

Deciduous trees provide an illustration of the spreading of Adventist literature around the world. On **January 3, 1875**, when the Seventh-day Adventist Church had only one printing press in Battle Creek, Michigan, Ellen White saw in vision printing presses in other countries printing the message in many languages. Years later, she visited Basel, Switzerland, and Oslo, Norway, and recognized their newly established publishing houses as among those she had seen in the vision. She had a similar experience in the 1890s when she visited Echo Publishing House in Australia.[3] And in 1878, she wrote that Adventist "publications must be multiplied, and scattered like the *leaves of autumn*. These silent messengers are enlightening and molding the minds of thousands in every country and in every clime."[4] As the deciduous forests cover the ground with their leaves during the autumn and winter seasons, so should we now help cover the whole world with Adventist publications.

Science and Religion

"He stretches out the north over empty space; He hangs the earth on nothing."
—Job 26:7

Many contemporary scientists argue that it is impossible to believe in God and be a serious scholar. But several scientists who helped lay the very foundations of modern science were creationists. A notable example is Sir Isaac Newton, who was born at Woolsthorpe Manor in Lincolnshire, England, on **January 4, 1643** (or December 25, 1642, on the Julian calendar). Considered by many the most influential scientist ever, Newton helped advance the fields of physics, astronomy, mathematics, and the natural sciences. He is widely known for his law of universal gravitation, his three laws of motion, and his studies on the refraction of light.

In 1676 Newton confessed, "If I have seen further, it is by standing upon ye sholders of Giants."[5] Later he added, "I do not know what I may appear to the world; but to myself I seem to have been only like a boy playing on the seashore, and diverting myself in now and then finding a smoother pebble or a prettier shell than ordinary, whilst the great ocean of truth lay all undiscovered before me."[6]

In contrast to modern scientists who believe that science has the final word about the origin and complexity of the universe, Newton affirmed, "But it is not to be conceived that mere mechanical causes could give birth to so many regular motions" as observed in the planetary system.[7] He also asserted, "Gravity may put the planets into motion, but without the Divine Power it could never put them into such a circulating motion as they have about the sun; and therefore for this, as well as other reasons, I am compelled to ascribe the frame of this system to an intelligent Agent."[8]

Aware of the limitations of human science and reason, Newton never lost his confidence in God as Creator and "Universal Ruler." He wrote more about religion than about science. In 1733 his famous work *Observations Upon the Prophecies of Daniel, and the Apocalypse of St. John* was published posthumously in London.

For Newton, "opposite to godliness is Atheism in profession, and idolatry in practice."[9] In other words, there is no real atheism but only a transference of worship. Those who do not worship God are either worshiping themselves or creating their own favorite gods, whoever or whatever those may be.

Wisdom Instead of Wealth

God appeared to Solomon, and said to him, "Ask! What shall I give you?"
And Solomon said to God: ". . . Now give me wisdom and knowledge."
—2 Chronicles 1:7–10

Can someone simultaneously be a person of science and a person of God? That was true of the African American George Washington Carver (ca. 1864–1943). A man of humble origins, Carver built a successful career as a botanist and inventor. He began each day with a prayer, asking God to reveal secrets to him about plants and vegetables. The story is told that he once prayed, "Mr. Creator, what was the universe made for?" And God replied, "You want to know too much." When Carver asked, "Mr. Creator, what is the peanut for?" God supposedly said, "That's more like it."[10]

Carver discovered more than three hundred uses for the peanut, including various kinds of foods, oil, paint, ink, soap, shampoo, facial cream, and plastics; he made more than one hundred products from the sweet potato, including flour, starch, and synthetic rubber. He was a world-class expert in botany and agriculture, and many sought his advice, including Mahatma Gandhi and Joseph Stalin. Thomas Edison and Henry Ford invited him to work for them. But Carver preferred to remain in his own laboratory—which he called "God's little workshop"—and, from there, to help his fellow human beings.[11]

He could have become substantially wealthy by patenting his discoveries, but he decided to leave them unpatented so that poor people could make the products he discovered without paying royalties. Carver died on **January 5, 1943**, leaving us an example of altruistic service. The epitaph on his grave on the Tuskegee University campus says: "He could have added fortune to fame, but caring for neither, he found happiness and honor in being helpful to the world."

What is the motivation of our own lives? The same King Solomon who asked God to grant him "wisdom and knowledge" (2 Chronicles 1:7–10) also said that "a good name is to be chosen rather than great riches" (Proverbs 22:1). The unselfish examples of the good Samaritan (Luke 10:25–37), of Dorcas (Acts 9:36–39), and of George Washington Carver should not remain as monuments of the past to merely be admired. They should motivate us to overcome our self-centered tendencies and live unselfish lives for the sake of humanity. By God's grace, you can make a difference too!

ORPHANS' TEARS

Pure and undefiled religion before God and the Father is this: to visit orphans
and widows in their trouble, and to keep oneself unspotted from the world.
—James 1:27

Life magazine of July 23, 1951, carried an article by Michael Rougier entitled "The Little Boy Who Wouldn't Smile." It is the touching story of Kang Koo Ri, a boy who lived with his parents and an older brother in a small house fifteen miles north of Seoul, South Korea. During the Korean War, when Kang was five years old, the village in which the family lived was destroyed, and a squad came to rescue the civilians who were still alive. At Kang's house, they shouted for any survivors, but there was no response. Looking more carefully, one of the soldiers saw the small naked figure of Kang crouched against the wall in the far corner, his eyes wide open. In another corner, they noticed a woman's body lying on a straw mattress, covered with maggots and flies. Kang's mother had evidently been dead for several days. But there was no sign of Kang's older brother or his father.[12]

"As Kang was carried away," the narrative continues, "he raised an arm in the direction of the house. Tears coursed down his cheeks and his body shook in spasms. The G.I.s thought that he was trying to say something, but no sound came. All the way back, he cried steadily, tears streaming from his eyes but no sound at all coming from his throat."[13] Back at the regimental command post, the chaplain described Kang as "a lot of very small bones held together by Lord knows what."[14] At the orphanage, he had no emotional strength to socialize. "Bewildered and speechless, he turned his back on the other children and walked away, his eyes wet with tears. There he stood, with one hand twisting the thumb of the other hand, his legs sagging slightly and his eyes on the ground."[15] Time passed, but Kang continued to ask to be taken back to his brother!

Kang is just one example of many thousands of war orphans who suffer from post-traumatic stress disorder. By an initiative of the French organization SOS Enfants En Détresse, **January 6** has been chosen as the World Day for War Orphans. According to James 1:27, it is our sacred duty to care for those lonely children of God who do not have anyone else to care for them. They need to see in us a reflection of God's love for a dying world.

ℕIKOLA 𝒯ESLA

"For which of you, intending to build a tower, does not sit down
first and count the cost, whether he has enough to finish it—lest,
after he has laid the foundation, and is not able to finish, all who see it begin
to mock him, saying, 'This man began to build and was not able to finish.' "

—Luke 14:28–30

M any projects have failed because creativity and idealism took precedence over planning and budgeting. A proverb says, "Stretch your legs according to the size of your quilt." A similar saying advises, "Stretch your arm no further than your sleeve will reach."[16] These sayings are not intended to kill your dreams and ambitions but only to remind you to live within your means and not dream of things you cannot achieve.

Nikola Tesla (1856–1943) was a talented inventor, engineer, physicist, and futurist. Born in the Austrian Empire (now Croatia), Tesla immigrated in 1884 to the United States to work with Thomas Edison. With financial backers, Tesla soon set up his own laboratories and companies to develop a range of electrical devices. With his brilliant mind, he "invented, predicted or contributed to development of hundreds of technologies that play big parts in our daily lives—like the remote control, neon and fluorescent lights, wireless transmission, computers, smartphones, laser beams, x-rays, robotics and, of course, alternating current, the basis of our present-day electrical system."[17]

With funding from a group of investors, in 1901, Tesla began to build a lab with a power plant and a tower able to transmit electricity all over the world. Eventually, the investors, worried about profit, withdrew their financial backing. Ultimately, in 1917, the US government demolished the unfinished tower for fear that German spies would use it to intercept communications during World War I. The great inventor lived the final years of his life in social isolation and financial poverty. He died on **January 7, 1943**, in his modest hotel room in New York City.

It's good to be idealistic and dream great dreams—if they can be achieved. Plan projects that will succeed and live within your budget, even if it means living a simpler life.

*U*NBIBLICAL *T*RADITIONS

"You nullify the word of God for the sake of your tradition."
—Matthew 15:6, NIV

Throughout the centuries, many unbiblical traditions have been ecclesiastically defended as biblical absolutes. Such dogmatic postures have distorted several of the Bible's teachings, inhibited the understanding of truth, and confused faith with credulity. This was evident in the Roman Catholic stance during the debate between geocentric (earth-centered) and heliocentric (sun-centered) theories of astronomy in the sixteenth and seventeenth centuries.

Ancient Greeks believed that the earth was the center of the solar system, which became the predominant view. By contrast, Polish astronomer Nicolaus Copernicus suggested that the sun was the center. In 1632, the heliocentric model was further endorsed in the book *Dialogue Concerning the Two Chief World Systems* by Italian astronomer and physicist Galileo Galilei (1564–1642). Despite his outstanding scientific contribution, Galileo was punished for heresy by the Roman Catholic Church. On June 22, 1633, the seventy-year-old astronomer went before the Inquisition in Rome, wearing the white shirt of a penitent. He was found "vehemently suspect of heresy, namely, of having believed and held the doctrine—which is false and contrary to the sacred and divine Scriptures—that the Sun is the centre of the world and does not move from east to west and that the Earth moves and is not the centre of the world."[18] Galileo's book was burned, and he was placed under house arrest until his death on **January 8, 1642**.

Some have argued that the Bible teaches the geocentric model. For instance, King David spoke of the sun as

like a bridegroom coming out of his chamber. . . .
Its rising is from one end of heaven,
And its circuit to the other end;
And there is nothing hidden from its heat (Psalm 19:4–6).

King Solomon added, "The sun also rises, and the sun goes down, and hastens to the place where it arose" (Ecclesiastes 1:5).

Do these statements teach that the earth is the center of the solar system? Not necessarily. These Bible verses use poetic, not scientific, language. Today, we commonly use the terms *sunrise* and *sunset* without defending a geocentric model. Why should we then expect the Bible to use language that we don't even use in our daily conversation? We also should avoid reading into the Bible our modern concepts, theories, and traditions.

ADVENTIST SCHOOLS

"And this is eternal life, that they may know You,
the only true God, and Jesus Christ whom You have sent."

—John 17:3

Evangelism and education go hand in hand. Through evangelism, we reach all social segments. Through education, we shape new generations. Looking at the world map, we can say that the Adventist Church is strong and healthy where both lines of work are healthy. This means that the right place for Adventist children to study is in Adventist schools. But what if our own church members no longer value Adventist education?

In the *Advent Review and Sabbath Herald* of **January 9, 1894**, Ellen White wrote, "When those who have reached the years of youth and manhood see no difference between our schools and the colleges of the world, and have no preference as to which they attend, though error is taught by precept and example in the schools of the world, then there is need of closely examining the reasons that lead to such a conclusion. Our institutions of learning may swing into worldly conformity. Step by step they may advance to the world; but they are prisoners of hope, and God will correct and enlighten them, and bring them back to their upright position of distinction from the world. I am watching with intense interest, hoping to see our schools thoroughly imbued with the spirit of true and undefiled religion."[19]

One year later, on **January 9, 1895**, Mrs. White wrote, "The end of all true education is expressed in the words of Christ: 'This is life eternal that they might know Thee, the only true God, and Jesus Christ, whom Thou hast sent.' [John 17:3]."[20] Spirituality should never be used as an excuse for poor academic performance, nor can academic excellence replace spiritual commitment. Each complements the other. If our schools are losing their spiritual identity, it is high time to rescue that identity so that they can fulfill the very purpose of their existence!

As a church and as families, we must unify our efforts in supporting Adventist education by raising the spiritual and academic levels of our schools and by encouraging every family to put their children in our schools. Let's criticize less and do more for the future generations of Adventists. Our students must be carefully prepared for this life and for eternity.

CROSSING THE RIVER

And Joshua said to the people, "Sanctify yourselves,
for tomorrow the LORD will do wonders among you."

—Joshua 3:5

The Rubicon River, in the north of Italy, marked the boundary between the Roman province of Cisalpine Gaul and Italy itself, which was controlled directly by Rome. No general of any Roman province could enter Italy as the head of his troops. To do so was a capital offense. But on **January 10**, 49 BC, Julius Caesar, with his legion, intentionally crossed the Rubicon and ignited civil war. Pompey and many of the Senate fled from Rome in fear. The idiom "crossing the Rubicon" is derived from that incident and means to make a difficult decision at a juncture from whence there is no way back.

Many centuries earlier, the Israelites also came to the borders of a river—the Jordan River—and had to cross it into the Promised Land. It was the time of year when the river was overflowing "all its banks" (Joshua 3:15). There were no bridges or boats to use. Only one thing could sustain them at that crucial moment: faith in the infallible word of God! "Joshua said to the people, 'Consecrate yourselves, for tomorrow the LORD will do wonders among you' " (Joshua 3:5, NASB). God opened the waters of the river, and the Israelites crossed on dry ground.

The crossing of the Jordan River has inspired innumerable sermons and many songs. This dramatic incident demonstrates that God can solve even our most unsolvable problems. Like the Israelites, we, too, need to trust in God, consecrate ourselves to Him, and then allow Him to work out His plans for our lives. Faith is the essential condition for Him to act effectively in our lives. As Jesus said to Martha, "Did I not say to you that if you would believe you would see the glory of God?" (John 11:40).

Some have noted a parallel between the Israelites' crossing of the Jordan into the land of Canaan and the saints being finally taken from this world to the heavenly Mount Zion. "They shall neither hunger anymore nor thirst anymore; the sun shall not strike them, nor any heat; for the Lamb who is in the midst of the throne will shepherd them and lead them to living fountains of waters. And God will wipe away every tear from their eyes" (Revelation 7:16, 17). You and I must be there as well!

𝒯HANKFULNESS

In everything give thanks; for this is the will of God in Christ Jesus for you.
—1 Thessalonians 5:18

Life becomes much more meaningful and attractive when adorned by the beautiful garment of thankfulness. As stated by William Arthur Ward, "Gratitude can transform common days into Thanksgiving, turn routine jobs into joy, and change ordinary opportunities into blessings."[21] The winds of competition, demand, and criticism have made our world a cold place to live. However, we can warm up the environment with kind words of appreciation and gratitude—words that can make a huge difference in the lives of those around us. But keep in mind that thankfulness is like a flower that blooms only when we expect nothing and appreciate everything.

Today, **January 11**, is International Thank-You Day, not to be confused with the Thanksgiving holidays in the United States, Canada, and a few other countries. The origin of Thank-You Day is unclear. Some suggest that greeting card companies promoted it as a holiday to increase their sales. Regardless of its origin, today is a good opportunity for us to reflect on the important subject of thankfulness.

There are at least three levels of thankfulness. The first and most superficial is the *rhetorical* level, in which one formally says "Thank you" without necessarily meaning it. The second is the *sincere* level, in which one feels and demonstrates gratitude for specific gifts and acts. The third and most substantial is the *lifestyle* level, in which a person is continuously thankful even for the most insignificant details in life. The Bible says, "In everything give thanks; for this is the will of God in Christ Jesus for you" (1 Thessalonians 5:18).

Too often, we hold back words of appreciation until those who are worthy of them are no longer with us. Since today is Thank-You Day, I would like to express my own appreciation to you for encouraging me by reading these devotionals. But I would also like to encourage you to send a thank-you note to someone who has made a difference in your life and perhaps still is making a difference. Your words of appreciation could brighten the path of those who love you and care about you. Be thankful today and every day.

GOD'S TRANSFORMING WORD

Create in me a clean heart, O God, and renew a steadfast spirit within me.
—Psalm 51:10

God's word has amazing creative and re-creative power. We are told that by God's command, the universe came into existence (Hebrews 11:3). Indeed, God "spoke, and it came to be" (Psalm 33:9, NIV). But the same amazing power is also present in God's Written Word, the Bible, which has been widely recognized for having transformed the lives of many people around the world.

On **January 12, 2013**, the History Channel aired a documentary movie entitled *101 Objects That Changed the World*.[22] This program listed the Bible as the number one object that has changed the world and, consequently, has most greatly impacted human lives!

A classic example of such change is Augustine's conversion experience. Augustine of Hippo (354–430) became one of the most influential early Christian theologians and philosophers. During his youth, he was enslaved by "the habit of satisfying an insatiable lust."[23] But his life was completely changed after reading Romans 13:13, 14: "Let us walk properly, as in the day, not in revelry and drunkenness, not in lewdness and lust, not in strife and envy. But put on the Lord Jesus Christ, and make no provision for the flesh, to fulfill its lusts."

Conversion brings peace and stability to our lives. In his *Confessions* (1.1.1), Augustine prayed, "For thou [O Lord] hast made us for thyself and *restless* is our heart until it comes to rest in thee." Ellen White says, "The surrender of all our powers to God greatly simplifies the problem of life. It weakens and cuts short a thousand struggles with the passions of the natural heart.[24]

Our relationship with God is not some sort of mystical experience that can be carried out apart from the Bible. As Jesus Christ is the *incarnate* Word of God (John 1:14), so the Bible is the *written* Word of God (John 5:39), and both are in perfect harmony. Saving faith is not a naive and groundless emotion. It is a personal relationship with Christ, firmly rooted in His Word. Set aside a special time every day to study God's Word, learn its wonderful teachings, and experience its amazing, transforming power in your own life.

ᵀOTAL ᵂAR

We do not wrestle against flesh and blood, but against principalities,
against powers, against the rulers of the darkness of this age,
against spiritual hosts of wickedness in the heavenly places.

—Ephesians 6:12

Only those who have experienced war can comprehend its brutality and horror. During World War II, the German army used an innovative military technique called blitzkrieg (which means "lightning war"), a devastating tactic based on speed and surprise. On **January 13, 1943**, Adolf Hitler declared "total war"—a willingness "to make any sacrifice in lives and other resources to obtain a complete victory."[25] Replacing male factory workers with women, he was able to add another 500,000 men to the German armed forces.

The Bible tells us that we are also in a total war against the spiritual forces of evil (Ephesians 6:12) and that the devil is filled with "great wrath, because he knows that he has a short time" (Revelation 12:12). This war involves every dimension of our lives and every moment of our time. Ellen White says that if our spiritual vision was quickened, we would see "angels flying quickly to the aid of these tempted ones, forcing back the hosts of evil that encompass them, and placing their feet on the sure foundation. The battles waging between the two armies are as real as those fought by the armies of this world, and on the issue of the spiritual conflict eternal destinies depend."[26]

But how can we gain victory over the hosts of evil? There is no victory without thoroughly preparing for battle ahead of time. For this reason, Paul, in Ephesians 6:10–20, describes the whole armor of the victorious Christian soldier. Remember that in this cosmic battle, "no man is safe for a day or an hour without prayer"[27] and that "we are not safe for one hour while we are failing to render obedience to the word of God."[28]

For those who surrender their lives unconditionally to God, His promise is that He "would sooner send every angel out of heaven to protect His people than leave one soul that trusts in Him to be overcome by Satan."[29] May this be our assurance!

ℒIFE OF SERVICE

*"Whoever desires to save his life will lose it, but whoever
loses his life for My sake and the gospel's will save it."*

—Mark 8:35

There are far more witty sayings about unselfish service than practical examples illustrating them in real life. One brave person who practiced what he taught was Albert Schweitzer (1875–1965). He was born on **January 14, 1875**, in the German province of Alsace-Lorraine and eventually became a renowned theologian, musician, philosopher, and physician. Dutch nurse Maria J. Lagendijk said, "He was a true Alsatian. He had the charm of a Frenchman and the solidity of a German."[30]

In 1904, Schweitzer read an article on the need for physicians in the French colony of Gabon in equatorial Africa. To everyone's dismay, he gave up his brilliant career as a professor at the University of Strasbourg and enrolled in medical school. In April 1913, he and his wife went to Lambaréné, where they built a jungle clinic. He later explained, "For years I had been giving of myself in words, and it was with joy that I had followed the calling of theological teacher and of preacher. But this new form of activity would consist not in preaching the religion of love, but in practicing it."[31]

Dr. Schweitzer was awarded the 1952 Nobel Peace Prize on December 10, 1953. But he returned to Africa and used the prize money for his leper hospital at Lambaréné. Shortly before she died, his wife asked him how long he was planning to stay in Africa. He replied, "As long as I draw breath."[32] He was fully convinced that "the most precious gift in life is to live not for ourselves but for the benefit of others, for truth and goodness."[33]

Regarding unselfish service, Schweitzer added, "Everyone must work to live, but the purpose of human life is to serve and to show compassion and the will to help others. Only then have we ourselves become true human beings."[34] "Example is not the main thing in influencing others, it's the only thing."[35] Reflect today on these statements and how they can impact your life.

$\mathcal{M}$IRACLE ON THE $\mathcal{H}$UDSON

*"Worthy is the Lamb who was slain to receive power and riches
and wisdom, and strength and honor and glory and blessing!"*
—Revelation 5:12

The afternoon of **January 15, 2009**, seemed like any other at LaGuardia Airport in New York City. But three minutes into a flight that had just taken off, a US Airways plane, Flight 1549, struck a flock of Canada geese, causing both jet engines to fail. Fire could be seen streaming from both. Without any chance of reaching a nearby airfield, Captain Chesley B. "Sully" Sullenberger III decided to "ditch" the airplane in the Hudson River. It was a cold day, 20°F (-7°C). The freezing water began streaming into the plane, so the crew rapidly evacuated the passengers onto the wings of the aircraft. Before leaving the plane, however, Sullenberger twice walked the length of the cabin to confirm that no one remained inside.

The whole survival and rescue process was a study in teamwork, led by Captain Sullenberger and supported by his crew and ground rescue personnel. Amazingly, all 155 people aboard survived, and only 2 needed to stay overnight in a hospital. Experts have praised it as "a magnificent piece of aviation professionalism,"[36] "the most successful ditching in aviation history,"[37] and "a heroic and unique aviation achievement."[38]

After hearing the news about this remarkable incident, I thought back on the cross upon which Christ died to redeem us. Then, in imagination, I thought of the future—the redeemed in heaven praising Him for His saving grace. Revelation 5 provides wonderful glimpses into the heavenly praises to the Lamb, setting the tone for our praise throughout eternity.

Arriving in heaven, Adam "looks about him and beholds a multitude of his family redeemed, standing in the Paradise of God. Then he casts his glittering crown at the feet of Jesus and, falling upon His breast, embraces the Redeemer. He touches the golden harp, and the vaults of heaven echo the triumphant song: 'Worthy, worthy, worthy is the Lamb that was slain, and lives again!' The family of Adam take up the strain and cast their crowns at the Saviour's feet as they bow before Him in adoration."[39] I pray that you and I will be there on that glorious occasion!

"No King but Caesar"

Pilate said to them, "Shall I crucify your King?"
The chief priests answered, "We have no king but Caesar!"

—John 19:15

C hristianity emerged at a time when Palestine was under Roman domination. We are told that Joseph and Mary went from Nazareth to Bethlehem due to a tax decree from Caesar Augustus (Luke 2:1–5), whose original name was Gaius Octavius (63 BC–AD 14). After defeating Mark Antony and Cleopatra, Octavius became the first sole ruler over the entire Roman Republic. On **January 16, 27 BC**, the Roman Senate voted new titles for him, officially making him Imperator Caesar Divi Filius Augustus. Historians usually refer to him as Caesar Augustus.

The Roman emperor was widely treated as a divine figure to whom temples, altars, and priesthoods were dedicated. He was considered either a god or a son of a god. But "the question of absolute divinity, that is, of divine nature, was not very relevant in pagan antiquity. What was expressed in imperial cults was rather relative divinity, that is, divine *status*, and the absolute power it entailed in relation to the worshippers."[40]

At Jesus' trial, Pilate asked, "Shall I crucify your King?" (John 19:15), forcing the crowd to decide whom they would be loyal to. The chief priests were present—the very ones whose daily ministration foreshadowed Christ's holy priesthood. They should have been the first to honor and defend Him. Instead, they shouted disgracefully, "We have no king but Caesar!" (verse 15).

Christ was rejected by the apostate priests, but not by God. Christ was glorified through His deepest humiliation (John 12:23, 24). Philippians 2:9–11 affirms, "God also has highly exalted Him and given Him the name which is above every name, that at the name of Jesus every knee should bow, of those in heaven, and of those on earth, and of those under the earth, and that every tongue should confess that Jesus Christ is Lord, to the glory of God the Father."

In contrast to those whose loyalty was to Caesar, the Bible refers to our Lord Jesus Christ as "the blessed and only Potentate, the King of kings, and Lord of lords" (1 Timothy 6:15). Revelation 17 says the Lamb will conquer the kings of the earth, "for He is Lord of lords and King of kings" (verse 14). May we remain loyal to Christ, regardless of what the crowds around us are shouting.

$\mathcal{A}$LMOST $\mathcal{M}$IDNIGHT

One keeps calling to me from Seir, "Watchman, how far
gone is the night? Watchman, how far gone is the night?"
—Isaiah 21:11, NASB

History is a story with a tragic beginning and a dramatic ending. In the beginning, humans separated themselves from God. In the end, humanity will face an apocalyptic encounter with God. But how close are we to that event? Influential segments of the scientific community are concerned about the impending destruction of the world.

On September 26, 1945, the Atomic Scientists of Chicago organized themselves to alert the public about "the scientific, technological and social problems arising from the release of nuclear energy."[41] The United States had just dropped nuclear bombs on the Japanese cities of Hiroshima and Nagasaki. In June 1947, the *Bulletin of the Atomic Scientists* (vol. 3, no. 6) started carrying on its front page the iconic Doomsday Clock to warn "the public about how close we are to destroying our world with dangerous technologies of our own making."[42]

Over the succeeding seventy years, the *Bulletin* has reset the minute hand of the clock 22 times, either backward or forward. On **January 17, 2017**, the hand was moved from three minutes to midnight to two and a half. This means that scientists, many of whom do not believe in God's intervention in human affairs, are convinced that the earth is no longer a safe place to live and that we are on the brink of major global catastrophe.

Curiously, the *Bulletin of the Atomic Scientists* for October 1949 carried under the Doomsday Clock the following statement by Robert Redi: "This is the time when things must be done before their time."[43] The scientific and ecological communities are very concerned about preserving the world from its destruction.

We, too, should care for God's creation. We know, however, that the world will not be destroyed by human power but by God's supernatural intervention. God will come to "destroy those who destroy the earth" (Revelation 11:18). We also know that the end of the world is closer now than when we embraced the faith (Romans 13:11–14). "Christ's coming is nearer than when we believed. Every passing day leaves us one less to proclaim the message of warning to the world."[44]

What Is Home?

Your wife shall be like a fruitful vine
In the very heart of your house,
Your children like olive plants
All around your table.

—Psalm 128:3

Today is a special day for me because, on Tuesday, **January 18, 1983**, my wife, Marly, and I got married. God has blessed our marriage, and our home has been enriched by three lovely children: Suellen, William, and Shelley. Over the years, my wife has beautified and sweetened our lives. Without her assistance, I never would have set aside time from my busy schedule to write these daily devotionals. So, I am deeply thankful to her. And I'm using our special occasion to reflect on how a house becomes a home.

Unquestionably, the family is the most important institution in our modern society. Yet, it is facing a deep crisis. Many families live together under the same roof and eat together at the same table but do not truly have a home. A popular saying suggests, "Fill a house with love and it becomes a home." And I would add that a stable home is a gift from God, built on His love and sustained by His values and principles.

The Austrian American operatic contralto Ernestine Schumann-Heink (1861–1936) has been credited for the tender text "What Is a Home?" This charming tribute defines "home" as:

A roof to keep out the rain. Four walls to keep out the wind. Floors to keep out the cold. Yes, but home is more than that. It is the laugh of a baby, the song of a mother, the strength of a father. Warmth of loving hearts, light from happy eyes, kindness, loyalty, comradeship. Home is first school and first church for young ones, where they learn what is right, what is good, and what is kind. Where they go for comfort when they are hurt or sick. Where joy is shared and sorrow eased. Where fathers and mothers are respected and loved. Where children are wanted. Where the simplest food is good enough for kings because it is earned. Where money is not as important as loving-kindness. Where even the teakettle sings from happiness. That is home. God bless it.[45]

There are no perfect families or faultless homes in our sinful world. But part of our end-time mission is to restore broken families and transform cold houses into warm homes. Preparation for Christ's second coming includes turning "the hearts of the fathers to the children, and the hearts of the children to their fathers" (Malachi 4:6). Our earthly homes must become support centers for our journey to our heavenly home.

SPREADING THE LIGHT

*"You are the light of the world. A city that is set on a hill cannot
be hidden. Nor do they light a lamp and put it under a basket,
but on a lampstand, and it gives light to all who are in the house."*

—Matthew 5:14, 15

Darkness is simply the absence of light. When light shines, darkness naturally vanishes. By spreading light, we help living things grow in a much more robust way. Actually, there is no life without light.

A major achievement in the process of bringing electric lighting into our houses took place on **January 19, 1883**, in Roselle, New Jersey. After much experimentation, Thomas Edison's first electric lighting system employing overhead wires began service. That achievement proved that an entire community could be lit by electricity from a shared, central generating station. Today, uncountable cities, towns, villages, and houses around the globe are served by some kind of electric lighting system.

Just as physical light is essential for our physical lives, so the light that shines from God's Word is essential for our spiritual lives. The Bible assures us that "God is light" (1 John 1:5) and "the Father of lights" (James 1:17). Likewise, Christ, who came to reveal the Father, not only said of Himself, "I am the light of the world," but also continued, "He who follows Me shall not walk in darkness, but have the light of life" (John 8:12). Since Christ and His teachings cannot be separated, we can conclude both are the light that should enlighten the world. As stated in Psalm 119:105, "Your word is a lamp to my feet and a light to my path."

When Jesus said we are "the light of the world" (Matthew 5:14), He did not mean that we should spread *our own* light to others. We should simply reflect His light—the light of His Word—to all around us. Then the light will never glorify us; rather, it will be a powerful means of leading people to glorify God. Christ declared, "Let your light so shine before men, that they may see your good works and glorify your Father in heaven" (verse 16).

Just as Thomas Edison created an electric lighting system that brought light into our homes, let us also carry God's light into the homes of those who are perishing in the darkness of this world. Together, we can light up this world!

*U*NITED IN *S*ERVICE

"That they all may be one, as You, Father, are in Me, and I in You; that
they also may be one in Us, that the world may believe that You sent Me."

—John 17:21

The horrors of World War II had finally ended, but the worries of the Cold War were still very much alive. There was indeed much political and military tension between the Western Bloc (capitalism) and the Eastern Bloc (communism). During those very unstable years, John F. Kennedy was elected as the thirty-fifth president of the United States. In his famous inaugural address at Capitol Hill in Washington, DC, on **January 20, 1961,** he challenged his own country and the nations of the Western Bloc to remain united and to support their common cause.

Kennedy first highlighted the value of unity. He stated, "United there is little we cannot do in a host of cooperative ventures. Divided there is little we can do—for we dare not meet a powerful challenge at odds and split asunder." Near the end of his speech, he emphasized the need for altruistic service with his memorable words, "And so, my fellow Americans, ask not what your country can do for you; ask what you can do for your country. My fellow citizens of the world, ask not what America will do for you, but what together we can do for the freedom of man."

It does not make much difference whether you agree with the political tone of this remarkable speech. What does matter is the realization that we all are directly involved in a huge, unceasing spiritual battle between good and evil and that we need to take a clear stand. According to the Bible, "We do not wrestle against flesh and blood, but against principalities, against powers, against the rulers of the darkness of this age, against spiritual hosts of wickedness in the heavenly places" (Ephesians 6:12).

As members of Christ's spiritual body (1 Corinthians 12:12–31), we can triumph only by remaining united in Christ (John 17:21) and supporting one another in unselfish service. We must closely follow the example of Christ, who "did not come to be served, but to serve, and to give His life a ransom for many" (Matthew 20:28). Instead of asking what the church can do for you, ask what you can do for the church and for those around you who are perishing in their sins. Unselfish love can and will make all the difference in our communities.

ℬAPTISM OF ℬELIEVERS

"He who believes and is baptized will be saved;
but he who does not believe will be condemned."

—Mark 16:16

One of the most solemn and meaningful Christian rituals is baptism. Christ was baptized as an adult by immersion (Matthew 3:13–17) and commanded His followers to do the same (Matthew 28:18–20). Only baptism by immersion can fully express the concept of true believers dying to sin; they are submerged in water and resurrected in newness of life as they come out of the water (Romans 6:3–6).

Several ancient European baptistries are well preserved, confirming that for centuries Christians continued to baptize adults by total immersion. Meanwhile, alternative practices began to emerge in the postapostolic period. In the late second century, infant baptism was being practiced in North Africa. In the middle of the third century, a bishop in Rome by the name of Novatian was baptized on his sickbed by someone pouring water on him. These exceptions to standard practices eventually became the official procedures of the Christian tradition.

In the sixteenth century, Anabaptists (who were also known as rebaptizers) began to practice *adult* baptism. On **January 21, 1525**, they performed their first baptismal ceremony at the house of Feliz Manz in Zurich. After prayer, the former priest George Blaurock rose and asked layman Conrad Grebel to baptize him with the Christian baptism. With a ladle, Grebel took water from a bucket and poured it on Blaurock in the name of the Father, Son, and Holy Spirit. Blaurock then proceeded to baptize the other members of the gathering. Later on, some of the Anabaptists also restored baptism by *total immersion*. This practice has been carried on by Baptists and some other Christian denominations, including the Seventh-day Adventist Church.

What a blessing it is to be baptized just as Christ was and then to remain faithful to our baptismal vows! "The fact that you have been *baptized* in the name of the *Father*, the *Son*, and the *Holy* Spirit is an assurance that, if you will claim Their help, these powers will help you in every emergency. The Lord will hear and answer the prayers of His sincere followers who wear Christ's yoke and learn in His school His meekness and lowliness."[46] Today, why not renew the commitment you made at your own baptism?

*U*NIVERSAL *I*NTELLIGENCE

"The eyes of the Lord are in every place, keeping watch on the evil and the good."
—Proverbs 15:3

What comes to your mind when you hear the word *espionage*? From a biblical perspective, you could recall the twelve Hebrew spies who explored the land of Canaan (Numbers 13) or the two spies hidden by Rahab in Jericho (Joshua 2). From a modern viewpoint, you might think of the Soviet KGB or the American CIA. Espionage aims to gather secret information about enemy countries and, sometimes, even friendly countries.

On **January 22, 1946**, United States president Harry S. Truman set up the Central Intelligence Group, eventually renamed the Central Intelligence Agency, the most powerful intelligence agency in the world. Today, the US Intelligence Community (IC) is a coalition of seventeen agencies and organizations (including the CIA) that work both independently and collaboratively to gather and analyze the intelligence necessary to conduct foreign relations and national security activities.

As sophisticated and efficient as the IC and other intelligence agencies might be, none of them can compare with God's intelligence network that oversees the whole universe! No wonder King David exclaimed, "Where can I go from Your Spirit? Or where can I flee from Your presence?" (Psalm 139:7). And King Solomon said, "The eyes of the LORD are in every place, keeping watch on the evil and the good" (Proverbs 15:3).

In contrast to human agencies, God's intelligence network is a friendly one, intended to rescue us from the forces of evil. "For I know the thoughts that I think toward you, says the LORD, thoughts of peace and not of evil, to give you a future and a hope" (Jeremiah 29:11). This means that the most sophisticated intelligence network in the whole universe is working on our behalf! We are absolutely protected by God, and nothing can ever happen to us outside the sphere of His all-encompassing knowledge and absolute foreknowledge. Praise God that He cares for each of us in such amazing and efficient ways!

Good Taste

*I also want the women to dress modestly, with decency and propriety, adorning themselves,
not with elaborate hairstyles or gold or pearls or expensive clothes, but with good deeds,
appropriate for women who profess to worship God.*

—1 Timothy 2:9, 10, NIV

People tend to read Paul's advice for "decency and propriety" (1 Timothy 2:9, 10, NIV) as referring to an old-fashioned dress code to be followed only in his day, but that is not necessarily the case. Paul is taking the universal principle of doing "all to the glory of God" (1 Corinthians 10:31) and applying it to the way we dress. It means that we should avoid all objectionable attire.

We live in a world where everything and everyone is overly exposed. Much contemporary fashion is designed to look sexy and appeal to people's sensual desires. Remember the anonymous addage, "Do not display in the showcase what is not for sale." Too often, nudity of the body reveals nakedness of the spirit. As faithful Christians, we must be sure that the message we are sharing about ourselves is, in fact, the one we want to communicate. Whenever we go to church, we need to remember its aisles are the aisles of God's house and not the runway of an Adventist fashion show.

Some people go to the other extreme, imagining that all modern fashion is wrong and unacceptable. In an article published in the *Adventist Review and Sabbath Herald* on **January 23, 1900,** Ellen White spoke of women "who are careless of their own apparel, and who think *it* a virtue to . . . dress without order and taste; and their clothing often looks as if it flew, and lit upon their persons. Their garments are filthy, and yet such ones will ever be talking against pride. They class decency and neatness with pride."[47] Please, never confuse "decency and neatness" with carelessness and lack of taste.

Almost all airlines and many other companies have either a specific uniform or dress code. As a church, we do not have and should never adopt one. Visitors are welcome to attend our services as they are, and we should avoid being judgmental. But the members of our congregations should glorify God in all they do, including the way they dress. But even if others do not follow this principle as they should, at least you and I should take it seriously.

$\mathcal{A}$LMOST $\mathcal{T}$HERE

Then the LORD *said to him, "This is the land of which I swore to give Abraham, Isaac, and Jacob. . . . I have caused you to see it with your eyes, but you shall not cross over there."*

—Deuteronomy 34:4

On November 13, 2015, Henry Worsley, a fifty-year-old retired British army soldier, began a 950-mile (1,530-kilometer) journey, crossing Antarctica through the South Pole. For more than two months, he pulled a 330-pound (150-kilogram) sled containing eighty days' worth of food, fuel, and survival gear. While all other polar explorers (including the famous Sir Ernest Shackleton) traveled as part of a group, Worsley was very close to becoming the first individual to walk the entire journey alone and unassisted.

But 30 miles (48 kilometers) short of his goal, Worsley wrote: "The 71 days alone on the Antarctic with over 900 statute miles covered and a gradual grinding down of my physical endurance finally took its toll today, and it is with sadness that I report it is journey's end—so close to my goal."[48] Calling for help, he was flown to the Clínica Magallanes in Punta Arenas, Chile. An abdominal infection (bacterial peritonitis) soon morphed into complete organ failure. Henry Worsley died on **January 24, 2016**.

After forty years of pilgrimage with the Israelites in the wilderness, Moses was called by God to the top of Mount Pisgah, from which he was shown the land of Canaan. Due to his previous lack of faith, Moses died just short of his goal—the Promised Land (Numbers 20:12; Deuteronomy 34:1–6). Even so, Moses was raised from the dead to inherit everlasting life (Jude 9) and appeared later with Elijah at Jesus' transfiguration (Matthew 17:1–7), and his name is listed as one of the heroes of faith (Hebrews 11:23–29).

Unfortunately, just as Worsley never reached his final destination, many people who dream, speak, and sing about heaven will never make it there. "Almost saved means totally lost," goes the saying. Let us thank God that *today* we have another opportunity to renew our commitment to Him and walk in His presence! He is giving us another opportunity because His compassions "are new every morning" (Lamentations 3:22, 23), and He is "not willing that any should perish but that all should come to repentance" (2 Peter 3:9). However, we must never forget that only those who endure "to the end shall be saved" (Matthew 24:13).

SERENITY IN THE STORM

Then He arose and rebuked the wind, and said to the sea,
"Peace, be still!" And the wind ceased and there was a great calm.

—Mark 4:39

The voyage on the *Simmonds* from England to America was proceeding as normal. On board were eighty English colonists and twenty-six Moravian Christians, as well as the missionary brothers John Wesley and Charles Wesley. The Moravians (who were Germans) lived a simple and unworldly form of Christianity and were active missionaries. John Wesley was much impressed with their radiant joy and deep devotion. They took no offense at being mistreated and did not respond to any rude word spoken against them.

In the early morning hours of Sunday, **January 25, 1736**, John Wesley joined the Moravians in their devotional. But, in Wesley's own words, suddenly, "the sea broke over, split the mainsail in pieces, covered the ship, and poured in between the decks, as if the great deep had already swallowed us up. A terrible screaming began among the English. The Germans calmly sang on. I asked one of them afterwards, 'Were you not afraid?' He answered, 'I thank God, no.' I asked, 'But were not your women and children afraid?' He replied, mildly, 'No; our women and children are not afraid to die.' "[49] That one event generated significant changes in Wesley's spiritual life and ministry. He had been trained for the ministry in Oxford, where, in 1729, he cofounded the "Holy Club" for those committed to overcoming sin and increasing holiness. Although he was an ordained Anglican minister and missionary, Wesley realized he was still missing the deep practical spirituality of the Moravians.

How deeply rooted is your religion? How do you react during life-threatening storms? In reality, "those who are engaged in service for the Master *need an experience much higher, deeper, broader, than many have yet thought of having. Many who are already members of* God's great family know little of what it means to behold His glory and to be changed from glory to glory."[50] While working for the Lord, we need to deepen our personal experience with Him every day. Only through a friendship with the Lord can we remain calm and confident that He is holding our hand during the stormy days as well as the sunny ones.

BAREFOOT IN THE SNOW

*If we confess our sins, He is faithful and just to forgive
us our sins and to cleanse us from all unrighteousness.*

—1 John 1:9

In May 2008, my wife and I visited the famous Canossa Castle in northern Italy on a sunny spring day. There I had an unplanned interview with Mario Bernabei, author of the book *Matilde e il castello di Canossa* (*Matilda and the Canossa Castle*). He highlighted some details about the relationship between the Countess Matilda of Canossa and Pope Gregory VII, including the humiliating way the pope treated Henry IV, king of the German Empire.

In contrast to the nice weather we were having that day, Henry IV arrived during the winter of 1076–1077, one of the coldest ever in that region. Having insulted the pope and rebelled against him, Henry was declared excommunicated and deposed from the throne by the pope. Knowing that the pope was visiting the castle, Henry went there to seek his forgiveness. Instead of welcoming the king into the warm castle, the pope left him outside for three days, **January 26–28, 1077.** Henry spent those three dyas in the snow, fasting, barefoot, humbly dressed, and his head uncovered. After this most severe penance, the pope finally admitted the king to his presence and granted him forgiveness.

Over the centuries, Canossa has been recognized as a symbol of the Church of Rome's claim to temporal supremacy and the acknowledgment of it by a powerful state head. But what other lessons can be drawn from this incident?

Some have noted the contrast between Gregory VII, a proud and arrogant *alleged* head of Christianity, and Christ, the humble and merciful *true* head of the church. Can you imagine if Christ treated us as the pope treated King Henry?

Whatever your sins, remember that no sin can escape the promise of 1 John 1:9—"If we confess our sins, He is faithful and just to forgive us our sins and to cleanse us from all unrighteousness." But what about the unpardonable sin mentioned in Matthew 12:31, 32, and Mark 3:28, 29? This sin is precisely the unwillingness to "confess our sins." But the beauty of salvation by grace through faith is that no *repented* and *confessed* sin remains unforgiven! This promise is for you and for me, and we should claim it right now.

ℋEAVENLY 𝒯ALENT

*Every good and perfect gift is from above, coming down from the Father
of the heavenly lights, who does not change like shifting shadows.*
—James 1:17, NIV

Wolfgang Amadeus Mozart was born on **January 27, 1756**, in Salzburg, Austria. He has been recognized as a great child prodigy, composer, and music performer. At the age of four, little Wolfgang could learn any minuet in half an hour. At age five, he began composing, and by six, he was already a celebrity. Wolfgang Amadeus Mozart died at the young age of thirty-five, but he left a legacy of some six hundred top-quality musical pieces in several genres. Mozart is undoubtedly one of the greatest musicians of all time and, in the opinion of some, perhaps the greatest ever.

The famous Swiss theologian Karl Barth was a fan of Mozart. He once speculated, "It may be that when the angels go about their task of praising God, they play only Bach. I'm sure, however, that when they are together *en famille*, they play Mozart and that then too our dear Lord listens with special pleasure."[51] Even without imagining Mozart's compositions in heavenly realms, one still must recognize that he had an exceptional musical talent that he used with extreme passion and dedication.

The beautiful German song "Nicht Jeder kann ein Mozart sein" ("Not Everyone Can Be a Mozart") recognizes that not everyone can become a genius like the great composer. But even a beginner's piece, played with one finger on the piano by a child, can become the most beautiful melody. What really matters is not so much how many talents we possess or how great some of them are but whether we are using them for the honor and glory of God and for the benefit of humanity.

"It is conscientious attention to what the world terms 'little things' that makes life a success. Little deeds of charity, little acts of self-denial, speaking simple words of helpfulness, watching against little sins,—this is Christianity. A grateful acknowledgment of daily blessings, a wise improvement of daily opportunities, a diligent cultivation of intrusted talents,—this is what the Master calls for."[52] Today, you can make a difference in the lives of those around you by sharing little acts of love with them!

THE BEST HALL OF FAME

*"Nevertheless do not rejoice in this, that the spirits are subject to you,
but rather rejoice because your names are written in heaven."*

—Luke 10:20

The memories of many famous people have been perpetuated in halls of fame, on monuments, or in portraits. Some people have designed famous projects carrying their own names, such as the famous Eiffel Tower on Champ de Mars in Paris. Originally built for a world fair celebrating the centennial of the French Revolution, it is now visited every year by some seven million people.

The Eiffel Tower is named after the engineer Gustave Eiffel, whose company designed and built the tower. The original plan was developed by Maurice Koechlin and Émile Nouguier, with additional insights by Stephen Sauvestre. Work on the foundation started on **January 28, 1887**, and the tower was completed in 1889. In 1957 a broadcasting aerial was added to its top. The tower is 1,063 feet (324 meters) tall (including the television antenna at its top) and weighs 7,300 tons. A total of 18,038 pieces were joined together using 2.5 million rivets. Despite initial criticism and protests by leading artists and intellectuals, the Eiffel Tower has become established as a prominent symbol of France.

In addition to Eiffel's, there are seventy-two names of French scientists, engineers, and mathematicians engraved on the tower in recognition of their outstanding contributions. This is one of the most remarkable halls of fame in all the world. But remember, "The world and its desires pass away, but whoever does the will of God lives forever" (1 John 2:17, NIV). This means that no human hall of fame, or even all halls of fame together, can be compared to the privilege of having our names written in the heavenly book of life.

Many need what they do not have, namely, *true religion*! "Profession alone is nothing. Names are registered upon the church books upon earth, but not in the book of life."[53] Perhaps you love "the praise of men more than the praise of God" (John 12:43). You and I must seek *less* human glory that vanishes and *more* of the heavenly glory that endures forever. When this is the case, we can rejoice because our names are "written in heaven" (Luke 10:20).

Slowing Down

Then, because so many people were coming and going that they did not even have a chance to eat, he said to them, "Come with me by yourselves to a quiet place and get some rest."
—Mark 6:31, NIV

Roads and traffic can test our patience and level of Christian behavior! So, let's start with a few questions: How do you feel when a slow driver in your lane holds you up? How do you react to the mistakes of other drivers? Do you generally feel that traffic should move faster than it does? The legendary race-car driver Mario Andretti once said, "If everything seems under control, you're just not going fast enough."

On **January 29, 1886,** Karl Benz applied for a patent for his Motorwagen, which became known as the first car ever. It was a three-wheeled automobile propelled by a gasoline-powered engine. Benz unveiled his invention to the public on July 3, 1886, on the Ringstrasse in Mannheim, Germany. The maximum speed for those early models was approximately 10 mph (16 kmph). Over the years, the car industry has greatly improved. Today the production, street-legal Bugatti Veyron 16.4 can reach a top speed of 268 mph (431 kmph)!

Cars reflect culture. They are faster today, mirroring our fast-paced society. Many believe that keeping things under control rarely creates greatness. Unquestionably, fast driving can be more exciting and take us to our destination more quickly. But remember, the faster you drive, the less you appreciate the view around you. High speed can become a lifestyle, not only with respect to driving but in every aspect of life. It is possible to move so fast through life that we don't pay attention to those around us.

Even though I don't know your personal lifestyle, I would encourage you to take Christ's invitation seriously. "Come with me by yourselves to a quiet place and get some rest" (Mark 6:31, NIV). Other than giving of yourself, the most precious gift you can give to God and your loved ones is your time. Time indicates priorities and demonstrates what is important. Not spending time with God shows that you have other "gods" who get more of your time than He does. Not spending time with your loved ones conveys the message that they are not as important to you as they think they are. Reflect on these thoughts and act today.

ONE BROTHERHOOD

For there is no distinction between Jew and Greek,
for the same Lord over all is rich to all who call upon Him.

—Romans 10:12

Our world is a huge battlefield between God and Satan. On one side, God is trying to save and unite humanity with the cement of His unconditional love. On the other side, Satan is trying to mislead and divide humanity with the wedge of his unlimited selfishness. He has caused deep social divides around the globe through evils such as exclusivism, tribalism, and racism.

In his speech at the German Reichstag on **January 30, 1939**, Adolf Hitler announced, "Today I will be once again a prophet: if the international Jewish financiers in and outside Europe should succeed in plunging the nations once again into a world war, then the result will not be the Bolshevizing of the earth, and thus the victory of Jewry, but the annihilation of the Jewish race in Europe!"[54] Hitler fulfilled his anti-Semitic prophecy in a most terrible way.

In stark contrast, authentic Christianity, counting all people as part of a single human family, overcomes cultural, ethnic, and social barriers. In the Old Testament, the Messianic era was portrayed as a time when Jews and Gentiles would worship together in God's temple, making it "a house of prayer for all nations" (Isaiah 56:7). Simeon, seeing the Child Jesus in the temple, prophesied that He came to bring salvation to "all peoples," including both Jews and Gentiles (Luke 2:30–32). Paul affirmed, "There is no distinction between Jew and Greek, for the same Lord over all is rich to all who call upon Him" (Romans 10:12). And further, "There is neither Jew nor Greek, there is neither slave nor free, there is neither male nor female; for you are all one in Christ Jesus" (Galatians 3:28).

God's love is powerful enough to bring us into one spiritual brotherhood. Those who are in Christ are "no longer strangers and foreigners, but fellow citizens with the saints and members of the household of God" (Ephesians 2:19). God's love empowers us to love everyone, whether they are Jews or Gentiles or even our own enemies (Matthew 5:43–48). You are invited today to be a stonemason for God, filling racial and social cracks with the cement of God's infinite love. Then, and only then, will the world be able to witness the transforming power of our religion.

UNCONDITIONAL FAITHFULNESS

They were stoned, they were sawn in two, were tempted, were slain with the sword. They wandered about in sheepskins and goatskins, being destitute, afflicted, tormented—of whom the world was not worthy. They wandered in deserts and mountains, in dens and caves of the earth.
—Hebrews 11:37, 38

Shakespeare asserted, "It is an heretic that makes the fire, not she which burns in't."[55] This was demonstrated when Cain murdered his own brother, Abel (Genesis 4:1–15), and in many similar cases since (Hebrews 11:30–38), including the slaughter of the Waldenses.

Ongoing attempts to force the Waldenses to conform to Catholicism had failed. So, on April 23, 1655, a brutal massacre took the lives of some 1,700 Waldenses in the Piedmont. This genocide generated a strong negative reaction throughout Europe. And, as if that were not enough, on **January 31, 1686**, the Duke of Savoy "decreed the destruction of all the Vaudois churches and that all inhabitants of the valleys should publicly"[56] renounce their heresies under penalty of death and banishment. Nevertheless, the Waldensian people remained faithful, despite these ongoing threats.

Ellen White describes it this way: "Though persecuted and driven from their homes, they conscientiously studied the word of God, and lived up to the light which shone upon them. When their possessions were taken from them, and their houses burned, they fled to the mountains, and there endured hunger, fatigue, cold, and nakedness. And yet the scattered and homeless ones would assemble to unite their voices in singing and praising God, that they were accounted worthy to suffer for Christ's name. They encouraged and cheered one another, and were grateful for even their miserable retreat. Many of their children sickened and died through exposure to cold, and the sufferings of hunger; yet the parents did not for a moment think of yielding their faith. They prized the love and favor of God far more than earthly ease or worldly riches. They received consolation from God, and with pleasing anticipations looked forward to the recompense of reward."[57]

Remember, only a religion that is worth dying for is worth living for! Let the amazing Waldensian example of courage and faithfulness to the Lord inspire your own religious life.

"Sing It Again"

Now I saw heaven opened, and behold, a white horse. And He who sat on him was called Faithful and True, and in righteousness He judges and makes war.

—Revelation 19:11

The majestic tune "Battle Hymn" arose out of the folk hymn tradition of the American camp meeting movement. One day, a friend challenged Julia Ward Howe (1819–1910), "Why do you not write some good words for that stirring tune?" She went to bed that night at the Willard Hotel in Washington, DC, thinking about the suggestion. Suddenly she awoke, grabbed a pencil and a piece of paper, wrote the lyrics, and went back to sleep. Julia could not imagine how successful that hymn would become!

The new "Battle Hymn of the Republic" was first published in *The Atlantic* on **February 1, 1862**. Soon it appeared in other newspapers and army hymnbooks. During the American Civil War, the Union armies marched to its cadence. When the prisoners of war in the Confederacy's Libby Prison got word of the Union victory at the Battle of Gettysburg, they shouted, wept, and sang the "Battle Hymn." The incident was later reported in a meeting where President Abraham Lincoln was present. With tears rolling down his cheeks, he exclaimed, "Sing it again!"

This hymn of victory, also titled "Mine Eyes Have Seen the Glory," echoes the words of Revelation 14:17–20. The first stanza reads as follows:

Mine eyes have seen the glory of the coming of the Lord;
He is trampling out the vintage where the grapes of wrath are stored;
He has loosed the fateful lightning of His terrible swift sword;
His truth is marching on.[1]

Just as the prisoners of Libby Prison sang this hymn anticipating their imminent freedom, the whole host of those redeemed by the blood of the Lamb will soon shout for joy when He appears in the clouds of heaven to free His faithful people. May you and I be among those who very soon will sing that amazing final hymn of triumph! Amen.

OUR WAITING TIME

He who testifies to these things says, "Surely I am coming quickly."
Amen. Even so, come, Lord Jesus!

—Revelation 22:20

Have you ever attended a Pathfinder survival camp with only scarce natural resources available? What a relief when the camp ends and you can enjoy your favorite meal again! But let's imagine that you were left alone in such a camp, having to remain there for several days, weeks, months, or even years. Unthinkable. However, this was the experience of Alexander Selkirk (1676–1721), a Scottish privateer and Royal Navy officer who was left as a castaway on an uninhabited island in the South Pacific Ocean.

As a youth, Selkirk displayed a quarrelsome and unruly disposition. As a seaman, his behavior did not improve much, and he ended up paying a high price for it. In 1704, the ship on which he served spent a few days on an island of the Juan Fernández archipelago, 420 miles (677.5 kilometers) off the coast of Chile, to stock up on fresh water and supplies.

Concerned about the seaworthiness of their vessel, Selkirk declared that he would rather stay on the island than continue aboard a dangerously leaky ship. Glad to be rid of him, Captain Stradling took Selkirk up on his offer and left him on the island with a musket, a hatchet, a knife, a cooking pot, a Bible, and some bedding and clothes. There he remained in loneliness, misery, and remorse for four years and four months. Finally, on **February 2, 1709**, two vessels, the *Duke* and the *Duchess*, arrived and rescued him.

This tragic story inspired Daniel Defoe to write his famous *The Life and Strange Surprising Adventures of Robinson Crusoe* (1719), and we can also glean some meaningful lessons from it. First, Selkirk should never have said that he would rather stay on the island than continue on the ship. Just as the captain took those words more seriously than Selkirk anticipated, people may also do the same with our rash statements. So, never say what you don't really mean.

Another lesson comes from Selkirk's final rescue. Our waiting time in this world can be much longer than we expect, but it will eventually end. As the *Duke* and the *Duchess* rescued him from that tedious island, so Christ will soon appear in the clouds of heaven to take us home. So, please do not be discouraged during this waiting time!

SPREADING GOD'S WORD

"What you see, write in a book and send it to the seven churches which are in Asia."
—Revelation 1:11

The Bible is God's Word written in human language. In ancient times, God asked Moses (Exodus 17:14) and other Bible prophets to write and send those inspired messages to their respective recipients. The apostle John was commissioned, "What you see, write in a book and send it to the seven churches which are in Asia" (Revelation 1:11). But since that time, the process of publishing and spreading the Bible has improved dramatically.

Johannes Gutenberg (ca. 1398–1468) was a German blacksmith, goldsmith, printer, and publisher. In 1439, he used movable-type printing in Europe for the first time in history. The Bible was not his first published work, but it was unquestionably his most important one. Gutenberg died on **February 3, 1468**, in his hometown of Mainz, Germany, leaving a grand legacy for humanity. His invention started the printing revolution, and the printing press is widely regarded as the most important invention of the second millennium, helping spread the writings of the Protestant Reformers.

Since Gutenberg's day, many things have changed. The twentieth-century communication theorist Marshall McLuhan stated, "Gutenberg made everybody a reader. Xerox made everybody a publisher."[2] Recent authors have added that personal computers have made everybody an author, and the internet has made everyone an editor and critic. In other words, today we can be almost everything at the same time—reader, publisher, author, editor, and critic. In our globalized world, the content of the Bible is available in a countless number of languages and translations. Meanwhile, sound interpretations and many misleading distortions of the Bible are both available.

Spreading God's Word means making its content available, whether in printed, electronic, or audio format. But more importantly, spreading God's Word implies allowing the Word to speak for itself, free from human distortion and biases. This means people must know the basic principles of sound biblical interpretation. As Philip helped the Ethiopian eunuch to understand Scripture (Acts 8:26–40), we are directed to "preach the word! Be ready in season and out of season. Convince, rebuke, exhort, with all longsuffering and teaching" (2 Timothy 4:2).

THE FLYING TAILOR

The prudent see danger and take refuge, but the simple keep going and pay the penalty.
—Proverbs 22:3, NIV

Franz Reichelt was an Austrian-born French tailor and parachuting pioneer who designed a new wearable parachute. After much negotiation with the local police, Reichelt got permission to conduct dummy test drops from the Eiffel Tower in Paris. So, on Sunday, **February 4, 1912**, he arrived at the tower at seven o'clock in the morning and announced that instead of performing the expected experiment, he himself would jump from it. Deeply concerned, his friends and spectators tried to dissuade him, but he did not change his mind. When questioned about the use of a safety rope or any other precautions, he simply replied, "I want to try the experiment myself and without trickery, as I intend to prove the worth of my invention."[3]

Reichelt's initial attempt to climb to the first floor of the tower was blocked by a guard who had witnessed previous unsuccessful dummy drops. But finally, they settled the issue, and he, along with two friends and a cinematographer, continued up to the first floor, a little more than 187 feet above the ground. Reichelt was confident that, to release his parachute, he only had to extend his arms in a cross position. At 8:22 A.M., observed by a crowd of some thirty journalists and curious people, he adjusted the apparatus with his friends' assistance, checked the wind direction, hesitated for about forty seconds, and then jumped. His half-open parachute immediately folded around his body, and he crashed into the icy ground at the foot of the tower. The autopsy revealed he had suffered a deadly heart attack shortly before impact—the tragic end of the so-called flying tailor.

There is much wisdom in the following words, usually attributed to Ronnie Oldham: "Excellence is the result of caring more than others think is wise, risking more than others think is safe, dreaming more than others think is practical, and expecting more than others think is possible."[4] However, the notion of "risking more than others think is safe" needs to be questioned. Sometimes it could be best, but not always. Perhaps we should listen more carefully to the counsels and warnings of those who already know the path we are just beginning to explore. If you decide to take a risk, always do it within the parameters of God's plan and never outside of them.

FLOOD GEOLOGY

*The waters swelled so mightily on the earth that all the high
mountains under the whole heaven were covered; the waters
swelled above the mountains, covering them fifteen cubits deep.*

—Genesis 7:19, 20, NRSV

Most scientists and many theologians deny the historicity of the Flood account in Genesis 6–8. For them, this is only a mythological story like the Babylonian flood tale called the *Epic of Gilgamesh*. By contrast, later Bible writers take the account of Noah and the universal flood literally in both the Old Testament (Psalm 104:6–9) and the New Testament (Matthew 24:37–39; Hebrews 11:7; 1 Peter 3:20; 2 Peter 2:5; 3:6).

The **February 5, 1867**, issue of the *Advent Review and Sabbath Herald* carried an article by D. T. Bourdeau entitled "Geology and the Bible." The author claimed, "Genuine Geology is as true as the Bible, and it does not contradict the Bible; for truth cannot contradict truth. Yet it is strange that some should pretend that there is a discrepancy between this science and the Bible; and it is stranger still that some who profess to believe the Bible, should adopt views purporting to be based on Geology, which are antagonistic to plain Bible facts, and yet claim that there is harmony between their views and the Bible."[5]

The scientific bases of Bourdeau's assertion were demonstrated by the self-taught geologist George McCready Price (1870–1963). Several of his books provided conclusive evidence that the geologic columns were formed not by a slow evolutionary process but by a worldwide flood. Price declared that his work was "to clear the old evolutionary structures from the ground" so that other creationists could build.[6] Many non-Adventist creationists have recognized his outstanding contribution to flood geology.

Evolutionists believe that the geological columns were formed over several evolutionary eras lasting millions of years. They believe that uncountable, more primitive forms of life existed and died prior to the appearance of human beings. If this were the case, then death would have already existed long before the sin of Adam and Eve (Genesis 3). On the other hand, the biblical account of the Flood, as it reads, is consistent with the biblical teaching that death came into the world through Adam's sin (Romans 5:12). Only from this perspective does the plan of salvation make sense!

THE PERSONALITY OF THE HOLY SPIRIT

"And I will pray the Father, and He will give you
another Helper, that He may abide with you forever."

—John 14:16

The nature of the Holy Spirit is a profound mystery, and we can understand it only to the extent that God's Word informs us. Early Seventh-day Adventists also had difficulty with the subject.

It was not until near the end of the nineteenth century that Adventists began to recognize the *personality* of the Holy Spirit. On **February 6, 1896**, Ellen White wrote a letter from Australia "to my brethren in America." In that letter, she referred to the Holy Spirit as "the third person of the Godhead."[7] Two years later (1898), she used the same expression in her classic book *The Desire of Ages*.[8]

In the June 9, 1896, issue of *Advent Review and Sabbath Herald*, George C. Tenney, then coeditor, wrote,

> We cannot describe the Holy Spirit. From the figures which are brought out in Revelation, Ezekiel, and other Scriptures, and from the language which is used in reference to the Holy Spirit, we are led to believe he is something more than an emanation from the mind of God. He is spoken of as a personality, and treated as such. He is included in the apostolic benedictions, and is spoken of by our Lord as acting in an independent and personal capacity, as teacher, guide, and comforter. He is an object of veneration, and is a heavenly intelligence, everywhere present, and always present. But as limited beings, we cannot understand the problems which the contemplation of the Deity presents to our minds.[9]

When Paul affirms that the Holy Spirit "makes intercession for us" in Romans 8:26, 27, he is suggesting that the Spirit has His own distinct personality. When the apostle speaks of "the mind of the Spirit," he eliminates any possibility of considering the Spirit only as abstract energy coming from the mind of God. If this were the case, then we would be speaking redundantly of *the mind of the mind* of God, which simply makes no sense.

Much more than mere energy, the Holy Spirit is the powerful Divine Helper who convicts the world "of sin, and of righteousness, and of judgment" (John 16:8); to pour out the love of God in our hearts (Romans 5:5), and to guide us "into all truth" (John 16:13). And there's more: He will abide with us forever!

OUR WONDERFUL HIGH PRIEST

For Christ did not enter a sanctuary made with human hands that was only a copy of the true one; he entered heaven itself, now to appear for us in God's presence.
—Hebrews 9:24, NIV

There are three basic questions about salvation that every Christian should be able to answer: What *did* Christ do for us on the cross? What *is* He doing for us now in the heavenly sanctuary? And what *will* He do for us at His second coming? Many Christians can explain what Christ did on the cross and what He will do at His second coming. But not so many understand what He is doing for our salvation now in the heavenly sanctuary.

One of the most helpful early Adventist expositions of this doctrine was O. R. L. Crosier's article "The Law of Moses," published in the *Day-Star* Extra on **February 7, 1846**. In this article, Crosier highlighted four basic concepts. First, the "sanctuary" mentioned in Daniel 8:14 is a heavenly sanctuary or temple (Hebrews 9:24; Revelation 11:19). Second, the heavenly sanctuary is a literal two-apartment sanctuary with a Holy Place and a Most Holy Place, as foreshadowed by the Mosaic tabernacle (Hebrews 9:1–9). Third, Christ is the Great High Priest of that sanctuary, making atonement for us by means of His own blood, which was shed on the cross (Colossians 1:20; Hebrews 9:11–23). And fourth, at the end of the twenty-three hundred symbolic days of Daniel 8:14, Christ went from the Holy Place into the Most Holy Place to receive the kingdom (Daniel 7:9–14). In a later article, Crosier explained that while Christ is now cleansing the *literal* temple of the New Jerusalem (Hebrews 9:22, 23), the Holy Spirit is cleansing the *spiritual* temple of God's people from their sins (1 Corinthians 3:16, 17; 6:19, 20).

But you may wonder, *If Christ already paid the price for all our sins at the cross, why does He still need to intercede for us in the heavenly sanctuary?* Christ died on the cross to save the whole world, but nobody will be saved against his or her will. Now Christ is graciously applying the merits of His sacrifice to all those who accept Him by faith. What a wonderful plan has been set up for our salvation.

Lord, what a disaster it would be if Your saving plan remained ineffective for me. I accept your sacrifice on the cross for my sins, and I invite you to be the High Priest of my life.

$\mathcal{A}$TONEMENT IN $\mathcal{A}$DVANCE

"Come, all you who are thirsty,
come to the waters;
and you who have no money,
come, buy and eat!
Come, buy wine and milk
without money and without cost."

—Isaiah 55:1, NIV

What an embarrassing situation when you finish eating at a nice restaurant and the bill comes, but you do not have enough money to pay it. How humiliating it is when you have to wash dishes to pay for your meal.

On **February 8, 1949**, Frank McNamara had a business dinner at New York's Major's Cabin Grill. When the bill arrived, he realized he had forgotten his wallet. He managed to find his way out of the pickle, but he decided there should be an alternative to cash. With his lawyer, Ralph Schneider, and friend Alfred Bloomingdale, McNamara eventually developed the Diners Club Card, primarily to be used for travel and entertainment purposes. Although some oil companies and department stores already issued their own proprietary cards, the Diners was the first credit card intended for widespread use.

According to the US Census Bureau, by 2000, there were 1.43 billion credit cards in use in the United States alone. Credit cards allow us to purchase in advance and pay later. Likewise, in Old Testament times, repentant sinners were genuinely saved with the assurance that the full redemption payment would be made on the cross of Calvary. Salvation in the Old Testament was effectual—even Enoch, Moses, and Elijah were taken to heaven centuries before Christ paid the redemptive price. But one wonders what would have happened to them if Christ had failed.

We are told that Christ assumed human nature with the possibility of sinning. Had He failed, "Satan would have triumphed, and the world would have been lost." But for our sakes, He "took the risk of failure and eternal loss."[10] How far-reaching the consequence of "eternal loss" would be we simply do not know, and we should avoid speculating.

Praise the Lord, Christ paid for the salvation of all humanity, including Old Testament believers who were saved in advance! No debt is left for any of us to pay. In fact, Christ overpaid the price of our salvation, for "where sin abounded, grace abounded much more" (Romans 5:20). Let us be thankful for and rejoice in His most gracious and precious gift.

*I*NSPIRED *L*EGACY

I, Tertius, who wrote this epistle, greet you in the Lord.

—Romans 16:22

Some people believe that all inspired writings were dictated word for word to the prophets by the Holy Spirit. In some instances, that was the case; but in general, the prophet himself or herself selected the words to convey the message. Speaking of her own experience, Ellen White explained, "Although I am as dependent upon the Spirit of the Lord in writing my views as I am in receiving them, yet the words I employ in describing what I have seen are my own, unless they be those spoken to me by an angel, which I always enclose in marks of quotation."[11]

Canonical prophets used secretaries and literary assistants. For instance, Jeremiah used Baruch as his secretary (Jeremiah 36). The Epistle to the Romans was authored by Paul (Romans 1:1) but physically written by Tertius (Romans 16:22). Likewise, Ellen White was helped at first by her own husband and later by other editorial assistants. One of their tasks was to gather previous materials she wrote so that she could use some of them in producing new materials. Ellen White compiled most of her books from her previous writings, and she always supervised the whole process. After her death in 1915, the trustees of her estate assumed that responsibility.

On **February 9, 1912**, Ellen White signed the final version of her last will and testament, appointing a self-perpetuating board of trustees, originally composed of William C. White, Clarence C. Crisler, Charles H. Jones, Arthur G. Daniells, and Frank M. Wilcox. Per the provision of Ellen White's will, the board would be responsible "for the improvement of the books and manuscripts held in trust by them, and herein provided; for the securing and printing of new translations thereof; for the printing of compilations from my manuscripts."[12] This means that she herself envisioned the production of new compilations from her writings according to the needs and challenges the church would face in the future.

So, when you find similarities and parallel statements in different places of the Bible or in the writings of Ellen White, do not be surprised. They carry God's message to us in the same way as when they were originally written. Let us read and study them respectfully as His word for us today.

Prophetic GPS

*Whether you turn to the right or to the left, your ears will hear
a voice behind you, saying, "This is the way; walk in it."*
—Isaiah 30:21, NIV

There was a time when finding some places could be quite a headache. But life and traveling became much easier with the improvement and popularization of the GPS. This space-based radio navigation system is operated by the United States Air Force and made available worldwide. "On **February 10, 1993**, the National Aeronautic Association selected the GPS Team as winners of the 1992 Robert J. Collier Trophy, the nation's most prestigious aviation award."[13] Undeniably, GPS is one of today's most important and useful technologies.

GPS devices can show us the route we should follow, warn us when we are in danger of leaving it, and bring us back to it if we miss a turn. There is a spiritual parallel: Jesus is "the way" (John 14:6), and the Holy Spirit is the divine Agent who keeps us faithful to Jesus and His word (John 16:13, 14). According to God's promise, "Whether you turn to the right or to the left, your ears will hear a voice behind you, saying, 'This is the way; walk in it' " (Isaiah 30:21, NIV). One of the most important instruments the Holy Spirit uses in carrying out this function is the gift of prophecy.

As Seventh-day Adventists, we believe that Ellen White's inspired writings are a prophetic GPS to guide us through the final and most challenging part of our journey to our heavenly home. As with a GPS device, which is only a tool to keep us on the right route, Mrs. White's writings are not intended to replace the Bible but to keep us faithful to it. They put boundaries on our biblical interpretation so that we do not distort the true meaning of God's Word. Disliking those boundaries, critics and revisionists undermine Ellen White's prophetic authority so that they can have the freedom to twist the biblical text.

We should never silence or distort God's wonderful prophetic word. As Christ said to the Seventy, "He who hears you hears Me, he who rejects you rejects Me, and he who rejects Me rejects Him who sent Me" (Luke 10:16). If Ellen White was a false prophet, we should reject her; but on the other hand, if she was a true prophet, we should accept her divinely inspired messages for us today.

$\mathcal{D}$EADLY $\mathcal{W}$OUND $\mathcal{H}$EALED

And I saw one of his heads as if it had been mortally wounded, and his deadly wound was healed. And all the world marveled and followed the beast.

—Revelation 13:3

Historically, Adventists have understood Revelation 13:3 as referring to the Roman ecclesiastical system and not to any individual pope. The French Revolution and Napoleonic Wars challenged the authority of the Roman Catholic Church, and in 1798, Pope Pius VI was taken into captivity by French troops. For more than 130 years, the papacy was deprived of any temporal authority. But that "deadly wound" was largely healed on **February 11, 1929,** when Cardinal Pietro Gasparri and Italian Prime Minister Benito Mussolini signed the Lateran Treaty, establishing Vatican City as an independent state and recognizing the pope as the head of that state.

The political influence of the papacy was further strengthened in 1984 when President Ronald Reagan and Pope John Paul II established formal diplomatic relations between the United States and the Holy See. In his book *The Keys of This Blood,*[14] Malachi Martin uncovered many of the Vatican's strategies for global political hegemony. It was no surprise when *Time* magazine named Pope John Paul II as "Man of the Year" in 1994. And in 2015, Pope Francis delivered a historic speech to the United States Congress.

The Second Vatican Ecumenical Council (1962–1965) aimed to restore "unity among all Christians," for "Christ the Lord founded one Church and one Church only,"[15] which "subsists in the Catholic Church, governed by the Successor of Peter and by the Bishops in communion with him."[16] Ecumenical and interreligious dialogues have since endeavored to bring religious groups into the fellowship of the Roman Catholic Church.

As chief of both church and state, the pope cannot say, "My kingdom is not of this world" (John 18:36). The union of religious and temporal powers has jeopardized religious freedom in the past and will do so again at the end of time (see Revelation 13). Remember, freedom is a blessing we value fully only after we lose it. It is our Christian duty to promote the separation of church and state with the purpose of fostering religious freedom for all.

BLESSED ASSURANCE

My heart is steadfast, O God, my heart is steadfast; I will sing and give praise.
—Psalm 57:7

Some obstacles seem too large to overcome and some periods of hardship too long to endure. While facing major challenges, you should ask yourself, "Am I allowing these obstacles to overcome me? Or am I willing to overcome them?"

Frances Jane Crosby, commonly known as Fanny Crosby, was born in Putnam County, New York, on March 24, 1820. Due to a medical error, she was blinded when she was only six weeks old. Nevertheless, she became a most inspiring example by overcoming this huge obstacle. When she was only eight years old, she had already written, "Oh, what a happy soul I am, / although I cannot see! / I am resolved that in this world / Contented I will be."[17] She believed that living her whole life unsighted would give her an amazing privilege: "When I get to heaven, the first face that shall ever gladden my sight will be that of my Savior!"[18] She died on **February 12, 1915**, leaving a far-reaching legacy of nearly nine thousand poems and hymns.

One of her most loved hymns was "Blessed Assurance." Its first stanza and refrain say,

Blessed assurance, Jesus is mine!
O, what a foretaste of glory divine!
Heir of salvation, purchase of God,
Born of His Spirit, washed in His blood.

This is my story, this is my song,
Praising my Savior all the day long.[19]

Crosby enriched her own spiritual life and the lives of others through hymns, and we should do the same. According to Ellen White, "The value of song as a means of education should never be lost sight of. Let there be singing in the home, of songs that are sweet and pure, and there will be fewer words of censure and more of cheerfulness and hope and joy. Let there be singing in the school, and the pupils will be drawn closer to God, to their teachers, and to one another."[20] In addition to following this advice in your home and school, lift your spirits by keeping a nice hymn in your mind throughout the day.

Saving Our Loved Ones

My son, keep your father's command
and do not forsake your mother's teaching.
Bind them always on your heart;
fasten them around your neck.
When you walk, they will guide you;
when you sleep, they will watch over you;
when you awake, they will speak to you.

—Proverbs 6:20–22, NIV

Many Christian families were once united by the same faith, the same values, and the same lifestyle. Parents and children would go to church together and worship together at home. But often, after the children go to high school and college, their values change. And afterward, the parents are left only with nostalgic memories of what religion once meant to their children. They fervently pray to God for the return of their children.

In early 1867, James and Ellen White spent six weeks at Greenville, Michigan, before moving there for a few years. Concerned for the spiritual welfare of her second son, James Edson White, on **February 13, 1867**, she wrote him a touching motherly letter:

I have more anxiety that you should become an humble Christian than to attain to an exalted position in this world. I am anxious for you to develop a character worthy of the better life. It is but a small matter to qualify yourself to live in this little short life. It is the life to come, the endless life, which should engage your highest ambition. And can it be that this little short, suffering life is of so much moment with you that it eclipses all the value of the immortal life promised on condition of faithful obedience? Will you, Edson, give yourself to God without reserve? Will you seek to develop a good Christian character? . . . Let your name be inscribed in the Lamb's Book of Life as one of His faithful, devoted soldiers, and it is all I ask. For this I pray daily. Will you, Edson, will you turn to your Redeemer with full purpose of heart?[21]

Is there someone in your own family who needs a conversion or reconversion experience? Perhaps even you? Looking at it from God's perspective, we should recognize that it is much wiser to "become an humble Christian than to attain to an exalted position in this world." How wonderful it would be if our families could remain united throughout eternity! Let's do our best to rebuild and solidify our families around the biblical values we all once embraced.

$\mathcal{V}$ALENTINE'S $\mathcal{D}$AY

And above all things have fervent love for one another,
for "love will cover a multitude of sins."

—1 Peter 4:8

Love is the fire that warms our hearts, the wind that drives our imaginations, and the water that refreshes our souls. Time spent together is never enough for those in love with each other. As the romantic saying goes: "If I had my life to live over again, next time I would find you sooner so that I could love you longer!"

Valentine's Day is commemorated on **February 14** as a special day of love and affection. According to an ancient legend, Saint Valentine tried to convert Roman Emperor Claudius II to Christianity and was sentenced to death. While in prison, he performed a miracle by healing Julia, the blind daughter of his jailer Asterius. On the evening before his execution, he supposedly sent her the first "valentine" card signed as "Your Valentine." Another legend suggests that Saint Valentine performed clandestine Christian weddings for soldiers who were forbidden to marry. Claudius II supposedly believed that married men did not make good soldiers.

Over time, Valentine's Day has become associated with romantic love and close friendship. The custom of sending cards, flowers, chocolates, and other gifts originated in the United Kingdom and was adopted in many other countries around the world. The US Greeting Card Association estimates that approximately 190 million valentines are sent each year in the United States. Half of them are given to family members other than husband or wife, usually to children. That figure goes up to 1 billion when the valentine-exchange cards made in school activities are included. Interestingly, schoolteachers receive the most valentine's cards.

We should remember that our words are meaningful only to the extent they are confirmed by our actions. So, let's take advantage of this day to *proclaim* and *demonstrate* our love and affection to those who are dear to us. You could also include a word of gratitude to someone who helped you through past difficulties but perhaps is no longer as close to you as he or she once was. By sending a message and perhaps a simple, inexpensive gift, we demonstrate that the recipient is special to us. Regardless of the response, we are sowing seeds of love!

THE TIME OF THE END

"But you, Daniel, shut up the words, and seal the book until the time of the end; many shall run to and fro, and knowledge shall increase."
—Daniel 12:4

Through the centuries, many Bible expositors have studied the apocalyptic prophecies of Scripture. But no other single event in modern times generated more interest in that topic than the imprisonment of Pope Pius VI on **February 15, 1798**, by French troops led by General Louis-Alexandre Berthier. Concerned about the French Revolution that was crushing Christianity in France, the pope condemned the revolution and even supported a league against it. In response, French soldiers conquered Rome, deposed the pope from his temporal authority, and even escorted him as a prisoner to various locations. He died in the citadel of Valence on August 29, 1799. Not until 1929 would the Vatican State be fully reinstated.

Bible expositors saw the imprisonment of the pope as the *end* of the 1,260 year-days of papal supremacy (Revelation 11:3; 12:6; cf. Daniel 7:25; Revelation 11:2; 12:14; 13:5) and the *beginning* of "the time of the end" (Daniel 8:17; 11:35, 40; 12:4, 9; cf. 8:19). That striking event generated major interest in Bible prophecies. The two sealed time prophecies in the book of Daniel—the 2,300 symbolic evenings and mornings (Daniel 8:14, 19, 26, 27) and the "time, times, and half a time" (Daniel 12:4–7)—were finally unveiled. From then on, time would be no longer just *regular* time (Greek, *kronos*) but rather *eschatological* time (Greek, *eschaton*). Thus, the time had become solemn, and there was a growing awareness of it.

Preachers around the globe emphasized the fulfillment of both the time prophecies and the cosmic signs of Christ's soon return (Matthew 24:29–31; Luke 21:25–28). But He did not return as soon as expected. And today, "the time of the end" has already been prolonged for more than two centuries. As foretold in the parable of the wise and foolish virgins (Matthew 25:1–13), the bridegroom's delay would cause all of the virgins to slumber and sleep. But the parable assures us that the bridegroom's coming was only delayed, not canceled. If that glorious event was *somewhat* near more than two hundred years ago, it is *much* nearer now. If in those days Advent believers already lived in eager anticipation, today we should live with even more expectancy. We must not, at this late date, give up our blessed hope.

EGYPTIAN ALLUREMENTS

"Come now, therefore, and I will send you to Pharaoh that
you may bring My people, the children of Israel, out of Egypt."

—Exodus 3:10

Those who watched the famous film *The Ten Commandments* have at least some idea of the splendors of ancient Egypt. Scholars list approximately 170 known pharaohs who ruled the country. Many of their burial sites have been plundered by thieves. However, on November 4, 1922, an archaeological team led by British Egyptologist Howard Carter discovered the tomb of Pharaoh Tutankhamun (ca. 1332–1323 BC), who ascended to the throne when he was about nine years old and died around the age of eighteen.

On **February 16, 1923**, Carter's team entered the sealed burial chamber of Tutankhamun, which was covered in gold and decorated with mystic symbols of protection. Inside the sarcophagus was the undisturbed mummy wrapped with 143 pieces of jewelry and covered with the famous blue and gold funerary mask. Nearly a decade after opening the tomb, Carter finished photographing and cataloging all pf its 5,398 items, including thrones, archery bows, trumpets, a lotus chalice, food, wine, sandals, fresh linen underwear, and a ceremonial sailing boat for the pharaoh's journey to the afterlife.

Ancient mystic Egyptians conceived of the human body as the home for the three parts of the soul—the *ka*, the *ba*, and the *akh*. Without the body as their physical meeting point, "the parts of the soul would become lost from each other, and the individual would cease to exist."[22] The mummification process, with its many rituals and prayers, aimed to keep the body whole for the afterlife. The tombs also held the basic means to make the journey to the world to come as comfortable as possible.

The ten plagues that preceded the Israelites' exodus from Egypt were God's judgments against the Egyptian superstitions (see Exodus 7–11). In contrast with the mummified Egyptian bodies, God will provide His followers with completely new and glorified bodies and a life with Him in heaven. "For our citizenship is in heaven, from which we also eagerly wait for the Savior, the Lord Jesus Christ, who will transform our lowly body that it may be conformed to His glorious body" (Philippians 3:20, 21). What a blessed assurance and wonderful hope we have!

AGENTS OF APOSTASY

"Dan shall be a serpent by the way,
A viper by the path,
That bites the horse's heels
So that its rider shall fall backward."

—Genesis 49:17

The experience of Eve in the Garden of Eden (Genesis 3:6) confirmed that "it is virtually impossible to live without being an evangelist, either for God or for Satan."[23] This principle was dramatically illustrated in the life of Dudley M. Canright (1840–1919), a foremost Adventist preacher in the 1870s and 1880s. Emotionally and spiritually unstable, he left the church and returned to it three times. Finally, at his own request, on **February 17, 1887**, his name was dropped from the church books in Otsego, Michigan, and he never returned.

As early as October 15, 1880, Ellen White wrote to him,

I was made sad to hear of your decision, but I have had reason to expect it. . . .

But if you have decided to cut all connection with us as a people, I have one request to make . . . : keep away from our people. . . .

I beg of you to go entirely away from those who believe the truth; for if you have chosen the world and the friends of the world, go with those of your own choice. Do not poison the minds of others and make yourself Satan's special agent to work the ruin of souls.[24]

Disregarding her request, Canright became one of the most bitter critics of the Seventh-day Adventist Church and Ellen White. Criticism harms our own dispositions and destroys our faith. We must be extremely careful. Ellen White warns us,

I saw that some are withering spiritually. They have lived some time watching to keep their brethren straight—watching for every fault to make trouble with them. And while doing this, their minds are not on God, nor on heaven, nor on the truth; but just where Satan wants them—on someone else. Their souls are neglected; they seldom see or feel their own faults, for they have had enough to do to watch the faults of others without so much as looking to their own souls or searching their own hearts. . . . Unless they reform, there will be no place in heaven for them, for they would find fault with the Lord Himself.[25]

Remember, faith and criticism cannot coexist. So, let's stop our criticism and build faith!

*T*HE *B*ATTLE *C*REEK *F*IRES

"Those whom I love I rebuke and discipline. So be earnest and repent."
—Revelation 3:19, NIV

There is something strange about your SDA fires, with the water poured on acting more like gasoline," declared Fire Chief Weeks of Battle Creek, Michigan.[26]

Why had the Battle Creek Fire Department been so unsuccessful in fighting the 1902 Adventist fires? In the early twentieth century, much turmoil was going on while Dr. John H. Kellogg was spreading his pantheistic view that nature is an extension of God. Kellogg and his associates attempted to control the whole church. Battle Creek had become an overcrowded center of church activities and problems. The town housed the General Conference headquarters, the Review and Herald Publishing Association, the huge Battle Creek Sanitarium, the Battle Creek College, and the large Dime Tabernacle.

Ellen White was much concerned about the centralization and advised church leaders to move the General Conference and other institutions to different locations. In November 1901, she warned, "Unless there is a reformation, calamity will overtake the publishing house, and the world will know the reason."[27] But her counsels were ignored.

In the early morning of **February 18, 1902**, the Battle Creek Sanitarium burned down. Instead of envisioning many smaller health-reform institutions in different locations, Kellogg decided to rebuild the sanitarium on an even larger scale. To help fund construction, he ordered five thousand copies of his book *The Living Temple* to be printed by the Review and Herald Publishing Association. Before they did so, however, the publishing house was also destroyed by a fire of unknown origin on December 30, 1902.

On January 5, 1903, Ellen White wrote to the brethren in Battle Creek, "Today I received a letter from Elder Daniells regarding the destruction of the Review office by fire. I feel very sad as I consider the great loss to the cause. . . . But I was not surprised by the sad news, for in the visions of the night I have seen an angel standing with a sword as of fire stretched over Battle Creek."[28]

God often uses tragedies to wake up His people. But what a blessing it would be if, without any disciplinary measures, we would proactively follow His prophetic word!

OUR POTENTIAL

Whatever your hand finds to do, do it with your might.
—Ecclesiastes 9:10

Some people make a huge difference in the world, and others almost none at all. Do you think a genius is *born* or *made*? To what extent are our own abilities inherited and developed? Some answers to these questions may be learned from the lives of those who left their mark on world history.

For example, on **February 19, 1878**, Thomas Edison was awarded US Patent No. 200,521 for the phonograph, a device that recorded music and allowed it to be played back. This was only one among 1,093 US patents he received during his lifetime.

Edison followed an interesting life philosophy, reflected in some popular sayings attributed to him. For example, he was convinced that if we did all the things we are capable of, we would literally astound ourselves. Regarding the value of hard work, he declared that genius is one percent inspiration and ninety-nine percent perspiration.

As to perseverance, Edison is often quoted as saying, "Our greatest weakness lies in giving up. The most certain way to succeed is always to try just one more time." And further, "Many of life's failures are people who did not realize how close they were to success when they gave up." He believed that even our failures could teach us great lessons.

Remember that honesty, creativity, thoroughness, and perseverance are basic components of building success. King Solomon advised, "Whatever your hand finds to do, do it with your might" (Ecclesiastes 9:10). In contrast, the prophet Jeremiah alerted, "Cursed is the one who does the LORD's work negligently" (Jeremiah 48:10, NASB).

Modern civilization is much more prone to pleasure and laziness than to hard work and major accomplishments. It seems that life has become an end in itself. Few people are concerned with leaving a positive legacy for future generations. But blessed are those who flee from mediocrity and superficiality! If we want to honor God with what we do, we should always do our best, as if we were employed by Him and working for Him.

Complex Marriage

But because of the temptation to immorality, each man should
have his own wife and each woman her own husband.

—1 Corinthians 7:2, RSV

When God created Adam and Eve, He established marriage as a sacred, monogamous, and enduring institution (Genesis 2:24; Matthew 19:4–6). But through the ages, some individuals and even communities have distorted that institution to satisfy their own sensual desires. A classic example is John Humphrey Noyes, a controversial Christian preacher and ideologist who, in early 1844, organized a utopist religious community in Putney, Vermont. In 1848, Noyes moved that community to Oneida, in upstate New York.

While studying at Yale Divinity School, Noyes concluded that Christ's second coming had taken place back in AD 70 and that now we are living in the age of the Spirit.[29] On **February 20, 1834**, he declared himself free of sin, and soon after, he began to preach a lifestyle free from all kinds of slavery and selfishness, including the slavery of monogamous marriage. For him, "in a holy community, there is no more reason why sexual intercourse should be restricted by law, than why eating and drinking should be—and there is as little occasion for shame in the one case as in the other."[30] The Putney Community and the Oneida Community practiced free love, or complex marriage, in which every man could be the husband of every woman, and every woman the wife of every man. The children born there belonged to the community. They did not know who their fathers were and were taken away from their mothers as soon as she discontinued breastfeeding them. Before being disbanded in 1880, the community had more than three hundred members.

Noyes didn't realize that true religion is not humanity reaching toward God but, rather, God's revelation to humanity. "The religion that comes from God is the only religion that will lead to God."[31] Noyes developed a so-called sinless community so he could freely satisfy his sinful instincts!

The very essence of religion is exclusive loyalty to one God (Exodus 20:3). Likewise, the very essence of marriage is enduring, exclusive faithfulness to one spouse (1 Corinthians 7:2). Loyalty to God and faithfulness to one's spouse are spiritual virtues that must not be confused with selfishness. They are expressions of love that need to be cultivated.

ℒonging for Your Salvation

"Seek the Lord while He may be found, call upon Him while He is near."
—Isaiah 55:6

Salvation is an individual choice, but it comes with deep social consequences. Have you ever thought about how many family members and friends are hoping to see you in heaven? Perhaps you are even praying for someone very close to you who has not accepted Jesus or who has left Him.

Ellen White and her twin sister, Elizabeth "Lizzie" Bangs, remained close but followed different paths. While Ellen dedicated her whole life to Jesus, Lizzie showed little interest in religious matters. Through the years, Ellen appealed to her many times. One of Ellen's most touching letters was written on **February 21, 1891**, the same year Lizzie died.

I love to speak of Jesus and His matchless love and my whole soul is in this work. I have not one doubt of the love of God and His care and His mercy and ability to save to the utmost all who come unto Him. That which I have seen of His precious love is a reality to me. . . .

Don't you believe on Jesus, Lizzie? Do you not believe He is your Saviour? That He has evidenced His love for you in giving His own precious life that you might be saved? All that is required of you is to take Jesus as your own precious Saviour. . . .

Dear sister, it is no wonderful thing that you have to do. You feel poor, suffering, and afflicted, and Jesus invites all of this class to come to Him. . . . The hands that were nailed to the cross for you are stretched out to save you. You need not fear as you lie on a bed of sickness and death. Friends may feel sorrowful, but they cannot save you. Your physician cannot save you. But there is One who died that you might live through eternal ages. Just believe that Jesus will hear your confession, receive your penitence, and forgive every sin and make you children of God. Jesus pleads in your behalf. Will you give yourself in trusting faith to Jesus? I long to take you in my arms and lay you on the bosom of Jesus Christ. . . .

. . . With Jesus as your blessed Friend you need not fear to die, for it will be to you like closing your eyes here and opening them in heaven. Then we shall meet never more to part.[32]

Please reflect today on this lovely appeal as if it were written to you!

OUR SUFFICIENT CREED

All Scripture is given by inspiration of God, and is profitable for doctrine,
for reproof, for correction, for instruction in righteousness, that the man
of God may be complete, thoroughly equipped for every good work.

—2 Timothy 3:16, 17

A creed is a brief, authoritative formula of religious beliefs and principles that strongly influence the way people think and live. Unfortunately, many Christian creeds, supposedly based on the Bible, have undermined the very authority and teachings of the Bible. Concerned about it, one nineteenth-century preacher emphasized the restoration of the Bible as the only true Christian creed.

On **February 22, 1846**, at the dedication of the Second Presbyterian Church in Fort Wayne, Indiana, Charles Beecher (1815–1900) delivered two discourses titled "The Bible a Sufficient Creed."[33] Beecher's discourses addressed (1) the Bible as a sufficient creed and (2) its substitution by any other creed as a step into apostasy. He stated that in our study of Scripture, we could use some helpful tools and resources, "remembering always that the strongest evidence *lies in the text itself.*"[34]

From the content of 2 Timothy 3:16, 17, Beecher pointed out that the Bible is intended (1) "for doctrine," covering the whole ground of the teaching of truth; (2) "for reproof," covering "the whole ground of the prevention, or extirpation of error"; (3) "for correction," covering "the entire ground of Church discipline, including the whole fabric of Church government"; and (4) "for instruction in righteousness," covering "the whole ground of training, of schooling, or education in personal holiness, commonly called experiential religion."[35] For Beecher, "the more truth is taught, the more error dies."[36] He challenged parents to "try the power of God's words upon the pliant natures" of their children and to "plant those living words deep."[37]

In contrast with the Roman Catholic and Protestant *closed* creeds, the Seventh-day Adventist Church has only a *revisable* Statement of Fundamental Beliefs. All revisions of those beliefs must be grounded in the Bible as our only creed. Scripture has a unique, transforming power that cannot be complemented by any ecclesiastical document.

ℐESUS ℒOVES THE 𝒰NWORTHY

But God demonstrates His own love toward us,
in that while we were still sinners, Christ died for us.

—Romans 5:8

William W. Prescott (1855–1944) was an influential educator, editor, and administrator who helped shape the Adventist educational system. In the **February 23, 1893**, *General Conference Daily Bulletin*, Prescott stated that "all our doctrines have their basis in a proper knowledge of the gospel, and grow out of a belief in Jesus Christ as a living personal Savior."[38] In his undated pamphlet entitled *Victory in Christ*, he left us the following insightful statement.

This is what touches my heart. It has always been easy for me to believe that God loves the world, and that Jesus loves His church, but I could never see any reason why He should love me. I have found, however, that there is no reason, so far as I am concerned. The explanation is simple enough when I look to Him and not to myself. He is love. Love is the very essence of His being. Love is His life. Love is the atmosphere in which He lives. He loves because He lives. His love does not seek out the worthy, but the unworthy. Therefore He loves me.

Jesus deals with us as individuals. His heart is large enough, His love is great enough, His knowledge is comprehensive enough, for the personal touch with each one. He knows me by name, just as He calls all the infinite number of stars by their names. He knows my experiences. He sympathizes with me in my trials and temptations. He loves me as if I were the only object of His love. . . .

. . . Each morning I choose to accept His love. Each morning I choose to love and work for Him. Each morning I say to Him, "Thy love has round [*sic*] me and drawn me, and I am Thine." I am at liberty to leave Him at any moment, but I am held by bonds that do not chafe—the silken cords of love. I do not wish to do anything in which I cannot cooperate with Him. He rules me with a rod of love, and life's joy and sweetness are found in the closest association with Him.

Do you know that He loves you? You are missing the best thing in life if your heart is not the shrine of His love.[39]

$\mathcal{P}$EACEMAKERS

"Blessed are the peacemakers, for they will be called children of God."
—Matthew 5:9, NIV

One of the most venerated Roman Catholic "saints" of all time is Francis of Assisi, who was born into a wealthy Italian merchant family. On **February 24, 1208**, Francis attended Mass, and that day the priest read Jesus' instructions to the Twelve (Matthew 10:5–10). From that day, Francis devoted himself to a life of poverty. He became an itinerant evangelist and later founded the monastic Order of Friars Minor. The famous "Peace Prayer of Saint Francis of Assisi," traditionally credited to his authorship, is thought-provoking for every believer.

O Lord, make me an instrument of Thy Peace!
Where there is hatred, let me sow love.
Where there is injury, pardon.
Where there is discord, harmony.
Where there is doubt, faith.
Where there is despair, hope.
Where there is darkness, light.
Where there is sorrow, joy.

Oh Divine Master, grant that I may not
so much seek to be consoled as to console;
to be understood as to understand;
to be loved as to love;
for it is in giving that we receive;
it is in pardoning that we are pardoned;
and it is in dying that we are born to Eternal Life. [40]

Today, God grants you another opportunity to be "the salt of the earth" and "light of the world" (Matthew 5:13, 14), and you can make a difference in the lives of those around you. May the love of God shine through you today and every day!

$\mathcal{T}$HE $\mathcal{P}$ASSION OF CHRIST

And when Jesus had cried out with a loud voice, He said, "Father, 'into Your hands I commit My spirit.'" Having said this, He breathed His last.

—Luke 23:46

The cross of Christ is the greatest monument to God's love in the whole universe. Stephen N. Haskell wrote, "Eternity can never fathom the depth of love revealed in the cross of Calvary. It was there that the infinite love of Christ and the unbounded selfishness of Satan stood face to face."[41] Even so, many attempts have been made to unveil at least some glimpses of the price Jesus Christ paid for our sins.

Much light was shed on the Roman method of crucifixion in Martin Hengel's book *Crucifixion*.[42] It was indeed a barbaric form of execution of the utmost cruelty, not intended for regular Roman citizens but only for rebellious foreigners and violent criminals and robbers. With the victims completely naked, it was applied in the cruelest, most shameful, and most sarcastic way possible. No wonder Paul spoke of Christ crucified as "a stumbling block to Jews and foolishness to Gentiles" (1 Corinthians 1:23, NIV).

On **February 25, 2004**, Mel Gibson's famous film *The Passion of the Christ* was released, providing a dramatic reconstruction of Christ's sufferings from the time Judas betrayed Him until the cross. Considered one of the most violent and powerful movies ever created, *The Passion of the Christ* was designed to grab the viewer's attention from start to finish. But the film focused much more on the physical brutality of Jesus' crucifixion than on the actual meaning of the cross. Remember, Christ was held on the cross not by the nails that pierced His hands and feet but by His great desire to save each of us!

An amazing transforming power flows from the cross. Therefore, "it would be well for us to spend a thoughtful hour each day in contemplation of the life of Christ. We should take it point by point, and let the imagination grasp each scene, especially the closing ones. As we thus dwell upon His great sacrifice for us, our confidence in Him will be more constant, our love will be quickened, and we shall be more deeply imbued with His spirit. If we would be saved at last, we must learn the lesson of penitence and humiliation at the foot of the cross."[43]

Why not take this inspired advice?

PUBLIC HUMILIATIONS

Also to You, O Lord, belongs mercy; for You render to each one according to his work.
—Psalm 62:12

Nothing that human beings do is perfect. But there are some public mistakes that are absolutely inexcusable. On Sunday, **February 26, 2017**, the Dolby Theater (formerly the Kodak Theater) in Los Angeles, California, was packed with celebrities for the eighty-ninth Academy Awards, or 2017 Oscars. Some 33 million viewers around the world were watching the much-expected event. On the stage, presenters Warren Beatty and Faye Dunaway announced the winners in various categories. They named *La La Land* the best-picture winner, and the film team rushed to the stage to receive their statuettes.

While they were still onstage hugging one another and thanking family and friends, *La La Land* producer Jordan Horowitz returned to the microphone and pointed out that, in fact, *Moonlight* had won the award. Then, he and his group handed their statuettes over to the real winners. Distractedly, Brian Cullinan had given Mr. Beatty the spare best-actress envelope instead of the best-picture envelope. The 2017 Oscars will likely be remembered not so much for its winners as for this major gaffe.

Another embarrassing event was the Miss Universe competition in Las Vegas, Nevada, on December 20, 2015. At the ceremony's climax, host Steve Harvey announced Ariadna Gutiérrez from Colombia as the winner. Amid much applause, outgoing titleholder Paulina Vega crowned her with the Miss Universe sash and tiara. But a few minutes later, Harvey admitted his error, and Paulina publicly removed the glorious emblems from Ariadna and put them on Pia Wurtzbach from the Philippines. Ariadna did not deserve to be treated like that.

In contrast to such faulty decisions and public humiliations, we are assured that "God is a just judge" (Psalm 7:11) and "judges the world with righteousness" (Psalm 9:8, NRSV). The apostle Paul affirms that "all of us must appear before the judgment seat of Christ" (2 Corinthians 5:10, NRSV). This implies that every case will be fairly decided prior to Christ's second coming, without any unfair or unnecessary surprises. Fairness and loyalty are the basis of God's judgment. You may trust that he will never overdo any penalty or withdraw any deserved reward. Everyone will be honestly rewarded according to his or her works.

ETERNAL REWARD

He shall see the labor of His soul, and be satisfied. By His knowledge
My righteous Servant shall justify many, for He shall bear their iniquities.
—Isaiah 53:11

Saturday, **February 27, 1988**, in London. The popular weekly BBC television program *That's Life!* featured the life of Nicholas Winton (1909–2015), who was sitting in the first row of the audience. At one point, TV presenter Esther Rantzen showed an old scrapbook Winton's wife, Grete, had found in their attic. The forgotten scrapbook carried the records, photos, names, and documents of the Czech Jewish children he had rescued during the Nazi occupation.

The story goes back to 1939, when the twenty-nine-year-old Winton went from his native London to Prague, Czechoslovakia. There he worked during the day as a stock-broker, and at night he rescued children, sending them by train to the United Kingdom. He saved 669 children until war broke out and kids could no longer leave Czechoslovakia. In fact, he kept his heroic deeds to himself for almost fifty years. Even his own wife, whom he married in 1948, didn't know about his rescue efforts until she found his scrapbook.

At the end of the *That's Life!* program, Rantzen asked the audience members who owed their lives to Winton to stand up. He was deeply moved when he realized that the studio audience was composed largely of the children he had rescued. From then on, those grown-up children considered him their honorary father. On December 31, 2002, he was knighted by Queen Elizabeth II in recognition of his work and became Sir Nicholas Winton. On October 28, 2014, he was awarded the highest honor of the Czech Republic. He died on July 1, 2015, at 106.

This touching experience reminds us of Christ, who left His heavenly throne, came to our dark and sinful world to rescue us from impending eternal death, and will soon take us to heaven. In His priestly prayer, He even asked, "Father, I want those you have given me to be with me where I am, and to see my glory, the glory you have given me" (John 17:24, NIV). The time is coming when we will meet Him face-to-face and even talk to Him. What a glorious meeting it will be with the redeemed from all nations and ages! We are told that "He shall see the labor of His soul, and be satisfied" (Isaiah 53:11). Will He see you there as well?

*T*HE *P*ERPETUAL COVENANT

"Therefore the children of Israel shall keep the Sabbath, to observe
the Sabbath throughout their generations as a perpetual covenant."

—Exodus 31:16

Humble beginnings can lead to huge results! This is how the rich arsenal of Seventh-day Adventist publications on the Sabbath began.

William Miller had stated in his "Lecture on the Great Sabbath" that "the Sabbath which remains is to be kept on the first day of every week, as a perpetual sign."[44] Millerite preacher Thomas M. Preble responded to this statement in an article, "The Sabbath," published in *Hope of Israel* on **February 28, 1845**. Shortly after, Preble expanded the article and published it in tract form and titled it *A Tract, Showing That the Seventh Day Should Be Observed as the Sabbath, Instead of the First Day; "According to the Commandment"* (1845).

Preble argued that (1) "only one kind of Sabbath was given to Adam, and only one remains for us" today (Hebrews 4:4–11); (2) on the cross, only the ceremonial sabbaths ceased, not the original moral Sabbath;[45] (3) "the disciples evidently kept the first day of the week as a *festival*, in commemoration of the resurrection of Christ, but never as *the Sabbath*";[46] (4) the post-apostolic change from Sabbath to Sunday was the work of the little horn who would change "times and laws" (Daniel 7:25);[47] (5) "if the children of God are the true Israel,"[48] then we should keep the Sabbath as well; and (6) we should begin "the Sabbath on Friday evening, and end on Saturday evening."[49]

Preble's article persuaded Joseph Bates from Fairhaven, Massachusetts, to accept the seventh-day Sabbath, and Bates later wrote his own tracts on the subject. Bates became the most influential Sabbath-keeping Adventist in leading other former Millerites to accept the Sabbath. Among them were the newly married couple James and Ellen White and J. N. Andrews, who eventually became the foremost Sabbath theologian in the denomination.

As a perpetual covenant between God and His faithful children, the seventh-day Sabbath has crossed the ages as an abiding channel of divine blessings to humanity. You, too, are invited to keep this day holy as a memorial of God's creation and redemption (Hebrews 4:4–11) and a foretaste of its eternal observance (Isaiah 66:22, 23). The Sabbath can bring new meaning to our busy lives!

AMAZING SPECTACLE

For we have been made a spectacle to the world, both to angels and to men.
—1 Corinthians 4:9

One of the most unique and fascinating places I have ever visited is Yellowstone National Park in the United States. It was established as a national park by the US Congress and President Ulysses S. Grant on **March 1, 1872**. "Yellowstone contains half of all the world's known geothermal features" and two-thirds of all the geysers on the planet.[1] While visiting the place, one is constantly tempted to say, "I wish that all of nature's magnificence, the emotion of the land, the living energy of place could be photographed."[2]

The word *geyser* comes from the Icelandic verb *geysa* (to gush)[3] and refers to a natural hot spring that regularly ejects a spray of steam and boiling water into the air. The most famous geyser at Yellowstone is Old Faithful, named by Henry D. Washburn in 1870. "This geyser erupts every 44 to 125 minutes"[4] and can spout "4,701 to 9,401 gallons of boiling water as high as 186"[5] feet into the air. Many expectant tourists watch the predictable geyser every day and are not disappointed by its performance.

The Bible says that we also are "a spectacle to the world, both to angels and to men" (1 Corinthians 4:9). Just as people come with expectations of Old Faithful, people also have expectations of us. They expect Christians to behave like Christians, and we shouldn't disappoint them. "Remember, our lives are the only Bible some people will ever read. Christians are to be living epistles, written by God and read by men."[6]

Rhetorical skills might convince and move multitudes for a time. But only our living example can give a lasting, transforming influence to our words. "The unstudied, unconscious influence of a holy life is the most convincing sermon that can be given in favor of Christianity. Argument, even when unanswerable, may provoke only opposition; but a godly example has a power that it is impossible wholly to resist."[7]

If you were the only Christian in the world, what would Christianity be like? Reflect on this question, and allow the Holy Spirit to transform your life as needed.

*T*HE *B*ASIS OF *O*UR *H*OPE

For we did not follow cunningly devised fables when we made known to you the power and
coming of our Lord Jesus Christ, but were eyewitnesses of His majesty.
—2 Peter 1:16

Several generations have enjoyed Frank Capra's captivating film *Lost Horizon*, which premiered in San Francisco, California, on **March 2, 1937**. Based on James Hilton's 1933 novel by the same name, the film tells the story of an airplane that runs out of fuel, eventually crashing into the snow-covered Himalayan Mountains. The pilot dies in the crash, but the few survivors are pulled from the wreckage and escorted by a group of Tibetans to the paradisiac valley of Shangri-la. Isolated from the outside world, the inhabitants grow in love and wisdom, living an almost perfect life of enduring harmony and joy.

The fantasy of Shangri-la highlights two basic values of human existence. One is the awareness that personal values and human relations are much more important than fleeting material possessions. As suggested by Martin Buber, while the world of experience is based on the words *I* and *It*, the world of relationships is grounded in the words *I* and *Thou*.[8] Thus, the materialistic stress of I and things should be balanced by an emphasis on I and You. After all, life finds its truest meaning in our relationships with God and others (Matthew 22:36–40).

The second basic value underscored by the film is the deep human longing for a better world. According to Emil Brunner, "What oxygen is for the lungs, such is hope for the meaning of human life. Take oxygen away and death occurs through suffocation, take hope away and humanity is constricted through lack of breath; despair supervenes, spelling the paralysis of intellectual and spiritual powers by a feeling of the senselessness and purposelessness of existence."[9]

In contrast to the fictional Shangri-la of *Lost Horizon*, our hope of eternal life does "not follow cunningly devised fables" (2 Peter 1:16). It is based on God's reliable promise of a perfect world with no more tears, pain, or death (Revelation 21:1–5). This promise gives meaning and purpose to our present life and assures us that all our loved ones who have died in Christ will finally be raised from the dead to inherit eternal life. What a glorious hope we have!

God's Leading

Show me your ways, Lord,
teach me your paths.
Guide me in your truth and teach me,
for you are God my Savior,
and my hope is in you all day long.

—Psalm 25:4, 5, NIV

God can lead our lives in unexpected and unpredictable ways. But how can we distinguish God's voice from mere intuition or even the voice of Satan trying to mislead us? Ellen White explains that "there are three ways in which the Lord reveals His will to us, to guide us, and to fit us to guide others."[10] First is His Word, the Holy Scriptures, which must be consulted before anything else. The second way is in His providential workings, which we can discern if we maintain a sanctifying relationship with God. And the third way is "through the appeals of His Holy Spirit, making impressions upon the heart, which will be wrought out in the character."[11]

The winds of the Great Depression were still blowing when C. H. Watson and W. H. Williams, General Conference president and under treasurer, respectively, were impressed to make some unscheduled banking transactions. On Thursday, **March 3, 1934**, Williams took the midnight train from Washington, DC, to New York City. The next morning, Friday, March 4, without telling anyone, he went to two different banks and sent three months' worth of funds in advance to most of the overseas missions of the Seventh-day Adventist Church. That afternoon, he returned to Takoma Park, Maryland.

The next morning (Sabbath), the newspaper headlines revealed that the banks were closed nationwide. After sunset, J. L. Shaw, General Conference treasurer, called an urgent meeting to discuss how to handle the financial crisis. Williams's explanation of what he had done on Friday brought much relief to the group. But what about the General Conference's own employee payroll? Williams reported that he regularly set aside funds, which he kept in envelopes of $1,000 each in a safety deposit box at the bank. This reserve would meet the payroll for three months.

The same Holy Spirit who inspired the Bible will never contradict the Bible. So, "if you are in doubt upon any subject you must first consult the Scriptures."[12] Through the sanctifying influence of the Scriptures, your conscience will become more and more sensitive to the impressions of the Holy Spirit.

"ᏋARTHEN ᏙESSELS"

But we have this treasure in earthen vessels, that the excellence
of the power may be of God and not of us.

—2 Corinthians 4:7

M any people wonder about the originality of the inspired writings: Can a true prophet copy from uninspired sources? If he or she does so, would those portions remain an uninspired island within the inspired writings? And furthermore, if a prophet does not provide the reference to the original source of information, would he or she be guilty of plagiarism?

Over the centuries, it was a common practice to use others' ideas without providing references to the original sources. A classic example is William Shakespeare, who, according to Ralph W. Emerson, "did owe debts in all directions, and was able to use whatever he found."[13] But in modern times, new regional and national acts have become stricter in regard to copyrights. In the United States, the Copyright Act of **March 4, 1909** (which went into effect on July 1, 1909) was the first federal law to effectively ensure literary, artistic, dramatic, and musical rights. So, it is quite unfair to judge classic authors (including prophets) based on our modern copyright laws and practices.

A thorough study of the Bible can unveil several instances in which its writers used uninspired sources. For instance, Paul quoted Epimenides of Crete (Acts 17:28; Titus 1:12), Aratus of Cilicia (Acts 17:28), and Menander (1 Corinthians 15:33). Jude quoted the pseudepigraph of 1 Enoch (Jude 14, 15). The book of Job contains several uninspired speeches accusing Job of doing evil. The Bible even quotes some of Satan's lies (Genesis 3:1–5; Matthew 4:3–11). Thus, prophetic inspiration does not imply absolute originality but only the divine assistance through the Holy Spirit for the reliable communication of truth and an unbiased account of facts.

We need at least a basic knowledge of how inspiration works in order to avoid distortions and misconceptions. Our focus should not be on the imperfect *container* that carries the message but rather on the *content* of the infallible message. "The treasure was entrusted to earthen vessels, yet it is, nonetheless, from Heaven. The testimony is conveyed through the imperfect expression of human language, yet it is the testimony of God."[14] The Bible does not just *contain* God's word; it actually *is* His word!

$\mathcal{M}$Y $\mathcal{D}$EAR CHILDREN

My son, keep your father's command,
And do not forsake the law of your mother.
Bind them continually upon your heart;
Tie them around your neck.

—Proverbs 6:20, 21

Children can have many friends but only two parents. Since friends play a non-disciplinary, supportive role, some teenagers expect their parents to behave as older friends. Far more than friends, parents have the sacred mission of teaching and preparing their children for life. Billy Graham stated, "A child who is allowed to be disrespectful to his parents will not have true respect for anyone."[15]

On **March 5, 1862**, Ellen White wrote a tender letter from Lodi, Wisconsin, to her children back home in Battle Creek, Michigan. She encouraged them to develop positive habits for daily life. She stated, "I am anxious you should encourage habits of order. Have a place for everything, and everything in its place. Take time to arrange your room, and keep it in order." She urged them to use their time wisely, for "Satan finds employment for idle hands and minds."[16] She closed her short letter with a touching spiritual appeal. She wrote, "Above all things, seek God. . . . Your parents have the deepest interest for you. But we cannot repent of your sins for you. We cannot take you to heaven. God alone in his love and infinite mercy can save you, and Jesus, the dear Saviour, invites you to his loving arms. He offers you salvation freely, if you will believe in him, love him, and render cheerful obedience."[17]

Many parents pray daily for the conversion or reconversion of their dear children. I know children who returned to God only after their parents had passed away with sorrowful hearts. Undoubtedly, it is far better to accept Christ later in life than never. But those children could have ignited a spark of joy in the hearts of their parents if they had made the decision earlier.

Reflecting on your own life, perhaps you should seriously consider this inspired advice: "Keep your father's command and do not forsake your mother's teaching" (Proverbs 6:20, NIV). Perhaps you need to surrender your life to God again and allow Him to lead you on the right path that you already know. If that is the case, then today is the best day to make the decision.

Sin of Omission

Anyone, then, who knows the right thing to do and fails to do it, commits sin.
—James 4:17, NRSV

The Irish statesman Edmund Burke said, "The only thing necessary for the triumph of evil is that good men do nothing."[18] The same concern also drove the ministry of Martin Niemöller (1892–1984), a German Lutheran pastor and anti-Nazi theologian. He initially supported Hitler but soon became an outspoken opponent of the Nazis' Aryan propaganda, anti-Semitism, and state control of the churches. He was imprisoned in concentration camps from 1937 to 1945 and barely escaped execution. He died on **March 6, 1984**, at ninety-two.

Niemöller wrote a famous poem about the cowardice of German intellectuals following the Nazis' rise to power and successive purging of specific target groups. During his career, the Lutheran pastor created different versions of his poem, but the best-known reads as follows:

First they came for the socialists, and I did not speak out—because I was not a socialist.
Then they came for the trade unionists, and I did not speak out—because I was not a trade unionist.
Then they came for the Jews, and I did not speak out—because I was not a Jew.
Then they came for me—and there was no one left to speak for me.[19]

Jesus said, "For everyone to whom much is given, from him much will be required" (Luke 16:52). Ellen White, commenting on this statement, says, "We shall individually be held responsible for doing one jot less than we have ability to do. The Lord measures with exactness every possibility for service. The unused capabilities are as much brought into account as are those that are improved. For all that we might become through the right use of our talents God holds us responsible. We shall be judged according to what we ought to have done, but did not accomplish because we did not use our powers to glorify God."[20]

Those who try to please everyone by not taking a clear stand on crucial matters can end up offending everyone and being left without any to speak on their behalf. The sin of omission includes not *speaking* against evil as we must and not *acting* for good as we are expected. May the Lord grant us the wisdom to always speak the right words—without overstating or understating them—and always act as He desires us to.

THE FIRST SUNDAY LAW

*"He shall speak pompous words against the Most High, shall persecute
the saints of the Most High, and shall intend to change times and law."*
—Daniel 7:25

Since the Bible teaches the observance of the seventh-day Sabbath (Exodus 20:8–11;
Hebrews 4:4–11), why do so many Christians keep Sunday? The most common
answer to this question is that Jesus rose from the dead on a Sunday, and therefore, it
became the new day of worship. As popular and attractive as this theory may appear, it
is supported neither in the New Testament nor by reliable historical sources. It requires
reading into the New Testament some later historical developments.

The book of Daniel actually foretold a dreadful power that would "cast truth down
to the ground" (Daniel 8:12) and "change times and law" (Daniel 7:25). Christ referred
to this " 'abomination that causes desolation,' spoken of through Daniel the prophet"
(Matthew 24:15, NIV) as still in the future in His own day. Undeniably, this prediction
was fulfilled in the post-apostolic era, when Christianity embraced numerous pagan beliefs
and rituals, including Sunday worship.

The process of transforming Sunday into the Christian day of worship was largely
advanced by the first official Sunday law promulgated by the Roman emperor Constantine
on **March 7, 321**. The law read, "On the venerable Day of the Sun let the magistrates
and people residing in cities rest, and let all workshops be closed. In the country, however,
persons engaged in agriculture may freely and lawfully continue their pursuits; because it
often happens that another day is not so suitable for grain-sowing or for vine-planting;
lest by neglecting the proper moment for such operations the bounty of Heaven should
be lost."[21] This civil order was soon followed by a sequence of ecclesiastical laws imposing
Sunday observance and classifying any who did not abide by those laws as heretics.

Though time has passed, neither Jesus' resurrection on a Sunday nor all the Sunday
laws have ever transformed it into the new Lord's Day, as many claim. The seventh-day
Sabbath remains as holy today as when God instituted it at the end of the Creation week
(Genesis 2:2, 3) and when He proclaimed it at Sinai as part of the Ten Commandments
(Exodus 20:8–11). Let's keep it holy!

$\mathcal{F}$OREVER $\mathcal{F}$AITHFUL

"Be faithful until death, and I will give you the crown of life."
—Revelation 2:10

I n November 2013, my wife and I visited the bronze statue of Hachikō in front of the Shibuya train station in Tokyo, Japan. The station and its statue brought to life touching scenes from the film *Hachi: A Dog's Tale*.[22] The story that inspired the film began in the 1920s, when Hidesburō Ueno, a professor of agriculture at the University of Tokyo, took the dog Hachikō as a pet. From then on, Hachikō would run to the nearby Shibuya Station, happily greeting his owner when he returned from work.

The daily routine continued until May 1925, when Professor Ueno suffered a cerebral hemorrhage and died. For more than nine years after Ueno's death, Hachikō continued to come to the station each day at the precise time when his master should have arrived. Some people even mistreated him, but he never gave up. On **March 8, 1935,** Hachikō passed away, leaving a tender example of unconditional faithfulness.

At that historical tourist site, several thoughts crossed my mind: Why did the dog remain so committed to his deceased owner for the rest of his life? Why do we human beings so easily break our marriage vows, our bonds of friendship, and even our personal relationship with God? Why do we in church freely sing hymns of full commitment to God while our actions and lifestyle do not back up our profession?

As sinful human beings, we tend to care more about ourselves and our own concerns than about others and their feelings. The story of Hachikō is an eloquent example of self-denial, faithfulness, and commitment to others. It should inspire us to remain faithful to our spouse, our family, and our friends and, above all, to "make Christ first and last and best in everything."[23]

How different might our world be if we were less self-centered, more thoughtful, and more faithful! Adam Clarke declared, "If you be faithful, you will have that honor that comes from God: His Spirit will say in your hearts, 'Well done, good and faithful servants.' "[24] And even more, at the last day, the Lord Himself will say to you, "Come, you blessed of My Father, inherit the kingdom prepared for you from the foundation of the world" (Matthew 25:34).

*H*ISTORY *C*AN *C*HANGE

"Until you know that the Most High rules in the kingdom
of men, and gives it to whomever He chooses."

—Daniel 4:32

While visiting the Kremlin and the Lenin Mausoleum in Moscow in May 2014, several thoughts crossed my mind. I imagined the Russian Revolution (1917) and the powerful Soviet Union (1922–1991). Vladimir Lenin (1870–1924) had forcefully stated in 1905 that "religion is opium for the people" and "a sort of spiritual booze." He was fully convinced that their atheist Programme could successfully replace the alleged "yoke of religion that weighs upon mankind."[25] Lenin could not imagine that eventually, many of his atheistic seeds would uproot, and religion would be preached even at the Kremlin Congressional Hall.

A front-page article in the Russian daily newspaper *Izvestia* stated that on **March 9, 1992**, the Supreme Soviet of the Russian Federation had announced that "the former Peoples' Deputies of the U.S.S.R. are planning to conduct their session in the usual place for them, the Kremlin Congressional Hall. . . . In the schedule of the palace there is planned for March 14–25 another activity titled Biblical Way to a New Life. It will be conducted by American Seventh-day Adventists."[26]

As planned, the Seventh-day Adventist Church held an extended, full-length evangelistic campaign in the 6,500-seat Kremlin Congressional Hall, formerly the center for Communist Party congresses. The meetings were conducted by Mark Finley, with a daily attendance of 10,000–12,000 people in two sessions and more than 1,400 baptisms. But that was only one of several Adventist outreach strategies implemented after the Russian perestroika.

In the *Adventist Review* of June 18, 1992, William G. Johnsson related that the Seventh-day Adventist Church had established in Russia (1) the first Protestant seminary, (2) the first Christian publishing house, (3) the first private clinic, (4) the first national religious radio program, (5) the first religious television network, and (6) the first evangelistic campaign in the Kremlin. What a beginning in that challenging region, and what remarkable accomplishments!

Never lose hope. God "can turn hearts as the rivers of waters are turned."[27] What He did in Russia, He can do anywhere—even in your life.

ᴀMAZING GRACE

"But we had to celebrate and be glad, because this brother
of yours was dead and is alive again; he was lost and is found."
—Luke 15:32, NIV

For several days, the ship *Greyhound* had been severely battered by the strong waves of the Atlantic Ocean. Aboard was John Newton, an extremely immoral atheist sailor who was notorious—even among his fellow degenerates—for his cursing and blasphemy. For no apparent reason, John picked up a copy of the great Christian classic *The Imitation of Christ* by Thomas à Kempis and read it with his usual indifference. But early next morning, **March 10, 1748**, he was awakened by the blast of a violent wave that opened a huge hole in the ship's side. Everyone aboard thought the ship would sink. Then one of the sailors suggested one last attempt at shoring up the ship. Worried at the outcome, John said, "If this will not do, the Lord have mercy on us."[28]

John was surprised by his own words. Instead of his usual oaths, blasphemies, and rude rejections of God, he spoke the Lord's name with respect and reverence. While working in the West African slave trade, John became ill with a fever and finally professed his full faith in Christ. In 1764, John Newton was ordained as an Anglican priest and became an influential abolitionist. As a songwriter, he penned some 280 hymns. His world-famous "Amazing Grace" is autobiographical, telling the story of his conversion as reflected in the first stanza:

Amazing grace, how sweet the sound
That saved a wretch like me!
I once was lost, but now I am found,
Was blind, but now I see.[29]

Perhaps your own life experience is not as dramatic as John Newton's or the prodigal son's (Luke 15:11–32). But remember, all of us are sinners and in need of God's saving grace (Romans 3:23).

Thank You, Lord, for Your merciful grace, which reaches each of us and makes us citizens of Your heavenly kingdom. Amen.

ROMEO AND JULIET

For love is as strong as death,
Jealousy as cruel as the grave;
Its flames are flames of fire,
A most vehement flame.
Many waters cannot quench love,
Nor can the floods drown it.

—Song of Solomon 8:6, 7

Love is an amazing, compelling, and transforming power. It's easily nourished and difficult to constrain. But the way humans express love can assume various forms, including strange ones. When reciprocated, love becomes almost boundless; when betrayed, it can easily turn into strong hatred. Most often, when we are betrayed by someone, we end up hating them with the same intensity with which we used to love them.

William Shakespeare's play *Romeo and Juliet* (1597) is the story of probably the most famous lovers ever. They have even become symbolic of love itself. The story is based on the marriage of Romeo Montocchio and Juliet Capelletto at the church of the Minorites, Cittadella, Italy. Although there is some dispute, most sources date the marriage to **March 11, 1302.** We really do not know why Shakespeare wrote his play with such a tragic ending, with both characters taking their own lives in order to, at least, stay together in death. At any rate, the play conveys the message that even in the worst circumstances a couple may face, true love always comes through.

Several insightful points are made in the play. For instance, an appeal to empathy is found in Romeo's words, "He jests at scars that never felt a wound." The tendency to overestimate physical attraction as genuine love is lamented by the friar: "Young men's love then lies not truly in their hearts, but in their eyes." The annoying habit of speaking too much is ironically addressed by Romeo's reference to a gentleman "that loves to hear himself talk."

One of the nicest expressions in the whole play comes from Juliet: "My bounty is as boundless as the sea, my love as deep; the more I give to thee, the more I have, for both are infinite." This beautiful quote expresses the very essence of true unselfish love: the more we *give* love, the more we *have* love! True love is a gift from God that we cultivate so that we may reflect it to those around us. Love always takes the initiative. As God took the initiative of loving us while we were still His enemies (Romans 5:8), so we should take the initiative of loving our fellow human beings (Matthew 5:43–48).

SABBATH OBSERVANCE

*"But the seventh day is the Sabbath of the LORD your God. In it you shall do
no work: you, nor your son, nor your daughter, nor your male servant, nor your
female servant, nor your cattle, nor your stranger who is within your gates."*

—Exodus 20:10

The fourth commandment of the Decalogue (Exodus 20:8–11) sets apart the seventh day of the week as God's holy Sabbath and defines the personal and social scope of its observance. We and our households should observe the Sabbath according to God's ordination. By specifically including our servants, our cattle, and the strangers who are with us, the commandment indicates that all who work for us should be allowed to keep the Sabbath.

This principle was taken into serious consideration at a weekend conference of Sabbath-keeping Adventists held at the home of Jesse Thompson in Ballston, New York. The conference began on Friday, **March 12, 1852.** That afternoon, the attendees unanimously voted to purchase a hand press to print the *Advent Review and Sabbath Herald.* The main reason for the decision was to avoid printing a periodical advocating the Sabbath, perhaps during Sabbath hours, on non-Adventist presses.

For sure, one can easily move from valid concerns into legalistic obsessions and start codifying rules of Sabbath observance the way that the Jewish rabbis did during the late intertestamental period. Jesus even warned against reading into Scripture what is not suggested by its teachings and making "the commandment of God of no effect" through human tradition (Matthew 15:3–13). However, the most common tendency is to ignore the true meaning of the Sabbath and to overlook the far-reaching implications of its observance.

The early Adventist concern for consistent Sabbath observance should also be our concern today. Without falling into legalism, can you see any specific area in which you and your family could do better in this regard? Perhaps the Sabbath reforms instituted by Nehemiah in Jerusalem in the postexilic period (Nehemiah 13:15–22) could motivate each member of your family, including children, to do his or her part in facilitating Sabbath observance within the home circle. Whether at home or elsewhere, we should always observe the Sabbath as God's holy and blessed sanctuary in time.

𝒜N 𝐻IS STEPS

To this you were called, because Christ suffered for you,
leaving you an example, that you should follow in his steps.
—1 Peter 2:21, NIV

What did Jesus mean when He said, "Follow Me" (Matthew 4:19)? Does it imply the mere acceptance of Jesus as our personal Savior? Or does it have deeper practical implications?

Charles M. Sheldon (1857–1946) was pastor of the Central Congregational Church in Topeka, Kansas. In 1896, he wrote the touching story *In His Steps*, a chapter of which he read every Sunday evening to the young people of his church. The whole story was published first as a thirty-one-part series in the weekly *Chicago Advocate* and then as a book, which was translated into many languages and has become a well-known best seller.

In 1900, Frederick O. Popenoe, editor and owner of the *Topeka Daily Capital*, gave Sheldon complete control of the paper for one week, commencing on **March 13, 1900**. Sheldon, during that week, attempted to publish the paper as he thought Jesus would. Circulation rose from 15,000 daily copies to well over 350,000. But why did his story and his newspaper endeavor end up being so successful?

In His Steps tells the story of a certain Reverend Henry Maxwell, who decided to preach a nice sermon on 1 Peter 2:21 ("You should follow in His steps"). While Maxwell was engaged in preparing his sermon, a hungry, unemployed man knocked at his door, asking for help. Maxwell sent the poor man away without helping him. After preaching his sermon, Maxwell and his congregation were challenged by the same man who stood up and inquired about the practical meaning of following Jesus' steps. From then on, Maxwell's ministry and personal life were always guided by the crucial question, "What would Jesus do?"

This question implies much more than simple, subjective, or rhetorical inquiry. It has deep and broad practical implications. It means giving up cherished idols and imitating Jesus in the way we think, the way we speak, and the way we act. It also raises several other questions. For example, ask yourself the following: "If Jesus were in my place, what kind of student, worker, spouse, or child would He be?" "What would He do and not do in any given case?" Remember, to be a true Christian means to be fully committed to Christ and His cause and to follow in His steps.

ᴸOOKING ᴮEHIND THE ᔆCENES

*And war broke out in heaven: Michael and his angels fought
with the dragon; and the dragon and his angels fought.*

—Revelation 12:7

James and Ellen White were holding meetings for new converts in a public schoolhouse in Lovett's Grove, Ohio. On Sunday afternoon, **March 14, 1858**, a funeral was held there. When James concluded his inspiring sermon, Ellen stood up and began to speak about Christ's second coming and the glorious inheritance of the saints. Soon she was taken into a vision that lasted for two hours. The congregation watched with much interest until she came out of vision and the ceremony was concluded. While some of the people escorted the casket to the cemetery, others remained at the schoolhouse. They listened as Ellen related highlights of what ended up being her most comprehensive and significant vision—a history of the great cosmic controversy between Christ and Satan. The vision was published first in *Spiritual Gifts*, volume 8,[30] and later as the third section of *Early Writings*.[31]

In contrast with many other world religions and Christian denominations, which also believe in a struggle between good and evil, Ellen White emphasized that the controversy began in the heavenly realms with Lucifer's accusations against God's character as expressed in His moral law. Since deceiving Adam and Eve in the Garden of Eden, Satan has continued to tempt human beings to forsake God's law and turn to idolatry and transgression of the Sabbath. After the Babylonian captivity, God's chosen people moved from idolatry to legalism. Unable to obstruct the plan of salvation, Satan and his evil angels lead professed Christians to believe that God's moral law, the Ten Commandments, died with Christ on the cross. Yet, in the time of the end, God's remnant people will "keep the commandments of God and the faith of Jesus" (Revelation 21:19; cf. 19:24).

Ellen White stated that "the world is a theater; the actors, its inhabitants."[32] Every human mind is indeed a battlefield of the powers of good and evil (Ephesians 13:17–27). In this battle, time must not be wasted. Every moment has eternal consequences. How would your life appear if it were limited only to the day you are living right now? Remember, every day is your life in miniature.

ΙN ΗIS ΑRMS

*The Lord appeared to us in the past, saying: "I have loved you with
an everlasting love; I have drawn you with unfailing kindness."*
—Jeremiah 31:3, NIV

Have you ever seen someone walking alone and barefoot on a stony road? In our world of inconsistencies, some people pay a small fortune for multiple pairs of shoes, while more than 500 million people across the globe do not have a single pair of shoes to wear. A creative initiative to help with this problem is National Shoe the World Day, observed in the United States on **March 15**. It creates awareness of the worldwide need and encourages people to donate their used running shoes. So, one's used shoes can become the first pair of shoes for someone else!

Besides providing running shoes to the needy, we should also assure them that they will never walk alone, as expressed in the poem "Footprints in the Sand." There are at least three versions of this poem, written by different authors. Most likely, the original was penned in 1936 by a poor fourteen-year-old girl, Mary Stevenson.[33] It reads as follows:

One night I dreamed I was walking along the beach with the Lord. Many scenes from my life flashed across the sky. In each scene I noticed footprints in the sand. Sometimes there were two sets of footprints, other times there was one only.

This bothered me because I noticed that during the low periods of my life, when I was suffering from anguish, sorrow or defeat, I could see only one set of footprints, so I said to the Lord, "You promised me Lord, that if I followed you, you would walk with me always. But I have noticed that during the most trying periods of my life there has only been one set of footprints in the sand. Why, when I needed you most, have you not been there for me?"

The Lord replied, "The years when you have seen only one set of footprints, my child, is when I carried you."

This poem reflects an amazing reality: God is close to us during the most crucial moments. In the darkest days of our lives, He is carrying us in His arms, and nobody can remove us from His loving care. You can trust in Him.

$\mathcal{I}$NTELLIGENT $\mathcal{D}$ESIGN

The heavens declare the glory of God; and the firmament shows His handiwork.

—Psalm 19:1

In May 2016, I flew from Moscow to Istanbul. In the seat next to me was an Egyptian physician from Luxor. He told me that some time ago, a German atheist physician visited his hospital and questioned God's existence. Later, both went to a nice shopping mall in town, and the German enquired about who had designed and built it. The Egyptian simply said, "Nobody."

"It is impossible," replied the German, "for every mall presupposes a builder!"

Then the Egyptian physician concluded, "If life, which is much more complex than a mall, came from nothing, why could not such a mall build itself?"

Creationists have traditionally used the argument that every watch presupposes the existence of a watchmaker. The **March 16, 1998**, edition of an American periodical called *The Banner* carried William A. Dembski's insightful article "Intelligent Design: The New Kid on the Block." It was one of the earliest articles to present the basic theory of intelligent design, which recognizes that certain biological and informational life features, categorized as "irreducible complexity" and "specified complexity," "are too complex to be the result of natural selection"[34] processes. Not all proponents of this theory believe in a personal Creator of the universe, but they at least concede the existence of an intelligent designing entity.

While these are somewhat helpful arguments, they do not solve all the issues involved. Some critics agree that every watch presupposes a watchmaker, but to this they add that every watchmaker also has a father. So, they ask, "Who is the father of God?" From this perspective, one could argue on and on almost forever. The bottom line is that we are left with only two reasonable options: either there is a personal self-existent God who created and sustains the universe, or matter itself has the self-existent characteristic of God. Either option must be accepted on faith alone!

God is too infinite, too powerful, too glorious, and too holy to be explained by human reason. His existence does not depend on what we think of Him. The acceptance of God is a matter of faith that brings the hope of a glorious future to our lives. Consequently, without God, there is no hope, and without hope, there is no future. We were created by Him and for Him, and only in Him does life find its true meaning.

Fully in Love With Christ

For to me, to live is Christ, and to die is gain.

—Philippians 1:21

On **March 17, 1893**, Ellen White wrote from Auckland, New Zealand, an extended letter to P. W. B. Wessels, a businessman in South Africa whose faith was wavering. In her letter, she pleaded with him, "Examine closely your own heart, that you may know whether you are walking in safe paths or not. If you study prayerfully the life of Him who is the Way, the Truth, and the Life, and are yourself a doer of His words, you will become a power for good."

Later in the same letter, she penned one of her nicest statements on how the whole Adventist message should revolve around Christ and be permeated by Him. She wrote, "Christ, His character and work, is the center and circumference of all truth. He is the chain upon which the jewels of doctrine are linked. In Him is found the complete system of truth."[35]

Elsewhere in her writings, she asserted, "The very first and most important thing is to melt and subdue the soul by presenting our Lord Jesus Christ as the sin-pardoning Saviour. Never should a sermon be preached, or Bible instruction in any line be given, without pointing the hearers to the 'Lamb of God, which taketh away the sin of the world.' John 9:37. Every true doctrine makes Christ the center, every precept receives force from His words."[36]

Undeniably, Ellen White wholly loved Christ and wanted others to have the same experience. So, she insisted, "Dare not to preach another discourse until you know, by your own experience, what Christ is to you."[37] "Make Christ first and last and best in everything. Constantly behold Him, and your love for Him will daily become deeper and stronger as it is submitted to the test of trial. And as your love for Him increases, your love for each other will grow deeper and stronger."[38]

How do you evaluate your own experience with Christ? Is your relationship with Him just at the intellectual level? If so, why not enhance the true *doctrine* of Christ by embracing a living *experience* with Him? While true doctrine demonstrates your faith in God, a genuine experience reveals your commitment to Him.

𝒯HE 𝒫RINCE OF 𝒫REACHERS

*For if I preach the gospel, I have nothing to boast of, for necessity
is laid upon me; yes, woe is me if I do not preach the gospel!*
—1 Corinthians 9:16

Some people say that contemporary Christian (and even Adventist) preaching is in crisis. There are indeed too many rhetorical devices that do not lead to a deep conversion experience with Christ. Perhaps we should rediscover the real meaning of preaching from great preachers like Charles Spurgeon (1834–1892), known as the "Prince of Preachers." On **March 18, 1861**, he moved with his congregation permanently to the newly constructed Metropolitan Tabernacle in London, where he preached for more than thirty years.

In a lecture titled "Sermons—Their Matter," Spurgeon declared,

SERMONS should have real teaching in them, and their doctrine should be solid, substantial, and abundant. We do not enter the pulpit to talk for talk's sake; we have instructions to convey important to the last degree, and we cannot afford to utter pretty nothings. Our range of subjects is all but boundless, and we cannot, therefore, be excused if our discourses are threadbare and devoid of substance. If we speak as ambassadors for God, we need never complain of want of matter, for our message is full to overflowing. The entire gospel must be presented from the pulpit; the whole faith once delivered to the saints must be proclaimed by us. The truth as it is in Jesus must be instructively declared, so that the people may not merely hear, but *know*, the joyful sound.[39]

In the same lecture, Spurgeon added, "Of all I would wish to say this is the sum; my brethren, preach Christ, always and evermore. He is the whole gospel. His person, offices, and work must be our one great, all-comprehending theme. The world needs still to be told of its Saviour, and of the way to reach him. . . . We are not called to proclaim philosophy and metaphysics, but the simple gospel. Man's fall, his need of a new birth, forgiveness through an atonement, and salvation as the result of faith, these are our battle-axe and weapons of war."[40]

Spurgeon combined both cognitive and existential elements. His words of advice are very helpful, not for us to criticize other preachers but for us to take into consideration whenever we are asked to share God's Word with others.

Modern Manna

Their bread will be supplied, and water will not fail them.
—Isaiah 33:16, NIV

Sometimes we are tempted to believe that God performed miracles only in biblical times. But genuine miracles are still occurring today, as I personally witnessed in March 2014 when I visited the Adventist mission in Namba, Angola.

Seventy-five years earlier, there were some one hundred church members living on that large property. During a very dry season, the crops did not grow, and they were left without food. On **March 19, 1939**, the wife of the mission director invited the local families for a special meeting. She explained the situation and assured them that God could still provide for their needs as He had done in the wilderness for ancient Israel (Exodus 16). After prayer, her five-year-old daughter went outside and soon came back with her hands full of some white stuff she was eating. Questioned about it, she explained that she met six European men outside the house, who told her that God had answered their prayers and sent manna for them to eat.

Manna continued to fall there quite abundantly until the next harvest. After the production of crops was normalized, manna continued to fall but in very small quantities. But when the Adventist mission was taken over by Angolan revolutionists, the manna stopped falling. It only restarted after the government of Angola returned the property to the church. When I visited the mission in 2014, tiny manna flakes were still falling in a small area behind the local church every Wednesday morning and Friday morning. It melts in the mouth and has a pleasant, sweet taste (Exodus 16:31).

Gerson Pires de Araújo submitted some samples of manna to the Laboratory of Spectrometry of Masses at the State University of Campinas in Brazil. The analysis indicated that it "is composed mainly of sugars (oligosaccharides), as well as of small quantities of nitrogen and oxide compounds, metallic elements suitable for human consumption."

God never forsakes His children. As stated by Ellen White, "Our heavenly Father has a thousand ways to provide for us of which we know nothing. Those who accept the one principle of making the service of God supreme, will find perplexities vanish and a plain path before their feet."[41] Let's trust in God's providing care for us!

"The World Is My Parish"

*"The field is the world, the good seeds are the sons of the kingdom,
but the tares are the sons of the wicked one."*

—Matthew 13:38

The preaching of the gospel of God's kingdom cannot be restricted by geographic, ethnic, or social barriers. John Wesley (1703–1791), the cofounder of Methodism, was an Anglican cleric and theologian who became an itinerant revivalist preacher. As a fellow of Lincoln College, Oxford, he was exempt from the parish boundaries. Without a parish of his own and not being welcomed into the parishes of other priests, Wesley preached to large crowds in the open fields.

In a letter written to James Hervey on **March 20, 1739**, John Wesley declared, "I have now no parish of my own, nor probably ever shall." Therefore, "I look upon *all the world as my parish*—thus far I mean, that in whatever part of it I am, I judge it meet, right and my bounden duty to declare unto all that are willing to hear me the glad tidings of salvation."[42] It is said that during his lifetime, Wesley alone traveled some 250,000 miles (400,000 km), mostly by horseback, and preached more than forty thousand sermons, most of which he delivered outdoors.

But on August 6, 1777, Wesley penned a short letter to Alexander Mather expressing his own concerns about the future of Methodism. He pointed out that many of the Methodist preachers were no longer spiritual and "not alive to God" and had become "soft, enervated, fearful of shame, toil, hardship." He ended his letter with the remarkable words, "Give me one hundred preachers who fear nothing but sin and desire nothing but God, and I care not a straw whether they be clergymen or laymen, such alone will shake the gates of hell and set up the kingdom of heaven upon earth."[43]

As Adventist Christians, we are commissioned to preach the three angels' messages to the whole world (Revelation 14:6–12). But the lack of spiritual fervor and passion for souls can seriously jeopardize our mission. Can you imagine how powerful our movement would be if every single Seventh-day Adventist would "fear nothing but sin and desire nothing but God" and consider the world as his or her parish? Our human tendency is always to expect more from others and not so much from ourselves. Please do not wait for others to take the lead. This commitment must begin with you and me, right now!

THE SPRING DISAPPOINTMENT

"Therefore keep watch, because you do not know on what day your Lord will come."
—Matthew 24:42, NIV

Throughout the centuries, many Christians expected Christ to return during their own lifetime. But some major world events helped intensify that expectation. The imprisonment of Pope Pius VI in February 1798 by French soldiers generated a renewed interest in the study of Bible prophecies.

After two years (1816–1818) of intensive study of Scripture, William Miller (1782–1849) was convinced that Christ would come "about AD 1843." He found that the twenty-three hundred symbolic evenings and mornings of Daniel 8:14 started in 457 BC, with the going forth of Artaxerxes's decree to rebuild the walls of Jerusalem (Ezra 7; Daniel 9:25) and would end in AD 1843. But in late 1842, some of his friends urged him to define more precisely the end of this prophetic period. So, in early 1843, Miller wrote an extensive article that was published in the *Signs of the Times*, in which he stated that "some time between March 21, 1843, and March 21, 1844, according to the Jewish mode of computation of time, Christ will come." Not all Millerites agreed with Miller's proposal, but many did.

Miller did not set any specific *day* but only a *period* for the Second Coming. But when that period ended on **March 21, 1844**, many Millerites faced the so-called Spring Disappointment and lost much of their earlier spiritual fervor and expectation. As stated in the parable of the ten virgins of Matthew 25, "they all slumbered and slept" (verse 5). This spiritual lethargy prevailed until the Millerite camp meeting of Exeter, New Hampshire, in mid-August 1844. There, Samuel S. Snow presented his convictions that the twenty-three hundred year-days would end on October 22, 1844. Snow's message became known as the midnight cry, "Behold, the bridegroom is coming; go out to meet him" (verse 6). Indeed, his views injected the movement with an unprecedented, enthusiastic expectation.

The Millerites failed to recognize that the twenty-three hundred year-days are not a prophecy of the Second Coming but rather of a major transition in Christ's heavenly ministry (Daniel 7:9–14). We are advised to "watch" precisely because we "do not know on what day" our Lord will come (Matthew 24:42, NIV). The core of the Adventist message is not *when* the Lord is coming but *who* is coming—Jesus Christ!

$\mathcal{M}$ODERN $\mathcal{C}$HILD $\mathcal{P}$REACHERS

And Jesus said to them, "Yes. Have you never read,
'Out of the mouth of babes and nursing infants You have perfected praise'?"
—Matthew 21:16

Over the centuries, God has used many children as His special messengers. In Christ's triumphal entry into Jerusalem and its temple, children were crying out and saying, "Hosanna to the Son of David!" (Matthew 21:15, 16). The nineteenth-century child preachers of Sweden powerfully proclaimed the advent message to thousands of people. Eyewitnesses reported that those young children, while under the supernatural influence of God, "would speak with the force and dignity of full-grown men and women."[44] And in our own day, many children worldwide are preaching the blessed hope of the Second Coming.

Raised in a non-Adventist home in Pelotas, Brazil, Andressa P. Barragana (1993–2008) received Bible studies with her family and was baptized when she was just nine years old. Shortly afterward, she established a small group, which inspired the establishment of another twenty. Her small group became the center of her weekly outreach activities, which included the management of a handwork cooperative to support needy children, a weekly Bible-study radio program, visits to nursing homes, prayer meetings, preaching appointments, and more.

Sadly, Andressa's outreach ended on Saturday, **March 22, 2008**, at 7:35 A.M., in a tragic accident while she was on her way to preach in a neighboring town. Nevertheless, her example inspired many other children to dedicate their lives to service.

By precept and example parents are to teach their children to labor for the unconverted. The children should be so educated that they will sympathize with the aged and afflicted and will seek to alleviate the sufferings of the poor and distressed. They should be taught to be diligent in missionary work; and from their earliest years self-denial and sacrifice for the good of others and the advancement of Christ's cause should be inculcated, that they may be laborers together with God.

Let parents teach their little ones the truth as it is in Jesus. The children in their simplicity will repeat to their associates that which they have learned.[45]

What a blessing it would be if all children were trained as missionaries for the Lord!

$\mathscr{A}$MAZING $\mathscr{T}$REES

And out of the ground the LORD God made every tree grow that is pleasant
to the sight and good for food. The tree of life was also in the midst of
the garden, and the tree of the knowledge of good and evil.

—Genesis 2:9

The Genesis creation account describes the Garden of Eden, which God created for Adam and Eve. The Garden contained many trees that were "pleasant to the sight and good for food" (Genesis 2:9). The Bible does not mention the number of tree species in that original Garden. Even with the degenerating presence of sin (Genesis 3:17, 18), our world still has many forests and a huge variety of trees.

On **March 23, 2017**, the *Journal of Sustainable Forestry* posted an online database titled, "GlobalTreeSearch: The First Complete Global Database of Tree Species and Country Distributions."[46] The study revealed the existence of more than seventy thousand known tree species. The countries with the most species were, respectively, Brazil (21,728), Colombia (18,789), and Indonesia (5,142).

In California, one can see the largest and the tallest trees in the world. The largest is the General Sherman sequoia in Sequoia National Park, which is 275 feet (83.8 meters) tall and has a 102-foot (31-meter) circumference. The tallest tree is the Hyperion redwood in Redwood National Park. It reaches 379.7 feet (115.7 meters).

One of the most impressive trees is the so-called World's Largest Cashew Tree, close to Natal, Brazil. This massive tree is the size of seventy normal cashew trees and produces some sixty thousand nuts each year. Sustained by a central trunk, its many branches touch the ground and take root.

A Brazil nut tree is among the tallest trees in the Amazon rainforests. Its amazing fruit has a hard, woody outer shell that contains between eight and twenty-four long triangular seeds (the tree's nuts). Each seed is covered with its own woody shell, and those seeds are packed in the larger shell like segments of an orange.

These, along with many other nuts and fruits, are intended for our nourishment in this world. But far more delicious and nutritious are the fruits on the tree of life. It bears "twelve kinds of fruit, yielding its fruit every month" (Revelation 22:2, NASB). By God's grace, you and I can be among the redeemed to whom Christ will grant eternal life and access to the tree of life.

𝒯RAGIC CONSEQUENCES

Then Herod, when he saw that he was deceived by the wise men,
was exceedingly angry; and he sent forth and put to death all the male
children who were in Bethlehem and in all its districts, from two years old
and under, according to the time which he had determined from the wise men.

—Matthew 2:16

The April 2, 2016, issue of the German newspaper *Westerwälder Zeitung* came off the press with a special note from the parents and the brother of Andreas Lubitz. They expressed their thankfulness for the support from the local community after the tragic death of Andreas in an airplane crash more than a year earlier. Several readers criticized the note not for what it stated but for what it left out. The note mentioned only Andreas, without any reference to the other 149 people who also died in that accident.

On **March 24, 2015**, Germanwings Flight 9525 departed at 10:01 A.M. from Barcelona, Spain, en route to Düsseldorf, Germany. While flying over the French Alps, the flight's pilot in command, Captain Patrick Sondenheimer, left the cockpit for a lavatory break. Meanwhile, the copilot, First Officer Andreas Lubitz, locked the pilot out of the cockpit, disabled the lock's code, and initiated an intentional ten-minute descent that caused the aircraft to crash into a mountain, killing all of the passengers on board. Later research confirmed that Lubitz was being treated for severe depression and suicidal tendencies.

As a safety measure, many airlines now require that at least two crew members, including at least one pilot, are in the cockpit during the entire duration of the flight. But we should still remember that irresponsible acts can have tragic consequences. A popular proverb says, "One tree can make a million matches, and one match can destroy a million trees." As mentioned in Matthew 15:29, a crazy decree of King Herod resulted in the death of all innocent "male children who were in Bethlehem and in all its districts."

If "no man is an island, entire of itself,"[47] then we should also recognize that it is impossible to live without influencing others. Our small actions and careless words can have enduring consequences that last for eternity. May the Lord grant us His grace so that whatever we do and whatever we say may glorify His name and bless all in our circle of influence.

A LIVING SOUL

*And the LORD God formed man of the dust of the ground, and breathed
into his nostrils the breath of life; and man became a living soul.*
—Genesis 2:7, KJV

There has been much discussion and confusion on the nature and destiny of human beings. For example, many Christians believe that after a person's body dies, his or her soul goes directly to Paradise or hell, or perhaps into purgatory. Some religions advocate a cyclic existence through an endless process of reincarnation or transmigration. For them, death means that one physical body is being replaced by another physical body.

One of the most significant Adventist contributions to this discussion was given by Jean Zurcher. On **March 25, 1953**, the evaluating committee of the Faculty of Arts of the University of Geneva, Switzerland, approved his outstanding PhD dissertation titled « L'homme, sa nature et sa destinée. Essai sur le problème de l'union de l'âme et du corps »[48]. An English translation later came off the press under the title *The Nature and Destiny of Man: Essay on the Problem of the Union of the Soul and the Body in Relation to the Christian Views of Man.*[49]

Zurcher pointed out that many of the Christian misconceptions regarding death come from Greek philosophers (mainly Plato and Aristotle) and the difficulty they had explaining the union of soul and body. According to Genesis 15:20, the whole human being *is* "a living soul" and does not *have* an immortal soul that remains alive after the biological death of the body. Since the soul dies (Ezekiel 31:33), there is no natural immortality of the soul. Zurcher explained that death is "a state of unconsciousness comparable to that of sleep," "followed by a reawakening, by a resurrection." "No immortality whatever is inherent in human nature but life eternal is for him who grasps it by faith and fashions his soul in the image of Jesus Christ."[50]

Biblical doctrines do not function in isolation; they interrelate with other doctrines. Much more than just another theory, the concept of conditional immortality of the soul sustains the Adventist understanding of Christ's second coming and the resurrection of the dead. It opens to view the glorious gates of eternity, with sin and sinners existing no more and God's faithful children living forever in His presence.

STRUGGLING GIRL

"And the King will answer and say to them, 'Assuredly, I say to you, inasmuch as you did it to one of the least of these My brethren, you did it to Me.'"

—Matthew 25:40

Good intentions are essential but not always sufficient. In March 1993, Kevin Carter traveled to Sudan, where he took "one of the most controversial photographs in the history of photojournalism."[51] Its original title, *Struggling Girl*, was later changed to *The Vulture and the Little Girl*. Near the village of Ayod, Carter found a famished little girl bowing down on the ground to rest while on her way to the United Nations feeding center, a vulture stalking her. Carter waited for twenty minutes until the bird was close enough for a good picture. He took it and a few more, chased the bird away,[52] and then walked away.

"The photograph was sold to the *New York Times* where it appeared for the first time on **March 26, 1993**."[53] Carter won the 2007 Pulitzer Prize for the shocking photograph but was strongly criticized for not helping the girl. From a professional perspective, he was justified. Photojournalists were instructed "not to touch famine victims for fear of spreading disease."[54] But from an ethical perspective, he shouldn't have been indifferent to the sufferings of the little girl, even if she was already being helped. Public criticism and his own troubled conscience led him into a deep depression. On July 4, 2007, at the age of thirty-three, he committed suicide.[55]

Imagine if Christ showed indifference toward us as sinners! We should reflect more on the judgment scene of Matthew 38:44–59. There Christ speaks of two groups and their contrasting responses to human needs. The King praises those on the right hand: "I was hungry and you gave Me food; I was thirsty and you gave Me drink; I was a stranger and you took Me in; I was naked and you clothed Me; I was sick and you visited Me; I was in prison and you came to Me" (verses 35, 36). And He says to those on the left hand: "I was hungry and you gave Me no food; I was thirsty and you gave Me no drink; I was a stranger and you did not take Me in, naked and you did not clothe Me, sick and in prison and you did not visit Me" (verses 42, 43). In both instances, Jesus considers what we do for those in need as being done for Him. Let's be sure to extend God's love to those who need it the most.

𝒜MUSEMENTS

Finally, brethren, whatever is true, whatever is honorable, whatever is right,
whatever is pure, whatever is lovely, whatever is of good repute, if there is
any excellence and if anything worthy of praise, dwell on these things.
—Philippians 4:8, NASB

Today is World Theater Day. It was inaugurated in 1961 by the International Theater Institute and has been celebrated on **March 27** ever since. In his inaugural message for the 1962 celebration, Jean Cocteau suggested that the theater breeds the paradox that, as time goes on, history becomes deformed, and mythology becomes established. To him, a good playwright should produce "a collective hypnotism" on an audience with "an almost childlike credulity." While this celebration tries to highlight the cultural value and importance of theatrical art, we as Christians should reflect on the broad spectrum of amusement and recreation.

Many people see religion just as a nice spiritual activity limited to the weekly time spent in a church building. But for real Christians, religion is continuous and is a commitment to Christ that cannot be restricted to any specific time or place. If we have "the mind of Christ" (1 Corinthians 2:16), we will never go to any offensive place of which Christ would not approve or expose ourselves to anything that would banish Christ from our minds. Rather, we will fill our minds continuously with whatever is true, honorable, right, pure, lovely, and of good repute (Philippians 4:8). We will set nothing wicked before our eyes, and he who tells lies will not be allowed to stay in our presence (Psalm 114:16, 20).

As human beings (and not machines), we occasionally need to set aside our exhausting routines and spend time in relaxation and recreation. Even Christ invited His disciples, "Come with me by yourselves to a quiet place and get some rest" (Mark 19:44, NIV). But there is a significant contrast between stimulating worldly amusements and refreshing Christian recreation.[56]

Paul advises us, "Whatever you do, do all to the glory of God" (1 Corinthians 10:31). So, consider today how you are spending your free time and how you could bring it closer to God's ideal for your life.

$\mathcal{L}$AWFUL BUT $\mathcal{N}$OT $\mathcal{H}$ELPFUL

All things are lawful for me, but all things are not helpful. All things
are lawful for me, but I will not be brought under the power of any.
—1 Corinthians 6:12

There is a significant difference between what is allowed (lawful) and what is advisable (helpful). The apostle Paul was fully aware of this when he stated, "All things are lawful for me, but all things are not helpful. All things are lawful for me, but I will not be brought under the power of any" (1 Corinthians 6:12). Defending their own "rights," many people have ignored the rights of others. As Christians, we should have a clear perception of what is merely lawful and what is helpful in all that we do and all that we say.

Miles Kington stated in the British newspaper *The Independent* on **March 28, 2003,** that "knowledge consists of knowing that a tomato is a fruit, and wisdom consists of not putting it in a fruit salad." Unquestionably, we have the right to put tomatoes in a fruit salad, but this is not what we usually do or what people like. We should be culturally sensitive and use common sense in all that we do. Our acts and behavior can follow the patterns of our culture and our ethics insofar that they do not conflict with the universal standards of God's Word.

The same principle should also be applied to our speech. Our words have the power to encourage or destroy others. It is easy to communicate the right information with impolite words or even with the wrong emphasis. Keep in mind that, as someone wisely stated, "knowledge is knowing *what* to say; wisdom is knowing *when* to say it; and respect is knowing *how* to say it." As stated by King Solomon, "Whoever guards his mouth and tongue keeps his soul from troubles" (Proverbs 21:23). And "a word fitly spoken is like apples of gold in settings of silver" (Proverbs 25:11).

So, what should be our attitude toward those who do not follow this principle? Our attitude is well defined by Jesus in His sermon on the mount (Matthew 5–7). He says that we should not "resist an evil person" but rather treat him or her in a loving manner, that we should extend loving respect extending even to our enemies (Matthew 5:38–48). As well stated by Solomon, "A soft answer turns away wrath, but a harsh word stirs up anger" (Proverbs 15:1). Only this type of practical religion can convince the world of the transforming power of the gospel.

𝒯HE SECRET 𝓕ORMULA

A gossip betrays a confidence, but a trustworthy person keeps a secret.
—Proverbs 11:13, NIV

Perhaps no other secret has generated so much curiosity and speculation over time as the famous Coca-Cola formula. On **March 29, 1886**, after preliminary experiments in his backyard, pharmacist John Pemberton (1831–1888) brewed the first batch of what would later become Coca-Cola. The first batch was created with kola nuts (for caffeine) and coca leaf. By early May, the formula was already selling in Jacob's Pharmacy in Atlanta and being promoted as a treatment for several health woes, including indigestion, headaches, hangovers, and even impotence.

Today, the Coca-Cola ingredients are listed on bottles and cans, but the "natural flavors"—also known as "20X" herbal extracts—remain intentionally vague. The recipe has been considered "one of the most closely guarded secrets in the world. There are claims that only two people know it at any given time and they can never travel on the same plane in case it crashes."[57] When one of them dies, the other one must share the formula with another trusted person. Despite the secrecy, many claim to have discovered the formula.

But one might ask the question: What secrets should we keep, and what secrets should we not? Is there a difference between good and bad secrets? Many industrial, trade, and military strategies are well kept, but what about our interpersonal relations? An anonymous quote says, "Keeping secrets from someone is no different than lying to them. It's still dishonest." Regina Brett adds, "If a relationship has to be a secret, you shouldn't be in it."[58] As Christians, our lives should be transparent, without hidden agendas. But that does not provide an excuse for anyone to start gossiping, as some enjoy doing.

Psychologists and counselors are legally required to keep the secrets of their clients. And Proverbs 11:13 warns us, "A gossip betrays a confidence, but a trustworthy person keeps a secret" (NIV). It is true that God will finally uncover all human secrets (Proverbs 12:3). But we should also remember that "many, many confessions should never be spoken in the hearing of mortals; for the result is that which the limited judgment of finite beings does not anticipate."[59] Let's be ethical with others and with ourselves!

Soothing Pain

A jar of wine vinegar was there, so they soaked a sponge in it,
put the sponge on a stalk of the hyssop plant, and lifted it to Jesus' lips.
When he had received the drink, Jesus said, "It is finished."
—John 19:29, 30, NIV

How would you feel if one of your legs were cut off above the knee without anesthesia? This was what Dr. Amos Twitchell, a noted surgeon from Keene, New Hampshire, did with four-year-old Uriah Smith. The twenty-minute operation was performed on the kitchen table of the Smith home. Praise God that times have changed, and today we have anesthesia to at least partially, if not completely, kill pain during such medical procedures.

American surgeon and pharmacist Crawford W. Long (1815–1878) noticed that people felt no pain when they injured themselves under the influence of ether. This led him to consider the use of sulfuric ether as an anesthetic. On **March 30, 1842**, Long excised two small tumors from James Venable, whom Long had anesthetized with ether, and he didn't feel any pain. Unaware of Long's prior work, on October 16, 1846, William T. G. Morton administered ether anesthesia before a medical audience at the Massachusetts General Hospital in Boston. Long did not announce his discovery until 1849 and never received full credit for it during his lifetime.

Shortly before the crucified Jesus died, He said, "I am thirsty!" Someone lifted a sponge with vinegar to Jesus' lips (John 19:28–30, NIV). Psalm 69:21 already predicted, "And for my thirst they gave me vinegar to drink." Ellen White explained, "To those who suffered death by the cross, it was permitted to give a stupefying potion, to deaden the sense of pain. This was offered to Jesus; but when He had tasted it, He refused it. He would receive nothing that could becloud His mind. His faith must keep fast hold upon God. This was His only strength. To becloud His senses would give Satan an advantage."[60]

Physically, pain is an alert that something is wrong and needs to be fixed. But we want the pain to go away while the problem is being solved. Spiritually speaking, we should not attempt to mask our pain while the problem of sin is being solved. The only true solution for our sin-related pain is personal repentance and forgiveness through God's infinite grace!

$\mathcal{P}$ROTECTING $\mathcal{C}$ARE

He will cover you with His pinions,
And under His wings you may seek refuge;
His faithfulness is a shield and bulwark.

You will not be afraid of the terror by night,
Or of the arrow that flies by day.

—Psalm 91:4, 5, NASB

Our world is a giant battlefield in the war between good and evil. Were it not for God's constant protection, we would be completely overwhelmed by the attacks of evil powers. Psalm 91 speaks of terror by night and arrows flying by day. But God protects His children and stays with them during both good and bad days.

In December 1847, the Fox family moved to Hydesville, New York. A few months later, the family was disturbed at night by inexplicable knockings and rappings like the sound of moving furniture. They increased in intensity, and on **March 31, 1848**, twelve-year-old Kate, the youngest of three sisters, noticed that the mysterious sounds responded to sounds that the girls made. Kate and her sister Maggie, fifteen, addressed the spirit as "Mr. Splitfoot," a nickname for the devil. They developed a communication code through which the spirit identified himself as a thirty-one-year-old peddler who was murdered and buried in the cellar of the house.

On August 24, 1850, Ellen White saw that "the 'mysterious rapping' was the power of Satan; some of it was directly from him, and some indirectly, through his agents, but it all proceeded from Satan." She identified that phenomenon as the beginning of modern spiritualism, which would take over the whole world at "the speed of lightning."[61] At the Hydesville Memorial Park—the site of the Fox home—one can see a foundation stone with the inscription, "The birthplace and shrine of modern spiritualism." Since that interaction between the Fox family and Satan, spiritualism and mysticism have grown astronomically, assuming many different forms and taking over much of the entertainment industry of the Western world.

As Bible-believing Christians, we should stay away from all such culturally acceptable delusions of the last days, intended "to deceive, if possible, even the elect" (Matthew 24:24). Please never ever enter "Satan's enchanted ground," even if it's just for curiosity and fun. Remember that under God's protecting care, we are more than safe and do not need to be concerned about the evil one's powers. His mighty angels will protect us.

ƑESTIVALS OF ℒIES

Like a madman who throws firebrands, arrows, and death, is the man who deceives his
neighbor, and says, "I was only joking."
—Proverbs 26:18, 19

Why do people lie and propagate false stories? Many times, it is just a matter of personal ignorance or of sharing some information without previously confirming its reliability. But deliberate lies and fake stories are usually intended either to deceive others and take advantage of them or simply to make fun of their naivete and credulity. Many cultures around the world have chosen **April 1** as April Fools' Day, on which fake stories are first reported and then explained to make fun of those who believed them.

Surprisingly, the "art" of lying for fun is even being promoted by lie contests. For instance, the World's Biggest Liar, in Cumbria, England, is an annual competition in telling lies. Politicians and lawyers are not allowed to compete because they "are judged to be too skilled at telling porkies."[1] The small town of Nova Bréscia, Brazil, is known as the national capital of lies, where every two years the Festival of Lies takes place. Stories must be original and as close as possible to the truth, leaving the audience in doubt of their veracity.

Professional and amateur lying is always focused on the psychosocial response of the audience. From a broader perspective, we can say that generally, there is nothing wrong with having fun with morally acceptable and inoffensive stories and jokes. The problem begins when they become a form of bullying or they put others down. It can become even worse when someone wants to cause harm, a motive described well by the German term *schadenfreude*, which refers to the feeling of pleasure or satisfaction derived from the misfortune of others.

The Bible addresses the matter of lying in very strong terms. To begin with, Christ called the Holy Spirit "the Spirit of truth" (John 16:13) and Satan "a liar and the father of lies" (John 8:44, NIV). King Solomon condemned lying even for the sake of joking (Proverbs 26:18, 19). When Ananias and Sapphira lied to the apostles, their act was considered a lie to the Holy Spirit, worthy of death (Acts 5:1–11). And we are informed that all liars will be left out of heaven (Revelation 21:27). Remember, regardless of their form, lies are lies and must be avoided.

DIVISIVE SPECULATIONS

*Not to teach false doctrines any longer or to devote themselves
to myths and endless genealogies. Such things promote controversial
speculations rather than advancing God's work—which is by faith.*
—1 Timothy 1:3, 4, NIV

God has entrusted us with a special Christ-centered message to be proclaimed to a sinful world that is nearing its destruction. Meanwhile, the devil uses all possible means to occupy us with endless *peripheral* speculations in order to distract us from the *core* of the gospel message and the fulfillment of our evangelistic mission. Among those distractions are the speculations about who will be the "last" pope.

Several individuals built creative prophetic scenarios around Pope John Paul II, who was pope for twenty-six years (1978–2005). Some suggested that he would eventually resign, another pope would assume the Vatican for a short time, and then John Paul II would reassume his function, becoming the last pope. But these speculative theories proved false. John Paul II continued as pope until his death on **April 2, 2005**. Instead of acknowledging their mistake, some of those individuals suggested that Pope Benedict XVI would remain just for a short while, and then Satan himself would simulate a pseudo resurrection of John Paul II and would rule the world as a human pope. Once again, the speculations failed when Benedict XVI, having been pope for almost eight years (2005–2013), was replaced by Pope Francis.

This is just one example of many fanciful speculations that have been proposed over the years. Gerhard F. Hasel noted, "In regards to unfulfilled prophecy, there is always the danger for the interpreter to speculate or to subtly become a prophet himself."[2] Jesus' warning against false prophets (Matthew 24:24) refers primarily to self-proclaimed prophets not sent by God. By extension, it can also refer to those who twist the meaning of Bible prophecy, either by imposing on it their own artificial interpretations or by ignoring parts of its content (Revelation 22:18, 19).

No wonder Paul advises us against "controversial speculations" that distract us from advancing God's work (1 Timothy 1:4, NIV). Instead of wasting our precious time with such divisive speculations, let's stick with the well-established prophetic message of the Bible and its enlightening power!

ᶜWᴇᴀᴛʜᴇʀ ᶠᴏʀᴇᴄᴀsᴛ

He also said to the crowds, "When you see a cloud rising in the west, you immediately say,
'It is going to rain'; and so it happens. And when you see the south wind blowing, you say,
'There will be scorching heat'; and it happens. You hypocrites! You know how to interpret the
appearance of earth and sky, but why do you not know how to interpret the present time?"
—Luke 12:54–56, NRSV

During Jesus' earthly ministry, temperature and weather forecasts were largely based on cloud and wind observations. Several modern meteorological techniques have made global weather forecasts much more precise and reliable. For example, on **April 3, 1995**, a low-earth orbit satellite called MicroLab 1 carrying a laptop-sized GPS receiver was launched into a circular orbit at an altitude of about 450 miles (724 kilometers). The satellite's technology can repeatedly sound the atmospheric layers by radio waves, retrieving important temperature, pressure, and water vapor data. The Ground-Based GPS Meteorology monitors water vapor in the lower atmosphere, showing the moisture and latent heat of our weather.

In Luke 12:54–56, Jesus rebuked the multitude because, although they could accurately predict weather and temperature, they were unable to interpret the meaning of their own "present time" (verse 56, NIV). When Jesus asked His disciples who people said He was, they replied, "Some say John the Baptist, some Elijah, and others Jeremiah or one of the prophets" (Matthew 16:14). In other words, people failed to realize that in Jesus Christ, the Messianic age had arrived, and they were indifferent to the nature of His kingdom (John 18:36).

Similarly, our generation has sophisticated meteorological systems but does not discern the signs of our own times. Scoffers say, "Where is the promise of His coming? For since the fathers fell asleep, all things continue as they were from the beginning of creation" (2 Peter 3:4). But could it be that even within our own ranks, we might find some "ectothermic amphibian" Adventists? Being "ectothermic" (cold-blooded), they have no clear perception of the temperature; being "amphibians," they try to enjoy the church and the world simultaneously.

We are rapidly approaching the stormy season of the end of time, and soon Christ will appear in the clouds of heaven. May the Lord open our eyes to the signs of our times and to the solemn days in which we live!

CHRIST THE REDEEMER

Christ Jesus is He who died, yes, rather who was raised,
who is at the right hand of God, who also intercedes for us.
—Romans 8:34, NASB

Each year tourists from around the world visit Rio de Janeiro, Brazil, which is world-renowned for its beautiful landscape, numerous attractions, and intense social life. At the top of Corcovado Mountain is the statue of Christ the Redeemer (Cristo Redentor), its open arms engulfing the city. The foundation stone of this colossal monument was laid on **April 4, 1922**. Nine years later, the iconic statue was completed. It was officially inaugurated on October 12, 1931, as a symbol of Christ, who loves and embraces all who come to Him. In 2007, the statute was proclaimed one of the New Seven Wonders of the World.

Over the years, the Christ the Redeemer statue has undergone periodic cleanings, repairs, and renovations. Even with a lightning rod on top, the statue is not totally immune to lightning and thunderstorms. According to the Brazilian National Institute for Space Research, an average of six lightning strikes hit the statue each year. In 2008, one of them damaged part of the statue's head and fingers, which had to be repaired.

This and other similar statues of Christ around the world are merely lifeless depictions of Him, periodically requiring care. In contrast, the real Christ whom we serve is "unblemished and spotless" (1 Peter 1:19, NASB) and "without sin" (Hebrews 4:15). He also remained sinless in His incarnation. Edward Heppenstall states: "The effect of Adam and Eve's sin, while it affected His physical constitution, did not reach Him morally and spiritually as it reaches us."[3] Otherwise, He could not be our Savior but would need a savior Himself.

While those statues need to be cared for, our living Christ is always interceding and caring for us. "He knows by experience what are the weaknesses of humanity, what are our wants, and where lies the strength of our temptations; for He was in all points tempted like as we are, yet without sin. He is watching over you, trembling child of God. Are you tempted? He will deliver. Are you weak? He will strengthen. Are you ignorant? He will enlighten. Are you wounded? He will heal."[4] What a wonderful Savior we have!

Costly Grace

"My grace is sufficient for you."

—2 Corinthians 12:9

Much is said today about grace. But what does it actually mean? One of the best descriptions of it came from the German Lutheran pastor, theologian, and martyr Dietrich Bonhoeffer (1906–1945). As a vocal antagonist of Hitler's regime, Bonhoeffer placed himself in an extremely dangerous situation in a time when most German religious leaders remained silent. Bonhoeffer was arrested on **April 5, 1943**, by the Gestapo and executed by hanging on April 9, 1945, just two weeks before the concentration camp in which he was being held prisoner was liberated. He lived only thirty-nine years but left a valuable literary legacy.

In chapter 1 of his book *The Cost of Discipleship* (1937), Bonhoeffer contrasts *cheap* grace and *costly* grace:

Cheap grace is the deadly enemy of our Church. . . .

. . . That is what we mean by cheap grace, the grace which amounts to the justification of sin without the justification of the repentant sinner who departs from sin and from whom sin departs. . . .

Cheap grace is the preaching of forgiveness without requiring repentance, baptism without church discipline, Communion without confession, absolution without personal confession. Cheap grace is grace without discipleship, grace without the cross, grace without Jesus Christ, living and incarnate.[5]

In contrast, costly grace

is *costly* because it calls us to follow, and it is *grace* because it calls us to follow *Jesus Christ*. It is costly because it costs a man his life, and it is grace because it gives a man the only true life. It is costly because it condemns sin, and grace because it justifies the sinner. Above all, it is *costly* because it cost God the life of his Son: 'ye were bought at a price,' and what has cost God much cannot be cheap for us. . . .

. . . Grace is costly because it compels a man to submit to the yoke of Christ and follow him; it is grace because Jesus says: "My yoke is easy and my burden is light."[6]

In addition to being a *costly* grace, God's saving grace is also an *active* grace that liberates us from the bondage of sin and gives us the right motivation for true obedience. As stated by Paul, salvation by grace through faith is "not of works" but "for good works" (Ephesians 2:8–10). Christ is the incarnation of God's grace. Therefore, to have Christ means to have God's wonderful grace with us.

ⱭN ꟿMPERISHABLE CROWN

Everyone who competes in the games goes into strict training. They do it to get
a crown that will not last, but we do it to get a crown that will last forever.
—1 Corinthians 9:25, NIV

In June 1998, I visited the Greek cities of Athens, Corinth, and Olympia. Close to the latter city, I saw the complex of the ancient Olympic Games, including the ruins of the Temple of Olympian Zeus and the old stadium. The first recorded Olympiad was held in 776 BC, and it occurred every four years during a religious festival honoring Zeus, the greatest of all Greek gods. The Olympic Games became the most important of all the athletic contests in the ancient world. But they were held for the last time in AD 393, after which the Roman emperor Theodosius I forbade their celebrations.

Fifteen centuries later, on **April 6, 1896**, the first modern Olympic Games opened in Athens. Since then, they have again been celebrated every four years, but in a different city around the world each time. Eleven women, representing the Vestal Virgins, go to the site of the ancient Olympics and ignite the Olympic flame with the light of the sun concentrated by a parabolic mirror. From Olympia, the torch is taken first to the Panathenaic Stadium in Athens and from there to the city where the Olympic Games will take place.

In 1 Corinthians 9:24–27, Paul used the image of those ancient games as an analogy for the Christian race. First, he urges the Christian to be a victorious runner. In the Olympic Games, "all the runners run, but only one gets the prize" (verse 24, NIV). But in the Christian race, all can be victorious. Second, Paul highlights that the Christian reward is worth the effort. In Olympia, the prize for the winner was a wild olive wreath; and in Corinth, it was an even more perishable crown of wilted celery. But the victorious Christian will receive "a crown that will last forever" (verse 25, NIV).

In Hebrews 11:39–12:2, all past victorious Christian runners are represented as watching our race and cheering us on to victory. We do not ignite our Olympic flame at the sanctuary of the Temple of Hera (Zeus's wife) but at the altar of the cross of Calvary, and we do not expect to receive just a perishable wreath but the imperishable "crown of righteousness" (2 Timothy 4:8). Run victoriously!

A Worthy Investment

Therefore, whether you eat or drink, or whatever you do, do all to the glory of God.
—1 Corinthians 10:31

Health is often like a savings account that we wait to invest in until it is no longer as valuable as it used to be. And yet, we still hope to get the best from it. As a quote often attributed to the Canadian clergyman A. J. Reb Materi aptly puts it, "So many people spend their health gaining wealth, and then have to spend their wealth to regain their health."

The World Health Organization (WHO) was founded on **April 7, 1948**, and is headquartered in Geneva, Switzerland. World Health Day is celebrated each year on April 7, marking the founding of WHO and drawing attention to important health issues facing the world. But what is health, and how can we promote it? According to WHO, "Health is a state of complete physical, mental and social well-being and not merely the absence of disease or infirmity."[7]

In her book *The Ministry of Healing*, Ellen White explains,

Too little attention is generally given to the preservation of health. It is far better to prevent disease than to know how to treat it when contracted. It is the duty of every person, for his own sake, and for the sake of humanity, to inform himself in regard to the laws of life and conscientiously to obey them. All need to become acquainted with that most wonderful of all organisms, the human body. They should understand the functions of the various organs and the dependence of one upon another for the healthy action of all. They should study the influence of the mind upon the body, and of the body upon the mind, and the laws by which they are governed.[8]

Mrs. White also states,

Pure air, sunlight, abstemiousness, rest, exercise, proper diet, the use of water, trust in divine power—these are the true remedies. Every person should have a knowledge of nature's remedial agencies and how to apply them. . . .
. . . Those who persevere in obedience to her laws will reap the reward in health of body and health of mind.[9]

These "true remedies" are the basis of the NEWSTART® health program that addresses (1) nutrition, (2) exercise, (3) water, (4) sunshine, (5) temperance, (6) air, (7) rest, and (8) trust in God.[10]

Knowing these things, why not improve your personal lifestyle by taking into serious and balanced consideration each of these eight basic principles of health?

RELIGIOUS DISCRIMINATION

We are hard-pressed on every side, yet not crushed; we are perplexed, but not in despair;
persecuted, but not forsaken; struck down, but not destroyed—always carrying about in the
body the dying of the Lord Jesus, that the life of Jesus also may be manifested in our body.
—2 Corinthians 4:8–10

Discrimination is a word easily pronounced but an experience very difficult to endure. It can simply mean your being left out or unwanted, making it evident that your absence is more desirable than your presence. In some cases, it may be that your death is preferred over your life. Whatever the case, discrimination always destroys human dignity.

The International Society for Human Rights (ISHR) is a secular organization originally founded on **April 8, 1972,** in Frankfurt, Germany, as the Society for Human Rights (Gesellschaft für Menschenrechte). Nine years later, in 1981, it reached international status,[11] and now some areas of focus include freedom of religion and freedom of press issues.[12] In 2009, the ISHR estimated that 80 percent of all acts of religious discrimination in the world are against Christians. A quite low estimate indicates that twenty Christians are being killed for their faith each day.

Massimo Introvigne, the founder of the Center for Studies on New Religions, pointed out that whereas atheistic communist regimes were the greatest persecutors of Christians in the twentieth century, Islamic ultrafundamentalists have taken their place in the twenty-first century. An anonymous Iraqi Christian revealed, "The attacks on Christians continue, and the world remains totally silent. It's as if we've been swallowed up by the night." John L. Allen Jr., the author of *The Global War on Christians* (published in 2016), regards the global persecution of churchgoers as "the unreported catastrophe of our time."[13]

After reading such reports, our tendency is to hate and discriminate against the discriminators and persecutors. But discrimination cannot overcome discrimination, for it increases the evil; only love can overcome it. Even so, we should pray for all those who are suffering for their faith around the world and do our best to suppress discrimination in all its forms, starting with ourselves. Love all, and do not consider others less human because they do not profess the same faith.

Speaking in Tongues

*And they were all filled with the Holy Spirit and began to speak
with other tongues, as the Spirit gave them utterance.*

—Acts 2:4

Many Christians today argue that those who are baptized with the Holy Spirit should speak in tongues as in apostolic times (Acts 2:1–13; 10:44–48; 19:1–7). But what kind of tongues did the early Christians speak? Did they speak in ecstatic unintelligible tongues or in human languages?

Although ecstatic tongues were already present in some ancient pagan religions and, later on, even in a few isolated Christian circles, a new emphasis on such tongues emerged from the famous Azuza Street Revival in Los Angeles, California. On **April 9, 1906**, William J. Seymour was holding charismatic prayer meetings in a couple of homes when Edward Lee and several other African Americans experienced the phenomenon. From there, the modern tongues movement spread around the world. But are these tongues of the same nature as those that were spoken by early Christians?

The apostle Paul teaches that the true gift of tongues is given to believers by the Holy Spirit with an the purpose of *outreach*, not so that they can achieve a special status *within* a monolingual community (1 Corinthians 14:9, 18, 19, 22, 27, 28). On the Day of Pentecost, the disciples actually spoke in known human languages so that each foreigner could listen to the gospel in his or her own language (Acts 2:4–13). In the case of Cornelius, the gift of tongues was a confirming sign that the gospel should also be preached to the Gentiles (Acts 10:44–48). The gift in Corinth helped spread the message in that important commercial center with many alien residents and foreign travelers (Acts 19:1–7).

No doubt, the true gift of tongues may be given even today, as has been the case in some missionary settings where no translator was available. But the presence of the Holy Spirit in one's life is made evident not so much through the spiritual *gifts*, which can be imitated by Satan (Exodus 7:8–13, 20–22; 8:6, 7), but rather in bearing the *fruit* of the Spirit (Galatians 5:22, 23). According to Ellen White, "To all who have accepted Christ as a personal Saviour, the Holy Spirit has come as a counselor, sanctifier, guide, and witness."[14] Regardless of your skills and gifts, you can be full of the Holy Spirit and bear His fruit.

CARING FOR SINNERS

"But go and learn what this means: 'I desire mercy and not sacrifice.'
For I did not come to call the righteous, but sinners, to repentance."
—Matthew 9:13

There is a human tendency to care more for the prosperous and to give the best presents to the wealthiest. But some people have broken this trend and committed themselves to serve the deprived and downtrodden social classes. One of these was William Booth (1829–1912), the founder and first general of the Salvation Army.

William Booth was born on **April 10, 1829**, in Nottingham, United Kingdom. In 1844, he had a conversion experience, and two years later, he became a lay revivalist preacher. In 1865, Booth and his wife, Catherine, founded the Christian Revival Society—which later became the Salvation Army—to reach the poorest and neediest, including alcoholics, criminals, and prostitutes. During its early years, the Salvation Army faced much opposition from the alcohol industry, which did not want the poorer classes to stop buying its product. His wife reported that Booth would "stumble home night after night haggard with fatigue, often his clothes were torn, and bloody bandages swathed his head where a stone had struck."

But Booth would not give up! In his last public address in the Royal Albert Hall, London, on May 19, 1912 (three months before his death), Booth declared, "While women weep, as they do now, I'll fight; while little children go hungry, as they do now, I'll fight; while men go to prison, in and out, in and out, as they do now, I'll fight; while there is a drunkard left, while there is a poor lost girl upon the streets, while there remains one dark soul without the light of God, I'll fight—I'll fight to the very end!"[15] Booth is also often credited for the quote, "The chief danger that confronts the coming century will be religion without the Holy Ghost, Christianity without Christ, forgiveness without repentance, salvation without regeneration, politics without God, heaven without hell."[16]

Appreciating the work of the Salvation Army, Ellen White also emphasized that God raised the Seventh-day Adventist Church to restore the biblical truth in an end-time setting. This means that its solemn mission cannot be replaced by any merely social gospel.[17] While caring for people's physical and social needs, we must also lead them "into all truth" (John 16:13; see also Matthew 4:24; 28:20).

DECEPTIVE APPEARANCES

But the LORD said to Samuel, "Do not look at his appearance or at his physical stature, because I have refused him. For the LORD does not see as man sees; for man looks at the outward appearance, but the LORD looks at the heart."

—1 Samuel 16:7

Whether we like it or not, we are judged by our appearance—by our height and weight, how we look and dress, and how we work and behave. Furthermore, as stated by the theoretical physicist Leonard Mlodinow, "Facial appearance translates to judgments of character."[18] However, as important as good looks might be, we must never forget that "appearances can be deceptive" and that "first appearance deceives many."

When the Lord sent the prophet Samuel to the house of Jesse to anoint a new king over the house of Israel (1 Samuel 16:1–13), the prophet was very impressed with the appearance of Eliab and even said, "Surely the LORD's anointed is before Him!" (verse 6). But the Lord warned Samuel, "Do not look at his appearance or at his physical stature, because I have refused him. For the LORD does not see as man sees; for man looks at the outward appearance, but the LORD looks at the heart" (verse 7).

Even Uriah Smith (1832–1903), widely recognized as the dean of prophetic interpretation in Seventh-day Adventist circles, failed in a similar matter. When the first automobiles pulled into Battle Creek, Michigan, some frightened horses bolted, injuring a woman. Convinced that the problem was the appearance of the vehicles, Smith designed a wooden horse's head to attach to the front of automobiles. On **April 11, 1899**, his "Design for a Vehicle-Body" was patented as US D30551 S for a term of seven years. But his invention did not work as expected. It turns out that the horses were scared not by the shape but rather by the noise of those early horseless carriages.

Hasty judgments can prevent us from seeing the inner beauty of people. Often behind an unattractive face, there is a loving heart and a shining personality. Much more important than our outward appearance is the aesthetic of a character that resembles the image and likeness of our Creator and Redeemer. And, if we could see all human beings through Christ's eyes, we would view them not as what they already are but as what they can still become if transformed by His amazing grace (Philippians 3:12–16).

⒠DEN TO ⒠DEN

But in keeping with his promise we are looking forward to
a new heaven and a new earth, where righteousness dwells.
—2 Peter 3:13, NIV

Images produce long-lasting memories that time cannot erase. A Chinese proverb says, "Hearing something a hundred times isn't better than seeing it once." A popular English saying adds, "A picture is worth a thousand words." Based on this principle, over the years, Adventist artists have portrayed many crucial elements of the plan of salvation.

One of the most insightful and inspiring collections of such pictures is the *Eden to Eden* art gallery in the main lobby of the General Conference of Seventh-day Adventists headquarters. Dedicated on **April 12, 2015,** the display has more than seventy paintings by various artists. The lower lobby has several pieces related to the Old Testament period. The art in the upper lobby and its hallway portrays the New Testament era. And the atrium displays images of the redeemed in the heavenly courts. The whole exhibit reaches its climax with Nathan Greene's original painting, *The Blessed Hope,* an amazing portrayal of Christ's second coming. Each painting carries a meaningful visual message, but the whole thematic sequence illustrates that we are now on the very border of eternity.

The *Eden to Eden* exhibit is a *microcosmic* representation of the plan of salvation, which will receive an unprecedented *macrocosmic* display at the end of the millennium when the New Jerusalem and God's throne will be on this earth (Revelation 21:1–3). Ellen White describes the scene:

Above the throne is revealed the cross; and like a panoramic view appear the scenes of Adam's temptation and fall, and the successive steps in the great plan of redemption.

. . .

The awful spectacle appears just as it was. Satan, his angels, and his subjects have no power to turn from the picture of their own work. Each actor recalls the part which he performed.[19]

Human history is coming to its end, and each of us is an actor on the stage of life. According to God's plan, everything is in place for our salvation. And now heaven and earth are carefully watching our performance (1 Corinthians 4:9; Hebrews 12:1, 2). May you and I faithfully persevere on our journey to the restored Eden. Please, don't allow anything or anyone to distract you from this goal!

$\mathcal{H}$EAVENLY $\mathcal{W}$ORSHIP

Then the seventh angel sounded: And there were loud voices in
heaven, saying, "The kingdoms of this world have become the kingdoms
of our Lord and of His Christ, and He shall reign forever and ever!"

—Revelation 11:15

One of the most majestic musical compositions of all time is George F. Handel's *Messiah*, best known for its "Hallelujah Chorus." Using the Bible-based, Christ-centered lyrics of Charles Jennens, Handel composed his masterpiece in only twenty-four days. At the end of the score, he wrote "SDG," an abbreviation of *Soli Deo Gloria*, which means "glory to God alone." The work was first performed in Dublin, Ireland, on **April 13, 1742**, for a very appreciative audience of seven hundred people.

According to a widespread tradition, the practice of standing during the "Hallelujah Chorus" began in March 1743 at the London debut performance, when King George II was supposedly so moved that he rose to his feet, and everyone else in the auditorium did the same. Some critics question this story due to the lack of contemporary historical evidence. Regardless of its origin, the practice has survived through the centuries and is still observed as a symbol of reverence to the exalted Christ.

The "Hallelujah Chorus" reflects the sublime expressions of heavenly praise described in the Revelation of John as rendered in the King James Version. For example, "The kingdoms of this world are become the kingdoms of our Lord and of His Christ; and He shall reign for ever and ever" (Revelation 11:15). "Alleluia: for the Lord God omnipotent reigneth" (Revelation 19:6). Based on John's visions of heavenly realms, Handel's chorus praises the enthroned Christ as "King of kings, and Lord of lords" (Revelation 19:16). It may be considered a slight foretaste of the music of heaven.

The whole plan of salvation was conceived and implemented so we can live in the very presence of God, "to enjoy the light and glory of heaven, to hear the angels sing, and to sing with them."[20] But much more important than simply knowing about the praises of heaven is preparing ourselves to praise God in heaven! After all, "heaven is worth everything to us, and if we lose heaven we lose all."[21] If we miss heaven, we miss the very purpose of our existence. By God's grace, you and I have to be there.

$\mathcal{T}$HE $\mathcal{M}$YSTERY OF $\mathcal{L}$IFE

I will praise You, for I am fearfully and wonderfully made;
marvelous are Your works, and that my soul knows very well.
—Psalm 139:14

Have you ever marveled at the complexity of the human body, with its many organs and interacting systems? Every single person has an extremely complex body with voluntary and involuntary muscles, an astonishing immune system with amazing healing capability, and an exceedingly mysterious brain that challenges all scientific research. How are thoughts and emotions generated? What makes every human being unique from all others?

Over the centuries, scientists have tried to understand the human body and its varied functions. For example, DNA research has uncovered foundational aspects of the genetic instructions related to the development, growth, and function of living organisms. The much-publicized Human Genome Project sought to sequence the entire human genome. On **April 14, 2003**, researchers announced that the process had been completed. However, according to the leaders of the Human Brain Project, "Understanding the human brain is one of the greatest challenges facing 21st-century science."[22]

On April 2, 2014, the British *Independent* explained, "We each have something approaching 100 billion nerve cells—neurons—in the human brain (more than the number of stars in the Milky Way). Each of them can be connected directly with maybe 10,000 others, totaling some 100 trillion nerve connections. If each neuron of a single human brain were laid end to end, they could be wrapped around the Earth twice over. Deciphering the biological conundrum of this most complex of organs makes unraveling the genome, for example, look like child's play."[23]

No wonder the psalmist David said that he was fearfully, wonderfully, and marvelously made by God (Psalm 139:14). As valuable as we are by design, much more value was added to us when God bought us with "the precious blood of Christ" (1 Peter 1:18, 19) to be "a temple of the Holy Spirit" (1 Corinthians 6:19). Given that God has invested so much in each of us, why should we not value ourselves and care adequately for our own health? "Therefore glorify God in your body and in your spirit, which are God's" (1 Corinthians 6:20).

OVERCONFIDENCE

Some trust in chariots and some in horses, but we trust in the name of the Lord our God.
—Psalm 20:7, NIV

The first half of the twentieth century was marked by intense competition among rival shipping lines. In 1908, the White Star Line commissioned the Harland and Wolff company in Belfast, Ireland, to build the largest and most luxurious steamship. On April 10, 1912, the new liner RMS *Titanic* (the word means enormous in size and strength) left Southampton, England, on its maiden voyage to New York. But four days later, while passing through the North Atlantic Ocean at 11:40 P.M., the ship collided with an iceberg that punched big holes in the starboard side of the ship. In the early morning of **April 15, 1912**, the *Titanic* broke in half and sank less than three hours after the accident.

Several wireless messages from other ships had warned the *Titanic* about icebergs along the way, but Captain Edward J. Smith kept the ship steaming full speed ahead, retiring to his room for the night around 9:20 P.M. Considered "unsinkable," the *Titanic* carried only twenty lifeboats—intended for rescuing survivors of other sinking ships. Despite some discrepancies regarding the exact number of people on board, about 710 people were rescued, and more than 1,500 perished in the disaster. Those who saw the 1997 film *Titanic* have a rough idea of the tragedy.

Important lessons can be learned from that disaster. The fact that the "unsinkable" ship sank should warn us against being overconfident in human achievements, including our own. David was fully aware of this tendency when he stated, "Some trust in chariots and some in horses, but we trust in the name of the Lord our God" (Psalm 20:7, NIV). Sooner or later, our best endeavors fade and die. Only the work we do as coworkers with God will last forever.

Captain Smith's self-sufficient disregard for the warnings from other ships had disastrous consequences. This demonstrates what can happen when we simply choose not to listen to reliable counsel and instructions. It also illustrates that small decisions can have huge consequences. Consider the far-reaching effects of Eve's decision to eat the fruit of the tree of knowledge of good and evil.

So, Lord, help us today and every day to make the right decisions according to Your will!

$\mathcal{P}$RAISING $\mathcal{V}$OICES

*Let the words of my mouth and the meditation of my heart be
acceptable in Your sight, O LORD, my strength and my Redeemer.*
—Psalm 19:14

We are called by God to proclaim the everlasting gospel in a world full of eloquent and convincing voices. To effectively fulfill our mission, we should pay attention not only to *what* we say (the content) but also to *how* we say it (the method). According to Ellen White, "We may have knowledge, but unless we know how to use the voice correctly, our work will be a failure. Unless we can clothe our ideas in appropriate language, of what avail is our education? Knowledge will be of little advantage to us unless we cultivate the talent of speech."[24]

In 1999, the Brazilian Society of Laryngology and Voice chose **April 16** as the annual day to celebrate the phenomenon of voice. Three years later, in 2002, Portuguese laryngologist Professor Mario Andrea, president of the European Laryngological Society, suggested that April 16 should receive much wider attention, and it became World Voice Day. Its aim is to demonstrate the enormous importance of the voice in the daily lives of everyone, encourage them to assess their vocal health, and persuade them to improve or maintain good voice habits.

A classic example of how personal effort can help us overcome speech problems is Demosthenes (384–322 BC), the greatest of ancient Greek orators. Plutarch, the Greek historian and biographer, relates that "Demosthenes had a speech defect, 'an inarticulate and stammering pronunciation.'" To overcome his problem, he "built an underground study where he exercised his voice, shaving half of his head so he could not go out in public." During this time, he practiced by "speaking with pebbles in his mouth and by reciting verses when running or out of breath. He also practiced speaking in front of a large mirror."[25]

Are there any aspects of your own voice and speaking skills that you need to improve? God can use us despite our human limitations and weaknesses. But by combining good techniques with perseverance, we can overcome many of our speech deficiencies. You and I should consecrate our voices to God, avoiding self-exaltation, and always use them to glorify God and uplift humanity.

ℛEVIVED BY ℋIS WORD

And when they had prayed, the place where they were assembled together was shaken; and they were all filled with the Holy Spirit, and they spoke the word of God with boldness.

—Acts 4:31

We are told that "a revival of true godliness among us is the greatest and most urgent of all our needs."[26] Recognizing this urgent need, the 2011 General Conference Annual Council voted to implement a plan called Revived by His Word. It was launched on **April 17, 2012**, and ended at the General Conference Session in July 2015. Every church member was encouraged to read one chapter of the Bible each day. At the 2015 session, a similar plan was instated—"Believe His Prophets," a five-year program to read through the Bible and selected Ellen White writings.

Every true revival in the history of Christianity has begun when people pled with God in fervent prayer and spent time in the earnest study of His Word. We are admonished that "never should the Bible be studied without prayer."[27] On the other hand, we should recognize that "the reading of the word of God prepares the mind for prayer."[28] Therefore, "I hope you will be an earnest, true Christian day by day, seeking God in prayer. Do not be so busy you cannot give time to read the Bible and seek the grace of God in humble prayer."[29]

We must recognize that revival and reformation go together. *Revival* generates the spiritual drive for reformation, and *reformation* is the result of any true revival. Revival without reformation is an empty spiritual illusion, and reformation without revival is nothing but ethical formalism. If it is true that in the past many preachers stressed reformation without revival, today the tendency is to preach revival without reformation. People want Christ as their Savior but not necessarily as their Lord.

Another basic feature of true revival is that it generates a deep feeling of personal humility and remorse. Whenever people become proud of themselves and judgmental of others, we can be sure that the Holy Spirit is not leading them. The aforementioned plans were formulated to encourage us to seek the Lord. But don't wait for others to stimulate spiritual growth; decide for yourself to seek the Lord now!

"HERE I STAND"

"Now when they bring you to the synagogues and magistrates and authorities,
do not worry about how or what you should answer, or what you should say.
For the Holy Spirit will teach you in that very hour what you ought to say."
—Luke 12:11, 12

One of the most dramatic moments of the Protestant Reformation occurred in 1521 in the city of Worms, Germany. Martin Luther's expositions of Scripture were undermining the authority and teachings of the Roman Catholic Church. On January 3, Pope Leo X had excommunicated Luther, and three months later, the reformer was called for a hearing before the Holy Roman Emperor Charles V at the Diet of Worms. Luther arrived in town on April 16, and on the next day, he appeared before the diet. He was shown a pile of books and then asked (1) whether he recognized them as of his authorship and (2) whether he was willing to reject their content. Agreeing that the books were from his pen, he asked for more time to reflect on the second question.

In the late afternoon of **April 18, 1521,** Luther was reintroduced to the diet and again confronted with the second question. After explaining that his books addressed different subjects, he was faced with the inquisitorial remarks, "Martin, how can you assume that you are the only one to understand the sense of Scripture? Would you put your judgment above that of so many famous men and claim that you know more than they all?"

Pressed for a straightforward answer, Luther replied, "Since then Your Majesty and your lordships desire a simple reply, I will answer without horns and without teeth. Unless I am convinced by Scripture and plain reason—I do not accept the authority of popes and councils, for they have contradicted each other—my conscience is captive to the Word of God. I cannot and I will not recant anything, for to go against conscience is neither right nor safe. God help me. Amen."[30]

Our postmodern and even post-postmodern world has spawned a rootless, uncommitted society. Not many people today are willing to defend the authority of Scripture, regardless of the consequences of taking such a stand. But in these last days, the world and the church need more people with such conviction. Are you willing to be one of them?

ℋUMAN ℐNTELLIGENCES

And God gave Solomon wisdom and exceedingly great understanding,
and largeness of heart like the sand on the seashore.

—1 Kings 4:29

With all the scientific research that has been done and with all the knowledge available today, neuroscientists still confess that it is virtually impossible to re-create human intelligence and grasp how the brain works. Even so, several psychological tests have been developed to assess human intelligence.

In the early twentieth century, Alfred Binet and Théodore Simon proposed a "grade scale of intelligence" for testing the intelligence of children. On **April 19, 1912**, at the V Congress for Experimental Psychology in Berlin, Germany, William L. Stern presented a paper, "The Psychological Methods of Intelligence Testing." In his paper, he used the expression "IQ = Intelligence Quotient" and suggested a formula to calculate it. But even more modern tests have their limitations. Some critics say that IQ stands for "Incomplete and Questionable"!

Moving beyond the notion of intelligence as mere rational thought, Howard E. Gardner identified seven different multiple intelligences in 1983.[31] But in 1999, Gardner increased that number to the following eight: linguistic, logic-mathematical, musical, spatial, bodily/kinesthetic, interpersonal, intrapersonal, and naturalistic. Yet, in 2003, Gardner himself confessed, "And as I try to understand happenings in areas ranging from genetics to cyberspace, I wish I had a lot more intelligence!"

Today, much is also made of artificial intelligence in machines. But this so-called intelligence comes from the human minds that conceive and develop the machines. If we could map the neurologic synapses of our own brain at any given moment, by the time we grasped them, our brains would have already developed new configurations. And this is an endless process.

Many modern psychologists believe that complex human intelligence is merely derived from natural evolutionary processes. But as Christians, we know that all of them come from God, the Source of "every good and perfect gift" (James 1:17, NIV), and should be used for His honor and glory (Jeremiah 9:23, 24). Are you using your intelligence and talent for God's honor and glory?

HEAVEN IS OUR HOME

"Then the king said to the servants, 'Bind him hand and foot, take him away, and cast him into outer darkness; there will be weeping and gnashing of teeth.' "
—Matthew 22:13

In September 2014, I visited some historical sites in Upper Austria. In the city of Braunau, my attention was drawn to an old house on a corner with a stone in front of it. Engraved on the stone was a German inscription that read, "For Peace, Freedom, and Democracy. Never Again Fascism, Millions of Dead Warn." Surprisingly enough, it was in this very house—some 125 years earlier, **April 20, 1889**—that a baby boy was born who was given the name Adolf Hitler. When his mother, Klara Hitler, took him in her arms for the first time, she never imagined the impact that her little boy would have on the world or how he would be remembered in history.

While at Hitler's birthplace, I thought of all the atrocities of World War II that I had first been deeply touched by during a 2004 visit to the Auschwitz-Birkenau death camps. I then imagined the final scene at the end of the thousand years described in Revelation 20, when the wicked of all the ages (including, most certainly, Adolf Hitler) will be raised to life. They will march up "over the breadth of the earth" and surround "the camp of the saints and the beloved city" (verse 9, NRSV). That will be the first and only time in history that all of the wicked human beings and every demonic power will be gathered together in one unholy union.

As startling as it may seem, we cannot escape the reality that being lost means that we not only miss out on the happiness of heaven but also that we become part of that wicked, demonic army, far more wretched than the infamous Nazi hordes of World War II. No wonder Jesus warned that at that time, "there will be weeping and gnashing of teeth" (Matthew 22:13). By no means can we continue playing games with our salvation! Nothing in this world, whether possessions or endeavors, can compare with the blessing of heaven.

Ellen White implores, "I saw that all heaven is interested in our salvation; and shall we be indifferent? Shall we be careless, as though it were a small matter whether we are saved or lost? Shall we slight the sacrifice that has been made for us?"[32] You and I must make it to heaven! That is our home.

$\mathcal{L}$OSING $\mathcal{O}$UR $\mathcal{I}$DENTITY

"But I have this against you, that you have left your first love."
—Revelation 2:4, NASB

S ociological studies of religion have demonstrated that religious movements usually emerge from a desire to reform the culture in which they exist. But by the second and third centuries of existence—after the pioneers and their associates are gone—these movements tend to lose their identity and be reabsorbed into the very culture they originally intended to reform. This process is easily seen in post-apostolic Christianity and post-Reformation Protestantism.

In the mid-nineteenth century, American Methodism was one of the most vibrant and dynamic Christian denominations. But with the passing of time, it began to lose its original fervor. On **April 21, 1972**, the General Conference of the United Methodist Church officially accepted doctrinal pluralism. The great Protestant principle of *sola Scriptura* (the exclusiveness of Scripture) was replaced by four equal sources of doctrinal authority. The Methodist Church asserted, "The Christian faith was revealed in Scripture, illuminated by tradition, vivified in personal experience, and confirmed by reason." By this action, the denomination opened itself to a variety of conflicting teachings and cultural values. Jerry L. Walls's insightful book *The Problem of Pluralism: Recovering United Methodist Identity*[33] points out how pluralism seriously undermined the Methodist identity.

The Seventh-day Adventist Church is today in its second century of existence and is being strongly influenced by contemporary culture. More than ever, we must take Paul's advice in Romans 12:2 seriously. *The Message* translation reads, "Don't become so well-adjusted to your culture that you fit into it without even thinking. Instead, fix your attention on God. You'll be changed from the inside out. Readily recognize what he wants from you, and quickly respond to it. Unlike the culture around you, always dragging you down to its level of immaturity, God brings the best out of you, develops well-formed maturity in you."

As Seventh-day Adventists, we live in a real world, and we live as people live today. But we must be careful that our culture does not undermine the universal principles and values of God's Word.

Caring for the Earth

Then God saw everything that He had made, and indeed it was very good.

—Genesis 1:31

The earth is our present home, and we should care for it. But many of its natural resources are being irresponsibly destroyed through "oil spills, polluting factories and power plants, raw sewage, toxic dumps, pesticides, freeways, the loss of wilderness, and the extinction of wildlife."[34]

In early 1969, a major oil spill off the coast of Santa Barbara, California, killed more than ten thousand seabirds, dolphins, seals, and sea lions. As a reaction to this disaster, activists pushed for environmental regulations, environmental education, and even an Earth Day. On **April 22, 1970,** the first Earth Day was celebrated in the United States, with some twenty million people uniting to promote environmental reform. The movement grew significantly. In 1990, some two hundred million people in 141 countries enhanced recycling efforts, helping "pave the way for the 1992 United Nations Earth Summit in Rio de Janeiro."[35]

In the document "Stewardship of the Environment," the Seventh-day Adventist Church officially condemned the irresponsible destruction of the earth's resources and suggested substantial lifestyle changes. The document declared, "Seventh-day Adventism advocates a simple, wholesome lifestyle, where people do not step on the treadmill of unbridled over-consumption, accumulation of goods, and production of waste. A reformation of lifestyle is called for, based on respect for nature, restraint in the use of the world's resources, reevaluation of one's needs, and reaffirmation of the dignity of created life."[36]

Adventists believe that the world is a result of God's creation, not an accident (Genesis 1; 2). In its original form, the world "was very good" (Genesis 1:31), and God commanded Adam "to tend and keep it" (Genesis 2:15). People of every generation—including our own—are stewards of God's creation and should preserve it in the best way possible. We should remember that nature reveals the character of its Creator, and in destroying it, we obscure that revelation. The fact that God will finally create "a new heaven and a new earth" (Revelation 21:1) should never be used as an excuse for careless stewardship. Let us help make our world a better place to live and a small foretaste of the glorious world to come!

ℭHE ℳAN IN THE ℬRENA

For a righteous man may fall seven times and rise again.

—Proverbs 24:16

People who make history usually combine both talent and perseverance. The famous American inventor Thomas Edison, when questioned about his mistakes, supposedly replied, "I have not failed. I've just found 10,000 ways that won't work."[37]

The value of perseverance was emphasized by Theodore Roosevelt in his speech "The Citizenship in a Republic," delivered at Sorbonne, Paris, on **April 23, 1910**. The most widely quoted portion of the speech is known as "The Man in the Arena" and reads as follows:

It is not the critic who counts; not the man who points out how the strong man stumbles, or where the doer of deeds could have done them better. The credit belongs to the man who is actually in the arena, whose face is marred by dust and sweat and blood; who strives valiantly; who errs, who comes short again and again, because there is no effort without error and shortcoming; but who does actually strive to do the deeds; who knows great enthusiasms, the great devotions; who spends himself in a worthy cause; who at the best knows in the end the triumph of high achievement, and who at the worst, if he fails, at least fails while daring greatly, so that his place shall never be with those cold and timid souls who neither know victory nor defeat.[38]

You and I live in the arena of the great controversy between good and evil, in an unceasing struggle "against spiritual hosts of wickedness" (Ephesians 6:12). Regardless of how talented and persistent we are, our best efforts in this battle will certainly fail if not strengthened and guided by God's almighty power. Ellen White writes that "the secret of success is the union of divine power with human effort. Those who achieve the greatest results are those who rely most implicitly upon the Almighty Arm."[39]

God is giving us a new day. Please, do not face it in your own human strength. You need His strength and guidance in all you do and say. With God as your partner, you can be more than victorious today. May the Lord be close to you at every moment! Amen.

EXPLORING THE UNIVERSE

Lift up your eyes on high,
And see who has created these things,
Who brings out their host by number;
He calls them all by name,
By the greatness of His might
And the strength of His power;
Not one is missing.

—Isaiah 40:26

After a long building and testing process, on **April 24, 1990**, the Hubble Space Telescope was launched into low-earth orbit as a joint project of NASA and the European Space Agency. Gravitating outside the earth's atmosphere, this space-based observatory has provided amazing images of the deeper universe. Some pictures are from galaxies 13.2 billion light-years away.

The scientific study of outer space (astronomy) has been enhanced by the development of the telescope and by the discovery of the physical laws that control the celestial bodies in their respective orbits. These ongoing achievements allow us to see today what no other generation before has seen. While time lasts, space science will continue to provide ever-clearer images of the universe. But throughout eternity, God's redeemed children will explore the universe by themselves, without any need for a telescope.

All the treasures of the universe will be open to the study of God's redeemed. Unfettered by mortality, they wing their tireless flight to worlds afar—worlds that thrilled with sorrow at the spectacle of human woe and rang with songs of gladness at the tidings of a ransomed soul. With unutterable delight the children of earth enter into the joy and the wisdom of unfallen beings. They share the treasures of knowledge and understanding gained through ages upon ages in contemplation of God's handiwork. With undimmed vision they gaze upon the glory of creation— suns and stars and systems, all in their appointed order circling the throne of Deity. Upon all things, from the least to the greatest, the Creator's name is written, and in all are the riches of His power displayed.[40]

Our limited brains cannot fully grasp the meaning of the two words *universe* and *eternity*. How amazing it is that God Himself came to this sinful planet to save you and me by His grace and has given us all eternity to explore His celestial handiwork! Is it not amazing?

*F*UNDAMENTAL *B*ELIEFS

But sanctify the Lord God in your hearts, and always be ready to give a defense to
everyone who asks you a reason for the hope that is in you, with meekness and fear.
—1 Peter 3:15

E arly Seventh-day Adventists never intended to craft a formal statement of fundamental beliefs. But through the years, more and more people were asking about the church's beliefs, and false assertions were distorting the integrity of the Adventist message. So, in 1872, Uriah Smith wrote *A Declaration of the Fundamental Principles Taught and Practiced by the Seventh-day Adventists*, with twenty-five statements. In 1889, those principles were slightly revised and expanded into twenty-eight propositions. A new statement of twenty-two "fundamental beliefs" appeared in the 1931 *Year Book of the Seventh-day Adventist Denomination*. And on **April 25, 1980**, the General Conference Session in Dallas, Texas, voted the first official statement of twenty-seven fundamental beliefs.

The nature of the new document was explained in its introductory paragraph: "Seventh-day Adventists accept the Bible as their only creed and hold certain fundamental beliefs to be the teaching of the Holy Scriptures. These beliefs, as set forth here, constitute the church's understanding and expression of the teaching of Scripture. Revision of these statements may be expected at a General Conference Session when the church is led by the Holy Spirit to a fuller understanding of Bible truth or finds better language in which to express the teachings of God's Holy Word."[41]

Crucial in this statement is the distinction between the Bible as the only unchangeable creed and the fundamental beliefs that can be revised. As examples of this type of revision, in response to animistic concerns and evil powers, the 2005 General Conference Session in Saint Louis, Missouri, added a new statement (number 11) on "Growing in Christ." Ten years later, the 2015 General Conference Session in San Antonio, Texas, revised the wording of several of the fundamental beliefs to make them clearer and more comprehensible.

While never intended to replace the Bible as our only creed, the 28 Fundamental Beliefs published in the *Seventh-day Adventist Church Manual* can help us concisely explain the basic Bible teachings of the church and the reason for our hope (1 Peter 3:15). You should know them well and be ready to share them with others.

IMMORTALITY OR RESURRECTION

*"The hour is coming in which all who are in the graves will hear His voice
and come forth—those who have done good, to the resurrection of life,
and those who have done evil, to the resurrection of condemnation."*
—John 5:28, 29

Many people wonder: If the human soul is naturally immortal, why does the New Testament teach a final resurrection of the dead? One of the most forceful answers to this question was provided by the leading European Protestant theologian and New Testament scholar Oscar Cullmann (1902–1999) at the Ingersoll Lecture on the Immortality of Man, held in Andover Chapel at Harvard University, on **April 26, 1955**. His lecture, titled "Immortality of the Soul and Resurrection of the Dead: The Witness of the New Testament," was first published in the *Harvard Divinity School Bulletin*[42] and later as a booklet.

Cullmann saw an irreconcilable tension between the Greek idea of the immortality of the soul and the Christian belief in the resurrection. For him, the Greek philosophical notion of the natural immortality of the soul could not be harmonized with the New Testament doctrine of the final resurrection of the dead. Interestingly, around AD 150, Justin Martyr (100–165) already warned that those "who say there is no resurrection of the dead, and that their souls, when they die, are taken to heaven" could not be considered Christians.[43]

In 1 Corinthians 15:16–18, Paul argues that "if the dead do not rise, then Christ is not risen" and, consequently, "those who have fallen asleep in Christ have perished." If at death the souls of the righteous are taken to heaven (as many believe), then there is no convincing reason even for Christ's own resurrection. In this case, Paul could not have spoken of those who died in Christ as having perished because they would already be in heaven with Christ.

But the good news of the New Testament is that death, as cruel and sad as it might be, was fully conquered by Christ through His own resurrection. "For if we believe that Jesus died and rose again, even so God will bring with Him those who sleep in Jesus" (1 Thessalonians 4:14). What a blessing to know that all our loved ones who died in Christ will finally be raised from the dead to receive eternal life!

$\mathcal{M}$ISSIONARY $\mathcal{W}$IVES

A wife of noble character who can find?
She is worth far more than rubies.
Her husband has full confidence in her
and lacks nothing of value.
She brings him good, not harm,
all the days of her life.

—Proverbs 31:10–12, NIV

We are deeply touched by the example of commitment and sacrifice of brave missionaries such as William Carey, who went to India in 1793; Robert Moffat, who was sent to South Africa in 1816; and David Livingstone, who sailed to Africa in 1841. But what about their wives and children? Many missionary wives paid a very high price—perhaps even higher than their missionary husbands—to serve the Lord in faraway mission fields. Living in pagan cultures and coping with long periods of loneliness, some wives suffered from serious emotional breakdowns.

Mary Moffat (1821–1862), daughter of the renowned Scottish missionary Robert Moffat, was born in Griquatown, South Africa, while her parents were serving there as missionaries. On January 2, 1845, Mary married another missionary named David Livingstone. Later, she was torn between joining her husband on his mission trips through the African continent and taking care of their children's education for several years in Britain. While with her husband in the camp of Shupanga, Zambezi, Mary fell ill and died on **April 27, 1862**. The inscription on her gravestone there reads: "Here repose the mortal remains of Mary Moffat, the beloved wife of Doctor Livingstone, in humble hope of a joyful resurrection by our saviour Jesus Christ." Mary sacrificed her life for the African mission field as much as her husband.

Ellen White says, "The mother's work often seems to her an unimportant service. It is a work that is rarely appreciated. Others know little of her many cares and burdens. Her days are occupied with a round of little duties, all calling for patient effort, for self-control, for tact, wisdom, and self-sacrificing love; yet she cannot boast of what she has done as any great achievement. . . . She feels that she has accomplished nothing. . . . Her name may not have been heard in the world, but it is written in the Lamb's book of life."[44]

We should all value and support the women who have worked and who are still working behind the scenes to support their missionary husbands!

Space Tourism

When I consider Your heavens, the work of Your fingers,
The moon and the stars, which You have ordained,
What is man that You are mindful of him,
And the son of man that You visit him?

—Psalm 8:3, 4

German philosopher Immanuel Kant (1724–1804) once said, "Two things fill the mind with ever new and increasing admiration and reverence, the more often and more steadily one reflects on them: the starry heavens above me and the moral law within me."[45] Human admiration and curiosity have led astronomers and space scientists to look as far as possible into the wonders of God's universe. But so far, professional astronauts have reached the moon and no further.

In 1961, Soviet cosmonaut Yuri Gagarin became the first man to fly into outer space. Inspired by that event, Dennis Tito (b. 1940) dreamed of going to space. Finally, on **April 28, 2001**, he joined the Soyuz TM-32 mission and spent seven days, twenty-two hours, and four minutes in space and orbited the earth 128 times. So, Dennis Tito, a billionaire, became the first space tourist, funding his own trip into space. But how much did this adventure cost him? Just for his ticket, he paid no less than $20 million. And remember, he never left the earth's orbit!

At the Second Coming, God's faithful children from all ages and from all places around the world will be taken through the starry skies to heaven (John 14:1–3). We are told that this space voyage from earth to heaven will take "seven days."[46] Some people speculate that a week is needed so that those who never kept a Sabbath could do so before entering the heavenly realms. In their imagination, that Sabbath would be kept on another planet. But nowhere in the Bible or in the writings of Ellen White is this ever suggested. All she says is simply that the ascension to heaven will take seven days. And how much do we have to pay for the trip through space? Nothing at all—God has already paid for it!

When flying into space, astronauts are confined to their small spaceships, along with just a few colleagues. In contrast, the saints will be taken to heaven by God's transportation. They will enjoy the company of all the redeemed from the earth, along with the holy angels and Jesus Christ Himself. No human endeavor or accomplishment can compare to this supreme reward. By God's grace, you and I will be there!

THE WEDDING GARMENT

"Let us rejoice and be glad and give the glory to Him, for the marriage of the Lamb has come and His bride has made herself ready." It was given to her to clothe herself in fine linen, bright and clean; for the fine linen is the righteous acts of the saints.
—Revelation 19:7, 8, NASB

Wedding ceremonies are designed to be as perfect as possible—the decorations, the participants, the ceremony, and, above all, the bride and her dress. One of the most glamorous was the wedding of Prince William, Duke of Cambridge, and Catherine (Kate) Middleton, on **April 29, 2011**, at Westminster Abbey, in London. Kate's wedding dress was designed by Sarah Burton, creative director of the luxury fashion house Alexander McQueen. The main body of the dress was made of ivory and white satin, with fifty-eight buttons of gazar and organza in the back. The bodice was decorated with floral motifs cut from machine-made lace. In designer Mark Badgley's words, "It's the kind of gown that will stand the test of time. Not all gowns do. Any bride across the world will want to wear it."[47] It's no surprise that soon after the royal wedding, replicas of the dress were produced for sale.

The Bible uses various wedding images to describe the relationship between Christ and His faithful church. In the parable of the wedding feast (Matthew 22:1–14), the church is portrayed not as the bride of the King's son but as the guests at the wedding feast. For that special occasion, all guests were required to wear a wedding garment. A guest without the garment was cast out into outer darkness. In the apocalyptic scene of the marriage of the Lamb (see Revelation 19:7–10), "fine linen is the righteous acts of the saints."

If "all our righteous deeds are like a filthy garment" (Isaiah 64:6, NASB), how can the wedding garment be defined as "the righteous acts of the saints" (Revelation 19:8)? According to Ellen White, that garment is "a gift from the king." "It is the righteousness of Christ, His own unblemished character, that through faith is imparted to all who receive Him as their personal Saviour."[48] As in the parable of the prodigal son (Luke 15:11–32), Christ wants to clothe us with the spotless garment of His own righteousness and prepare us for His wedding feast.

CULTURAL APPEALS

And do not be conformed to this world, but be transformed by the renewing of your mind,
that you may prove what is that good and acceptable and perfect will of God.
—Romans 12:2

One of the greatest challenges for God's people over the centuries has been remaining loyal to Christ when their faith is in conflict with contemporary social values. Culture has always tempted God's people, but the counterculture of the 1960s and 1970s became a time of extreme rebellion against traditional values.

Disillusioned with the contemporary culture, and especially weary of the Vietnam War (1955–1975), many American young people latched on to the motto "Make Love, Not War." Escaping their families, some decided to live in hippie communes and attempted to find the ideal environment in which to express their sinful desires through free love, drugs, and psychedelic rock music. The ultimate expression of the countercultural movement was the Woodstock Music Festival held in Bethel, New York, from August 15 to 18, 1969.

The long and disastrous Vietnam War finally ended with the fall of Saigon on **April 30, 1975**, leaving more than fifty-eight thousand Americans dead. The hippie movement eventually disappeared, but many of the countercultural winds of the 1960s and 1970s continue to blow today. Our contemporary society is overstimulated by sounds and images and is characterized by a sex-obsessed culture. Furthermore, the postmodern mind questions the absolute values of the Bible.

Surrounded by so many cultural temptations, we must take the words of Psalm 119:9 seriously: "How can a young person stay on the path of purity? By living according to your word" (NIV). *The Message* paraphrase of Romans 12:2 adds, "Don't become so well-adjusted to your culture that you fit into it without even thinking. Instead, fix your attention on God. You'll be changed from the inside out. Readily recognize what he wants from you, and quickly respond to it. Unlike the culture around you, always dragging you down to its level of immaturity, God brings the best out of you, develops well-formed maturity in you."

In His priestly prayer, Jesus asked the Father, "I do not pray that You should take them out of the world, but that You should keep them from the evil one" (John 17:15). May His prayer be our own today and every day!

A Heart for Africa

*For the love of Christ compels us, because we judge thus: that if One
died for all, then all died; and He died for all, that those who live should
live no longer for themselves, but for Him who died for them and rose again.*
—2 Corinthians 5:14, 15

The history of Christianity has been brightened by brave missionaries like David Livingstone (1813–1873), who carried the gospel torch into the most remote places of the African continent. He arrived in Cape Town in 1841, and shortly afterward, he began moving northward to spread the gospel through "native agents." Some three years later, he was attacked and injured by a lion.[1] But he did not give up!

"On January 2, 1845, Livingstone married [Robert] Moffat's [oldest] daughter, Mary, and she accompanied him on many of his journeys"[2] until her death in 1862. But "so impassioned was his commitment to Africa that his duties as husband and father were relegated to second place."[3]

Having served his beloved Africa for more than thirty years, Livingstone died from malaria and dysentery on **May 1, 1873**, in the southeast of Lake Bangweulu (modern Zambia). His loyal attendants Chuma and Susi removed his heart and buried it under a tree near the spot where he died and then carried his body all the way to Bagamoyo (modern Tanzania), from where it was transported to London and eventually buried in Westminster Abbey. But his heart remained where it had always been—in Africa!

Livingstone was not as successful in generating direct conversions as in exploring the mission field and sowing gospel seeds for later missionaries to harvest. He declared, "Our work and its fruits are cumulative. We work towards another state of things. Future missionaries will be rewarded by conversions for every sermon. We are then pioneers and helpers. Let them not forget the watchmen of the night—us, who worked when all was gloom, and no evidence of success in the way of conversion cheered our paths. They will doubtless have more light than we, but we served our Master earnestly, and proclaimed the same gospel as they will do."[4]

Did Livingstone regret all the years he served in Africa? Not at all. He bravely stated, "People talk of the sacrifice I have made in spending so much of my life in Africa. Can that be called a sacrifice which is simply paid back as a small part of a great debt owing to our God, which we can never repay?"[5] If Christ sacrificed Himself for us, why can we not sacrifice ourselves in the places most in need of the good news?

Countercultural Challenges

You must understand this, that in the last days distressing times will come.
—2 Timothy 3:1, NRSV

Our civilization is characterized by an antithetical mixture of technological progress and moral decline. Should this surprise us? Not at all, because Jesus mentioned that the same depravity that preceded the Flood would reappear just prior to His second coming (Matthew 24:37–39). End-time human behavior—actually, misbehavior—is also well described in 2 Timothy 3:1–7 and 2 Peter 2:1–22. This decline became more evident in the 1960s and 1970s, particularly during the turmoil of 1968.

There were ongoing conflicts in Paris between students and authorities at the Paris University at Nanterre. On Thursday, **May 2, 1968**, the administration shut down the university, which led to massive protests in the city. Similar sociopolitical riots also occurred in Prague, Berlin, Chicago, and other places around the world. That same year also saw the assassinations of Martin Luther King Jr. and Robert Kennedy, aggressive antiwar movements; the Black Power protests; and an upsurge of the women's liberation movement.

Historians refer to 1968 as the year that shook and changed the world and the year that never ended. Indeed, the world would no longer be the same!

The countercultural winds of that critical period are still blowing today, but with increasing intensity. Fundamental religious and moral values are being cast to the ground. Every form of authority is now being challenged. Since we are followers of Christ, the greater the challenges, the more intense our convictions should be. This is precisely the time when all true Christians should rise up and be "the salt of the earth" and "the light of the world" (Matthew 5:13–16).

See, darkness covers the earth
    and thick darkness is over the peoples,
but the LORD rises upon you
    and his glory appears over you (Isaiah 60:2, NIV).

Let us demonstrate to the world the transforming power of God's amazing grace!

ℛELIGIOUS SCULPTURES

"And you shall make two cherubim of gold; of hammered
work you shall make them at the two ends of the mercy seat."
—Exodus 25:18

The second commandment of the Decalogue reads, "You shall not make for yourself a carved image—any likeness of anything that is in heaven above, or that is in the earth beneath, or that is in the water under the earth" (Exodus 20:4). But how should we understand this statement?

One of the most famous Adventist sculptors was the British-born Alan Collins (1928–2016). Several of his works are displayed in the Guildford Cathedral in England and some at Adventist university campuses in the United States. For instance, on Sunday afternoon, **May 3, 1981**, Collins's bronze sculpture *Good Samaritan* was unveiled on the campus of Loma Linda University. On April 25, 1998, another impressive bronze sculpture, *Legacy of Leadership*—depicting J. N. Andrews and his two children leaving for Europe in 1874—was unveiled in front of Pioneer Memorial Church at Andrews University.

Victor Issa's twelve-piece bronze sculpture *The King Is Coming* was unveiled at the 2000 General Conference Session in Toronto, Canada. It depicts ten individuals representing all the continents of the world, with radiant faces beholding Christ's second coming. After the session, the sculpture was permanently placed in the lobby of the General Conference headquarters in Silver Spring, Maryland.

Some people wonder whether these sculptures are a transgression of the second commandment. But we should remember that this prohibition was written on a table of stone placed within the ark of the covenant, which had two golden sculptures of cherubim on top. So, the commandment does not forbid all visual aids, many of which even adorned the earthly sanctuary. The command is meant in the sense of "You shall not make for yourself an idol" (Exodus 20:4, NASB).

God instructed Moses to make "a bronze snake" (Numbers 21:9, NIV). But later, when the Israelites were venerating it, King Hezekiah destroyed it (2 Kings 18:4). The problem is not so much *what* we see but *how* we see it. Even nice people and useful things can end up being venerated. Regardless of their nature, all idols must be removed from our lives, but some visual aids can be helpful and inspiring as we wait to set our eyes on Jesus.

"MY PATMOS"

*I, John, both your brother and companion in the tribulation and
kingdom and patience of Jesus Christ, was on the island that is called
Patmos for the word of God and for the testimony of Jesus Christ.*

—Revelation 1:9

Have you ever faced a frustrating experience that ended up becoming a real blessing in your life? Have you seen the sun shining through very dark clouds? Remember that some of our fondest dreams must be frustrated so that God can grant us something far better and more rewarding. This is what happened to Martin Luther after the famous 1521 Diet of Worms.

On April 18, Luther had stated at the diet that his conscience was "captive to the Word of God"[6] and that he would not recant. Eight days later, he and his group began their homeward journey. Frederick the Wise, the Elector of Saxony, knew the threat Luther was facing and set up a secret plan to remove him from the reach of his enemies. On the evening of May 3, while Luther was entering some woods, four or five armed horsemen attacked the wagon and captured Luther. They first dressed him as a knight and then took him to the Wartburg Castle, near Eisenach, where he arrived on **May 4, 1521**. There he was kept sequestered in a locked cell, as if he were a dangerous criminal, till his hair and beard had grown enough to hide his identity. He called himself by the nickname of Knight George (Junker Jörg).

Luther remained in the Wartburg Castle for ten months. He referred to it as "my Patmos,"[7] an allusion to the island where John wrote the book of Revelation. Isolated from the outside world and away from his busy life in Wittenberg, Luther had enough time to produce something he could not have done otherwise. In just eleven weeks, he translated the whole New Testament from Greek into German. While there, he also wrote several books without access to his library. Therefore, these writings had a strong biblical basis.

Truly, God can transform frustrating experiences into very real blessings. On the remote island of Patmos, the apostle John wrote the book of Revelation. Secluded in the Wartburg Castle, Luther translated the New Testament into German. While living in distant Australia, Ellen White produced her classic book *The Desire of Ages*. Never doubt God's power and providential leading—He can bless you and use you wherever He places you!

HACKSAW RIDGE

"How God anointed Jesus of Nazareth with the Holy Spirit and with power, who went about doing good and healing all who were oppressed by the devil, for God was with Him."
—Acts 10:38

Sabbath, **May 5, 1945**, was a challenging day in Okinawa. Japanese troops were fiercely defending their last remaining barrier—Okinawa and the Maeda Escarpment, a huge cliff that the soldiers called Hacksaw Ridge. When American soldiers reached the top of the cliff, the enemy met them with a vicious counterattack. American officers ordered an immediate retreat. All of the soldiers obeyed except one—Desmond Doss—who, risking his own life, went back into the firefight to rescue as many wounded soldiers as he could. He saved at least seventy-five lives that day.

Several days later, Doss himself was severely wounded by a Japanese grenade that landed at his feet and by a sniper's bullet that shattered his arm. In pain and losing blood, he sent other wounded soldiers out of the fray ahead of himself. He was willing to die so others could live. Doss paid a lifelong price for his heroic actions. For five and a half years, he underwent treatment for tuberculosis he contracted during the war. Eventually, a lung and five ribs had to be removed. Nevertheless, he was at peace in his conscience.

As an unarmed Seventh-day Adventist combat medic, Doss did not fire or even carry a gun. Rather than killing, he chose to heal, even during Sabbath hours (Matthew 12:12). On October 12, 1945, Doss received the Medal of Honor from United States president Harry S. Truman. In fact, Doss was the first conscientious objector to receive that honor, which was followed by several other accolades. His story is told in the books *The Unlikeliest Hero* (republished in 2016 as *Redemption at Hacksaw Ridge*), by Booton Herndon, and *Desmond Doss: Conscientious Objector*, by Frances M. Doss.[8] This amazing story was brought to the big screen in the famous film *Hacksaw Ridge*.

True war heroes are not always those who kill many enemy soldiers. They may also be people who rescue lives, as Desmond Doss did. He was a war hero because he followed and practiced the example of Christ, who "went about doing good and healing all who were oppressed by the devil, for God was with Him" (Acts 10:38). The world needs more heroes like that!

Without Religion

*"For God knows that in the day you eat of it your eyes will
be opened, and you will be like God, knowing good and evil."*

—Genesis 3:5

Psychologists have wrestled with the question, Did God create man, or did man create God? Sigmund Freud (1856–1939), the founder of psychoanalysis, was born to Jewish parents in Freiburg, Moravia, in the Austrian Empire, on **May 6, 1856**. As one of the most influential and controversial thinkers of the twentieth century, Freud challenged the concept of God and the nature of religion. He envisioned a mature society filled with people living moral lives free from religion.

Based on the child's need for "a father's protection," Freud viewed the notion of God as a human projection of this need; that is, as "the figure of an enormously exalted." According to Freud, religion is "an illusion" and can be compared to "a childhood neurosis."[9] While other atheists strongly denied the existence of God and the meaning of religion, Freud suggested an attractive and convincing psychological process for people to migrate from that infant *religious* camp into the mature *unreligious* society.

No wonder Tony Campolo called Sigmund Freud "the apostle of disbelief" and declared, "There is no doubt that religion had already waned under the onslaught of the Enlightenment, but it was Freud who provided the radically new understanding of human nature that made any religious explanation of the whats and whys of our personhood seem naïve."[10]

From a biblical perspective, the whole notion of maturing away from God and His Word echoes the speech of the serpent in the Garden of Eden. Subtly, the serpent first characterized God's word as too restrictive and unreasonable and then offered a more liberated and reasonable approach. In Genesis 3:5, the serpent argued, "For God knows that in the day you eat of it your eyes will be opened, and you will be like God, knowing good and evil."

Freud died in 1939, but many of his faithful disciples continue to label God and religion as he did. Perhaps you are even under psychosocial pressure to give up your supposed "infant religion." Never be ashamed of your loyalty to God and His Word (Luke 9:23–26)!

♂OYFUL ♂ADORATION

Oh come, let us sing to the LORD! Let us shout joyfully to the Rock of our salvation.
—Psalm 95:1

magine yourself in Vienna, Austria, on **May 7, 1824**. Without explaining why, a friend takes you to the Theater am Kärntnertor. As soon as you enter the concert hall, you sense great excitement and eager anticipation at the huge event. The orchestra is larger than usual. At the appointed time, the conductor comes to the stage—none other than the great Ludwig van Beethoven, about to premiere his Symphony no. 9. Some criticized him for adding a choir and soloists to a symphony, which he did in the final movement.

By that time, Beethoven was completely deaf! He couldn't even hear his own musical composition performed. A hidden conductor (Michael Umlauf) sat out of sight, secretly keeping time for the musicians. When the performance ended, Beethoven was several bars behind and still conducting. Seeing this, the contralto soloist approached him and turned him around to accept the audience's enthusiastic cheers and applause. Even without hearing the applause, he could at least see the gestures of ovation. He left the stage with tears in his eyes, deeply touched.

The Ninth Symphony's lyrics were originally from "Ode to Joy" (1785) by the famous German poet Friedrich Schiller. The poem speaks of all people being united in universal brotherhood and ends with the majestic words,

Brothers, above the starry canopy
There must dwell a loving Father.
Do you fall in worship, you millions?
World, do you know your creator?
Seek Him in the heavens;
Above the stars must he dwell.

Later, the lyrics "Joyful, joyful, we adore Thee" by Henry van Dyke, were put to the melody. Today, it is considered one of the most beautiful hymns of all time.

Distracted by so many activities, we can easily lose the spirit of adoration derived from a true Creator-creature relationship. But Psalm 95:1 invites us, "Oh come, let us sing to the LORD! Let us shout joyfully to the Rock of our salvation." The hymn "Joyful, Joyful, We Adore Thee" calls all creatures and even creation itself to joyfully adore their Creator.[11] If you know the hymn, why not sing it now and keep it in mind today? Have a joyful time with your Creator-Redeemer!

THE PRINCE AND THE PAUPER

*And being found in appearance as a man, He humbled Himself
and became obedient to the point of death, even the death of the cross.*
—Philippians 2:8

Life is full of contrasts and paradoxes. Sometimes even our best plans backfire, as illustrated in the film *The Prince and the Pauper*, officially released on **May 8, 1937**, and followed by several remakes. Based on Mark Twain's 1881 novel of the same title, the movie portrays an imaginary scene. "In Tudor England, two boys are born on the same day in the most different circumstances. . . . Tom . . . is the [*pauper*] son of vicious criminal John Canty . . . , while Edward Tudor . . . is [a *prince* and the heir to the throne] of King Henry VIII of England. . . . They meet and are astounded by their striking resemblance to each other. As a prank, they exchange clothes, but the Captain of the Guard . . . mistakes the prince for the pauper and throws him out of the palace grounds. Tom is unable to convince anybody except for the Earl of Hertford . . . of his identity. Everyone else is convinced that [the "prince"] is mentally ill. When Henry VIII dies, Hertford threatens to expose Tom unless he does as he is told. [Fearing for his own future,] Hertford also blackmails the Captain"[12] into finding and assassinating Edward, the real prince.

But "Edward finds an amused, if disbelieving, protector in Miles Hendon. . . . With [his] help, Edward manages to re-enter the palace just in time to interrupt the coronation ceremony and prove his identity. Edward becomes King Edward VI while Tom is made a ward of the new king; Hertford is banished for life, and Hendon is rewarded for his services."[13]

This beloved story gives us a vague idea of the mystery of incarnation, as described by Paul in Philippians 2:5–11. This wonderful passage speaks of Christ, who left the heavenly courts, came to our sinful world, and even assumed our human nature. He lived as the humble people of that time lived. He was rejected by many whom He came to save. In contrast to the aforementioned prince, Christ continued His humiliation all the way to the cross, where He died with thieves. But then, He triumphantly rose from the dead, ascended back to heaven, and was enthroned as "King of kings and Lord of lords" (Revelation 19:16).

Praise the Lord for this amazing humiliation and exaltation, which we will study throughout eternity!

THE WOUNDS IN HIS HANDS

And one shall say unto him, What are these wounds in thine hands? Then he shall answer,
Those with which I was wounded in the house of my friends.
—Zechariah 13:6, KJV

The **May 9, 2013**, issue of the *Adventist Review* presented an impressive painting of Jesus on its cover. It was slightly blurred with some glasses overlaid, allowing the viewer to see part of the face of Jesus more clearly through the lenses. Who was the creator of the original illustration? None other than Harry Anderson, an extremely talented and famous Adventist illustrator who painted some of the most beautiful portraits of Jesus.

Harry Anderson (1906–1996) was born to Swedish parents in Chicago, Illinois, on August 11, 1906. In 1944, he joined the Seventh-day Adventist Church and soon after began painting for the Review and Herald® Publishing Association. He painted about three hundred religious-themed illustrations for the church. By 1945, Anderson had completed *What Happened to Your Hand?* which is probably his most famous work. In that painting, Jesus is portrayed with three modern children.

This modern setting in *What Happened to Your Hand?* generated quite a bit of opposition, even from the staff of the Review's art department. But much of that bias disappeared after one of the staff members reported an enlightening experience. One evening at home, his little daughter was looking at her copy of *The Children's Hour*. When she came to that painting, she ran to him and said, "Daddy, I want to sit on Jesus' lap too." He immediately realized that the modern illustration could help children better identify with Jesus.

Ellen White explains that at the final judgment, Jesus will show the wicked "His hands with the marks of His crucifixion. The marks of this cruelty He will ever bear. Every print of the nails will tell the story of man's wonderful redemption and the dear price by which it was purchased."[14] But even now, "in our behalf He presents before His Father the marks of the crucifixion which He will bear throughout eternity."[15]

The Lord said to Zion, "I have inscribed you on the palms of My hands" (Isaiah 49:16). Likewise, we have in Jesus' hands a symbol of His unconditional love for us and the assurance that He will never forsake us.

ℬLESSED 𝒜DVERSITIES

Out of weakness [they] were made strong.

—Hebrews 11:34

German forces had just invaded the territory of the Netherlands. On Friday after-noon, **May 10, 1940,** the governor-general of the Dutch East Indies announced over the radio that, in their colonies, all male Germans over the age of sixteen would be arrested. As a German Seventh-day Adventist missionary in that field, Siegfried H. Horn (1908–1993) knew that he could be imprisoned at any moment. Even so, he went to church that evening on his motorcycle and preached on the sufferings of Jesus. As soon as he arrived back home, the police came. He was arrested and did not see his beloved wife for more than six years!

During World War II, Horn was a prisoner of war, first of the Dutch in Indonesia and then of the English in India. Having access to books in prison, Horn developed his skills in biblical languages and taught his fellow inmate. Following the war, he immigrated to the United States, where he completed his education. He studied for a short while at Johns Hopkins University with Professor William A. Albright and, in 1951, earned a PhD in Egyptology from the University of Chicago.

For twenty-five years, Dr. Horn taught archaeology and the history of antiquity at the Seventh-day Adventist Theological Seminary on the campus of Andrews University. He wrote several articles and the commentaries for Genesis, Exodus, Ezra, and Nehemiah in the *Seventh-day Adventist Bible Commentary*. He was the primary author of the *Seventh-day Adventist Bible Dictionary*. He also started the seminary's doctoral programs, introduced the Andrews University Archaeological Museum, was the founding editor of the *Andrews University Seminary Studies* journal, and initiated and directed the archaeological diggings at Tell Hesban (the biblical Heshbon) in Jordan.

Crises do not necessarily imply a negative outcome. They can generate a new beginning or a new direction in life. While some people remain victims of disastrous circumstances, others find ways to use them to their own advantage. For Horn, the years he spent as a prisoner of war redirected his whole career. You should not view life's crises as obstructive walls; they can be steps upward, leading to a brighter future. Remember, you can "do all things through Christ who strengthens" you! (Philippians 4:13).

*I*GNORING THE *P*ROPHETIC *W*ORD

Yet He sent prophets to them, to bring them back to the LORD;
and they testified against them, but they would not listen.
—2 Chronicles 24:19

There is a human tendency toward not taking God's word as seriously as one should. It was the problem of the antediluvians (Hebrews 11:7), the contemporaries of Jesus (Matthew 23:29–36), and those running the Battle Creek Sanitarium at the turn of the twentieth century.

In early 1900, Ellen White stated that "the Lord took Dr. Kellogg in hand to do a special work," but under his leadership, the Battle Creek Sanitarium was losing its original identity.[16] On February 18, 1902, the sanitarium was destroyed by fire, and Mrs. White identified the tragedy as God's judgment. Two days later, she warned, "A solemn responsibility rests upon those who have had charge of the Battle Creek Sanitarium. Will they build up in Battle Creek a mammoth institution, or will they carry out the purpose of God by making plants in many places?"[17]

Disregarding Ellen White's warnings, Dr. Kellogg and his associates decided to rebuild an even larger sanitarium in Battle Creek. All of the circumstances seemed to favor their decision, including the overall popularity of the plan, financial benefits to both Adventist and non-Adventist communities, and massive sales of Kellogg's book, *The Living Temple*. So, on Sunday, **May 11, 1902**, an estimated ten thousand persons witnessed the cornerstone of the new Battle Creek Sanitarium being laid.

Soon, however, unfulfilled promises and financial crises showed that it was much easier to plan the sanitarium project than to finance it. The publication of *The Living Temple* was controversial from the very start, and Dr. Kellogg increasingly distanced himself from the thinking and the leadership of the church. Eventually, he took absolute control of the sanitarium, and on November 10, 1907, he was disfellowshiped from the Battle Creek Tabernacle.

Just as the antediluvians could have saved their lives by heeding Noah's prophetic warnings, many headaches related to the Battle Creek Sanitarium could have been avoided by following Ellen White's prophetic counsels. Remember, the prophetic word might not seem the most logical or practical to us; but in the long run, it is always the best and most trustworthy!

The Lady With the Lamp

"So he went to him and bandaged his wounds, pouring on oil and wine;
and he set him on his own animal, brought him to an inn, and took care of him."
—Luke 10:34

Life is worth living if it's centered on others and not on ourselves. Ellen White said, "We shall pass through this world but once; any good that we can do, we should do earnestly, untiringly, in the spirit that Christ brought into His work."[18]

Florence Nightingale (1820–1910) was born on **May 12, 1820**, in Florence, Italy. Her name was inspired by her birthplace. She studied nursing in Kaiserswerth, Germany, and began her work in London. During the Crimean War (1853–1856), she and her team of nurses vastly improved sanitary conditions at a British base hospital, reducing its death rate by two-thirds. They established a kitchen to attend to the dietary needs of the patients, a laundry to provide clean linens for them, and a classroom and library for intellectual stimulation and entertainment. Nightingale unceasingly cared for the soldiers. In the evenings, she carried a lamp while ministering to patient after patient. The soldiers were both moved and comforted by her endless compassion and called her the Lady With the Lamp and the Angel of the Crimea.

She combined earnest professionalism with dedicated love. Her strategies helped improve nursing practices, and her caring efforts inspired many generations of nurses. Today, some nursing graduation ceremonies still culminate with the lighting of a Nursing Candle and the recitation of the Nightingale Pledge in honor of Florence Nightingale, "the Lady With the Lamp."

Nightingale stated, "I attribute my success to this—*I never gave or took any excuse.*"[19] She advised, "So I never lose an opportunity of urging a practical beginning, however small, for it is wonderful how often in such matters the mustard-seed germinates and roots itself."[20] She also emphasized the importance of combining empathy and cooperation. "Let us, in the spirit of friendly rivalry, rejoice in their progress, as they do, I am sure, in ours. All can win the prize. One training school is not lowered because others win. On the contrary, all are lowered if others fail."[21]

The example of Florence Nightingale should inspire us to go out today and shine for Jesus. You can make a great difference in someone's life!

$\mathcal{M}$ARIAN $\mathcal{A}$PPARITIONS

"Then the angel said to her, 'Do not be afraid, Mary, for you have found favor with God.
And behold, you will conceive in your womb and bring forth a Son, and shall call His name
Jesus.'"

—Luke 1:30, 31

The Bible declares that God chose Mary to be the mother of the incarnate Son of God, who was generated by the Holy Spirit (Matthew 1:20, 21). But the Roman Catholic Church established the extrabiblical dogma of the Immaculate Virgin Mary who, "when the course of her earthly life was finished, was taken up body and soul into heavenly glory."[22] This notion favored the acceptance of many supernatural Marian apparitions through the centuries.

On Sunday, **May 13, 1917**, the Virgin Mary supposedly appeared for the first of six times near Fatima, Portugal, to three Portuguese shepherd children: Lucia dos Santos and her cousins Francisco and Jacinta Marto. In the first apparition, "Our Lady" asked them to pray the Rosary every day; in the second, she commissioned Lucia to spread through the world the devotion to the Immaculate Heart of Mary; and in the third, the children were taken in vision to the edge of the earth, where they saw the inferno with uncountable demons and souls in human form being burned in huge fires.

In the third apparition, the children were warned, "You have seen where the souls of poor sinners go. To save them, God wishes to establish in the world the devotion to my Immaculate Heart. If people do what I tell you, many souls will be saved and there will be peace."[23]

Such Marian apparitions are acceptable to those who believe in the Catholic dogmas of the natural immortality of the soul and Virgin Mary as a heavenly mediator on behalf of humanity. But those manifestations are unacceptable for those who trust the biblical teaching of the unconsciousness of the dead (including Mary) until their final resurrection.

In an age of increasing supernatural apparitions, our only safeguard is biblical truth (Isaiah 40:8; Revelation 22:18, 19)—not in the supposed sayings of Virgin Mary. After all, "Shouldn't people ask God for guidance? Should the living seek guidance from the dead? Look to God's instructions and teachings! People who contradict his word are completely in the dark" (Isaiah 8:19, 20, NLT). May the Lord protect us from all counterfeit experiences!

Mother's Day

Then Pharaoh's daughter said to her, "Take this child away and nurse him for me,
and I will give you your wages." So the woman took the child and nursed him.
—Exodus 2:9

Caring mothers are the incarnation of God's love within humanity. Abraham Lincoln confessed, "All that I am, or hope ever to be I get from my mother—God bless her."[24] On Sunday, May 10, 1908, Anna Jarvis, who led the movement to establish Mother's Day, held a memorial ceremony to honor her mother, Ann, who had died on May 9, 1905, and all other mothers. That ceremony is considered the first official observance of Mother's Day in the United States.

On May 9, 1914, American president Woodrow Wilson established a national Mother's Day holiday to be celebrated each year on the second Sunday of May. On that day, the United States flag should be displayed on all government buildings, private homes, and other suitable places "as a public expression of our love and reverence for the mothers of our country."[25]

One model mother in biblical times was Jochebed (Numbers 26:59). For some twelve years, she educated her child Moses for God.

She endeavored to imbue his mind with the fear of God and the love of truth and justice, and earnestly prayed that he might be preserved from every corrupting influence. She showed him the folly and sin of idolatry, and early taught him to bow down and pray to the living God, who alone could hear him and help him in every emergency.

. . . From his humble cabin home he was taken to the royal palace, to the daughter of Pharaoh, "and he became her son." Yet even here he did not lose the impressions received in childhood.[26]

Likewise, we should prepare our children to face the challenges of our contemporary world.

In 2023, on **May 14,** several countries are celebrating Mother's Day. So, I would like to praise God for the three wonderful mothers He gave me—my own mother, Frieda, who brought me to life and cared for me in my early years; my mother-in-law, Cenira, who became my second mother; and my wife, Marly, who is the mother of our three children. They are all very dear to me! You, too, can pay a special tribute to the mothers in your own heart.

May the Lord bless all mothers who are reading this devotional. I would like to wish you much health and joy and the blessing of having your families united in Christ. Happy Mother's Day!

ℬUTANTAN ℐNSTITUTE

God made him who had no sin to be sin for us, so that
in him we might become the righteousness of God.

—2 Corinthians 5:21, NIV

Snakes generate different reactions in those who see them. Some people love snakes, but others fear them. In the late 1980s, my wife and I visited the famous Butantan Institute in the city of São Paulo, Brazil, the largest immunobiological and biopharmaceuticals producer in Latin America and one of the largest in the world. Founded on February 23, 1901, it is renowned for its collection of poisonous snakes and also includes venomous lizards, spiders, insects, and scorpions collected over the course of more than a hundred years.

With extracts from the reptiles' and insects' poisons, the institute develops vaccines against many diseases, such as tuberculosis, rabies, tetanus, and diphtheria. The center also produces antidotes for poisonous serpent bites. Unfortunately, on **May 15, 2010,** a fire in the Building of Collections destroyed more than 70,000 species of serpents, as well as more than 450,000 species of arthropods, including scorpions, Opiliones, myriapods, and spiders.

The process of extracting serpents' poison to produce antidotes against serpents' bites illustrates what Christ did on the cross. By carrying our sins without becoming a sinner, He provided us with the effective antidote against sin (2 Corinthians 5:21). This principle was well illustrated by the fiery serpents that were killing the Israelites in the wilderness and the bronze serpent on the pole, which gave life to those who looked at it (Numbers 21:4–9). Jesus said, "As Moses lifted up the serpent in the wilderness, even so must the Son of Man be lifted up, that whoever believes in Him should not perish but have eternal life" (John 3:14, 15).

The disastrous destruction of the large number of serpents at the Butantan Institute in 2010 reminds us of the final destruction of "that serpent of old, called the Devil and Satan," and his evil angels at the end of the millennium (Revelation 12:9; 20:7–10). God's triumph over evil, first promised in the Garden of Eden (Genesis 3:15) and assured on the cross (John 12:31), will then be finally and forever accomplished. Then the poison of sin will be completely eradicated from the universe, never again to infect anyone.

$\mathcal{T}$HE $\mathcal{H}$IGHEST $\mathcal{M}$OTIVATION

And whatever you do, do it heartily, as to the Lord and not to men.

—Colossians 3:23

Will Durant stated, "Excellence, then, is not an act but a habit."[27] It is the habit of always improving on whatever we do. That was the philosophy of Antonio Stradivari (c. 1644–1737), the great Italian luthier (violin maker), whose instruments are still renowned for their outstanding tonal quality.

On **May 16, 2006**, a Stradivari violin from 1707 sold for US$3.5 million at a New York City auction. Another Stradivari violin on display at the Ashmolean Museum in England is worth nearly US$15 million. Why are authentic Stradivari (in Italian) or Stradivarius (in Latin) instruments so valuable?

Experts explain that the quality of handmade instruments depends on the ability to choose the right wood, the proper tools, the best shape for the instrument, and a good varnish. Regarding the wood, Hungarian luthier Tibor Szemmelveisz says, "There can be huge differences in quality, even in slices from the same tree, depending on whether the slice comes from the southward or northward-facing side of the tree, or from the upper or lower side on a slope."[28]

Many people would like the accolades Stradivari earned for his accomplishments, but few would pay the price of his commitment. To make a valuable contribution in life, we must overcome our natural tendency toward laziness and mediocrity and improve continuously.

A famous statement by an unknown author reads, "Excellence is the result of caring more than others think is wise, risking more than others think is safe, dreaming more than others think is practical, and expecting more than others think is possible. It is the commitment to high quality performance that produces outstanding results of lasting value. Excellence is believing in continuous improvement and never being satisfied with anything being less than it can be. It is quality as a way of life."

Some people are more self-motivated than others. Regardless of where we are on the scale, we have a higher motive for continuous improvement—to glorify God. In the words of Paul, "And whatever you do, do it heartily, as to the Lord and not to men" (Colossians 3:23). Whatever God does, He always does perfectly; and we, as His ambassadors, should always do our best as well.

ᏔHE ᏔEASTS OF ᏔSRAEL

*"These are the feasts of the LORD, holy convocations which
you shall proclaim at their appointed times."*

—Leviticus 23:4

People usually like to celebrate birthdays and holidays with family and friends. In addition, many people enjoy celebrating after completing a special project. In ancient times, God set apart several annual feasts for the Israelites. They were divided into two main cycles (see Leviticus 23). First came the *spring* feasts—Passover, Unleavened Bread, and Pentecost. Later were the *autumn* feasts—the Feast of Trumpets, the Day of Atonement, and the Feast of Tabernacles. All the men of Israel were supposed to celebrate three of them in Jerusalem—Passover, Pentecost, and the Feast of Tabernacles.

Of special relevance in interpreting the significance of the Hebrew feasts was a letter from William Miller published in the Millerite periodical *Signs of the Times* on **May 17, 1843**. He suggested that as the *spring* feasts were fulfilled at Christ's first advent and in His suffering, the *autumn* feasts should be fulfilled in relationship to Christ's second advent. Regarding the first cycle of feasts, the New Testament declares that Christ died on the cross as "the Lamb of God" (John 1:29) and as "our Passover" (1 Corinthians 5:7). He was raised from the dead as "the firstfruits of those who have fallen asleep" (1 Corinthians 15:20). And the Holy Spirit came upon the disciples on the Day of Pentecost (Acts 1:8; 2:1–4).

Similarly, the second cycle of feasts started being fulfilled at the beginning of the end-time era of Christ's second coming. As the Feast of Trumpets announced the soon arrival of the Day of Atonement, the great Second Advent movement proclaimed that the twenty-three hundred symbolic year-days of Daniel 8:14 would end in 1844 when the sanctuary should be cleansed. That year marks the beginning of the antitypical Day of Atonement. In turn, the Feast of Tabernacles is still to be fulfilled during the thousand years, when the saints will remain in heaven (Revelation 20) before they settle permanently on this earth made new (Revelation 21:1–4).

We are living today in the great antitypical Day of Atonement. Just as the ancient Israelites were expected to "afflict" their souls (Leviticus 16:29; 23:27), we should consecrate our lives in full commitment to the Lord and be ready for His soon appearing!

ᵀITHES AND ᴼFFERINGS

So He called His disciples to Himself and said to them, "Assuredly, I say to you that this poor widow has put in more than all those who have given to the treasury; for they all put in out of their abundance, but she out of her poverty put in all that she had, her whole livelihood."
—Mark 12:43, 44

God instituted the system of tithes and offerings with the triple purpose of breaking our selfishness, sustaining the gospel ministry, and fostering mission. Even so, some people argue that misuse of those funds in church channels justifies the giver in sending his or her means directly to alternative, "more reliable" projects and ministries.

The **May 18, 1869**, issue of the *Advent Review and Sabbath Herald* carried a short article by J. N. Andrews, "The Tithing System." Regarding the origin of that system, Andrews suggested that "the tithing system did not originate with the Levitical priesthood, but with that of Melchisedek, under which we now are [Hebrews 7]. We are therefore under obligation to do as much as this, as Christians; and if any wish to give as much as the poor widow, they will not lose their reward."[29]

The priesthood in the days of Jesus had become extremely corrupt. Jesus could have discouraged the poor widow from helping that priesthood. Instead, He praised her for what she did (Mark 12:41–44; Luke 21:1–4). Ellen White explains, "Those self-sacrificing, consecrated ones who render back to God the things that are His, as He requires of them, will be rewarded according to their works. Even though the means thus consecrated be misapplied, so that it does not accomplish the object which the donor had in view,—the glory of God and the salvation of souls,—those who made the sacrifice in sincerity of soul, with an eye single to the glory of God, will not lose their reward."[30]

And she pleads with us, "Let none feel at liberty to retain their tithe, to use according to their own judgment." "God has not changed; the tithe is still to be used for the support of the ministry. The opening of new fields requires more ministerial efficiency than we now have, and there must be means in the treasury."[31] So, let's bring all our faithful tithes and offerings into God's assigned storehouse (Malachi 3:10).

$\mathcal{T}$HE $\mathcal{D}$ARK $\mathcal{D}$AY

"But in those days, after that tribulation, the sun will be darkened, and the moon will not give its light; the stars of heaven will fall, and the powers in the heavens will be shaken."
—Mark 13:24, 25

People usually prefer sunny days over rainy and cloudy ones. Many pagans and mystics even venerate the sun as the king star and the source of light to the world. In contrast, God has darkened the sun in some crucial moments of human history. For instance, the ninth plague against the land of Egypt caused three days of absolute darkness (Exodus 10:21–23). While Jesus was on the cross, "the sun was darkened" for three hours (Luke 23:44, 45). And when the fifth apocalyptic angel pours out his bowl of God's wrath on the earth, the kingdom of the beast will become "full of darkness" (Revelation 16:10).

Speaking of end-time signs that would precede His return, Jesus mentioned that "the sun will be darkened, and the moon will not give its light" (Mark 13:24, 25; cf. Joel 2:31). Adventist authors have associated this specific sign with the aptly named Dark Day of **May 19, 1780**, as confirmed by Ellen White in her book *The Great Controversy*.[32] That phenomenon was observed over the New England states and parts of Canada. Eyewitnesses reported that the day became completely dark, extending its darkness into the next morning. During the real nighttime, the moon appeared colored red. Some believe that the Dark Day was caused by a combination of smoke from forest fires, a thick fog, and cloud cover.

If the Dark Day was caused by natural factors, how can it be a sign of the time of the end? Remember that at the opening of the sixth apocalyptic seal, Revelation says, "There was a great earthquake; and the sun became black as sackcloth of hair, and the moon became like blood. And the stars of heaven fell to the earth, as a fig tree drops its late figs when it is shaken by a mighty wind" (Revelation 6:12, 13). Fulfilling this prophecy, both the Great Lisbon Earthquake of November 1, 1755, and the meteor storm of November 13, 1833, had natural causes. If so, why could not the Dark Day of 1780 have a similar cause?

God uses both natural and supernatural events to wake us up from our careless security and spiritual lukewarmness. He has done it countless times in the past, and if needed, He can do it again today!

THE DEITY OF CHRIST

For in Him dwells all the fullness of the Godhead bodily.

—Colossians 2:9

Many theological debates and distortions arise from the human tendency to over-emphasize one side of the "coin" over the other. The Christological discussions within the ancient church were a classic example of this. Many wondered, How can Christ be at the same time both God and man? How much was He divine, and how much was He human?

Much confusion was brought into the discussion by Arius (AD 256–336), a priest in Alexandria, Egypt, who believed that Christ was more than human but less than divine. He believed that, way back in eternity, God created the Son, who in turn created everything else. The Council of Nicaea was formally opened on **May 20, 325**, and dealt with the "Arian heresy." After being in session for a month, the council promulgated the original Creed of Nicaea, affirming that Jesus Christ was "begotten, not made, cosubstancial with the Father";[33] and anathematizing those who suggested that "there once was when he was not."[34]

In the Reformed tradition, the Westminster Confession of 1647 stated, "In the unity of the Godhead there be three persons, of one substance, power, and eternity: God the Father, God the Son, and God the Holy Ghost. The Father is of none, neither begotten nor proceeding; the Son is eternally begotten of the Father; the Holy Ghost eternally proceeding from the Father and the Son."[35] However, can we say that our Lord Jesus Christ is "eternally begotten of the Father"?

In John 3:16, the original Greek word *monogenēs* has been inaccurately translated as "only begotten" (KJV) when its true meaning is "only" (RSV) or "one and only" (NIV). Since He has and always has had life in Himself, Christ could refer to Himself as the source of life (John 14:6). For this reason, in Isaiah 9:6, He is called "Mighty God" and "Everlasting Father." Paul says that "in Him dwells all the fullness of the Godhead bodily" (Colossians 2:9). And Ellen White affirms that "in Christ is life, original, unborrowed, underived."[36]

What a wonderful and mighty Savior we have! Being always God in the highest sense, He could reassume "all authority in heaven and on earth" and promise us, "Surely I am with you always, to the very end of the age" (Matthew 28:18, 20). We can fully trust the way He cares for us and leads us.

Church Organization

And Moses chose able men out of all Israel, and made them heads over the people: rulers of thousands, rulers of hundreds, rulers of fifties, and rulers of tens.

—Exodus 18:25

The rapid growth of the Sabbath-keeping Adventist movement brought the need for an organizational structure that could integrate the scattered local Adventist communities. But several pioneers still echoed the words of George Storrs, an influential Millerite preacher who, in February 1844, had stated, "No church can be organized by man's invention but what it becomes Babylon *the moment* it is *organized*."[37] In response to this concept, Ellen White pointed out that some feared that they would "become Babylon if they organize," but it was rather the lack of organization that had transformed many churches into a "perfect Babylon, confusion."[38]

The formation of an organizational structure took place at three basic levels. The first was the organization of local churches. While groups of Sabbath-keeping Adventists had begun to form in the mid-1840s, it was only in the 1850s that those groups started to elect deacons, local church elders, and treasurers. The second level was the formation of state conferences. In 1861, the first Seventh-day Adventist conference was established in Michigan; and in 1862, six more new conferences were organized. The third level of the early organizational development was the formation of a General Conference, which took place in Battle Creek, Michigan, on **May 21, 1863**. The organization of union conferences and union missions, as well as divisions, did not take place until the early twentieth century.

Some may ask, "Do we still need an organizational church structure?" Ellen White declares, "Let none entertain the thought that we can dispense with organization. It has cost us much study and many prayers for wisdom, that we know God has answered, to erect this structure. It has been built up by His direction, through much sacrifice and conflict. Let none of our brethren be so deceived as to attempt to tear it down, for you will thus bring in a condition of things that you do not dream of. In the name of the Lord I declare to you that it is to stand, strengthened, established, and settled."[39]

ＪOHN ＷYCLIFFE

"And you will be hated by all for My name's sake.
But he who endures to the end will be saved."

—Matthew 10:22

True Christian heroes remain unconditionally faithful to Christ and His Word even under the most severe pressure. One inspiring example is John Wycliffe (1320–1384), a theology professor at Oxford. He boldly proclaimed the headship of Christ, the authority of the Scriptures, and salvation by grace through faith. Concerned with those teachings, on **May 22, 1377**, Pope Gregory XI issued five bulls condemning the work of Wycliffe for promoting "certain erroneous and false propositions and conclusions, savoring even of heretical pravity, tending to weaken and overthrow the status of the whole church, and even the secular government."[40]

In response to the pope's bulls, Wycliffe stated, "I profess and claim to be by the grace of God a sound (that is, a true and orthodox) Christian and while there is breath in my body I will speak forth and defend the law of it. I am ready to defend my convictions even unto death. In these my conclusions I have followed the Sacred Scriptures and the holy doctors, and if my conclusions can be proved to be opposed to the faith, willingly will I retract them."[41]

On May 4, 1415, the Council of Constance retroactively excommunicated Wycliffe and banned his writings. His works were to be burned, and his remains removed from consecrated ground. This order, confirmed by Pope Martin V, was carried out in 1428—forty-three years after Wycliffe's death! In the presence of several ecclesiastical authorities, his remains were taken out of his grave in Lutterworth, burned to ashes, and cast into the nearby brook Swift. Someone wrote an epitaph at his former grave declaring him "the devil's instrument, church's enemy, people's confusion."[42]

In *The Church History in Britain* (published originally in 1655), Thomas Fuller states, "Thus this brook [Swift] hath conveyed his ashes into Avon, Avon into Severn, Severn into the narrow seas, they into the main ocean; and thus the ashes of Wicliffe are the emblem of his doctrine, which now is dispensed all the world over."[43] And by God's grace, we, too, have inherited this wonderful legacy of truth. Even though we are not compelled to pay such a high price for our faith, we should have the same commitment Wycliffe had. Let's carry his torch until the end!

"AND CAN IT BE"

"For you shall go out with joy,
And be led out with peace;
The mountains and the hills shall break forth into singing before you,
And all the trees of the field shall clap their hands."

—Isaiah 55:12

C onversion is such a profound and amazing experience with Christ that not even Satan with all his hosts can fully grasp its meaning.[44] One of those amazing experiences was the conversion of Charles Wesley (1707–1788) on Sunday, May 21, 1738. He even confessed, "I now found myself at peace with God, and rejoiced in hope of loving Christ."[45]

Out of a new heart came a new song about his spiritual pilgrimage. He wrote in his journal for Tuesday, **May 23, 1738**, "I waked under the protection of Christ, and gave myself up, soul and body, to him. At nine I began a hymn upon my conversion, but was persuaded to break off, for fear of pride. Mr. Bray coming, encouraged me to proceed in spite of Satan. I prayed Christ to stand by me, and finished the hymn."[46]

Charles Wesley did not identify the specific hymn he composed on that occasion. But it is quite evident that he referred to his amazing hymn "And Can It Be?" This composition tenderly describes how a sinful individual is justified by Christ's righteousness and can boldly approach the eternal throne. The first stanza and the refrain say,

And can it be that I should gain
an int'rest in the Savior's blood?
Died He for me, who caused his pain?
For me, who Him to death pursued?
Amazing love! how can it be
That Thou, my God, shouldst die for me?[47]

Many Old Testament psalms are prayers reflecting the spiritual experiences of the psalmists. So, why not take "And Can It Be?" or another hymn you like and reflect on it today, making it your prayer or praise expression? Involved with your many daily activities, you can keep your mind on God.

ᎷANHATTAN

"Again, the kingdom of heaven is like treasure hidden in a field, which a man found and hid; and for joy over it he goes and sells all that he has and buys that field."
—Matthew 13:44

Imagine you are one of more than 137,000 tourists who visit Manhattan Island every day. At the heart of New York City, Manhattan is considered the world center for capitalism. If you are interested in economic and international affairs, you should visit the United Nations headquarters and the two world-leading stock exchanges—the New York Stock Exchange and NASDAQ Stock Market. Regardless of your personal interests, you would most certainly also want to visit Times Square, Broadway, Central Park, Grand Central Terminal, and the Empire State Building. However, not many would look for a real estate agency. Residential property prices on the island often exceed $1,400 per square foot!

The name Manhattan means "island of many hills." The island originally belonged to the Native American Lenape tribe. But, according to some estimates, on **May 24, 1626**, Peter Minuit bought the island for the Dutch West India Company by trading goods valued at sixty guilders (a former currency of the Netherlands). Some authors have suggested that the whole island was bought for the equivalent of about US$24. Allowing for inflation, today, that would equal a little more than US$1,000. At any rate, Minuit could not have imagined how valuable his island would eventually become!

In the short parable of the hidden treasure (Matthew 13:44), Jesus compared the kingdom of heaven to a treasure worth far more than all earthly possessions combined—including all of Manhattan Island. Some people might deduce from this parable that a genuine Christian should not own any earthly possessions. But the parable of the great supper (Luke 14:15–24) clarifies that the real issue is not whether one owns a new piece of land or some oxen or whether a person should get married. The problem is in allowing those things to replace our unconditional commitment to receiving God's kingdom.

Just as Peter Minuit made an investment in Manhattan Island, we are expected to invest our talents in God's cause, even when we don't know what the outcome will be (Matthew 25:14–30). Do your best for God and leave the results with Him. You will not be disappointed.

THE POWER OF PRAYER

"If you ask anything in My name, I will do it."

—John 14:14

Prayer is God's method of keeping us in tune with Him and the condition for receiving His most precious blessings. Studying Scripture, one can see that there are some blessings God gives us whether we pray or not (Matthew 5:45). But most blessings are reserved for those who ask with a pure heart (Proverbs 28:9). Christ highlighted this condition when He stated, "If you ask anything in My name, I will do it" (John 14:14).

George Müller (1805–1898) went further than most might expect in living a life of complete dependence on God. George was born in Germany, but when he was twenty-three years old, he moved to London to work as a missionary to the Jews. Things did not work out as he had hoped, and on **May 25, 1832**, he moved to Bristol, England. There he established and directed the Ashley Down Orphanage, where he cared for 10,024 orphans over the course of his lifetime. He also opened 117 schools, providing Christian education to more than 120,000 children. His orphanage system was run on prayer alone—Müller never asked for money. He kept a record of more than fifty thousand answered prayers and said that none of his prayers remained unanswered.

Among the most well-known answers to prayer came one morning when three hundred children were ready to go to school, but there was no food for breakfast. Müller asked the children to sit at the empty table and then gave thanks for the meal. When they finished praying, a baker knocked on the door with sufficient fresh bread to feed everyone, and the milkman's cart broke down in front of the orphanage, so he gave the orphanage ten large cans of milk.

While sailing to America, Müller told the captain of the ship about an appointment he had in Quebec on the upcoming Saturday afternoon. The captain replied that, due to heavy fog, it would be impossible to arrive on time. Müller replied, "No, my eye is not on the density of the fog, but on the living God, Who controls every circumstance of my life."[48] He prayed, and in less than five minutes, the fog disappeared from the sky. The captain became a Christian.

Müller lived a life of intentional prayer, and we can do the same. God may not always answer our prayers in just the way we would like, but He never leaves a sincere prayer unanswered. You can trust Him!

RELIGION OF THE HEART

*"I have been crucified with Christ; it is no longer I who live,
but Christ lives in me; and the life which I now live in the flesh I live
by faith in the Son of God, who loved me and gave Himself for me."*
—Galatians 2:20

Religion is much more than merely a rational acceptance of certain doctrinal beliefs. It is more than sporadic emotional expressions at worship services and prayer meetings. Rather, it is a true conversion experience that leads to a daily and unconditional commitment to Christ. It means being crucified to the world and living a new life in Christ, allowing Him through His Word to control our thoughts, words, and actions.

This life of devotion was the emphasis of Nicolaus von Zinzendorf (1700–1760), an influential Pietist bishop of the Moravian Church who was born on **May 26, 1700**, in Dresden, Germany. Dissatisfied with the dry Lutheran orthodoxy of his time, Zinzendorf stressed religion of the heart, profoundly influencing John Wesley, the founder of Methodism.

As the apostle Paul surrendered his whole life to Christ (Galatians 2:20), so did Zinzendorf. Reflecting on the meaning of Christ's sacrifice on the cross and relating it to his own salvation, the great Moravian revivalist stated, "Thanks to the blood of the Lamb. Thanks be to God, which gives us the victory through our Lord Jesus Christ. He has redeemed us. We may have committed never so many sins, they are all drowned in the ocean of the blood of Christ."[49]

With such adoration for Christ, Zinzendorf could not accept a passive or isolated religion. He asserted, "There can be no Christianity without community." His love for Christ gave him a strong passion for mission. A statement often attributed to Zinzendorf reads, "Mission, after all, is simply this: Every heart with Christ is a missionary, every heart without Christ is a mission field."

Reflecting on those meaningful words of Zinzendorf, we should ask ourselves: How are we responding to Christ's sufferings on our behalf? Perhaps your religion has been more of an intellectual enterprise and not a truly life-changing experience with Christ. Whatever your current state, remember that you are not your own. You were bought by Christ, and you should live and work for Him. He should guide every moment of your life.

God's Orchestra

His intent was that now, through the church, the manifold wisdom of God
should be made known to the rulers and authorities in the heavenly realms.
—Ephesians 3:10, NIV

As you consider the condition of your local church, what analogy would best portray it? For example, Paul compared the church to the human body with all its various organs and members (1 Corinthians 12:12–31). Others refer to it as a spiritual hospital with many sick patients. A friend once told me that his local church was like the popular 7-Eleven convenience store—members participate only on the *seventh day* at *11:00* A.M.

At a time when Christianity had lost much of its original identity, John Calvin (1509–1564) inspired and supervised the reformation of the ecclesiastical, educational, and political structures of Geneva, Switzerland. What Luther was to the German-speaking reformation, Calvin was to its French-speaking counterpart. Calvin died on **May 27, 1564**, in Geneva, but he left an impressive legacy of efficient church organization for Christianity.

One of Calvin's most insightful analogies was his comparison of the church to an orchestra. In his commentary on Psalm 135:13, 14, he said, "The whole world is a theatre for the display of the divine goodness, wisdom, justice, and power, but the Church is the orchestra, as it were—the most conspicuous part of it; and the nearer the approaches are that God makes to us, the more intimate and condescending the communication of his benefits, the more attentively are we called to consider them."[50]

This statement should lead us to meaningful reflection. Let us imagine for a moment that your church is indeed an orchestra. So, how well tuned are the instruments? Are all members of the orchestra playing the same work in the same key? Furthermore, how impressed would the audience be with the music that is being performed? According to Mark Dever, "The Church is the gospel made visible."[51] So, what kind of gospel does your church make visible?

Your local congregation is God's orchestra for the community in which it is located. Perhaps you should consider some practical strategies to improve it so it can perform the best music in the most beautiful way possible. Remember, God deserves nothing less than our best.

The Power of Joyfulness

A joyful heart is good medicine, but a broken spirit dries up the bones.
—Proverbs 17:22, NASB

The smiley face is one of the most popular emojis in modern media. Its use is almost mandatory in electronic messages to visually convey the emotional intent of the sender. But in many cases, while faces are smiling, hearts are crying. So, in addition to using joyful smiley faces in our messages, we should, in fact, cultivate joyful hearts. A joyful expression can enhance our aesthetic beauty as well as our physical and emotional health (Proverbs 15:13; 17:22).

Popular American physician, lecturer, and social activist Hunter Doherty Adams (nicknamed Patch Adams) was born in Washington, DC, on **May 28, 1945**. As a teenager, he became frustrated with people's greed and love of money and with social inequality. He had to overcome his own personal traumas through social activism and bringing joy to sick patients suffering extreme pain, especially children. With the help of friends, he founded Gesundheit Institute—a free community hospital promoting compassionate connections with patients and emphasizing humor and playing. His innovative health practices were portrayed in the 1998 film *Patch Adams*.

Adams explains, "Research has shown that laughter increases the secretion of the natural chemicals, catecholamines and endorphins, that make people feel so peppy and good. It also decreases cortisol secretion and lowers the sedimentation rate, which implies a stimulated immune response. Oxygenation of the blood increases, and residual air in the lungs decreases. Heart rate initially speeds up and blood pressure rises; then the arteries relax, causing heart rate and blood pressure to lower. Skin temperature rises as a result of increased peripheral circulation."[52] But, for loneliness, "Friendship is clearly the best medicine."[53]

Remember that a person can be funny but unfriendly and can smile without caring. As someone once quipped, "A smile is worth a thousand words, but a single word can end a thousand smiles." Instead of living only for ourselves, we can make the world better by bringing joy to others. In this cold, competitive world, we must cultivate a joyful and caring heart that overflows with compassion to those around us. A smile can turn the light of the soul on, but only friendship can keep that light on. Let us be more joyful and friendlier!

On Top of the Mountain

I lift up my eyes to the mountains—
where does my help come from?
My help comes from the LORD,
the Maker of heaven and earth.

—Psalm 121:1, 2, NIV

Alpinists are people who like to climb high mountains that are often covered in snow and ice. Mount Everest, the highest mountain in the world, has long been considered the ultimate challenge. Its peak is 29,035 feet above sea level, and climbing it is extremely dangerous. Besides freezing temperatures and the obvious potential for long falls from cliffs and into deep crevasses, climbers suffer the effects of the extremely high altitude, often called mountain sickness.

Early climbers attempting to climb Mount Everest either gave up or never returned. On **May 29, 1953**, at 11:30 A.M., after seven weeks of climbing, the New Zealand alpinist Edmund Hillary and his Nepalese guide Tenzing Norgay became the first to reach the top of Mount Everest. With a low air supply, the two men stayed at the top of the world for only fifteen minutes. They enjoyed the view and took photographs. On their way down, Hillary triumphantly said to another New Zealander on the expedition, "Well, George, we've knocked [it] off."[54]

Mountains and mountaineering can teach us meaningful lessons. While climbing the social ladder, we should remember the well-known saying, "The higher you climb on the mountain, the harder the wind blows." The top of a high mountain is a lonely place. The experience of Moses and the Israelites in the wilderness demonstrated that even honest and qualified leaders face misunderstanding, criticism, and opposition. Successful leaders must be creative, but innovation generates opposition.

Looking at it from a spiritual perspective, we know there was a time in Judah's history when people built for themselves pagan shrines "on every high hill" (1 Kings 14:23). But in Psalm 121:1, 2, the psalmist says, "I lift up my eyes to the mountains—where does my help come from?" (NIV). And then, he proclaims that his help does not come from the mountains but rather "from the LORD, the Maker of heaven and earth" (NIV). As majestic and dangerous as high mountains might be, they are powerless and helpless in themselves. Only He who "weighed the mountains in scales and the hills in a balance" (Isaiah 40:12) can help you face your most challenging needs. Bring your problems and entrust them to the Maker of heaven and earth.

ᏦᎪᎢᎪ ᏒᎪᏀᎣᏚᎣ

"For I am not ashamed of the gospel of Christ, for it is the power of God to salvation for everyone who believes, for the Jew first and also for the Greek."

—Romans 1:16

Every General Conference session of the Seventh-day Adventist Church is a unique event with delegates, special guests, and other visitors from around the world. The 1936 and 1954 sessions were both held in San Francisco, California, and the high point of both were the presentations of Kata Ragoso (also spelled Rangoso), a delegate from the Solomon Islands in the South Pacific, who became an ordained minister and mission president.

On **May 30, 1936**, Ragoso told the assembly that he and his people had been caught in the depths of paganism. They "lived a life of sin," and their "thoughts were evil continually."[55] They worshiped evil spirits, were addicted to all kinds of vices, and practiced violent acts, including head-hunting. But, twenty-five years earlier, the missionary G. F. Jones had come to their island and preached the Adventist message. By God's grace, they "cast off the fetters of paganism"[56] and experienced a complete transformation—even in the areas of diet and hygiene.

Ragoso attested,

We are now able to live happily and peacefully because of the wonderful gospel that has been brought to us. I want to tell you definitely this afternoon that none of my people who have accepted this glorious message desire to return to the worship of idols and to paganism.

Today 5,000 of my people are rejoicing with you in this message of a soon-coming Savior. Over 100 of them are ministers, teachers, and departmental workers among our own kith and kin.[57]

The everlasting gospel is much more than just a wonderful theory; it is the marvelous transforming power of God. Ellen White, writing of the conversions that Christ is making in human lives through His mercy and abundant grace, says they are "so amazing that Satan, with all his triumphant boasting, with all his confederacy of evil united against God and the laws of His government, stands viewing them as a fortress impregnable to his sophistries and delusions. They are to him an incomprehensible mystery."[58] Wonderful grace has changed uncountable lives throughout the ages. You and I need this transforming power in our own lives daily!

ʙROKEN Sᴛʀɪɴɢꜱ

"Have I not commanded you? Be strong and of good courage; do not be afraid, nor be dismayed, for the Lᴏʀᴅ *your God is with you wherever you go."*

—Joshua 1:9

E xceptional musical performances usually derive from the combination of three basic components—the piece that is being played, the quality of the instrument that is being used, and the skills of the artist who is playing. An excellent instrument in the hands of a poor musician does not help much. On the other hand, even a common instrument in the hands of a virtuoso can make a great difference.

Niccolò Paganini (1782–1840) was an extremely skilled Italian violinist and composer. Some consider him the most famous violin virtuoso of all time. On **May 31, 1794**, Paganini made his public debut in his hometown, Genoa, when he was eleven years old. Probably due to Marfan syndrome, his fingers were long and flexible, allowing him to develop new, very difficult performance techniques. But he also liked to entertain the audience with various musical tricks. For instance, he could play his "Witches' Dance" on one string after cutting the other three on stage with a pair of scissors. At any rate, people were always impressed with his amazing performances.

Some people are so skilled and successful in their respective careers that they could be compared to Paganini. But most of us are perhaps more like his violin with broken strings. Looking at ourselves, we see only our own weaknesses and limitations. We might doubt that God can use us. And others may even confirm our own doubts, pushing our already low self-esteem even further down.

As in the case of Paganini, what really counts is not so much how many strings are left but the hands of the artist. God can use you even if only one single string is left. But even if all your strings are gone, He can add as many new strings to your life as needed. The only condition for you to perform well is to place yourself in His hands and allow Him to do His will in your life. Then give Him all the honor and glory for all of your achievements. God's promise for you today is, "Be strong and of good courage; do not be afraid, nor be dismayed, for the Lᴏʀᴅ your God is with you wherever you go" (Joshua 1:9).

OUR DEEPEST NEEDS

As the deer pants for the water brooks, so pants my soul for You, O God.
—Psalm 42:1

Norma Jeane Mortenson (later baptized as Norma Jeane Baker) was born in Los Angeles, California, on **June 1, 1926.** Unfortunately, she was abandoned by her biological mother, grew up not knowing who her father was, and was later placed with foster parents who had mental problems. Norma spent most of her childhood in an orphanage and several foster homes. Some biographers believe she was a victim of early childhood sexual abuse. At the tender age of sixteen, she married James Dougherty, who went away to fight in World War II. Those childhood traumas and that life of turmoil left indelible marks on her personality.

Documentary photographer David Conover is credited for having discovered Norma as a model, and Ben Lyon arranged a screen test for her with 20th Century Fox. When she was twenty years old, she was given the stage name Marilyn Monroe—Marilyn, after the actress Marilyn Miller, and Monroe, her biological mother's maiden name. Over the years, Marilyn Monroe built an extremely successful career as a Hollywood sex symbol and movie star. But on the morning of August 5, 1962, she was found dead in her Los Angeles home, apparently due to a drug overdose.

Monroe's life confirmed the undeniable reality that physical beauty and public notoriety cannot meet our deep emotional and existential needs. In 1951, Monroe wrote in one of her notebooks, "Alone!!!!! I am alone—I am always alone, no matter what."[1]

In his poem "Mal Secreto" (Secret evil), Raimundo Correia suggests that if we could see through the mask of the face the "pain that dwells in man's soul and destroys all dreams," perhaps "so many people who now make us envious, would then move us to pity!"[2] The truth is that many human hearts are bleeding from moral and social wounds that refuse to heal.

The preface to Ellen White's *The Desire of Ages* speaks of the "inexpressible longings" of every human heart that cannot "be satisfied by pleasure, by wealth, by ease, by fame, [or] by power."[3] Those longings come from God to lead us to Jesus Christ, who alone can bring real meaning to our lives. If your past still hurts, your present is unstable, and your future is uncertain, surrender your life to Jesus and allow Him to take care of all your burdens.

𝒫LEASING CONCESSIONS

"When you come into the land which the LORD your God is giving you,
you shall not learn to follow the abominations of those nations."
—Deuteronomy 18:9

E veryone knows it's easier to go downhill than uphill. Likewise, it is easier to compromise our religious values in the society in which we live than to preserve them. For this reason, Moses warned the Israelites before they entered the land of Canaan, "When you come into the land which the LORD your God is giving you, you shall not learn to follow the abominations of those nations" (Deuteronomy 18:9). But how does compromise occur?

In the *Signs of the Times* dated **June 2, 1881**, Ellen White wrote, "Many feel that they must make some concessions to please their irreligious relatives and friends. As it is not always easy to draw the line, one concession prepares the way for another until those who were once true followers of Christ are in life and character conformed to the customs of the world. The connection with God is broken. They are Christians in name only. When the test hour comes, then their hope is seen to be without foundation. They have sold themselves and their children to the enemy. They have dishonored God, and in the revelation of His righteous judgments, they will reap what they have sown. Christ will say to them, as He said to ancient Israel, 'Ye have not obeyed My voice. Why have ye done this?' "[4]

People's intentions are innocent—just "to please their irreligious relatives and friends"— and can even assume an evangelistic air. They believe that by conforming more closely to the lifestyle of their relatives and friends, it will be easier to reach them with the Adventist message. But we can never forget that "conformity to worldly customs converts the church to the world; it never converts the world to Christ."[5] The outcome is very predictable—"one concession prepares the way for another" on the road downhill toward "the customs of the world."

When our Christian standards and moral values are at stake, our stand should be as firm and uncompromising as that of Daniel and his friends in the Babylonian court (Daniel 1; 3). You must be motivated by principle. Never sell your soul merely to please relatives and friends!

Gethsemane

He withdrew about a stone's throw beyond them, knelt down and prayed,
"Father, if you are willing, take this cup from me; yet not my will, but yours
be done." An angel from heaven appeared to him and strengthened him.
—Luke 22:41–43, NIV

Christ's earthly ministry was ending, and He would soon face His cruel death on the cross. In the Garden of Gethsemane, He fought one of His most dramatic battles against the hosts of evil. The *Signs of the Times* issue for **June 3, 1897**, carried Ellen White's touching article "Gethsemane." Prayerfully, reflect on the following quotations from that article:

It was here that the mysterious cup trembled in Christ's hand. Here the destiny of a lost world hung in the balance. Should he refuse to stand as man's surety? Satan encircled his humanity with a horror of great darkness, tempting him to think that God had forsaken him. . . .

. . . The worlds unfallen and the heavenly angels watched with intense interest as the conflict drew to its close. Satan and his confederacy of evil, the legions of apostasy, watched intently this great crisis in the work of redemption. The powers of good and evil waited to see what answer would come to Christ's thrice-repeated prayer. In this awful crisis, when everything was at stake, when the mysterious cup trembled in the hand of the Sufferer, the heavens opened, a light shone forth amid the stormy darkness of the crisis hour, and an angel who stands in the presence of God, occupying the position from which Satan fell, came to the side of Christ. What message did he bring? . . . Did he tell him that he need not drink the bitter cup, that he need not bear the guilt of man?

The angel did not come to take the cup from Christ's hand, but to strengthen him to drink it, with the assurance of the Father's love. He came to give power to the divine-human Suppliant. He pointed him to the open heavens, telling him of the souls that would be saved as the result of his sufferings. . . . He assured him that his Father is greater and more powerful than Satan, that his death would result in the utter discomfiture of Satan, and that the kingdom of this world would be given to the saints of the Most High. He told him that he would see of the travail of his soul, and be satisfied, for he would see a multitude of the redeemed, saved, eternally saved.[6]

ETERNAL LOVE

Love never ends.
—1 Corinthians 13:8, NRSV

The name of American industrialist Henry Ford (1863–1947) is forever associated with the Ford Motor Company and the development of the assembly-line method of industrial mass production. But not much is said about his wife, who supported him for fifty-nine years.

On April 11, 1888, Henry Ford married Clara Jane Bryant, and the couple initially lived on farmland given to Henry by his father. By 1891, they had moved to Detroit, Michigan, where Ford began working as an engineer for Edison Illuminating Company. With a flexible, on-call work schedule, Ford began developing his Quadricycle, a four-wheel, self-propelled vehicle with a gasoline engine. During those early years, the Fords lived in ten different rental homes. Clara believed in her husband and supported him, even with no concrete evidence that his inventions would ever succeed.

Finally, on **June 4, 1896,** Ford test-drove his Quadricycle down Detroit's Grand River Avenue. James Bishop, his chief assistant, bicycled ahead of him to alert passing carriages and pedestrians of the oncoming automobile. In 1903, the Ford Motor Company was incorporated, and in 1908 Ford introduced the Ford Model T. That was just the beginning of an extremely successful business enterprise.

Henry Ford could never have become what he was without the support of his beloved wife. He said of her, "If anyone thinks I've done anything in life, they should remember that my wife has been a great helper. I don't believe I would have got far without her. She has always believed in me and backed me in whatever I've attempted."[7] In 1940, James Bone asked Ford what he would like to do "in a future incarnation." Without reluctance, Ford answered, "The only thing is I should like to be sure of having the same wife."[8] Henry and Clara Ford not only helped launch the car industry but also left their legacy of a solid marriage.

Genuine love is not an unreliable feeling that is shaken by adversity. It is an unconditional commitment. Such commitment is expressed well in Ruth's plea to her mother-in-law Naomi: "Do not press me to leave you or to turn back from following you! Where you go, I will go; where you lodge, I will lodge; your people shall be my people, and your God my God. Where you die, I will die—there will I be buried. May the LORD do thus and so to me, and more as well, if even death parts me from you" (Ruth 1:16, 17, NRSV). May this unconditional love unite the marriages of our church!

COMPREHENSIVE HEALTH

Beloved, I pray that you may prosper in all things and be in health, just as your soul prospers.
—3 John 2

The year 1863 brought serious challenges for Seventh-day Adventists! Early that year, two of James and Ellen White's children got diphtheria, causing severe sore throats and high fevers. Meanwhile, the American Civil War (1861–1865) was raging on, and the Military Draft Act of March 3, 1863, was a serious threat for all who refused to join the Union Army. If that was not enough, much energy was spent on developing a church organizational structure. It culminated in the establishment of the General Conference of Seventh-day Adventists in May 1863. No wonder James White and other leaders were exhausted and needed to fortify their own health.

On Friday evening, **June 5, 1863**, Ellen White was at the Aaron Hilliard home in Otsego, Michigan, when she received her most comprehensive health reform vision. It outlined a "general plan" of "reformation in habits and practices."[9] She saw that "it was a sacred duty to attend to our health" and to speak "against intemperance of every kind,—intemperance in working, in eating, in drinking and in drugging." Much emphasis was placed on the need for cultivating "a cheerful, hopeful, peaceful frame of mind" to strengthen one's health. Several other aids to good health were pointed out, including pure soft water as "God's great medicine."[10]

This vision was the beginning of a new Adventist lifestyle that continued to develop as it was enhanced by subsequent visions and scientific discoveries. As most of us know by experience, changing habits and reeducating tastes are not always easy tasks. Being "a great meat eater," Ellen White had a hard time giving up meat and enduring the taste of bread. When she struggled with the temptation, she put her arms across her stomach and said to herself, "I will not taste a morsel. I will eat simple food, or I will not eat at all."[11]

Our sinful nature tends to twist God's principles to fit our own habits and tastes, but we must stay in control of our appetites. God wants us to be as healthy as possible in every dimension of life (3 John 2). Why don't we bring ourselves, by His grace, into conformity with His principles? After all, it is "a sacred duty"!

ᴜPHOLDING THE ᴮIBLE

*That through these [exceedingly great and precious promises] you may be partakers of the
divine nature, having escaped the corruption that is in the world through lust.*

—2 Peter 1:4

The 1909 General Conference Session took place on the campus of Washington
Missionary College (now Washington Adventist University) in Washington, DC.
Ellen White came all the way from Saint Helena, California, to the session, where she
spoke eleven times. At eighty-one years old, she felt that this would be her last opportunity
to speak to an assembly of the worldwide church.

On Sunday afternoon, **June 6, 1909**, at three o'clock, Ellen White gave a farewell
sermon entitled, "Partakers of the Divine Nature." She stated,

We have had many precious meetings here, and we need to make the very best
account of our privileges. We shall very probably never all meet again on this earth;
but I want to meet this people in the kingdom of God. . . .

May the Lord help us to live in accordance with His Word. We all need the truth
as it is in Jesus. Let us represent Christ and the truth wherever we go, that we may
stand in that position where we can glorify God. . . .

O what a scene of rejoicing it will be when the Lamb of God shall place upon
the heads of the redeemed the victor's crown! Never, nevermore will you be led into
temptation and sin. You will see the King in His beauty. And those whom you have
helped heavenward will meet you there. They will throw their arms about you and
acknowledge what you have done for them. . . .

Brethren, we shall separate for a little while, but let us not forget what we have
heard at this meeting. . . . Let us remember that we are to be partakers of the divine
nature, and that angels of God are right around us, that we need not be overcome
by sin. . . . I pray God that this may be the experience of each one of us and that in
the great day of God we all may be glorified together.[12]

Having finished her sermon, Ellen White was on her way to her seat. Suddenly, she
returned to the pulpit and picked up the Bible from which she had read. She opened it,
held it out in her hands trembling with age, and said, "Brethren and Sisters, I commend
unto you this Book."[13] Without another word, she closed the Bible and walked from the
platform. Those were her last words spoken to a world assembly of the church.

*I*MMEASURABLE *L*OVE

"For God so loved the world that He gave His only begotten Son,
that whoever believes in Him should not perish but have everlasting life."
—John 3:16

D o you have a favorite Bible text? If so, what does it mean to you? One of the most widely quoted verses in the Bible is John 3:16. Church of Scotland minister William Barclay called it "the very essence of the gospel," and other writers have called it "the Bible in miniature."

On the evening of **June 7, 1885**, Charles H. Spurgeon preached a powerful sermon on John 3:16 at the Metropolitan Tabernacle in London. He stated, "What was there in the world that God should love it? There was nothing lovable in it. No fragrant flower grew in that arid desert. Enmity to him, hatred to his truth, disregard of his law, rebellion against his commandments; those were the thorns and briars which covered the waste land; but no desirable thing blossomed there." But "amid the ruins of humanity there was space for showing how much Jehovah loved the sons of men. . . . When the great God gave his Son he gave God himself, for Jesus is not in his eternal nature less than God. When God gave God for us he gave himself. What more could he give? God gave his all: he gave himself. Who can measure this love?"[14]

J. Edwin Hartill derived twelve "greatest" superlatives from John 3:16:

"For God"—the greatest lover
"So loved"—the greatest degree
"The world"—the greatest company
"That He gave"—the greatest act
"His only begotten Son"—the greatest gift
"That whosoever"—the greatest opportunity
"Believeth"—the greatest simplicity
"In him"—the greatest attraction
"Should not perish"—the greatest promise
"But"—the greatest difference
"Have"—the greatest certainty
"Everlasting life"—the greatest possession[15]

What an amazing concentration of superlatives expressed in just twenty-five words! John 3:16 can become even more meaningful if you replace the words *world* and *whoever* with your own name. After all, God loves you personally!

So Many Gods

"You shall have no other gods before Me."

—Exodus 20:3

Our world is full of gods, all competing with the only true God. For example, ancient Greeks envisioned the existence of twelve gods in Olympus and many other lower gods, all with human forms and passions. Aristotle stated, "People make the lives of the gods in the likeness of their own—as they also make their shapes."[16] A century earlier, Xenophanes declared, "But if horses or oxen or lions had hands or could draw with their hands and accomplish such works as men, horses would draw the figures of the gods as similar to horses, and the oxen as similar to oxen, and they would make the bodies of the sort which each of them had. Ethiopians say that their gods are snub-nosed and black; Thracians that theirs are blue-eyed and red-haired."[17]

The two Greek philosophers are right about the gods and idols that human beings have created for themselves (Isaiah 44:9–20). The trouble starts when, confused and frustrated by so many gods created over time, one believes the only true God is just another human projection.

In her book *A History of God*, Karen Armstrong suggested that the prophets of Israel ascribed "their own feelings and experiences to God" and "monotheists have in some sense created a God for themselves."[18] On **June 8, 2009**, Robert Wright's book *The Evolution of God* was released with a similar humanist perspective. Wright says, "Abrahamic monotheism grew organically out of the 'primitive' by a process more evolutionary than revolutionary."[19]

Crucial to the whole discussion is the question, Is what the Bible says about God just a *human creation* of God or a *divine revelation* from God? Both Armstrong and Wright would propose the former option, but the Bible itself asserts the latter. We are assured that "prophecy never had its origin in the human will, but prophets, though human, spoke from God as they were carried along by the Holy Spirit" (2 Peter 1:21, NIV).

Those who insinuate that the God of the Bible is an imagined god are creating their own human god—themselves. That has to be the case, because anyone or anything that takes the place of God becomes the god. And God's commandment is clear: "You shall have no other gods before Me" (Exodus 20:3). The only way to avoid idolatry is to believe in the one true God.

✐ESTIFYING TO THE ✐MPEROR

"For last night there stood by me an angel of the God to whom I belong and whom I worship, and he said, 'Do not be afraid, Paul; you must stand before the emperor; and indeed, God has granted safety to all those who are sailing with you.' "
—Acts 27:23, 24, NRSV

History has been shaped by people of strong convictions and unashamed boldness, as in the case of the apostle Paul. To the church in Rome, he wrote, "I am not ashamed of the gospel of Christ" (Romans 1:16). To the elders of the church in Ephesus, he stated that he was so committed "to testify to the gospel of the grace of God" that he did not count his own life dear to himself (Acts 20:24). Paul's teachings were backed by his example, as when he appealed to Caesar (Acts 25:11, 12).

The Caesar, or Roman emperor, to whom Paul appealed was none other than the powerful and cruel Nero (AD 37–68). In her book *The Acts of the Apostles*, Ellen White describes Paul's trial before the emperor, whose name made the world tremble.[20] In that critical hour, Paul was left to stand alone (2 Timothy 4:16, 17). But what a striking contrast between one of the most degraded rulers ever and one of the greatest Christians ever! Paul persuasively presented the truths of the gospel and of divine judgment. For a moment, even the heart of Nero was touched by the gospel message.

Only a few years later, both men sealed their destinies. In AD 67, Nero sentenced Paul to be decapitated, and the apostle gave up his life, fully assured that he would eventually be raised from the dead to receive his "crown of righteousness" (verses 6–8). Nero, having agitated his country's ruling class and his own army commanders, fled from Rome in panic and committed suicide on **June 9,** AD **68.** Unlike Paul, Nero's ultimate destiny will be final annihilation along with the rest of the wicked.

Ellen White affirmed, "What the church needs in these days of peril is an army of workers who, like Paul, have educated themselves for usefulness, who have a deep experience in the things of God, and who are filled with earnestness and zeal. Sanctified, self-sacrificing men are needed; men who will not shun trial and responsibility; men who are brave and true."[21] Are you willing to be one of those brave workers?

$\mathcal{A}$LEXANDER THE $\mathcal{G}$REAT

"For what will it profit a man if he gains the whole world, and loses his own soul?"
—Mark 8:36

S ome people have ruined their brilliant public careers by not being able to control
themselves. A classic example of this is Alexander the Great (356–323 BC), who was
educated by the famous Greek philosopher Aristotle and became a symbol of successful
conquering power. At the age of twenty, Alexander became king of Macedon. Shortly
afterward, he invaded and conquered the Greek city-states. He expanded his domain
significantly by conquering first the Persian Empire in the east and then Egypt in the south,
where he founded Alexandria, the city named after him. Pushing farther east, he hoped to
conquer India, but his exhausted troops refused to fight any longer, and he had to give up
his ambitious plan. While in Babylon, Alexander died in the palace of Nebuchadnezzar II
on **June 10, 323** BC, at just thirty-two years old, having developed a fever and struggled
with illness for twelve days.

The real cause of Alexander's illness remains hidden. Some modern scholars have
suggested that he could have contracted typhoid fever or malaria or even smallpox.
However, some historians are convinced that the wine he drank in his debauchery at
a party hosted by a friend named Medius was intentionally poisoned. Other historians
reject this theory, claiming that twelve days would be too long for a poisoned person to
survive. The ancient Greek historian Diodorus said that Alexander was struck with pain
after "he drank much unmixed wine in commemoration of the death of Heracles."[22]
Whatever the case, Alexander conquered the world in twelve years but was conquered
by a fever that took his life in twelve days!

Alexander's tragic end provides important lessons. Jesus raised the crucial question,
"For what will it profit a man if he gains the whole world, and loses his own soul?" (Mark
8:36). Remember, "a wise man will not be governed and controlled by his appetites and
passions, but will control and govern them."[23]

SUSTAINED BY PRAYER

Then the disciples came to Jesus privately and said, "Why could we not cast it out?"
So Jesus said to them, "Because of your unbelief. . . .
This kind does not go out except by prayer and fasting."
—Matthew 17:19–21

A true missionary is an instrument used by the Holy Spirit in the sacred task of leading sinners from the kingdom of Satan into the kingdom of Jesus Christ (Colossians 1:13, 14). Many skilled missionaries and preachers have used their impressive talents and the best resources available and yet have failed. How can we explain that?

On **June 11, 1883**, Ellen White wrote a letter to her son Willie, highlighting evangelistic challenges that the church in California was facing. With the framework of the great controversy between God and Satan in mind, she stressed that such missionary endeavors could be truly successful only through unceasing prayer. She wrote,

We talk to the workers that they must do their missionary work with a spirit of prayer, and that they must come close to the people and not feel that after giving a paper or securing names their work is done. They have Satan and his angels close at their elbows to counteract every effort they may make. As they walk the streets, they must pray for grace and for the angels of God to be round about them. Unless they do, the craft of the devils will turn aside the efforts made, and the truth [will] not find access to hearts, and thus the whole city may be warned in vain. . . .

One man [John Knox], when the church in Scotland was making some resolutions to compromise the faith, to concede their staunch principles, was determined never to yield a jot or tittle. He went upon his knees before God and thus pleaded, "Give me Scotland or I die." His importunate prayer was heard. Oh, that the earnest prayer of faith may arise everywhere, "Give me souls buried now in the rubbish of error, or I die! Bring them to the knowledge of the truth as it is in Jesus."[24]

There is a tendency today to rely more on our sophisticated outreach strategies than on the power of the Holy Spirit. Some charismatic Pentecostal preachers even try to manipulate the work of the Holy Spirit. Instead of trying to use the Holy Spirit, why not allow Him to use us? Working with humility in a spirit of prayer, like John Knox, will generate eternal results!

EVERY DAY OUR BEST

" 'And I'll say to myself, "You have plenty of grain laid up for
many years. Take life easy; eat, drink and be merry." '
"But God said to him, 'You fool! This very night your life will be demanded
from you. Then who will get what you have prepared for yourself?' "

—Luke 12:19, 20, NIV

Imagine it is Sunday, **June 12, 2005**, and you are at Stanford Stadium for Stanford University's 114th commencement. Surprisingly, the keynote speech is being delivered by a guest speaker who doesn't even have a college degree! Just a few years ago, he was forced out of the company he helped found, and, recently, he was diagnosed with pancreatic cancer. He just tells three stories from his own life experiences, yet his fifteen-minute speech is destined to become one of the most famous discourses ever presented at that prestigious university.

Who was the speaker? You may already know it was Steve Jobs (1955–2011), the chief executive officer and cofounder of Apple and Pixar Animation Studios. The American journalist Walter Isaacson described him as "a creative entrepreneur whose passion for perfection and ferocious drive revolutionized six industries: personal computers, animated movies, music, phones, tablet computing, and digital publishing."[25] He was the main conceptualizer of several Apple products, including iMacs, iPhones, iPads, iPods, iPhoto, iMovie, and iTunes.

In his Stanford speech, Jobs said, "Remembering that I'll be dead soon is the most important tool I've ever encountered to help me make the big choices in life. Because almost everything—all external expectations, all pride, all fear of embarrassment or failure—these things just fall away in the face of death, leaving only what is truly important."[26] He confessed, "For the past 33 years, I have looked in the mirror every morning and asked myself: 'If today were the last day of my life, would I want to do what I am about to do today?' "[27] He died on October 5, 2011, at only fifty-six years old, but he left an extremely rich technological legacy.

As urged by Ellen White, "We should watch and work and pray as though this were the last day that would be granted us. How intensely earnest, then, would be our life. How closely would we follow Jesus in all our words and deeds."[28] What changes can you make in your life to best implement this advice?

*H*E *C*AME TO *R*ESCUE *U*S

"For the Son of Man has come to seek and to save that which was lost."
—Luke 19:10

In March 2016, I visited the Natural History Museum of Bern, Switzerland. My main purpose was to see the taxidermy mount of Barry (1800–1814), the most famous mountain rescue dog in history. This male Saint Bernard was born at the Great Saint Bernard Pass Hospice on the Alpine border between Switzerland and Italy. At 8,200 feet (about 2,500 meters) above sea level, with freezing temperatures and snowstorms, this region presented immense challenges for travelers attempting to travel the pass. People from the hospice went out with their dogs each day to look for lost travelers. Barry, the most tireless of them all, has been credited with rescuing more than forty people.

Over the years, paintings and storybooks have kept his memory alive. Legends suggest that he used to carry a small barrel filled with a stiff drink around his neck, that he once found a half-frozen boy and carried him to the hospice on his own back, and that while he was rescuing his forty-first person, who happened to be one of Napoleon's soldiers, the man mistakenly confused the rescue dog with a wolf and killed him with a bayonet. Nevertheless, these myths cannot undermine Barry's extraordinary legacy. On **June 13, 2014**, two hundred years after his death, the Bern Museum opened a permanent exhibition titled *Barry, the Legendary St Bernard.*

As I gazed at Barry, my thoughts went back more than two hundred years. I imagined him rescuing travelers in the snowy Alps. Then my thoughts drifted to another rescue—one that happened some two thousand years ago when the Son of God left the heavenly courts and came to this dangerous world to reclaim it with His saving grace. At that moment, I offered a silent prayer, thanking God first for what He had done through that rescue dog for lost travelers and then through His Beloved Son for all of humanity.

Scripture assures us that Christ's rescue mission was so effective that "where sin abounded, grace abounded much more" (Romans 5:20) and that He is "able to save to the uttermost those who come to God through Him" (Hebrews 7:25). Regardless of our sinful past, Christ has "delivered us from the power of darkness and conveyed us into the kingdom of the Son of His love, in whom we have redemption through His blood, the forgiveness of sins" (Colossians 1:13, 14).

$\mathcal{U}$PLIFTING THE $\mathcal{S}$ABBATH

So there remains a Sabbath rest for the people of God.
—Hebrews 4:9, NASB

As a teenager in his native city of Rome, Samuele Bacchiocchi was frequently ridiculed and rejected for being a "heretic" Seventh-day Adventist who kept the Sabbath. This challenged him to pursue an extensive, in-depth investigation of the history, theology, and meaning of the Sabbath. The process reached its climax on **June 14, 1974**, when he defended his doctoral dissertation on the rise of Sunday observance in early Christianity at Pontifical Gregorian University in Rome, Italy. Bacchiocchi was indeed the first (and perhaps the only) non-Catholic to graduate from this prestigious university, founded in 1551 by Ignatius of Loyola.

From his exhaustive investigation of the Bible and ancient historical sources, Bacchiocchi concluded that "the adoption of Sunday in place of the Sabbath did not occur in the primitive Church of Jerusalem by virtue of apostolic authority, but approximately a century later in the Church of Rome. An interplay of Jewish, pagan and Christian factors contributed to the abandonment of the Sabbath and adoption of Sunday observance instead."[29]

Even so, many Christian authors still argue that the apostolic church began to keep Sunday shortly after Christ's resurrection. Yet, by reading the four Gospels' account of the resurrection, written many years later, one can find only ordinary references to "the first day of the week" (Matthew 28:1; Mark 16:1, 2; Luke 23:54–24:1; John 20:1, 19, 26), with no allusion whatsoever to Sunday worship. The disciples met together on that very same day with the doors shut, not to celebrate the resurrection but because they were afraid of the Jews (John 20:19, 26).

These and other pieces of biblical evidence confirm the abiding nature of the seventh-day Sabbath as the covenantal sign between God and His children. The Sabbath was originally instituted for all humanity at the end of the Creation week (Genesis 2:1–3), it comes to us every week as God's unchanged sanctuary in time (Isaiah 58:12–14), and it will continue to be observed after the world is restored to its original perfection (Isaiah 66:22, 23). Every Sabbath, we are invited to enter God's delightful rest and to receive its wonderful blessings (Hebrews 4:4, 9–11).

CHAMELEON SYNDROME

"And they shall teach My people the difference between the holy and the unholy, and cause them to discern between the unclean and the clean."
—Ezekiel 44:23

M any animals camouflage themselves by blending in with various features of their surroundings. Potential victims do it instinctively to hide from predators. On the other hand, predators camouflage themselves to surprise their victims. For self-defense, some chameleons can adjust their colors in relation to the vision of the specific predator species by which they are being threatened. Likewise, many Christians minimize the opposition of the world by attempting to blend in with the surrounding culture. By doing so, they obscure the sinfulness of sin.

The **June 15, 1876**, issue of *Signs of the Times* carried an insightful article by Ellen White titled "Christ's Teachings." In this article, she warned,

The greatest danger of the world is, that sin does not appear sinful. This is the greatest evil existing in the church; sin is glossed over with self-complacency. Blessed indeed are they who possess a sensitive conscience; who can weep and mourn over their spiritual poverty and wanderings from God; who are poor in spirit and can receive the reproof God sends them; and who, with confessions and brokenness of heart, will take their places, all penitent, in humiliation at the cross of Christ. God knows it is good for men to tread a hard and humble path, to encounter difficulties, to experience disappointments, and to suffer affliction. Faith strengthens by coming in conflict with doubt, and resisting unbelief through the strength of Jesus.

Excusing sin does not change its sinful nature; it only makes us more vulnerable to it. According to Ellen White, "Conformity to worldly customs converts the church to the world; it never converts the world to Christ. Familiarity with sin will inevitably cause it to appear less repulsive."[30] Addressing this conformity to the world, Ezekiel 44:23 says that the leaders of God's people must teach them "the difference between the holy and the unholy, and cause them to discern between the unclean and the clean." But before we can effectively teach this distinction to others, we must be able to recognize it and be convinced of it ourselves.

ℱAITH ℱHAT 𝒥USTIFIES

Therefore, having been justified by faith, we have peace with God through
our Lord Jesus Christ, through whom also we have access by faith into this
grace in which we stand, and rejoice in hope of the glory of God.

—Romans 5:1, 2

J esus Christ died for the whole world, and His saving grace is available to all human beings. If this is the case, why will not all human beings be saved? Justification by faith is the dividing line between being saved and remaining lost. It is by faith alone that we can appropriate to ourselves the saving grace of Jesus Christ. But what is justifying faith?

German theologian Artur Weiser wrote, "Faith is always man's reaction to God's primary action."[31] In other words, God first reveals Himself to us, and we then accept His revelation by faith. According to Ellen White, "Faith is the gift of God, but the power to exercise it is ours. Faith is the hand by which the soul takes hold upon the divine offers of grace and mercy."[32]

In his table talk of **June 16, 1539**, Martin Luther stated, "Faith justifies not as a work, or as a quality, or as knowledge, but as assent of the will and firm confidence in the mercy of God. For if faith were only knowledge, then the devil would certainly be saved because he possesses the greatest knowledge of God and of all the works and wonders of God from the creation of the world."[33]

Remember, faith *without* doctrinal knowledge leads to rootless and unstable credulity. It is like a boat without a rudder in the middle of the ocean. On the other hand, faith *restricted to* such knowledge becomes dry and presumptuous. It generates self-proclaimed Christians with big brains and empty hearts. In contrast, justifying faith *presupposes* right doctrinal knowledge, but it reaches *beyond* that knowledge into the very presence of God, where Jesus Christ as our Great High Priest is offering His saving grace to every true believer.

One of our greatest temptations is to assume that the right doctrine of salvation can save us. But we must combine the right doctrine *about* Christ and a saving experience *with* Him. Praise God if you already have that experience. If not, you can pray as the man who said to Jesus, "I do believe; help me overcome my unbelief" (Mark 9:24, NIV).

ᏠHE ᏸROKEN STONE

They also said, "Men of Galilee, why do you stand looking into the sky?
This Jesus, who has been taken up from you into heaven, will come
in just the same way as you have watched Him go into heaven."
—Acts 1:11, NASB

M any faithful Adventist missionaries have sacrificed their lives in carrying the ever-lasting gospel to the remotest places of the world. The **June 17, 1909**, issue of the *Advent Review and Sabbath Herald* announced that the General Conference voted Ferdinand A. Stahl of Ohio as a missionary to Bolivia.[34] A few days later, he and his wife, with their two children, left for the mission field. They dedicated themselves to amazing medical-missionary and teaching work among the Indians of Lake Titicaca and other regions of Bolivia and Peru.

In his book *In the Land of the Incas*, Stahl tells of his experience with the local people in a place called Umucho. After Stahl told them that Jesus was coming soon to reclaim His faithful people, the natives responded very positively. At the end of the service, the chief asked Stahl when he could come back to teach them more. Stahl was reluctant to commit, but the chief insisted. So, Stahl promised, "If I do not return, someone else will."[35]

The chief asked, "But how am I to know that someone else will teach us the same things?"[36]

Stahl picked up a small stone, broke it in two, and gave one half of it to the chief. He added that whoever should come to teach them would bring the other half of the stone.[37] Three years later, Stahl returned to the Umucho district and went to see the chief, who was away for a few weeks. But his wife came and asked, "Oh, why did you stay away so long?"[38] The tribespeople had been very eager to learn more about the Adventist message. Shortly after arriving, Stahl declared,

Bolivia surely is a good field for labor, because it is a very needy one. It has been my privilege to make a country trip, and I have observed the same conditions everywhere—gross darkness, people living for they know not what. . . .

. . . But these difficulties are an inspiration to us. The greater the difficulties, the more help we can claim from God. The greater the hardships, the more closely we cling to Christ, who knows all about them, having suffered all things for us.[39]

A self-sacrificing spirit should inspire our efforts too.

𝒯HE 𝒲IRE 𝓕ENCE

Now may the God of patience and comfort grant you to be like-minded
toward one another, according to Christ Jesus, that you may with one mind
and one mouth glorify the God and Father of our Lord Jesus Christ.
—Romans 15:5, 6

F ences usually divide and separate people—those on one side of the fence are separated
from those on the other side. But with a change of perspective, a fence can also be
a symbol of unity.

Michel Quoist (1918–1997) was born on **June 18, 1918**, in Le Havre, France. He
became a Roman Catholic priest and writer, author of the best-selling book *Prayers of Life*,
originally published in 1954. In his prayer "The Wire Fence," Quoist highlights unity:

The wires are holding hands around the holes;
To avoid breaking the ring, they hold tight the neighboring wrist,
And it's thus that with holes they make a fence.
Lord, there are lots of holes in my life.
There are some in the lives of my neighbors.
But if you wish, we shall hold hands,
We shall hold very tight,
And together we shall make a fine roll of fence to adorn Paradise.[40]

But genuine unity cannot be achieved by human effort. Ellen White says that it can
be accomplished only through Christ. She explains,

The cause of division and discord in families and in the church is separation from Christ.
To come near to Christ is to come near to one another. The secret of true unity in the
church and in the family is not diplomacy, not management, not a superhuman effort to
overcome difficulties—though there will be much of this to do—but union with Christ.

Picture a large circle, from the edge of which are many lines all running to the
center. The nearer these lines approach the center, the nearer they are to one another.

Thus it is in the Christian life. The closer we come to Christ, the nearer we shall
be to one another. God is glorified as His people unite in harmonious action.[41]

May our union with Christ hold us close together as families and as church members!

$\mathcal{T}$HE 1888 $\mathcal{M}$ESSAGE

If indeed you have heard Him and have been taught by Him, as the truth is in Jesus.
—Ephesians 4:21

Several Seventh-day Adventist independent ministries are dedicated to proclaiming "the 1888 message." Such claims refer to the doctrinal presentations and discussions during the General Conference Session in Minneapolis, Minnesota (which was held from October 17 to November 4, 1888), as well as the Ministerial Council that started a week earlier. The topics addressed included the identification of the ten prophetic horns of Daniel 7, the law in Galatians 3, and righteousness by faith. But how should we understand that message?

On August 5, 1888, Ellen White wrote an open letter to the delegates who would attend the 1888 General Conference Session. She began by saying, "We are impressed that this gathering will be the most important meeting you have ever attended. This should be a period of earnestly seeking the Lord and humbling your hearts before Him. I hope you will regard this as a most precious opportunity to pray and counsel together." Later in the letter, she added, "The correct interpretation of the Scriptures is not all that God requires. He enjoins upon us that we should not only know the truth, but that we should practice the truth as it is in Jesus."[42]

During the meetings, Ellen White heartily endorsed the Christ-centered messages presented by Alonzo T. Jones and Ellet J. Waggoner. But some read into her support more than she had intended. Her endorsement was for the *messages* presented, not the human *messengers*.

On **June 19, 1889**, Ellen White addressed this in a sermon in Rome, New York. She explained, "I have had the question asked, What do you think of this light that these men are presenting? Why, I have been presenting it to you for the last forty-five years—the matchless charms of Christ. This is what I have been trying to present before your minds. When Brother Waggoner brought out these ideas in Minneapolis, it was the first clear teaching on this subject from any human lips I had heard, excepting the conversations between myself and my husband."[43]

For Mrs. White, the central emphasis of the 1888 message was the same theme she had always presented—"the matchless charms of Christ" and "the truth as it is in Jesus." A deep and *personal* experience with Him is at the heart of righteousness by faith.

CARING FOR HEALTH

*Do you not know that your body is the temple of the Holy Spirit who is in you, whom you
have from God, and you are not your own? For you were bought at a price; therefore glorify
God in your body and in your spirit, which are God's.*

—1 Corinthians 6:19, 20

The church was financially depleted. Why should a third medical institution be placed
in southern California? On October 10, 1901, Ellen White wrote in her diary that
she saw a pleasant sanitarium in southern California with fruit trees on the grounds.
Some patients were in wheelchairs, and others were outdoors under shade trees with
birds singing. The place seemed familiar to her, as if she had spent months there. In
1904, Seventh-day Adventists bought a property near San Diego where the Paradise
Valley Hospital and the Glendale Adventist Medical Center would eventually be built.
But neither of them was what Mrs. White had seen in vision.

Following Ellen White's leading, Pastor John A. Burden borrowed $1,000 on a personal
note for a down payment that he made on May 29, 1905, securing the Loma Linda
Hotel and surrounding property. Two weeks later, on June 12, Mrs. White arrived at
Loma Linda for the first time. "Willie, I have been here before," she stated to her son. He
responded, "No, Mother, you have never been here." She added, "Then this is the very
place the Lord has shown me, for it is all familiar. We must have this place. We should
reason from cause to effect. The Lord has not given us this property for any common
purpose."[44]

On **June 20, 1905**, delegates of nearly all twenty-two churches of the Southern California Conference endorsed the purchase, which was finally settled at $38,900. The
sanitarium opened in November of that year. But Ellen White envisioned the institution
as more—she urged that it become a medical school. For her, "the healing of the sick
and the ministry of the Word are to go hand in hand."[45] She added, "The medical school
at Loma Linda is to be of the highest order" and should enable the students "to pass the
examinations required by law of all who practice as regularly qualified physicians."[46]

Over the years, Loma Linda University has been driven by this noble ideal of excellence.
Its history reminds us of what God can do for us if we follow His lead, even under adverse
circumstances. God knows the future, though it is still unknown to us!

A TIMELESS MESSAGE

"But about that day or hour no one knows, not even the angels in heaven, nor the Son, but only the Father. Be on guard! Be alert! You do not know when that time will come."
—Mark 13:32, 33, NIV

Jesus warned against predicting the time of His return. But many have ignored the warnings and ventured into that kind of speculation. After the October 1844 disappointment, Sunday-keeping Adventists proposed at least twenty-one new dates for the Second Coming. Even within Sabbath-keeping Adventist circles, Joseph Bates suggested that the seven times the high priest sprinkled the blood before the mercy seat (Leviticus 16:14) represented seven years that should be reckoned from the fall of 1844 to the fall of 1851. But every speculation has failed!

By November 1850, Ellen White had written, "The Lord showed me that TIME had not been a test since 1844, and that time will never again be a test."[47] On **June 21, 1851**, while at Camden, New York, she received a vision warning against attempting to place the fulfillment of any time prophecy beyond October 1844. She explained, "The Lord showed me that the message must go, and that it must not be hung on time; for time will never be a test again. I saw that some were getting a false excitement, arising from preaching time, that the third angel's message can stand on its own foundation, and that it needs not time to strengthen it, and that it will go with mighty power, and do its work, and will be cut short in righteousness."[48]

Despite these and many other subsequent admonitions by Ellen White, some individuals always find a way to justify their personal fascination with time-setting. Some argue that Jesus forbade us only from knowing "the day and hour" of His coming (Matthew 24:36; Mark 13:32) but not the specific year. Others claim that we cannot know the specific date of the Second Coming but that some time prophecies, such as the 1,290 and 1,335 days (Daniel 12:11, 12), are still to be fulfilled in the future.

Some prophetic theories might sound very logical and convincing. But those who take Christ's warnings and Ellen White's admonitions seriously will not venture into such ungrounded fantasies. The Adventist message does not need this kind of crutch to move forward.

"MOTHER OF GOD"

*Now the birth of Jesus the Messiah took place in this way. When
his mother Mary had been engaged to Joseph, but before they lived
together, she was found to be with child from the Holy Spirit.*

—Matthew 1:18, NRSV

I f Mary, the mother of Jesus, were raised from the dead, how do you think she would react to all that has been said about her over the centuries? In the Gospel record, we find an angel telling her, "Rejoice, highly favored one, the Lord is with you; blessed are you among women" (Luke 1:28). But much has been added by Christian tradition and endorsed by ecclesiastical decisions.

Four major ecclesiastical decisions contributed to the exaltation of Mary. First, she was given the title "Mother of God." The Third Ecumenical Council, convening at the Church of Mary in Ephesus, Anatolia, opened on **June 22, AD 431**. That assembly officially recognized Mary as "God-bearer" and condemned those who considered her only as "Christ-bearer."

The next church proclamation upheld Mary's perpetual virginity. The Second Council of Constantinople in 553 called her "the holy and glorious Mother of God and *ever virgin* Mary."

The third doctrinal advance was the dogma of Mary's Immaculate Conception. The papal bull *Ineffabilis Deus* of 1854 declared that since the first instant of her conception, "the Blessed Virgin Mary" "was preserved free from all stain of original sin."[49]

The fourth assertion was to recognize Mary as a "Mediatrix of Divine grace." The papal encyclical *Iucunda Semper Expectatione* (released in 1894) stated, "The recourse we have to Mary in prayer follows upon the office she continuously fills by the side of the throne of God as Mediatrix of Divine grace."[50] Furthermore, Catholic cardinals and bishops have petitioned the Vatican to also recognize Mary as co-Redeemer and co-Mediator with Christ.

As blessed as Mary was in being the mother of Jesus, the Bible does not endorse any of these assertions. And they are based on the unbiblical notion of the natural immortality of the soul. Nowhere does the New Testament venerate Mary as the mother of God. If unfallen angels do not accept worship (Revelation 22:8, 9), how could she as a human? And we have only "one Mediator between God and men, the Man Christ Jesus" (1 Timothy 2:5). As stated by Peter, "there is no other name" besides Christ by which we can be saved (Acts 4:12).

ᴀ ᴅᴏᴜʙʟᴇ ʟɪꜰᴇ

Draw near to God and He will draw near to you. Cleanse your hands, you sinners; and purify your hearts, you double-minded.

—James 4:8

Some people lead a double life. One is their *public* life—how they want to be viewed by others. The other is their *hidden* life, which is kept secret. But why do people behave like this? James Harvey Robinson (1863–1936) suggested, "Speech gave man a unique power to lead a double life; he could say one thing and do another."[51] But double lives usually evolve from the human tendency to cover up sinful and immoral behaviors.

There have always been a variety of ways for people to maintain hidden parallel lives. But, on **June 23, 2003**, the website Second Life went live. This and similar immersive internet-based websites allow people to escape from the real world into the virtual world, where they can start new and exciting "relationships" and pursue whatever fantasies they please. In most cases, parallel relationships are kept secret from parents, spouses, and children.

In his insightful book *John Ploughman's Talk*, Charles H. Spurgeon included a chapter entitled "Men With Two Faces," in which he warns, "You may trust some men as far as you can see them, but no further, for new company makes them new men. Like water, they boil or freeze according to the temperature."[52] And he adds, "It is not all who go to church or meeting that truly pray, nor those who sing loudest that praise God most, nor those who pull the longest faces who are the most in earnest."[53]

I, of course, don't know if you are leading a double life. Perhaps not. But if you are allowing a cherished sin to corrupt your spiritual and moral integrity, then I invite you to surrender your private life to the Lord today. Ask Him for strength to overcome your weakness. You can do it privately. No one else needs to know about it.

The inspired counsel for us today is, "Draw near to God and He will draw near to you. Cleanse your hands, you sinners; and purify your hearts, you double-minded" (James 4:8). God can bring consistency to your inconsistencies so that your private life is in full harmony with your public image. The price you must pay for giving up your sin is nothing compared to the peace of mind that will be yours!

SUCCESS WITH HUMILITY

Thus says the LORD:
"Let not the wise man glory in his wisdom,
Let not the mighty man glory in his might,
Nor let the rich man glory in his riches."

—Jeremiah 9:23

One of the greatest challenges in life is how to combine success with humility. One person who seemed to understand this balance was the race car driver Juan Manuel Fangio, born on **June 24, 1911**, in Balcarce, Argentina. During the 1950s, Fangio won the Formula One World Championship five times.[54] His career was shaped largely by his motto: "You must always believe you will become the best, but you must never believe you have done."[55]

Lionel Messi, one of the most successful soccer players ever, was born on **June 24, 1987**, in Rosario, Argentina, and is extremely skilled and very well paid. Messi won the Ballon d'Or award—soccer's highest prize—more often than anyone else. Commenting in *MoneyWeek* magazine, Messi stated: "Money is not a motivating factor. Money doesn't thrill me or make me play better because there are benefits to being wealthy. I'm just happy with a ball at my feet. My motivation comes from playing the game I love. If I wasn't paid to be a professional footballer, I would willingly play for nothing."[56]

Whether we are active in sports or in any other human endeavor, we should always ask ourselves, "At the bottom line, what motivates my behavior? Why am I trying to be better than everybody else?" According to Jeremiah 9:23, there is nothing wrong with being "wise," "mighty," or even "rich," as long as it does not become an obsession and a source of self-exaltation. According to Ellen White, "men are not [to] be exalted as great and wonderful. It is God who is to be magnified."[57] And "self-surrender is the substance of the teachings of Christ."[58]

Growing in Christ means becoming less self-centered and more Christ-centered. This means that we should never consider ourselves stars that make our own light but planets that reflect the wonderful light of Christ, the "Sun of Righteousness" (Malachi 4:2). All our skills and achievements should bring glory and honor to God, the Creator and Sustainer of our lives. In Paul's words, "Whether you eat or drink, or whatever you do, do all to the glory of God" (1 Corinthians 10:31).

$\mathcal{M}$URPHY'S $\mathcal{L}$AW

Even though I walk
through the darkest valley,
I will fear no evil,
for you are with me;
your rod and your staff,
they comfort me.

—Psalm 23:4, NIV

Have you ever had a day when everything seemed to go wrong? If it was just a day, you should be very thankful. For some people, the "unlucky day" seems like it lasts forever.

Roy Cleveland Sullivan (1912–1983) was born in Greene County, Virginia. He was hit by lightning in 1942 when he was thirty years old; a second time in 1969; a third in 1970; a fourth in 1972; a fifth in 1973; a sixth in 1976; and, finally, a seventh on **June 25, 1977**. All seven strikes were documented by the superintendent of the Shenandoah National Park. Sullivan claimed that even as a child, he had been struck by lightning, but it was never documented. For those who are curious about the mathematical chances, the probability of a person being struck by lightning seven times would be $1:10^{28}$.

Superstitious people might conclude that Sullivan was cursed. Others could say he was a victim of Murphy's Law, which states that if anything can go wrong, it will. This "law" was coined by an American, Captain Edward A. Murphy (1918–1990), who, in 1949, was working with a team of engineers on a US Air Force project designed to find out how much sudden deceleration a person can stand in a crash. When an engineer wrongly installed some cables and wires on the project, Murphy blamed him, saying, "If there is any way to do it wrong, he will." However, others had made similar statements before.

Whatever truth Murphy's Law may contain, it is too general and too pessimistic. Yes, one could apply the law to Roy Sullivan, but what about the overwhelming majority of the world population who never experience even a single lightning strike? Furthermore, the law does not take into account God's loving discipline of His creatures (Revelation 3:19).

Even when things go wrong, we should never forget that God cares for us all of the time, on our sunny days and during the cloudy ones. As stated by King David,

Even though I walk
through the darkest valley,
I will fear no evil,
for you are with me;
your rod and your staff,
they comfort me (Psalm 23:4, NIV).

Look at the beautiful roses along the way and ignore the thorns!

June 26

$\mathcal{P}$ROTON $\mathcal{T}$HERAPY

For all have sinned and fall short of the glory of God, and all are justified
freely by his grace through the redemption that came by Christ Jesus.
—Romans 3:23, 24, NIV

The World Health Organization identifies cancer as the second leading cause of death globally. This generic term refers to a large group of diseases characterized by the abnormal growth of cells beyond their usual boundaries. These cells can invade adjoining parts of the body and even spread to other organs.[59] Loma Linda University in Southern California is a world leader in cancer treatment.

In 1970, Dr. James M. Slater and his cancer-therapy team began developing a system that could take full advantage of the potential for treating patients with heavily charged particles. The purpose was to accurately guide an external radiation beam to an invisible target inside the patient. In 1985, as part of his ambitious undertaking, Dr. Slater proposed that the university build the world's first in-hospital proton accelerator that would be capable of a more precise form of radiation treatment.

Despite strong initial opposition, the $45 million Proton Therapy Center was eventually built—the first of its kind in the nation. The first patient, who had an ocular tumor, was treated on October 23, 1990. The treatment of brain tumors began in March 1991, and treatments using a rotation gantry began on **June 26, 1991**. More than 150 people are treated each day at the center.

The ongoing efforts to cure cancer, or at least to keep it under control, can teach us significant spiritual lessons. What cancer is to the body, sin is to our spiritual and moral lives. Billy Graham stated, "Sin is like cancer. It destroys step by step. Slowly, without realizing its insidious onslaught, it progresses until finally the diagnosis is pronounced: sick to death."[60]

Thankfully, however, Christ's sacrifice to cure us of our sins is infinitely more efficient than proton therapy is to fight cancer. According to Paul, "All have sinned and fall short of the glory of God." But he goes on to joyfully say, "All are justified freely by his grace through the redemption that came by Christ Jesus" (Romans 3:23, 24, NIV). While some cancers are still incurable, every sin repented of is 100 percent curable through Christ's sacrifice on the cross. Praise the Lord for it!

"The Blind Shall See"

In that day the deaf shall hear the words of the book, and the eyes
of the blind shall see out of obscurity and out of darkness.

—Isaiah 29:18

We have this wonderful promise that in God's everlasting kingdom, "the deaf shall hear" and "the blind shall see" (Isaiah 29:18). A foretaste of it was seen during Christ's earthly ministry (Matthew 11:2–5). But even today, we can make a difference in the lives of those with special needs.

Helen Adams Keller (1880–1968) was born in Tuscumbia, Alabama, on **June 27, 1880**. When she was only nineteen months old, she contracted an illness—diagnosed as "brain fever"—that left her both deaf and blind. Beginning in 1887, Anne Sullivan became Helen's teacher and companion, helping her develop the ability to communicate. In 1904, Keller became the first deaf and blind person to earn a bachelor of arts degree. As an icon for overcoming blindness, dumbness, and deafness, she visited with many dignitaries and traveled the world, presenting lectures on optimism and hope and promoting humanitarian causes.

Over time, Keller developed a very positive and inspiring attitude. Her statements express a rich life experience. On overcoming problems, she stated, "Although the world is full of suffering, it is full also of the overcoming of it."[61] Based on her own struggles, she could say, "Character cannot be developed in ease and quiet. Only through experience of trial and suffering can the soul be strengthened, vision cleared, ambition inspired, and success achieved."[62]

Keller also emphasized the value of identifying and using our opportunities. She warned, "When one door of happiness closes, another opens; but often we look so long at the closed door that we do not see the one which has been opened for us."[63] About her own attitude, she said, "To what is good I open the doors of my being, and jealously shut them against what is bad."[64]

And she recognized that "the best and most beautiful things in the world cannot be seen or even touched, but just felt in the heart."[65]

As mentioned earlier, Helen Keller overcame her physical limitations thanks largely to Anne Sullivan, whose eyes and ears provided her with vision and hearing. While we wait in hope for the final restoration from all our physical limitations (Revelation 21:4), we can also make a difference in the lives of those with special needs.

𝒯HE 𝒧ANGUAGE OF 𝒞LOTHES

The royal daughter is all glorious within the palace; her clothing is woven with gold. She shall be brought to the King in robes of many colors.
—Psalm 45:13, 14

On **June 28, 1837**, at only eighteen years old, Queen Victoria was crowned as monarch of the powerful United Kingdom and Ireland. No more than 5 feet (1.52 meters) tall, she reigned for sixty-three years and influenced the lifestyle (including the clothing styles) of the Victorian era. Before her reign (1837–1901), "men were the focus of fashion, but with a queen in power, women surged to the forefront. The role of a wife became to show off her husband's status and wealth to the public, with the husband himself receding into the background."[66]

Many other leading figures and stars have influenced people's lifestyles. But religious dialog about fashion and clothing tends to be hot, divisive, and even competitive. Some believe that a true Christian should never follow the world's fashion. Others argue that one can dress as he or she likes because what matters is the *inner* person and not the *outer*. Unquestionably, the inner person is the source of outer behavior (Mark 7:21–23). But clothes are much more than just a means of covering our bodies. They reveal our personal taste, social status, and moral values.

In her book *The Language of Clothes*, Alison Lurie states, "For thousands of years human beings have communicated with one another first in the language of dress. Long before I am near enough to talk to you on the street, in a meeting, or at a party, you announce your sex, age and class to me through what you are wearing—and very possibly give me important information (or misinformation) as to your occupation, origin, personality, opinions, tastes, sexual desires and current mood. I may not be able to put what I observe into words, but I register the information unconsciously; and you simultaneously do the same for me."[67]

So, if a Christian is "the salt of the earth" and "the light of the world" (Matthew 5:13–16), how should he or she dress? There are helpful Bible principles dealing with this subject (1 Timothy 2:9, 10; 1 Peter 3:3, 4). But in a nutshell, a true Christian should dress in his or her culture as the people with high moral values and good reputations do in that specific culture.

$\mathcal{E}$VANGELISTIC $\mathcal{E}$THICS

Paul replied, "Whether quickly or not, I pray to God that not only you but also all who are listening to me today might become such as I am—except for these chains."
—Acts 26:29, NRSV

E vangelism is the heartbeat of the church and the very reason for its existence. But how far can we go in evangelizing people without infringing on their religious liberty? This crucial question is briefly addressed in the document "A Seventh-day Adventist Statement on Religious Liberty, Evangelism, and Proselytism," released at the General Conference Session in Toronto, Ontario, Canada, which opened on **June 29, 2000**. The document recognizes that "freedom of religion is a basic human right,"[68] meaning that no coercive evangelistic method should ever be used. Seventh-day Adventists believe that "faith and religion are best disseminated when convictions are manifested and taught with humility and respect, and the witness of one's life is in harmony with the message announced, evoking a free and joyous acceptance by those being evangelized."[69]

When inviting others to join their church, Seventh-day Adventists should be respectful of other churches. C. Mervyn Maxwell (1925–1999) declared,

When Adventists invite a friend to leave his denomination and become a Seventh-day Adventist, they don't expect him to give up everything he knows as a Methodist or Baptist or Presbyterian or Catholic. Far from it! Every beautiful facet of truth he learned about Jesus in his former church, he should cherish even more warmly in the Seventh-day Adventist Church, adding to the glorious things he already knows the great and virtual truth discovered by Seventh-day Adventists.

When an Adventist says he has "the truth," he is not boasting. It isn't his truth. It's God's truth; truth which God has revealed, not to satisfy curiosity, but to be spread everywhere to everyone who will listen, to everyone for whom Christ gave His life and whom He lives to save.[70]

Some people overemphasize religious freedom to the point of undermining Christ's great gospel commission (Matthew 28:18–20). Others stress proselytism to the extent that people can no longer decide for themselves. We should preach the gospel with the same conviction and intentionality as Paul but always allow people the right to decide for themselves.

WALLS AND BRIDGES

*For he himself is our peace, who has made the two groups one
and has destroyed the barrier, the dividing wall of hostility.*
—Ephesians 2:14, NIV

China has some of the most impressive man-made structures in the world. One is the famous Great Wall of China, which began to be built around 221 BC under the order of Emperor Qin Shi Huang. As a means of preventing incursions from barbarian nomads into the Chinese Empire, the wall was significantly expanded over the centuries. A preliminary survey suggested that it was only 5,500 miles (8,851 kilometers) long. But in 2012, more accurate archaeological studies revealed that the historic structure (including a series of fortifications) was actually 13,170 miles (21,195 kilometers) long.

Another impressive Chinese structure is the Danyang-Kunshan Grand Bridge, a 102-mile (164-kilometer) elevated high-speed rail line between Shanghai and Nanjing. It crosses the Yangtze River Delta with its lowland rice paddies, canals, rivers, and lakes. Constructed in a mere four years by up to ten thousand laborers, the bridge was finished in 2010 and opened for commercial service on **June 30, 2011**. It is by far the longest bridge ever made. So, China has both the longest wall and the longest bridge in the world.

The gospel also invites us to build both strong *spiritual walls* to separate us from sin and concrete *social bridges* to bring us closer to sinners in need of salvation. But when it comes to interpersonal relationships, "We build too many walls and not enough bridges."[71] There are indeed many wall builders, carelessly separating marriages, families, and close friends. But there are also bridge builders who overcome all kinds of obstacles to reconcile broken relationships.

Jesus was an extremely social person who broke down many of the societal walls of His day. "In every human being He discerned infinite possibilities. He saw men as they might be, transfigured by His grace."[72] "If we would humble ourselves before God, and be kind and courteous and tenderhearted and pitiful, there would be one hundred conversions to the truth where now there is only one."[73]

How different would our world be if you and I were to become bridge builders to share God's saving love with those who are perishing!

TRUE MODERN MIRACLES

A thousand may fall at your side, and ten thousand at your right hand;
but it shall not come near you.
—Psalm 91:7

Modern charismatic miracles occur exclusively onstage in huge auditoriums and are broadcast to as many people as possible. God, however, does not depend on marketing strategies to work on behalf of His faithful servants (Matthew 7:21–23). In her inspiring book *A Thousand Shall Fall*, Susi Hasel Mundy tells the amazing story of how God miraculously protected her father, Franz Hasel, and their family in Hitler's Germany during World War II.[1]

As a Seventh-day Adventist pacifist, Franz Hasel "was drafted and assigned to Pioneer Company 699, Hitler's elite troops who built bridges at the front lines."[2] On **July 1, 1941**, the Pioneer Company was ordered to cross the Polish border and enter Ukraine. After days of marching, many of the soldiers were exhausted. Those unable to continue were simply left behind to die from illness or to be killed by the Russians. Franz was also worn out and burning with fever. His socks were in shreds, and huge blisters covered his swollen feet.

With no hope for the future, Franz prayed, "Dear Lord, You know that my life is committed to You. When I left home, I felt assured that You would bring me back safely to my family. Now You have given me another promise. But here I am, sick and unable to continue. Unless You help me, I am lost. I know that You are a promise-keeping God. I commit myself into Your hands."[3] Soon afterward, he fell asleep. At the wake-up call at 3:15 A.M., to his amazement, his feet were completely healed—covered with healthy skin and no scars! This was only one of the many threatening circumstances through which God protected him.

Of the twelve hundred men who comprised the Pioneer Company, only seven survived, and Franz was one of them. Franz indeed experienced God's protective care as promised in Psalm 91:7—"A thousand may fall at your side . . . ; but it shall not come near you." Back home, Franz's wife and children also witnessed the fulfillment of verse 10—"No evil shall befall you, nor shall any plague come near your dwelling." Unquestionably, God's power has not weakened, and His promises will never wear out. He cares for you and will never ever forsake you. He can protect you today as He did the Hasel family.

*L*IFE'S *T*URNING *P*OINTS

"Now it happened, as I journeyed and came near Damascus at about noon,
suddenly a great light from heaven shone around me. And I fell to the ground
and heard a voice saying to me, 'Saul, Saul, why are you persecuting Me?' "

—Acts 22:6, 7

Have you ever faced a threatening situation that radically changed the course of your life? Some bad situations are generated by our own mistakes. Others can result from following misleading advice. And some are completely out of our control—they just happen! Regardless of the cause, from that point on, our lives are often no longer the same.

Respecting his father's wishes, Martin Luther enrolled at the University of Erfurt to study law. He had a promising career ahead of him. Six weeks later, he took a short vacation to visit his parents in Mansfeld. On his return trip on **July 2, 1505**, Luther ran into a horrific thunderstorm and was thrown to the ground by a flash of lightning. Desperately he cried, "Help me, Saint Anna, I will become a monk!"[4] Because his father was a miner and Saint Anna was the patron of miners, Martin swore his vow to her.

Some skeptics consider Luther's thunderstorm experience a mere legend, but he described it as a fact. We can't know for sure whether, prior to this, he was already considering the possibility of becoming a monk. At any rate, it was a major turning point in his career and life. On the evening of July 16, he had a farewell dinner with his friends. The next morning, he entered the Augustinian Monastery at Erfurt—a city with so many monasteries that it was called "Little Rome." That was the beginning of a long spiritual journey from which he would emerge as a powerful Protestant Reformer.

"Life begins at the end of your comfort zone."[5] A terrifying lightning strike convinced Luther to give up his law studies and begin a new monastic life. A startling theophany (a personal appearing of Christ) near Damascus converted Saul from a persecutor of Christians to a tireless apostle of Christ. Likewise, God can take us out of our comfort zones and use us in His cause.

He is pleading with us today, "Whom shall I send? And who will go for Us?" Why should we wait for drastic measures to awaken us? May your answer and mine be as Isaiah's: "Here am I! Send me" (Isaiah 6:8).

$\mathcal{N}$EW $\mathcal{J}$ERUSALEM

Then I, John, saw the holy city, New Jerusalem, coming down out of heaven from God, prepared as a bride adorned for her husband.
—Revelation 21:2

M any Christians still believe that Israel will play a crucial role in the end-time eschatological scenario. For them, the Old Testament prophecies about the restoration of Jerusalem and the establishment of the Messianic kingdom (Zechariah 12–14) will be literally fulfilled. But for that to happen, the State of Israel must be established, and the temple of Jerusalem rebuilt on its original site on Mount Moriah (2 Chronicles 3:1).

Theodor Herzl (1860–1904) was an Austro-Hungarian journalist and political activist. He founded the World Zionist Organization and promoted Jewish migration to Palestine with the purpose of forming a Jewish state. He died on **July 3, 1904**. He is generally regarded as the father of the State of Israel, established forty-four years later.

In his popular book *The Late Great Planet Earth*, Hal Lindsey suggested that in 1948 the final prophetic countdown began, and forty years later (ca. 1988), an alleged tribulation of seven years would begin, at the end of which (ca. 1995) Christ would come to reign on a literal throne in the earthly Jerusalem.[6] But all those dates passed, and nothing happened. What went wrong with Lindsey's prophetic interpretation?

In Daniel 9, Gabriel spoke of the rebuilding of Jerusalem and the temple at the end of the seventy years the Babylonian captivity (Daniel 9:2). That was the starting point for both the seventy weeks of Daniel 9:24–27 and the twenty-three hundred symbolic days of Daniel 8:14. But nowhere does the Bible speak of the establishment of the State of Israel as the starting point for any end-time prophetic period, as suggested by Lindsey. Many Old Testament prophecies about the restoration of Jerusalem and the temple were fulfilled by the Jews who returned from the Babylonian captivity, as described in the books of Ezra and Nehemiah.

The eschatological expectations of the New Testament are not tied to the State of Israel or the Middle East. The New Jerusalem is a heavenly reality. Abraham waited for the heavenly city "whose builder and maker is God" (Hebrews 11:10). And God's children from all ages and from all over the world will serve Him before His throne in the heavenly temple (Revelation 7:15) in the New Jerusalem (Revelation 21:2). This is our glorious inheritance!

𝒯HE 𝓛EIPZIG 𝒟EBATE

He answered, "What's written in God's Law? How do you interpret it?"
—Luke 10:26, *The Message*

Have you ever argued with someone who does not see things from your perspective? Without common ground, the discussion can go on and on, almost forever, without much progress being made. That is what happened to Martin Luther at the famous 1519 Leipzig Debate, considered one of the greatest debates in history.

Tension was mounting between the emerging Protestant movement and the Roman Catholic Church. After some dialogue, both groups agreed to have an academic debate in Leipzig, Germany. The event officially opened on June 27, with Johann Eck defending the Roman Catholic Church and Andreas Carlstadt representing the Wittenberg Protestant party. With his rhetorical skills, Eck was persuading the audience. With his monotonous reading, Carlstadt was providing good content for the records but losing ground with the listeners.

Already in good standing with many observers, Eck believed that the time had come to bring Luther himself into the arena. On the morning of **July 4, 1519**, "the two greatest debaters of Germany" began to dispute. Luther realized that he was living out some of the most crucial days of his life. Too much was at stake for him to lose that debate! With no common ground between the disputers, a consensus was never reached. While Luther remained faithful to the reading of Scripture, Eck twisted the Bible to support the authority of the pope and Catholic tradition. The debate ended on July 14, with the audience divided according to their own personal prejudices and conflicting means of Bible interpretation.

We can learn some important lessons from this debate. First, it is not necessarily those who have the best rhetorical skills or who are most grounded in truth who prevail. In many cases, rhetoric is used to cover up illogical and distorted information. A second lesson we can learn is that, before we study the Bible with someone, we should make sure that he or she accepts its authority and is willing to allow it to interpret itself.

In a world with so many conflicting interpretations of the Bible, we are called by God to uplift "the Bible, and the Bible only, as the standard of all doctrines and the basis of all reforms."[7]

ᴅOLLY THE SHEEP

Through him all things were made; without him nothing was made that has been made. In him was life, and that life was the light of all mankind.
—John 1:3, 4, NIV

G od is the Source of life. His powerful word brought all living beings throughout His vast universe into existence. "By the word of the Lᴏʀᴅ the heavens were made, and all the host of them by the breath of His mouth." "For He spoke, and it was done; He commanded, and it stood fast" (Psalm 33:6, 9). As created beings themselves, humans are unable to create any form of life. But they have genetically manipulated existing life-forms.

On **July 5, 1996,** Dolly the sheep was born through a series of genetic and reproductive experiments implemented by the Roslin Institute in Edinburgh, Scotland. She "was cloned from a cell taken from the mammary gland of a six-year-old Finn Dorset sheep and an egg cell taken from a Scottish Blackface sheep."[8] Since then, many other large mammals have been successfully cloned. Those experiments could open the door for the development of a new genetically modified human generation.

In February 1997, President Bill Clinton asked the American National Bioethics Advisory Commission to study the legal and ethical issues involved. The commission concluded that it was "morally unacceptable for anyone in the public or private sector, whether in a research or clinical setting, to attempt to create a child using somatic cell nuclear transfer cloning."[9]

On November 11, 1997, UNESCO's Universal Declaration on the Human Genome and Human Rights asserted, "Practices which are contrary to human dignity, such as reproductive cloning of human beings, shall not be permitted."[10] In January 1998, French president Jacques Chirac called for a global prohibition of human cloning.[11] But how long will the scientific community abide by those restrictions?

Unquestionably, genetic experiments have helped solve some genetic diseases previously considered incurable. But some genetic experiments are disrespectful to God and His amazing creation, which originally "was very good" (Genesis 1:31). We should remember that God created humanity in His own image and likeness (verse 26), and we should respect it as such. Let us allow God to be God and His creation to remain as He originally intended.

WITNESSING THROUGH THE FLAMES

For I am already being poured out as a drink offering, and the time of my departure is at hand. I have fought the good fight, I have finished the race, I have kept the faith. Finally, there is laid up for me the crown of righteousness, which the Lord, the righteous Judge, will give to me on that Day, and not to me only but also to all who have loved His appearing.
—2 Timothy 4:6–8

If you were to visit the imperial city of Constance in southern Germany in early July 1415, you would see that the town was overrun with people. They were there for the famous Council of Constance (1414–1418), which was convened (1) to settle the issues between three rival popes—Gregory XII, Benedict XIII, and John XXIII—each claiming to be the true successor of Peter; (2) to reform ecclesiastical government and moral life; and (3) to eradicate heresy.

On Saturday, **June 6, 1415**, in the early morning, Jan Hus, an influential professor at the University of Prague, appeared before the council that had assembled in the Cathedral of Constance. Hus was officially sentenced as an ecclesiastical outcast and criminal. Six bishops carried out the rite of degradation. They removed his vestments, destroyed his tonsure, put a cap covered with pictures of the devil and inscribed with the word "heresiarch" on his head, and committed his soul to the devil. Escorted through the streets of Constance, Hus could see his books being burned at the public square.

At the place of execution, the reformer's arms were fastened behind his back; his neck was bound to the stake by a chain, and straw and wood were heaped up around his body. For the last time, the offer of life was renewed if he would recant. But Hus responded, "I shall die with joy today in the faith of the Gospel which I have preached." As the flames arose, twice he sang, "Christ, thou Son of the living God, have mercy upon me." The wind blew the fire into Hus's face, silencing his voice. He died praying and singing. Hus's execution stirred the Bohemian nation, and his reformation cause was carried on by the Hussites and later by Martin Luther.

Jan Hus reflected the spirit of the martyrs who preferred to die rather than betray their Lord and Savior. Hus shall receive his "crown of righteousness" (2 Timothy 4:8). What about you and me? Do we have the same spirit?

A Lucky Day?

Then God blessed the seventh day and sanctified it, because in it
He rested from all His work which God had created and made.

—Genesis 2:3

Since ancient times, the number seven has been considered a symbol of completeness and perfection. The climax of joy and contentment is often referred to as "being in seventh heaven." No wonder there was so much mystical expectation about Saturday, **July 7, 2007**. That date happened to be the seventh day of the week, plus the seventh day of the seventh month of the seventh year of the millennium—expressed numerically: 7/7/07.

Many gamblers believed that the day would be a lucky day. The wedding-planning website, TheKnot.com, had thirty-eight thousand couples register 7/7/07 as their wedding date—more than triple the number of couples being married on any other day of the year. In addition, Live Earth: The Concerts for a Climate in Crisis was held in several places around the world.

Meanwhile, in many Brazilian cities, the Seventh-day Adventist Church organized special events emphasizing the seventh-day Sabbath as the Dia Mundial da Alegria (World Day of Joy). I participated in that major crusade, preaching on the meaning of the Sabbath at the campus church of São Paulo Adventist University—Engenheiro Coelho. What a joy to celebrate the Sabbath on the seventh day, according to the commandment (see Exodus 20:8–11).

The Sabbath comes to us every week, interrupting our frenetic and competitive life routine and reminding us of our spiritual priorities. It is God's sanctuary in time, telling us that *life* is more important than *things* and inviting us to spend special time with Him and with our fellow human beings. The Sabbath is a channel of God's blessings to humanity and a prototype of the Sabbath the redeemed will keep throughout eternity (Isaiah 66:22, 23).

God's invitation and promise for us today is,

"If you keep your feet from breaking the Sabbath
    and from doing as you please on my holy day,
if you call the Sabbath a delight
    and the Lord's holy day honorable,
and if you honor it by not going your own way
    and not doing as you please or speaking idle words,
then you will find your joy in the Lord,
    and I will cause you to ride in triumph on the heights of the land
and to feast on the inheritance of your father Jacob" (Isaiah 58:13, 14, NIV).

$\mathcal{N}$O $\mathcal{E}$VERLASTING $\mathcal{H}$ELL

"That will leave them neither root nor branch."

—Malachi 4:1

H ave you ever imagined what it would be like to spend eternity suffering in hell? Many Christian preachers and authors have portrayed hell in the most dramatic way possible. For example, on **July 8, 1741**, Jonathan Edwards, a famous eighteenth-century American theologian and preacher, frightened his audience in Enfield, Connecticut, with his famous sermon "Sinners in the Hands of an Angry God." He stated straightforwardly that at any moment, the impenitent listeners could be swallowed into "the glowing flames of the wrath of God," having to unceasingly suffer in hell for "millions and millions of ages."[12] No wonder the audience begged so loudly for God's mercy that Edwards was unable to finish his sermon.

Much of the medieval notion of hell was expressed in Dante Alighieri's epic poem *Divine Comedy*, in which he says hell is inside the earth and reached through nine circles of suffering. In his booklet *The Sight of Hell*, English Roman Catholic priest John Furniss (1809–1865) illustrates the length of eternal torment using a "great solid iron ball, larger than the heavens and the earth. A bird comes once in a hundred millions of years and just touches the great iron ball with a feather of its wing."[13] The burning of sinners in hell continues even after that iron ball is worn away by such occasional touches of a feather! But if life on this earth is so short (Psalm 90:9, 10), why would God punish the impenitent sinners so severely and for all eternity?

As a child and teenager, Ellen Harmon (later White) was much troubled with the notion of an eternally burning hell. In her mind, "the justice of God eclipsed His mercy and love" until she understood the biblical teaching that human beings are not naturally immortal and that all impenitent sinners will be destroyed.[14] Later on, she even wrote that the exclusion of the wicked from heaven and their final destruction are acts of God's mercy to them.[15]

Sin and suffering had a beginning and were not part of God's original plan. They will be completely eradicated and God will "make all things new" (Revelation 21:5) so that the universe can be restored to its original perfection. Love will forever triumph over sin!

ℋandling the 𝒲ord

Do your best to present yourself to God as one approved, a worker who does
not need to be ashamed and who correctly handles the word of truth.
—2 Timothy 2:15, NIV

As a young person, I enjoyed attending the Sabbath afternoon youth program at our local country church. Among other fun activities, there was a contest to be the fastest to find and read specific Bible passages. Almost without exception, my older sister, Eleda, won the contest. It seemed like her Bible always opened automatically to the different verses. Imagine how impossible this would have been centuries ago with the early Bibles, divided only by books, with no chapters or verses.

Stephen Langton (ca. 1150–1228) was an influential archbishop of Canterbury who died on **July 9, 1228**. "He is credited with having divided the Bible into the standard . . . arrangement of chapters used today."[16] Then, in 1448, Jewish rabbi Mordecai Nathan subdivided the Old Testament into verses. And in 1551, Robert Stephanus (also known as Robert Estienne), keeping Nathan's divisions of the Old Testament, added similar subdivisions to the New Testament. The first complete Bible with chapter and verse divisions was the Geneva Bible of 1560, an influential Protestant translation into English prior to the King James Version.

But what does it mean to "correctly handle" God's Word? Correct handling comprises at least four important aspects: (1) to demonstrate familiarity with the Bible; (2) to respect the Bible as God's Word; (3) to interpret its content correctly; and (4) to allow its truth to transform our lives. "As you take the Bible in your hands, remember that you are on holy ground."[17]

Much more than just another good book, the Bible must be the light of your whole life (Psalm 119:105). "Make the Bible the man of your counsel. Your acquaintance with it will grow rapidly if you keep your minds free from the rubbish of the world. The more the Bible is studied, the deeper will be your knowledge of God. The truths of His word will be written in your soul, making an ineffaceable impression."[18]

God's Word brings joy, meaning, and hope to our lives. It is the divine bridge that connects time with eternity (Isaiah 40:6–8) and the only condition for everlasting life.

Missionary Volunteers

Then I heard the voice of the Lord saying, "Whom shall I send? And who will go for us?"
And I said, "Here am I. Send me!"

—Isaiah 6:8, NIV

Caring for the youth means caring for the future of the church. In 1879, in a little country church in Hazelton, Michigan, fourteen-year-old Luther Warren and seventeen-year-old Harry Fenner, aiming to help their less-spiritual friends, organized the first Seventh-day Adventist young people's society. Following their example, youth societies began appearing across the country and abroad.

Responding to the crucial need to organize the burgeoning Adventist youth work, the Sabbath-School and Young People's Convention was held **July 10–21, 1907**, at Mount Vernon, Ohio. The presentations and discussions emphasized youth engagement in the Adventist mission to the world. After careful study and deliberation, the convention adopted this resolution:

"Resolved, That the young people's organization in the General Conference and in the union and local conferences be known as the Young People's Missionary Volunteer Department and that the organization in the local churches be known as the Seventh-day Adventist Young People's Society of Missionary Volunteers."[19]

General Conference President Arthur G. Daniells, who attended the convention, noted that the name identified (1) our denominational name, "Seventh-day Adventist"; (2) the church segment involved, "Young People's Society"; and (3) the aim of the department, "Missionary Volunteers." Over the years, the Missionary Volunteers, known today as Adventist Youth, has become one of the most dynamic nourishing and outreach forces of the church.

Ellen White appealed, "In order that the work may go forward in all its branches, God calls for youthful vigor, zeal, and courage. He has chosen the youth to aid in the advancement of His cause. To plan with clear mind and execute with courageous hand demands fresh, uncrippled energies. Young men and women are invited to give God the strength of their youth, that through the exercise of their powers, through keen thought and vigorous action, they may bring glory to Him and salvation to their fellow-men."[20]

How is the Adventist Youth Society in your own local church? Is it still strong and dynamic? If not, what can you do to help it regain its strength and missionary fervor?

Caring for Our Time

So teach us to number our days, that we may gain a heart of wisdom.

—Psalm 90:12

We human beings exist within the dimension of time and measure our existence in years. Ancient civilizations used sundials to mark the hours of the day. Over the centuries, mechanical clocks were developed, which eventually were spring-driven or perpetuated by a pendulum.

Big Ben in London is the largest four-faced *chiming* clock in the world. Big Ben is actually the nickname of the Great Bell in the clock, but by extension, it can also refer to the clock itself and even to the clock tower. The clock was started on May 31, 1859, and Big Ben first chimed the hour on **July 11, 1859**. But two months later, the Great Bell cracked and was silent for four years. During that period, the hour was struck on the fourth quarter bell.

Over time, conventional mechanical clocks have been largely replaced by electronic ones and even quartz clocks and watches. Modern atomic clocks have reached an amazing level of precision. It is believed that strontium atomic clocks will neither gain nor lose a second for the next fifteen billion years. Today, we also hear about such standard times as Greenwich Mean Time, Time International Atomic, and Coordinated Universal Time, which aim at keeping our atomic clocks coordinated with the relationship between the earth and sun.

As significant as measuring time might be, the most important factor relating to time is how we spend it. Ellen White counseled, "You can live this life only once."[21] "Life is mysterious and sacred. It is the manifestation of God Himself, the source of all life. Precious are its opportunities, and earnestly should they be improved. Once lost, they are gone forever."[22]

Time is God's sacred gift to each of us. We should consider it as precious as life itself is to us. We cannot exist outside of time. We cannot extend, shorten, or recover time. The only thing we can and should do is determine our priorities and manage our lives to the best of our abilities within the time we still have.

The clock does not stop. Every moment has eternal consequences. So, pause for a moment and reflect on how you have been spending your time. May the Lord help us to always spend our time wisely!

*T*HE *L*IFE OF *C*HRIST

He was in the world, and the world was made through Him, and the world
did not know Him. He came to His own, and His own did not receive Him.

—John 1:10, 11

The incarnation of God the Son is the most amazing mystery that has ever occurred. How could the Creator and Maintainer of the whole universe assume human nature and live among us as a poor human being? The life and humanity of Christ is indeed the most sublime topic we can reflect on. No other subject has such a positive transforming power.

Since the early days of her prophetic ministry, Ellen White had written much about Christ. But she spent much of her time in Australia (1891–1900) with her comprehensive project on the life of Christ. On **July 12, 1892**, she noted in her diary, "This afternoon I wrote a number of pages on the life of Christ. I long for a large portion of the Spirit of God, that I may write the things which the people need."[23] That was the beginning of a major project that would result in the publication of three of her most inspiring books—*Thoughts From the Mount of Blessing* (1896), *The Desire of Ages* (1898), and *Christ's Object Lessons* (1900).

On Friday, July 15, 1892, she penned a letter to O. A. Olsen, president of the General Conference, in which she acknowledged, "I walk with trembling before God. I know not how to speak or trace with pen the large subject of the atoning sacrifice. I know not how to present subjects in the living power in which they stand before me. I tremble for fear lest I shall belittle the great plan of salvation by cheap words. I bow my soul in awe and reverence before God and say, 'Who is sufficient for these things?' "[24]

With the help of her editorial assistant, Mrs. White gathered the content of many articles she had already written on the subject, reliable quotes from other authors, and aspects of the life of Christ shown to her in vision. Much new information she wrote under the guidance of the Holy Spirit. Finally, in October 1898, *The Desire of Ages* came off the press as one of the world's most wonderful expositions of Christ's life and ministry.

Today, we have many trustworthy reflections on the life of Christ, including the four New Testament Gospels and the three aforementioned books. Consider devoting your attention to a reading plan and study on the life of our beloved Savior Jesus Christ.

Number Thirteen

And while He was still speaking, behold, a multitude; and he who was called Judas,
one of the twelve, went before them and drew near to Jesus to kiss Him.
But Jesus said to him, "Judas, are you betraying the Son of Man with a kiss?"
—Luke 22:47, 48

Today is **July 13**. Many people consider thirteen to be an unlucky number. They will not sit in row thirteen on airplanes or stay on the thirteenth floor in hotels. Some people are especially afraid of Friday the thirteenth and may even stay home, avoiding all business. But how did such superstitions begin?

There are several theories regarding "unlucky thirteen." For example, in contrast with twelve, seen by many as a symbol of completeness, thirteen is, by some, considered a number of incompleteness. Some mystics argue that Jesus and the twelve apostles made up a group of thirteen, and when the betrayer, Judas, left, the group went down to the ideal number—twelve. Some believe that the day on which Judas betrayed Jesus was Friday, Nisan 13, on the Jewish calendar. On April 13, 1970, one of the oxygen tanks of Apollo 13 exploded, and its mission had to be aborted. On Friday, October 13, 1307, Philip IV of France arrested hundreds of the Knights Templar.[25] Other similar examples could be added to the list. And Thomas W. Lawson's novel *Friday, the Thirteenth* (1907) helped advance the superstition surrounding that specific day.

Combining the above theories with the bad reputation of August in some cultures, Friday the thirteenth of August is seen as especially fearful. For instance, in Brazil, August is known as the unlucky month of mad dogs, so dogs are usually vaccinated against rabies. Portuguese brides avoid getting married in August because that was the month when sailors used to go on long voyages, and the newly married ladies did not want to be left alone without a honeymoon.

Undoubtedly, many disasters have happened on Friday the thirteenth, but approximately the same number happen on every other day of the year. It all depends on your perspective. The problem begins when coincidence is taken as the norm, and exceptions are considered the rule. For those who trust in God and put their lives in His hands, there is no reason to be concerned over such ungrounded superstition. After all, "if God is for us, who can be against us?" (Romans 8:31).

$\mathcal{F}$ORGOTTEN $\mathcal{B}$ABIES

"Can a mother forget the baby at her breast
and have no compassion on the child she has borne?
Though she may forget,
I will not forget you!"

—Isaiah 49:15, NIV

On the stage of life, we must forget our flawed performances of the past and avoid distracting ourselves from the important role we play in the present. Some distractions don't cause much damage, but others have irreversible consequences and cause never-ending remorse.

Unfortunately, even the most attentive parents can make a fatal mistake. On **July 14, 2016**, ABC News posted Nicole Pelletiere's alarming article " 'Forgotten Baby Syndrome': A Parent's Nightmare of Hot Car Death."[26] The author tells the tragic story of Sophia Rayne "Ray Ray" Cavaliero, who, shortly after her first birthday on May 25, 2011, was left in a car in Austin, Texas, and forgotten. Her mother, Kristie Reeves, was preparing for a conference call at home. So, she sent Ray Ray with her father, Brett Cavaliero, who was supposed to drop her off at daycare. The little girl was even wearing a beautiful new dress her teacher had given her for her first birthday.

At 1:15 P.M., Reeves met her husband at his office and picked him up for lunch. While she recalled how pretty Ray Ray looked in her new dress, Brett became strangely quiet. Suddenly, he asked Reeves to drive back to his office. She imagined that he had forgotten something. But when she asked what was going on, he replied, "I can't remember dropping Ray Ray at day care this morning." Reeves immediately called 911. The paramedics worked for forty minutes, trying to revive the girl, and then they took her to the local children's hospital. Shortly after, she was declared dead from heatstroke.

Tragically, forgotten baby syndrome is more common than we would expect. Ray Ray was only one of the thirty-three children that died in the United States that year from being left in a hot car.

In Isaiah 49:15, we find a wonderful promise. Even though parents might forget their own children, God never forgets us. "He knows each individual by name, and cares for each as if there were not another upon the earth for whom He gave His beloved Son."[27]

Some parents have a favorite child (Genesis 37:3, 4), but God does not have favorites. Every one of us, including you, is His favored child.

*T*HE *S*TONES *A*RE *C*RYING *O*UT

"I tell you," he replied, "if they keep quiet, the stones will cry out."
—Luke 19:40, NIV

One of the most significant archaeological discoveries of all time is the Rosetta Stone, housed in the British Museum since 1802. Some scholars say that the stone was found on **July 15, 1799**, by the French captain Pierre-François Bouchard. Others argue that it was discovered on July 19 or even in August. Despite the minor discrepancies, we do know that it was found in July or August 1799 in the village of Rosetta, in the Nile Delta, during Napoleon's Egyptian campaign.

The Rosetta Stone is an ancient Egyptian granodiorite stele with a decree from 196 BC honoring Ptolemy V as a god. The inscription is engraved in three languages: ancient Egyptian hieroglyphics, demotic, and Greek. Thomas Young decoded the demotic script, which helped Jean François Champollion decipher the hieroglyphs in 1822. This provided the key to reading many other hieroglyphic inscriptions of ancient Egypt, where the Israelites had lived and been held captive for centuries.

This, along with other archaeological discoveries, allowed the stones to "cry out" at a critical moment in world history. At the time, the method of higher criticism (later known as the historical-critical method) was bringing into question the divine origin of the Bible and denying many of its historical accounts. On the other hand, archaeological discoveries in the Middle East began to confirm the historicity of several of those accounts.

Some might ask, Does the Bible really need to be endorsed by external sources? Accepting the Bible as the self-authenticated Word of God, one should allow it to critically evaluate all other sources of knowledge, not the other way around. Nevertheless, archaeology has contributed significantly to helping reconstruct the historical and cultural background of biblical events and to understanding how people lived in biblical times—how they built their houses, how they worked, how they got married, and more. For instance, Martin Hengel's insightful book *Crucifixion* detailed the methods of Roman crucifixion, shedding new light on Jesus' cruel death on the cross.[28]

Thank You, Lord, for the archaeological discoveries that support the historicity of the Bible and help us better understand its historical and cultural background!

𝒩ew 𝒫rophets?

"And it shall come to pass afterward
That I will pour out My Spirit on all flesh;
Your sons and your daughters shall prophesy,
Your old men shall dream dreams,
Your young men shall see visions."

—Joel 2:28

As Seventh-day Adventists, we believe that Ellen G. White (1827–1915) was called by God to provide special prophetic assistance for the end-time restoration of Bible truth. As she saw prophecies being fulfilled, she expected Jesus to return while she was still alive. But with the passing of time, she became increasingly convicted that perhaps she would have to rest. On Sabbath morning, July 10, 1915, her son Willie prayed with her, after which she whispered to him, "I know in whom I have believed" (see 2 Timothy 1:12). Later, she spoke a few words to some women in the room. On Friday afternoon, **July 16, 1915**, at 3:40 P.M., she died peacefully after a very fruitful seventy-year prophetic ministry.

In the last years of her life, Ellen White was frequently asked whether God would raise another true prophet. She consistently answered that the Lord had not given her light on that specific matter. In 1907, she wrote, "Abundant light has been given to our people in these last days. Whether or not my life is spared, my writings will constantly speak, and their work will go forward as long as time shall last. My writings are kept on file in the office, and even though I should not live, these words that have been given to me by the Lord will still have life and will speak to the people."[29]

Ellen White died more than a century ago, and some Adventists wonder whether we should expect another prophet. They usually quote Joel 2:28, a verse in which God promised to pour out His Spirit "on all flesh," and that people would prophesy, dream dreams, and see visions. Does it imply that everyone will become a prophet? I don't think so. God sometimes gives limited prophetic revelations to people—as in the case of Pharaoh (Genesis 41:1–36) and Nebuchadnezzar (Daniel 2)—without calling them to become prophets.

It is best to leave this question with "God, who is too wise to err and too good to do us harm."[30] Meanwhile, let us read, study, and practice the principles in the prophetic writings already available to us. They are more than sufficient to guide us safely to our heavenly home.

ℕEVER ℙART 𝒜GAIN

Then we who are alive and remain shall be caught up together with them in the
clouds to meet the Lord in the air. And thus we shall always be with the Lord.
—1 Thessalonians 4:17

Some goodbyes leave an empty space in our hearts. It is hard to see someone we want to spend every minute with depart. It is painful to ask someone to stay if we know he or she really wants to leave us. And it is heartbreaking to say goodbye to someone when we know we will never say hello to them again. Yes, we are all longing for a land where the word *goodbye* is unknown.

Isaac Watts (1674–1748) was born in Southampton, United Kingdom, on **July 17, 1674**. Known as the "Father of English hymnody," Watts wrote approximately six hundred hymns. In 1707, he penned his beautiful "Never Part Again." Its first stanza and original refrain read as follows,

There is a land of pure delight,
Where bliss eternal reigns,
Infinite day excludes the night
And pleasures banish pain.

We're trav'ling to Immanuel's land,
We soon shall hear the trumpet sound,
And soon we shall with Jesus reign,
And never, never part again.[31]

This was one of William Miller's favorite hymns. He asked his family members to sing it to him again and again before his death in 1849. Over the years, many General Conference sessions and Adventist camp meetings closed with this hymn and the thoughtful question, "Could this be our last session or meeting, and could the next one be in heaven?"

Jesus did not return as soon as the Adventist pioneers had expected. But remember, His second coming is much closer now than when Isaac Watts wrote the lyrics of this beautiful song or when William Miller sang it. It is also much closer than when those Adventist sessions and camp meetings were concluded with this hymn. Undoubtedly, very soon, Jesus will appear in the clouds of heaven to take us home, and then we surely will "never part again"!

MARIE CURIE

But he was pierced for our transgressions,
he was crushed for our iniquities;
the punishment that brought us peace was on him,
and by his wounds we are healed.

—Isaiah 53:5, NIV

Maria Skłodowska was born in 1867 in Warsaw, Poland, and there began her scientific training and practice. In 1891, she went to Paris, France, where she continued her studies of physics, chemistry, and mathematics at the University of Paris and conducted her subsequent scientific work. After marrying Pierre Curie, she became known as Marie Curie. In 1903, Marie, along with her husband and Henri Becquerel, received the Nobel Prize in Physics for their work on radioactivity. She also won the 1911 Nobel Prize in Chemistry for her work on polonium and radium. Marie Curie was the first woman to be awarded a Nobel Prize and the only woman ever to have received two of them.

On **July 18, 1898**, Marie and her husband publicized their discovery of an element that they named polonium in honor of her native Poland. Five months later, on December 26, the couple announced a second new element, which they called radium (the Latin word for "ray"), from which they also coined the term *radioactivity*. Curie died in 1934 of aplastic anemia stemming from radiation exposure caused by the test tubes of radium she carried in her pockets during research and from the mobile X-ray units she set up during her service in World War I. Not having all the understanding and safety measures we have today, she died from exposure to the very element she discovered and researched.

The Bible tells us that Jesus came to this world to resolve the problem of sin, and the only way of doing it was by dying for our sins. We are told that "God made him who had no sin to be sin for us, so that in him we might become the righteousness of God" (2 Corinthians 5:21, NIV).

He was pierced for our transgressions,
    he was crushed for our iniquities;
the punishment that brought us peace was on him,
    and by his wounds we are healed (Isaiah 53:5, NIV).

Even so, He remained "without sin" (Hebrews 4:15). At His incarnation, Christ took all the effects of sin but was not infected by sin. If He had sinned, He could not be our Savior but would need a savior for Himself. But praise God that our sinless Savior carried our sins without becoming a sinner!

WOMEN'S RIGHTS

There is neither Jew nor Greek, there is neither slave nor free,
there is neither male nor female; for you are all one in Christ Jesus.
—Galatians 3:28

The Creation account declares that both man and woman were created by God in His own image and likeness (Genesis 1:26, 27). The fact that Eve was made from one of Adam's ribs implies parity and companionship (Genesis 2:21–24). As well stated by Matthew Henry (1662–1714), "The woman was made of a rib out of the side of Adam; not made out of his head to rule over him, nor out of his feet to be trampled upon by him, but out of his side to be equal with him, under his arm to be protected, and near his heart to be beloved."[32] But sin distorted the relationship between men and women (Genesis 3:16), and through the ages, countless females have been invalidated and oppressed by men.

The Seneca Falls Convention held in the Wesleyan Chapel in Seneca Falls, New York, on July 19–20, 1848, asserted that by creation, "woman is man's equal." The "Declaration of Rights and Sentiments" presented and signed by one hundred of the three hundred attendees at the convention denounced several "injuries and usurpations on the part of man toward woman" and claimed that women, being "enlightened in regard to the laws under which they live," had the right to speak in public meetings, to participate in the elective franchise, and more.[33]

Men and women are equal not only by creation but also by redemption. Indeed, creation and redemption are the two great equalizers of human beings. Both men and women were created by God, and both are saved through Christ's atoning sacrifice on the cross. Paul says, "There is neither male nor female," for all are "one in Christ Jesus" (Galatians 3:28). But even so, the Bible keeps a clear sexual distinction between males and females that should not be broken (Leviticus 18:22; 20:13). Any attempt to break this distinction is a corruption of God's creation (Romans 1:24–28).

During His earthly ministry, Christ respected and upheld women. He protected them against social and religious discrimination (John 4:1–42; 8:1–11). Any form of sexual abuse and social discrimination against women is a direct offense to God as their Creator and Sustainer!

"The Greatest Week in History"

"And I, if I am lifted up from the earth, will draw all peoples to Myself."
—John 12:32

Astronautic space exploration had just begun, but in his 1961 "Special Message to the Congress on Urgent National Needs," American president John F. Kennedy urged, "This nation should commit itself to achieving the goal, before this decade is out, of landing a man on the moon and returning him safely to the earth."[34] Eight years later, on **July 20, 1969**, astronauts from Apollo 11 successfully landed on the moon. As the first person to walk on its surface, Neil Armstrong described that experience as "one small step for a man, one giant leap for mankind."[35]

On July 24, the capsule carrying Neil Armstrong, Michael Collins, and Edwin Aldrin splashed down in the Pacific Ocean, returning all three astronauts back to earth safely. They were extracted from the ocean and kept under a twenty-one-day quarantine on the aircraft carrier USS *Hornet* as a precaution against "moon germs." Through a small glass window, President Nixon saluted them and said: "This is the greatest week in the history of the world since the Creation. . . . As a result of what you have done, the world has never been closer together."[36]

Today, there are people who believe the moon landing was all a hoax because some of the images shown "from the moon" that day had been prerecorded in the flight simulator. But whatever the conspiracy theorists say, it is undeniable that the Apollo 11 mission was a major scientific achievement. However, it was not as important as suggested by President Nixon. It can never be compared with the events of the Passion Week when the very destiny of humanity was in the balance. Yes, Apollo 11 carried three men to the moon, but the cross of Christ gives all of humanity free access to the very presence of God in heaven.

The Apollo 11 mission generated worldwide excitement and expectation. As a kid growing up in southern Brazil, I eagerly followed live radio coverage of the event. But neither this nor any other event in human history has ever brought more people "closer together" than the cross of Christ. We are told by Paul in 2 Corinthians 5 that, at the cross, "God was in Christ reconciling the world to Himself" (verse 19). Then Paul makes this appeal: "On Christ's behalf, be reconciled to God" (verse 20). This is your chance! Don't delay your decision any longer.

GODS WHO ARE NO GODS

"And you see and hear how this fellow Paul has convinced and led astray
large numbers of people here in Ephesus and in practically the whole province
of Asia. He says that gods made by human hands are no gods at all."
—Acts 19:26, NIV

Ephesus was a port city and an important trade center in the Mediterranean. Its famous Temple of Artemis was one of the Seven Wonders of the Ancient World. The original structure was built around 550 BC. It was allegedly burned down by a certain Herostratus on **July 21, 356** BC—the same night on which Alexander the Great was born. The Ephesians decided to build an even larger and more magnificent temple in place of the burned one. Alexander offered financial help to the project, but the proud Ephesians refused it, with someone reportedly saying, "How can one god present gifts to another god?" The new building was surrounded by marble steps that led to a terrace. Inside stood 127 marble columns and a statue of the Greek goddess Artemis (known to the Romans as the goddess Diana), protector of the hunt, women, and virgins.

Paul came to Ephesus on his third missionary tour, and his preaching soon disrupted the popular worship of Artemis. Acts 19:23–41 tells us that Demetrius, who made silver shrines of Artemis, incited an uprising against Paul. He told his fellow craftsmen, "There is danger not only that our trade will lose its good name, but also that the temple of the great goddess Artemis will be discredited; and the goddess herself, who is worshiped throughout the province of Asia and the world, will be robbed of her divine majesty" (verse 27, NIV). Inflamed by Demetrius's speech, the crowds shouted for about two hours, "Great is Artemis of the Ephesians!" (verse 34, NIV).

The Ephesian craftsmen were upset by Paul's teaching "that gods made by human hands are no gods at all" (verse 26, NIV). "When the uproar had ended, Paul sent for the disciples and, after encouraging them, said goodbye and set out for Macedonia" (Acts 20:1, NIV). It looked as though the goddess Artemis and her Ephesian craftsmen had triumphed—but it wasn't to last forever. Although the Temple of Artemis was again rebuilt after it was sacked and destroyed by the Ostrogoths in AD 268, Paul's religion won out. The great temple fell into insignificance as Christianity spread throughout Asia and Europe.

Remember, man-made gods and their shrines come and go, as do their makers. But those who anchor their faith in the only true God and His Word will remain forever.

OVERCOMING TEMPTATIONS

Therefore submit to God. Resist the devil and he will flee from you.

—James 4:7

Temptation is a powerful and persistent force. Many people, instead of resisting it, simply offer apologies and excuses for falling into it. For instance, Irish playwright and novelist Oscar Wilde had one of his characters quip, "I can resist everything except temptation."[37] American movie actress Mae West jokingly confessed, "I generally avoid temptation, unless I can't resist it."[38] Such statements, however, ignore the transforming power of the gospel.

In a sermon preached in Harbor Heights, Michigan, on **July 22, 1891**, Ellen White warned, "The temptations will surround us just as long as we live. Satan will try us in one way, and if he doesn't overcome us he will try us in another way. And thus his efforts will never cease."[39] Years earlier, in 1858, she stated, "The power of Satan now to tempt and deceive is ten-fold greater than it was in the days of the apostles."[40] Knowing this, we must identify our own weaknesses and learn how to overcome them by God's grace.

Minister and author Randy Alcorn wisely pointed out, "It's always easier to *avoid* temptation than to *resist* it."[41] Just as Adam and Eve should have stayed away from the tree of knowledge of good and evil (Genesis 2:15–17), we must stay away from all avoidable circumstances that might lead us into sin. Nevertheless, temptations, predictable and unpredictable, will try to overcome us, and we have no power of ourselves to withstand Satan's strategies. The victory can be gained only if we first submit ourselves to God and then, empowered by Him, resist the devil (James 4:7).

Christ is our unfailing example in overcoming temptation, for He was "tempted in every way, just as we are—yet he did not sin" (Hebrews 4:15, NIV). He faced temptation with prayer (Matthew 26:36–46), unconditional faithfulness to God's word (Matthew 4:1–11), and singing songs of faith.[42] These should be our strategies as well.

If we place ourselves in God's hands, He will shield us from "all the fiery darts of the wicked one" (Ephesians 6:16). "He will not let you be tempted beyond what you can bear." And "he will also provide a way out so that you can endure it" (1 Corinthians 10:13, NIV). Every temptation we overcome strengthens us to overcome others. Be strong in the Lord!

A True Adventist

*"However, do not rejoice that the spirits submit to you,
but rejoice that your names are written in heaven."*
—Luke 10:20, NIV

Since its early inception, the Seventh-day Adventist Church has experienced rapid numerical growth and significant geographical expansion. The *Advent Review and Sabbath Herald* issue for **July 23, 1857,** carried a short article titled "The Cause," in which James White reported that the number of Sabbath-keeping Adventists back in 1847 was only "about one hundred."[43] That number had increased to around two hundred by 1850, two thousand in 1852, and thirty-five hundred by 1863. In 2017, the church had a worldwide membership of more than twenty million. Praise the Lord for this amazing growth!

As a church, we have a solid organization and a very consistent Bible message. But how many of us church members live in conformity with that message? Christ's parables of the kingdom (see Matthew 13) reveal that not all who come into the church are truly converted and will persevere until the very end.

In 1867, Ellen White warned, "Names are registered upon the church books upon earth, but not in the book of life. I saw that there is not one in twenty of the youth who knows what experimental religion is."[44] In the early 1890s, she added, "It is a solemn statement that I make to the church, that not one in twenty whose names are registered upon the church books are prepared to close their earthly history, and would be as verily without God and without hope in the world as the common sinner."[45]

These statements should not be used to statistically calculate how many of our local church members will be in heaven and how many will not. Remember that the final separation between the wheat and the tares and between the good and the bad fish is an end-time task performed by God's angels and not by any human being (Matthew 13:27–30, 47–50). The previously quoted statements were given as solemn warnings for each of us to examine our own lives and overcome our lukewarm, Laodicean spiritual condition (Revelation 3:14–22).

Today, we need more who will reform their own lives and fewer who attempt to reform the lives of others. Being a genuine Adventist is not so much a matter of *saying* but rather of *living*. May your name and mine remain in the Lamb's book of life (Revelation 21:27).

𝒯HE 𝓛AST 𝒫OEM

"And God will wipe away every tear from their eyes; there shall be no more death, nor sorrow, nor crying. There shall be no more pain, for the former things have passed away."
—Revelation 21:4

S ome people deviously come into our lives, crush our feelings, and then walk away as if nothing has happened. Someone has said, "Feelings don't walk away. People do." Another confessed, "My biggest mistake is thinking that people care for me as much as I do for them."

Annie R. Smith (1828–1855) was an extremely sweet and talented young lady. In 1851, she sent her poem "Fear Not, Little Flock" to James White. He liked the poem so much that he not only published it in the *Advent Review and Sabbath Herald* but also invited her to come to Rochester, New York, as a copy editor for that paper. There she fell in love with the handsome young preacher J. N. Andrews, who apparently had feelings for her too—but they never married. In November 1855, suffering from tuberculosis, Annie returned to her home in West Wilton, New Hampshire. As the months passed, her strength sharply declined.

On Tuesday morning, **July 24, 1855**, Annie wrote her last poem:

Oh! shed not a tear o'er the spot where I sleep;
For the living and not for the dead ye may weep;
Why mourn for the weary who sweetly repose,
Free in the grave from life's burden and woes?

Annie peacefully died two days later. On August 26, 1855, Ellen White wrote to J. N. Andrews, "I saw that you could do no better now than to marry Angeline. . . . Annie's disappointment cost her her life. I saw that you [John] were injudicious in her [Annie's] case."[46] It is evident that although Andrews was no longer close to her when Annie's life ended, she still had feelings for him. Don't toy with the feelings of others. They may end up paying a heavy price!

Despite all her emotional pain and physical suffering, Annie's last poem confirms that she ended her days at peace with God. As so well expressed in some of her previous writings, she was looking forward to that glorious day when "God will wipe away every tear" from the eyes and from the hearts of His suffering children. What a blessed hope we have!

THE IMITATION OF CHRIST

*Then Jesus spoke to them again, saying, "I am the light of the world.
He who follows Me shall not walk in darkness, but have the light of life."*
—John 8:12

Our world is full of heroes, actors, and models—humans who can easily distract us and even mislead us. If we consider ourselves Christians, then Jesus Christ should be our Hero and Model. He is One worthy of being imitated. As Ellen White said so well, "We have only one perfect photograph of God, and this is Jesus Christ."[47]

In the fourteenth century, Gerard Groote founded a Catholic pietist religious community in the Netherlands called The Brethren of the Common Life. They devoted themselves to the study and teaching of Scripture, doing charitable work, and copying religious and inspirational works. Thomas à Kempis was a member of that community. He was born in Germany in about 1380 and died in the Netherlands on **July 25, 1471.** His classic book *The Imitation of Christ* encourages practical religion and true piety.

Kempis challenges us, "What good does it do to speak learnedly about the Trinity if, lacking humility, you displease the Trinity? Indeed it is not learning that makes a man holy and just, but a virtuous life makes him pleasing to God. I would rather feel contrition than know how to define it. For what would it profit us to know the whole Bible by heart and the principles of all the philosophers if we live without grace and the love of God? Vanity of vanities and all is vanity, except to love God and serve Him alone."[48]

We need to continuously grow in Christ. "If you cannot recollect yourself continuously, do so once a day at least, in the morning or in the evening. In the morning make a resolution and in the evening examine yourself on what you have said this day, what you have done and thought, for in these things perhaps you have often offended God and those about you."[49] Kempis also warns against the presumptuous theory of sinless perfection, "Every perfection in this life has some imperfection mixed with it and no learning of ours is without some darkness."[50]

Practical religion and true piety are found in simply imitating Christ. He assured us that "it is enough for a disciple that he be like his teacher, and a servant like his master" (Matthew 10:25). Let's imitate Him today and every day.

$\mathcal{W}$E $\mathcal{H}$AVE $\mathcal{T}$HIS $\mathcal{H}$OPE

Looking for the blessed hope and glorious appearing of our great God and Savior Jesus Christ.
—Titus 2:13

Seventh-day Adventists are people of hope. Over the years, they have heartily preached and sung of Christ's glorious second coming. An excellent example of this was the 1962 General Conference Session in San Francisco, California. "We Have This Hope" was the theme. Wayne H. Hooper (1920–2007), a member of the King's Heralds Quartet from the *Voice of Prophecy* radio broadcast, was asked to write the theme song for that conference. After much prayer, he composed both the lyrics and the tune for a song with the same title, "We Have This Hope." The 1962 General Conference Session opened on Thursday evening, **July 26, 1962**, when the delegates to the session sang it for the first time. It begins with these inspiring words: "We have this hope that burns within our hearts, Hope in the coming of the Lord."[51]

"We Have This Hope" is one of the most-loved Adventist hymns and has even been used as the theme song for several other sessions (1966, 1975, 1995, 2000, and part of the 2015 session). It has been translated into several other languages. Before the 1995 General Conference Session, with "United in Christ" as its theme, Hooper was asked to write a second stanza, which was added to the song.

What really matters is the message of the song and what it means for us. We are now much closer to the Second Coming than when this song was first sung in 1962. Are we excited about it? Ellen White challenges, "Every day that passes brings us nearer the end. Does it bring us also near to God?"[52] Take time to reflect on this question today.

ᏢASSION FOR ᏜISSIONS

In journeys often, in perils of waters, in perils of robbers.
—2 Corinthians 11:26

H ow would you feel about being called to serve the Lord in some inhospitable region far away, permeated with tropical diseases and deadly snakes? What if you had to leave behind your home, relatives, and friends and walk into an uncertain future?

That was the experience of Leo and Jessie Halliwell, who served the Lord in Brazil for thirty-eight years, most of which were spent in the Amazon region. In their small medical and missionary boat, the *Luzeiro* (*Light Bearer*), the couple sailed up and down the huge Amazon River between the cities of Belém and Manaus. It is estimated that they treated more than a quarter-million Brazilians and Indians for tropical and other diseases while spreading the Adventist message to those isolated communities on the banks of the great river.

In his inspiring book *Light Bearer to the Amazon*, Leo Halliwell wrote, "We are thankful that the Lord has given us health to work in the Amazon region. We count it not a sacrifice, but a privilege; and we dedicate the rest of our lives to helping finish the work in the North Brazil Union."[53] In 1958, the Halliwells retired back to the United States, leaving behind an amazing legacy of unselfish service to the poor and needy.

On the evening of **July 27, 1959**, the National Order of the Southern Cross was awarded to Leo and Jessie Halliwell. It is the highest award conferred by the Brazilian government on foreigners who render outstanding service to the country. In his speech, the government representative described the Halliwells as "exceptional persons" who "rank among the few who can give everything, expecting nothing in return." In reply, Leo Halliwell stated, "I can only say that when we first arrived in Brazil, almost forty years ago, we found the Brazilian people to be very kind, loving, and courteous. . . . Today our best friends are in Brazil. We are in the States, but our heart is down in Brazil. Our best friends are right up there along the Amazon River in northern Brazil."[54]

The Halliwells and many other Adventist missionaries had and still have a real passion for their mission fields. What about you? Have you ever considered becoming a missionary? Whether overseas or at home, you should be a missionary for the Lord!

"ᵀHEIR ᵂORKS ᶠOLLOW ᵀHEM"

Then I heard a voice from heaven saying to me,
"Write: 'Blessed are the dead who die in the Lord from now on.' "
"Yes," says the Spirit, "that they may rest from their labors, and their works follow them."
—Revelation 14:13

On the floor of the Saint Thomas Church in Leipzig, Germany, one can see a brass plate with the inscription "Johann Sebastian Bach," marking the place where he was buried. It's just a name, but a name that speaks for itself, evoking memories of the great composer and his amazing musical legacy.

Remarkably, on July 28, two very influential Baroque-music icons passed away. The first was the Italian composer and violin virtuoso Antonio Vivaldi (1678–1741), who died in Vienna, Austria, on **July 28, 1741**. He created some five hundred concertos, including the famous *The Four Seasons* for violin and chamber orchestra. The second icon to pass on July 28 was the German composer and musician Johann Sebastian Bach (1685–1750), who died in Leipzig, Germany, on **July 28, 1750**. Experts say that 1,128 pieces of music by Bach are available today, and many others have been lost. Can you imagine how many people have performed or enjoyed the works of these two composers? They died a long time ago, but "their works follow them."

You may never be as famous as Vivaldi or Bach, but your influence is perhaps more important than you realize. Consider this statement: "How little you know the bearing of your daily acts upon the history of others. You may think that what you do or say is of little consequence, when the most important results for good or evil are the consequence of our words and actions. The words and actions looked upon as so small and unimportant are links in the long chain of human events."[55] God takes into account "the influence exerted for good or for evil," as well as "its far-reaching results."[56]

If your name were to appear on a brass plate like the one I saw in the Saint Thomas Church, what do you think people would remember about you? What is your legacy? Whatever the extent of our influence might be, all of us are called to exercise a saving influence on those around us. I hope that all those who follow in our footsteps will be led to the everlasting kingdom!

WEDDING VOWS

But Ruth said:
"Entreat me not to leave you,
Or to turn back from following after you;
For wherever you go, I will go;
And wherever you lodge, I will lodge;
Your people shall be my people,
And your God, my God.
Where you die, I will die,
And there will I be buried.
The LORD do so to me, and more also,
If anything but death parts you and me."

—Ruth 1:16, 17

Do you remember the nicest wedding ceremony you ever attended? What made it stand out above all others? Beautiful decorations, well-dressed people, touching moments all capture our focus at a wedding, but nothing attracts our attention like the sight of the bride in her dress. Some people believe that the larger and more ostentatious a wedding ceremony, the happier the couple will be in life. But that is not necessarily the case!

One of the most magnificent wedding ceremonies ever took place on **July 29, 1981**, at Saint Paul's Cathedral in London. The "wedding of the century," as it was called, was attended by 3,500 guests and watched by some 750 million TV viewers worldwide. The bride's engagement ring consisted of fourteen solitaire diamonds surrounding a 12-karat oval blue Ceylon sapphire, set in 18-karat white gold. Her wedding dress became known as one of the most famous dresses in the world. Indeed, everything seemed perfect for Prince Charles and Lady Diana Spencer to live happily ever after. The couple had two lovely sons (Princes William and Harry), and Diana said she believed that "family is the most important thing in the world." But tragically, Charles and Diana separated in 1992 and divorced in 1996.

Almost all couples promise to love, honor, and cherish their spouses for a lifetime, regardless of the circumstances—"as long as you both shall live," "till death us do part." Some even include Ruth's vow to Naomi (see Ruth 1:16, 17) as their own marriage covenant. Given these heartfelt pledges, why do people change their minds so easily and no longer honor their vows? One problem is that, often, marriage is nothing more than a means of self-gratification.

Some churches perform wedding recommitment services for married couples. But there is no need to wait for these services, which are held only occasionally. Couples should renew their vows regularly at home. Plan a simple ceremony recommitting yourselves to God and to each other, and God's blessing will rest on you and your family.

*T*HE *D*AY OF *F*RIENDSHIP

"A new commandment I give to you, that you love one another;
as I have loved you, that you also love one another."

—John 13:34

Friends make life worth living. Popular speaker and author Steve Maraboli suggested, "Friends are medicine for a wounded heart and vitamins for a hopeful soul." A popular proverb (frequently attributed to the ancient Greek dramatist Euripides) says, "Friends show their love in times of trouble, not in happiness." In other words, they remain at our side when everyone else disappears.

In 2011, the United Nations General Assembly proclaimed **July 30** as the International Day of Friendship. The decision was based on "the idea that friendship between peoples, countries, cultures, and individuals can inspire peace efforts and build bridges between communities."[57] Friendship is also one of the most powerful tools for leading people to Christ.

The cover article of *Ministry* magazine for December 1977 is entitled, "Why Not Use the Net Too?"[58] In that article, Clark B. McCall, pastor of the Herman, California, Seventh-day Adventist Church at the time, told of his successful "kindness-call" program, inspired by Ellen White's statement, "If we would humble ourselves before God, and be kind and courteous and tenderhearted and pitiful, there would be one hundred conversions to the truth where now there is only one."[59]

McCall asked his church members to offer a weekly volunteer kindness service. The list of services included making phone calls, babysitting, providing transportation and assistance with housework, and making general visits. This friendship approach gradually wore down the wall of prejudice and resulted in several Bible studies. McCall explained that using this approach, one of his churches experienced a huge increase in baptisms over the previous year.

If they are to bear fruit, friendship and goodness must be intentional. We are told that Christ "mingled with men as one who desired their good. He showed His sympathy for them, ministered to their needs, and won their confidence. Then He bade them, 'Follow Me.' "[60] Try using friendship evangelism as a regular strategy to bring people to Christ. Pray for someone you would like to reach through this pleasant and effective strategy.

ᒍOURNEY ᒍNTO THE ᑌNKNOWN

Now the LORD had said to Abram:
"Get out of your country,
From your family and from your father's house,
To a land that I will show you."

—Genesis 12:1

amily should be the social unit in which life begins and love never ends—a place where parents and children can always enjoy their most precious moments together. But the presence of sin has undermined God's ideal, and even well-established families suffer the pain of separation. Sooner or later, the time comes when grown children move away to continue their studies, work at new jobs, and establish their own families. Parents are left with empty-nest syndrome, while children face the challenge of learning to fly by themselves.

At the clinic where my wife and I went when she was pregnant with our son William, there was a little framed quote, "A child is a flower that blossoms in your life and then disappears into an adult." Pure reality! However, just as parents miss their cute babies, older children may also face stress and sadness when they leave home and begin their journey into the unknown.

Ruth E. Van Reken was born in the United States on **July 31, 1945**, and then raised for thirteen years in Nigeria. Her parents were missionaries, and she was sent away to boarding school when she was only six years old. In her touching book *Letters Never Sent* (released in 1988), she published retrospective letters describing her feelings of belonging everywhere and, at the same time, nowhere. She begins her first letter, dated September 1951, by saying:

"Dear Mom and Dad, I feel awful. Something inside is squeezing me so bad I can hardly breathe. You said it would be fun to get on the plane and go to boarding school, but so far it isn't. I couldn't stop crying on the airplane, but I didn't want the other kids to know. I kept my face to the window, so they might think I liked watching the clouds. When I got to school this afternoon, I was still crying and I just couldn't stop."[61]

Birds cannot remain forever in their nest. The time comes when they need to fly on their own. But when they do, they should never forget their origins. Likewise, if you have already left or are soon leaving the home of your parents, remember to stay connected with those who love and care about you. Family bonds are sacred and should be kept healthy.

August 1

$\mathcal{N}$OT A $\mathcal{B}$ROKEN $\mathcal{S}$HAFT

Zeal for your house consumes me, and the insults of those who insult you fall on me.
—Psalm 69:9, NIV

A meaningful quote attributed to the famous Italian humanist publisher Aldus Manutius (1449–1515) wisely said, "It is not work that kills; but no work and overwork."[1] Adventist pioneer James White (1821–1881) would fall into the second category. Holding to the motto "Better wear out than rust out," he pushed himself over the years more than his strong body could tolerate. At age forty-four, James suffered a severe stroke of paralysis. Once he had recovered, he continued to work as hard as always.[2]

In 1881, his wife, Ellen, tried to convince him that they should move away from the burdens of Battle Creek. But he replied, "Where are the men to do this work? Where are those who will have an unselfish interest in our institutions, and who will stand for the right, unaffected by any influence with which they may come in contact?" With tears in his eyes, he added, "My life has been given to the up-building of these institutions. It seems like death to leave them. They are as my children, and I cannot separate my interest from them. These institutions are the Lord's instrumentalities to do a specific work."[3]

One Sabbath morning, James and Ellen were together in the pulpit of the Battle Creek Tabernacle. Two days later, on **August 1, 1881**, he suddenly became ill, and the following Sabbath, he died at the Battle Creek Sanitarium.[4] While the diagnosis was that he died from malaria, behind his illness were the years of overworking as he helped develop the church. Because James died at the age of sixty without "completing" his ministry, some proposed putting up a broken shaft on his grave. But Ellen responded, "Never! . . . Never! He has done, singlehanded, the work of three men. Never shall a broken monument be placed over his grave!"[5]

With sadness, she wrote, "Side by side we had labored in the cause of Christ for thirty-six years; and we hoped that we might stand together to witness the triumphant close. But such was not the will of God. The chosen protector of my youth, the companion of my life, the sharer of my labors and afflictions, has been taken from my side, and I am left to finish my work and to fight the battle alone."[6]

Remember, sometimes we need to slow down to go further!

ℋONORING GOD IN ℱUFFERING

*Therefore let those who suffer according to the will of God commit
their souls to Him in doing good, as to a faithful Creator.*

—1 Peter 4:19

P romoters of the so-called positive confession ideology suggest that our words have
supernatural power to change circumstances and shape destinies. Assuming that
because every sin, sickness, disease, sorrow, and grief was laid on Jesus (Isaiah 53:3–5),
those preachers encourage their audiences to make this confession: "Today I am forgiven,
healed, healthy, and well." To them, only a lack of faith can prevent someone from being
physically healed.

On **August 2, 1982**, the American theologian and philosopher Francis Schaeffer
(1912–1984) penned a consoling letter to a pastor whose wife, Sharon, had multiple
sclerosis. Schaeffer wrote,

I do believe that at times the Lord gives direct healing, and I have seen something of
this in my own ministry through the years. This is surely to the praise of the Lord,
and we thank Him. But there is the constant, pernicious danger of this slipping into
the idea that if a person is a true believer and has sufficient faith, he will always be
healed. This is clearly not what the Bible teaches. The New Testament has various
places that show conclusively that not all of the Christians in that day were healed.
What this idea does is to forget that God is not a computer, but a personal Heavenly
Father who must be allowed to answer in His personal and infinite loving wisdom.
I have seen some of God's most faithful and loving people wiped out by people
telling them that if they are not cured, it is because of lack of spirituality or a lack
of prayer. This sometimes certainly is the case, but to tell people who have an acute
illness that is always the case is often to heap guilt on their head when they certainly
do not need this. . . .

There is nothing more cruel than a group of people pouring guilt on someone
who is ill just when they do not need it.[7]

The positive confession teaching selfishly offers a crown without a cross (Matthew
16:24). In contrast, the apostle Paul patiently endured the thorn in his flesh and took
pleasure in his infirmities (2 Corinthians 12:7–10). And the apostle Peter encourages us
to rejoice in being partakers of Christ's sufferings (1 Peter 4:13). Let us allow God to be
God in our lives and accept His plans for us.

ℛADICAL ℳEASURES

There is a way that appears to be right, but in the end it leads to death.
—Proverbs 14:12, NIV

E verything had been carefully planned for a nice weekend together on Tangier Island, Chesapeake Bay, Virginia. Miriam Wells and John Wesley Taylor V anticipated a wonderful time with their son on the island. On Friday morning, **August 3, 2012,** they passed through the Washington, DC, metropolitan area and then took a four-lane highway to the marina from which a boat would take them to the island. Since the highway was almost deserted, Miriam set the cruise control at 60 mph.

The trip was going well until Miriam realized that the cruise control was stuck at that speed, and the brake was no longer disengaging it. She tried different options, but nothing seemed to work. John quickly suggested she safely pull the car over and turn the engine off. With the engine turned off, the car glided to a stop. John phoned their mechanic to try to figure out what might have gone wrong with the cruise control. The mechanic gave him precise instructions on how to locate and deactivate the faulty cable. Even without cruise control, the family was able to arrive on time at the marina.

There are moments in life when the only thing we can do is turn off the engine and stop. When moral issues are involved, for instance, we have to make a radical decision to stop the immoral behavior. The decision may involve a short-term loss but could avert a future disaster. Other times, such as when we are diagnosed with a terminal disease, our only remaining option may be to calmly accept reality. In the words of Viktor E. Frankl, "When we are no longer able to change a situation, we are challenged to change ourselves."[8]

Life is indeed a sequence of decisions. Some are easy to make, while others are far more difficult. Regardless, it is always helpful to remember Reinhold Niebuhr's "Serenity Prayer," which begins with the plea, "God, give me grace to accept with serenity the things that cannot be changed, courage to change the things which should be changed, and the wisdom to distinguish the one from the other." We can also keep in mind the anonymous prayer, "Lord, help me remember that nothing will happen today that we can't handle together."

RECEIVERS BECOME GIVERS

The next day Jesus decided to leave for Galilee. Finding Philip, he said to him, "Follow me."
. . . Philip found Nathanael and told him, "We have found the one Moses wrote about in the
Law, and about whom the prophets also wrote—Jesus of Nazareth, the son of Joseph."
—John 1:43–45, NIV

The **August 4, 1853**, issue of the *Advent Review and Sabbath Herald* carried an interesting note about the spreading of the Adventist message in Michigan. It stated, "I have just returned from Hastings. We had there five meetings. The Lord greatly blessed us with his Holy Spirit. The saints were comforted and refreshed. Sinners trembled and wept. Two confessed the truth in meeting, and two more declared their intentions of keeping the Sabbath of the Lord our God, and more are under conviction that we have the truth. . . . Some will be baptized the first opportunity. . . . We think that the message of the third angel is fast rising here, and the Lord is opening the way for the loud cry."[9]

Who wrote these words? They came from the pen of David Hewitt, the first Seventh-day Adventist in Battle Creek, Michigan. Interestingly, in 1852, when Joseph Bates decided to preach the Adventist message in Battle Creek, he used a unique strategy. He went to the local postmaster, who supposedly knew everyone in town, and asked him who was "the most honest man in town." The postmaster replied that David Hewitt was just such a person. So, Bates went to the Hewitts' house and shared with them the Adventist message. They gladly accepted it,[10] and, as confirmed by the note above, David became a dedicated Adventist missionary.

In John 1:43–51, we read about Jesus calling Philip, who, in turn, called Nathanael. This illustrates the nature of the gospel mission: those who receive become givers! In reality, "Every true disciple is born into the kingdom of God as a missionary. He who drinks of the living water becomes a fountain of life. The receiver becomes a giver. The grace of Christ in the soul is like a spring in the desert, welling up to refresh all, and making those who are ready to perish eager to drink of the water of life."[11]

We cannot keep the gospel message just for ourselves as a hidden treasure; it must be shared with others (Matthew 25:14–30). What are your personal plans to share this marvelous message?

RESCUED IN THE ATACAMA

And when he came to the den, he cried out with a lamenting voice to Daniel.
The king spoke, saying to Daniel, "Daniel, servant of the living God, has your God,
whom you serve continually, been able to deliver you from the lions?"
—Daniel 6:20

The world was eagerly following the news from the San José mine in the Atacama Desert, northern Chile. On **August 5, 2010**, at 2:05 P.M., the main access to the copper mine was blocked by the collapse of about 700,000 tons of diorite rock—twice the mass of the Empire State Building. Alternative passages were blocked by fallen rock or threatened by ongoing rock movement. A group of thirty-three miners was trapped 2,300 feet underground. Emergency food supplies stocked in the shelter were intended to last only two or three days, and there was also a dangerous shortage of water and air. Would there be any survivors?

Aboveground, close to the entrance of the mine, the Campamento Esperanza (Camp Hope) developed. There, more than two thousand family members, workers, and members of the press were assisted by the local Seventh-day Adventist pastor Carlos Parra Díaz. The rescue process took much longer than expected. After seventeen days, rescue crews broke into the mine with a six-and-a-half-inch drill bit. The miners taped a piece of paper to the drill bit. Written in red were these words: "Estamos bien en el refugio los 33" (We are well in the shelter, the 33). Rescuers sent supplies down through the hole and drilled bigger holes. After sixty-nine days underground, all thirty-three miners were rescued in steel rescue capsules. People celebrated as each miner emerged. At the cost of US$20 million, it was one of the most challenging mining rescue missions in history.

Just as those miners were trapped in the San José mine, all humanity, through the fall of Adam and Eve, has been imprisoned in sin and condemned to die. But God developed an amazing rescue plan to save humanity. Christ came to this world, died on the cross, rose from the dead, and consecrated "a new and living way" for us to access heaven (Hebrews 10:20). The rescue plan is so efficient that Paul says, "Where sin abounded, grace abounded much more" (Romans 5:20).

Can you imagine the celebration when the redeemed of all ages finally enter the heavenly courts? You and I must be among the victorious rescued by God's amazing grace!

𝒦ing 𝒟avid

Jesus said to him, "Thomas, because you have seen Me, you have believed. Blessed are those who have not seen and yet have believed."

—John 20:29

C ritics had long questioned several historical Bible records that had never been confirmed by contemporary extrabiblical documents. For example, with no archaeological confirmation of his existence, King David was regarded as just one of many mythological figures. But in July 1993, at the site of Tel Dan in northern Israel, an excavation directed by Israeli archaeologist Avraham Biran discovered a fragment of a stone monument, or stela, commemorating the victory of an Aramean king over the "king of Israel" and the "king of the House of David" (Judah).

The *New York Times* came off the press on **August 6, 1993**, with an article titled, "From Israeli Site, News of House of David." It reported that biblical scholars described the discovery as "phenomenal," "stunning," and "sensational." In November 2016, the Biblical Archaeology Society stressed that "the stela's fragmented inscription . . . proved that King David from the Bible was a genuine historical figure and not simply the fantastic literary creation of later Biblical writers and editors. Perhaps more important, the stela, set up by one of ancient Israel's fiercest enemies more than a century after David's death, still recognized David as the founder of the kingdom of Judah."[12]

This raises a crucial question: Should we trust extrabiblical sources more than the Bible account itself? Or should it be the other way around? If we believe the Bible to be just another ancient religious-cultural expression, then we *should* expect outside confirmation of its historical accounts. But if we accept the Bible's own claim of being the infallible Word of God (2 Peter 1:19–21; Revelation 22:18, 19), then we should accept its historical records without question.

Only in the Bible do we find "a history of our race unsullied by human pride or prejudice." Only there "the curtain is drawn aside, and we behold, behind, above, and through all the play and counterplay of human interests and power and passions, the agencies of the all-merciful One, silently, patiently working out the counsels of His own will."[13] Unconditional acceptance of God's Word will strengthen our faith and transform our lives.

$\mathcal{T}$HE $\mathcal{L}$OVE OF GOD

For I am convinced that neither death nor life, neither angels nor demons, neither the present
nor the future, nor any powers, neither height nor depth, nor anything else in all creation,
will be able to separate us from the love of God that is in Christ Jesus our Lord.

—Romans 8:38, 39, NIV

Skilled authors and able songwriters have used their most eloquent language to describe the love of God. One of these was Frederick M. Lehman (1868–1953). He was born in Mecklenburg, Germany, on **August 7, 1868**, and immigrated to the United States with his family when he was four. He wrote hundreds of songs and compiled five songbooks. Yet he recognized that God's love surpasses all human depictions. In 1917, in Pasadena, California, he wrote the wonderful hymn "The Love of God." The refrain of his hymn proclaims, "O love of God, how rich and pure! How measureless and strong!"[14]

These words echo what Ellen White wrote more than thirty years earlier:

All the paternal love which has come down from generation to generation through the channel of human hearts, all the springs of tenderness which have opened in the souls of men, are but as a tiny rill to the boundless ocean when compared with the infinite, exhaustless love of God. Tongue cannot utter it; pen cannot portray it. You may meditate upon it every day of your life; you may search the Scriptures diligently in order to understand it; you may summon every power and capability that God has given you, in the endeavor to comprehend the love and compassion of the heavenly Father; and yet there is an infinity beyond. You may study that love for ages; yet you can never fully comprehend the length and the breadth, the depth and the height, of the love of God in giving His Son to die for the world. Eternity itself can never fully reveal it.[15]

Contemplate God's love. Open yourself to its transforming influence. Your life will never be the same!

Self-Sufficiency

So, if you think you are standing firm, be careful that you don't fall!
—1 Corinthians 10:12, NIV

Some people know how to climb the ladder of success but not how to get off it. Alvin Toffler (1928–2016) warned, "Nothing is more dangerous than yesterday's success."[16]

Alonzo T. Jones (1850–1923) accepted the Adventist message and was baptized at Walla Walla, Washington, on **August 8, 1874.** In 1878, he was ordained as a minister and became an influential thought leader. Together with Ellet J. Waggoner, he played a crucial role in preaching righteousness by faith at the 1888 General Conference Session in Minneapolis and afterward. But his association with Dr. John H. Kellogg fueled self-sufficiency and his post-1901 anti-organization bitterness. Jones tirelessly attempted to undermine Arthur G. Daniells's leadership as General Conference president.

As early as September 19, 1892, Ellen White had stated, "It is quite possible that Elder Jones or Waggoner may be overthrown by the temptations of the enemy; but if they should be, this would not prove that they had had no message from God or that the work that they had done was all a mistake."[17] Unfortunately, they lacked humility and failed to live the message they themselves had preached so effectively to thousands of other people. Eventually, all three—Kellogg, Waggoner, and Jones—ended up leaving the church.

In 1907, Jones was asked to turn in his ministerial credentials, and the following year he was disfellowshiped from the church. He requested a hearing at the 1909 General Conference Session in Washington, DC. There he presented a long self-justifying and accusatory speech and met with key church leaders three times. At last, after an extended appeal for reconciliation, President A. G. Daniells reached his hand across the table and said, "Come, Brother Jones, come." Jones arose and slowly extended his hand, then he suddenly pulled it back and declared, "No, never!" and sat down again.[18] Jones never rejoined the church.

Far more important than starting well is ending well. Pride and self-sufficiency have a high price. A. T. Jones's story could have had a different ending had he remained humble and thankful for what the Lord had accomplished through him.

ℒEANING 𝒯OWER

*"And everyone who hears these words of mine and does not act on
them will be like a foolish man who built his house on sand."*
—Matthew 7:26, NRSV

Sometimes we are tempted to start a new project without giving enough thought to its implications and long-lasting consequences. That was the case with the famous Leaning Tower of Pisa in Italy. Its foundation was started on **August 9, 1173**, but the tower itself was not completed until more than two hundred years later. The building has seven standard stories and a smaller bell chamber at the top. The tower is about 185 feet (57 meters) tall and weighs 14,500 tons (6,577 kilograms). It was built on unstable ground composed of soft clay and occasional layers of sand. Early on during construction, the ground started giving way, and the building began to lean. Many efforts were made to prevent the tower from tumbling.

Just as the Tower of Pisa was built on unstable ground, the spiritual lives of many professed Christians rest on a superficial and faulty form of subjective religion. Jesus addressed this issue at the close of His famous sermon on the mount. In Matthew 7:21, we read, "Not everyone who says to Me, 'Lord, Lord,' shall enter the kingdom of heaven, but he who does the will of My Father in heaven." The distinction becomes even more clear-cut in the parable of the two builders, also known as the parable of the two foundations (verses 24–27).

Some people believe that the parable revolves around merely the personal acceptance or rejection of Jesus Christ. And it's true that "no other foundation can anyone lay" besides Jesus Christ (1 Corinthians 3:11). But the real issue here goes beyond the mere acknowledgment and confession of Him as "Lord, Lord." It is directed at anyone "who hears these words of mine and puts them into practice" in contrast to one "who hears these words of mine and does not put them into practice" (Matthew 7:24, 26, NIV).

We should never forget that "the religion that comes from God is the only religion that will lead to God."[19] Human ideologies come and go like the waves of the ocean. Only "the word of our God stands forever" (Isaiah 40:8). Those who build their lives on the firm foundation of God's Word will shine "like the stars forever and ever" (Daniel 12:3).

RECONVERSION

"But we had to celebrate and be glad, because this brother
of yours was dead and is alive again; he was lost and is found."
—Luke 15:32, NIV

Brothers and sisters living under the same roof can develop distinct characters and follow different paths, as in the case of Esau and Jacob (e.g., Genesis 25:21–34). In James and Ellen White's family, their oldest son, Henry Nichols, had a more stable personality, while his brother, James Edson, was full of ups and downs, especially in financial matters. But even his spiritual life was not as it should be. Over the years, Ellen sent him several letters appealing to him, but without many positive results.

One time Edson even confessed in a letter to his mother, "I am not at all religiously inclined." Ellen realized that Satan was leading her son astray. She prayed fervently on his behalf and sent him a long, appealing letter. She said, "Your religious history need not have been vacillating, but firm and true; but you would be independent and take your own course. You have been strong one hour, vacillating the next. I am now determined to press upon your notice and make you hear: 'This is the undertow.' "[20] This appeal turned his life around.

On **August 10, 1893**, Edson wrote to his mother: "I have surrendered fully and completely, and never enjoyed life before as I am [enjoying it] now. I have for years been under a strain, with so much to accomplish, and it has stood right in my way. Now, I have left it all with my Saviour, and the burden does not bear me down any longer. I have no desire for the amusements and pleasures that made up the sum of my enjoyments before, but have an enjoyment in the meetings with the people of God such as I never had before." A few days later, he added, "I have proved my own way and it is a poor way. I now want God's way, and I know it will be a good way." From then on, Edson lived a stable spiritual life.

Perhaps you, too, have tried unsuccessfully to manage your life in your own way. Don't wait. Surrender your life and all your plans to God right now. If needed, you can even have a reconversion experience as dramatic as the prodigal son's (Luke 15:11–32). Our heavenly Father is more than willing to embrace you and transform you into a citizen of His everlasting kingdom.

"MY DEAR SON"

Hear, my child, your father's instruction, and do not reject your mother's teaching.
—Proverbs 1:8, NRSV

When you think of your parents (or whoever raised you), what comes to your mind? Do you still remember their wise counsel and helpful guidance? What moral values did they believe you would carry for life? Do you still keep their written correspondence to you?

On **August 11, 1868**, Ellen White wrote an insightful letter on character development to her nineteen-year-old son Edson. She began by saying, "I am thankful to our heavenly Father for the efforts you are making to overcome every defect of character. It is the overcomers who will see Jesus as He is, and be made like Him."[21] She then advised him to continue to "walk in the light which God has given."[22] He should not only pray but also live his prayers.

As a loving mother, Ellen encouraged her son to keep a clear conscience. She counseled, "Make the will of God your rule of conduct in all things—in small matters as well as great. . . . How pleasant, how satisfactory, will be the recollection all through life that though exposed to many and fierce temptations, your hands were unstained by dishonesty, and your heart undefiled by cherishing temptation."[23]

On the topic of finances, Ellen added, "Extravagance must have resources, and if money cannot be obtained honestly, it will be obtained dishonestly. A love of pleasure, of fine clothing, has brought many a youth to prison, and even to the gallows. Always make it a point to live within your income. Do without things rather than incur a debt. Never purchase an article until you can pay for it."[24]

Ellen directed her son's attention to the moral integrity exemplified by Joseph, who "learned to govern, by first learning to obey." She concluded, "My dear son, do not get above the simplicity of a humble Christian life. Let the character of Joseph be your character; let his strength to resist temptation be your strength. Your efforts will be successful if you make them in the strength of God. Jesus is a present help. May the blessing of Jesus ever rest upon you, is the prayer of your Mother."[25]

Today is a good day to reflect on the wise advice you received from your parents and other true Christians. By God's grace, this day can be a new beginning in your life!

*I*NVESTING IN THE *Y*OUTH

Let no one despise your youth, but be an example to the believers
in word, in conduct, in love, in spirit, in faith, in purity.
—1 Timothy 4:12

M any great leaders of the world have recognized the value and potentiality of shaping the minds of the new generations. Some have done it for a good cause, and others, for a bad one, as in the case of Adolf Hitler and his Hitlerjugend (Hitler Youth). On September 14, 1935, he told a group of fifty-four thousand boys and girls gathered in Nuremberg, "You are the future of the Nation, the future of the German Reich!"[26] But already in his book *Mein Kampf* (published originally in German in 1925), Hitler stated, "Youth furnishes the building material and the plans for the future."[27] No wonder that by 1936, 97 percent of all public-school teachers in Germany belonged to the National Socialist Teachers League.

In contrast, many Christian youth organizations have inspired new generations to live biblical values and fulfill the gospel mission. Some of the most influential ones are the Young Men's Christian Association (better known as the YMCA), founded in 1844 in London for the healthy development of "body, mind, and spirit," and the Student Volunteer Movement for Foreign Mission, organized in 1886 to recruit college and university students in the United States for missionary service abroad. For many years, the Missionary Volunteer Society of the Seventh-day Adventist Church was driven by the motto, "The Advent message to all the world in this generation."

In December 1999, the United Nations General Assembly voted **August 12** as International Youth Day. This is part of the United Nations' strategy "to increase the quality and quantity of opportunities available to young people for full, effective, and constructive participation in society."[28] What a blessing it would be if Adventist youth had similar opportunities in their local churches!

Ellen White declared, "With such an army of workers as our youth, rightly trained, might furnish, how soon the message of a crucified, risen, and soon-coming Saviour might be carried to the whole world!"[29] Every Adventist congregation should be a missionary training school for the next generation. What has your church done to make this a reality?

ℳORAL ᗪECLINE

"For as in the days before the flood, they were eating and drinking, marrying and giving in marriage, until the day that Noah entered the ark, and did not know until the flood came and took them all away, so also will the coming of the Son of Man be."

—Matthew 24:38, 39

I s our world today better or worse than it was two hundred years ago? The answer to this question depends on your perspective. From a technological viewpoint, our world has improved significantly. But socially speaking, moral values have declined remarkably. Yet, there are strong marriages, like islands in our social ocean, though whipped about by every immoral storm.

Billy Graham and Ruth Bell were married on **August 13, 1943**. Their inspiring marriage lasted for nearly sixty-four years before Ruth died on June 14, 2007. Asked about her husband's frequent absences from home, Ruth once remarked, "I'd rather have a little of Bill than a lot of any other man."[30] The day before her death, Billy stated, "Ruth is my soul mate and best friend, and I cannot imagine living a single day without her by my side. I am more in love with her today than when we first met over 65 years ago as students at Wheaton College."[31] Unfortunately, not many modern couples build such a romantic and long-lasting marriage!

In the mid-1970s, the dean of men at the boarding school where I was enrolled regularly quoted Ruth Graham's famous statement, "If God doesn't punish America, He'll have to apologize to Sodom and Gomorrah." Without question, things have gotten much worse since then! If Ruth Graham was concerned about the moral decline of the world at that time, what would she say today? For example, in the past, people spoke only of two genders: masculine and feminine. But by mid-2014, the *Telegraph* reported that British Facebook users could choose from seventy-one different gender options!

Christ warned that the antediluvian lifestyle of "eating and drinking, marrying and giving in marriage" would be practiced just before the end of the world (Matthew 24:37–39). The moral decline of our world demands that either God must intervene in human affairs or humanity will destroy itself. But Christ is coming soon to destroy the wicked (Revelation 21:8) and establish His kingdom of righteousness (Daniel 7:13, 14). Praise the Lord!

ℋᴇ Ðɪᴇᴅ ꜰᴏʀ ℳᴇ

For Christ also suffered once for sins, the just for the unjust, that He might bring us to God, being put to death in the flesh but made alive by the Spirit.
—1 Peter 3:18

No human sacrifice can be compared to the infinite sacrifice of Christ on the cross of Calvary. Even so, we have examples of people who died for others. At the end of July 1941, three prisoners escaped from the Auschwitz concentration camp in southern Poland. To deter further escape attempts, the Nazi SS deputy camp commander ordered ten of the remaining prisoners to be starved to death. One of them was Franciszek Gajowniczek, who pled, "My wife! My children!" Touched by his words, Franciscan friar Maximilian Kolbe (1894–1941) volunteered to take his place.

"After two weeks of dehydration and starvation, only Kolbe remained alive." To clear the area, on **August 14, 1941**, the guards gave him a lethal injection of carbolic acid. He died at age forty-seven, and his remains were burned the next day.[32] He voluntarily died for Franciszek Gajowniczek (1901–1995), who lived another fifty-three years. At ninety-three years old, Gajowniczek recalled that day: Father "Kolbe told the commandant, 'I want to go instead of the man who was selected. He has a wife and family. I am alone. I am a Catholic priest.' "[33]

This account reminds us of what Christ did for us two thousand years ago. Ellen White put it this way: "The world's Redeemer was treated as we deserve to be treated, in order that we might be treated as he deserved to be treated. He came to our world and took our sins upon his own divine soul, that we might receive his imputed righteousness. He was condemned for our sins, in which he had no share, that we might be justified by his righteousness, in which we had no share. The world's Redeemer gave himself for us. Who was he?—The Majesty of heaven, pouring out his blood upon the altar of justice for the sins of guilty man."[34]

Christ did not die an ordinary death. He died the second death in our place so that all who are in Him will not suffer that death (Revelation 20:6). "God has given us eternal life, and this life is in His Son" (1 John 5:11).

Thank You, Lord Jesus Christ, that You came to suffer and die for me! Through Your amazing sacrifice, I can be justified and have eternal life. Amen.

Colossal Dreams

Now the rest of the acts of Hezekiah—all his might, and how he
made a pool and a tunnel and brought water into the city—are they
not written in the book of the chronicles of the kings of Judah?

—2 Kings 20:20

Not all trees bear fruit at the same time. Some, like a fig tree, can bear fruit in two years. An avocado tree growing from seed can take anywhere from five to thirteen years before it is mature enough to produce fruit. Likewise, not all of our grandest dreams materialize as fast as we would like. Two amazing hydraulic-engineering projects illustrate this principle well.

The first is the Siloam Tunnel, also known as Hezekiah's Tunnel. Jerusalem was under siege by the Assyrians, led by King Sennacherib. To ensure a safer water supply, King Hezekiah ordered the excavation of a rock tunnel conveying water from the Gihon Spring to the Pool of Siloam. At 1,749 feet (533 meters) long and with a drop of only 12 inches (30.5 centimeters), this curving tunnel was excavated by two teams—one group excavated from one end while the other dug from the opposite end, and they met in the middle. This impressive project was all completed during King Hezekiah's reign.

Another major project was the Panama Canal, connecting the Atlantic and the Pacific Oceans. Pedro Arias Dávila, the governor who founded the city of Panama in 1514, was charged by the Spanish crown with the task of finding a natural site to unite the two oceans. Over time, a number of important steps had to be taken. Finally, on **August 15, 1914**, the 48-mile (77.25-kilometer) canal was inaugurated, and the first vessel officially crossed it. Although the two oceans are at the same level, the canal has three locks that raise the ships to the level of Lake Gatún and then lower them on the other side. It took four centuries before the original plan was fully realized.

As mentioned, not all trees bear fruit at the same time. Not all dreams can be implemented in the same span of time. Some of your best ideas may take more than a lifetime to become realities. Be humble enough to do your best in everything you do, even if others will be the ones to receive the honor for a project you initiated or carried on. If your intention is to glorify God in whatever you do (Matthew 5:16; 1 Corinthians 10:31), you will not be discouraged when you don't receive praise for your accomplishments.

AVOIDING TRAGEDIES

"But if the watchman sees the sword coming and does not blow the trumpet, and the people are not warned, and the sword comes and takes any person from among them, he is taken away in his iniquity; but his blood I will require at the watchman's hand."

—Ezekiel 33:6

On the tragic morning of September 11, 2001, when the hijacked commercial airplanes crashed into the World Trade Center and the Pentagon, Zacarias Moussaoui was sitting in a jail in Minnesota facing immigration charges. He arrived in the United States in February 2001 and raised suspicion after paying large sums of cash to a flight-training school. He insisted on receiving training to fly a "big bird"—that is, a Boing 747 Jumbo—despite an obvious lack of skills even with small planes. His strange conduct raised much concern.

Moussaoui was arrested in Minnesota on **August 16, 2001**, around four o'clock in the afternoon, on charges of violating the terms of his visa. Checking with foreign intelligence agencies, the Minneapolis FBI field office learned that Moussaoui could have terrorist connections. The field office immediately contacted FBI headquarters in Washington, requesting approval to launch a full-scale investigation, including a search of Moussaoui's laptop records and possessions. But the request was denied. Not until after the September 11 attacks was the investigation authorized and carried out, confirming that the laptop contained the whole terrorist strategy!

Sometimes distractions and omissions can have devastating consequences. Many of the unsolvable problems we face today are those that were not solved while they could have been. The fact of the matter is that we tend to be more reactive than proactive. Not very many are able to foresee the harvest in the seed or the destructive fire in the spark. In the case of Moussaoui, top FBI agents believed that the field operatives were overstating their case.

In spiritual matters, we are accountable before God to "sound a clear call" (1 Corinthians 14:8, NIV). God expects us not only to warn others but also to heed the warnings addressed to us. We need God's wisdom to neither overstate nor neglect the issues we face. A word of warning spoken to the right person at the right time in a clear and forthright way may not always be appreciated, but it could prevent huge problems in the future.

𝒯HE CASE OF 𝒜ZARIA CHAMBERLAIN

For God will bring every work into judgment,
including every secret thing, whether good or evil.

—Ecclesiastes 12:14

Michael and Lindy Chamberlain were just beginning their family campout at Uluru (also known as Ayers Rock), Northern Territory, Australia. They were having an enjoyable time with their two boys, Aidan and Reagan, and their two-month-old baby girl, Azaria. But on the night of Sunday, **August 17, 1980**, Azaria was taken from the family tent, and she was never found. Lindy reported to the local police that she had seen a dingo—a wild Australian dog—slip out of the tent and, sure enough, a week later, a tourist found Azaria's bloody jumpsuit, boots, diapers, and undershirt. The initial investigation concluded that no member of the Chamberlain family was responsible for her death. But the story did not end there. It set off the most publicized trial in Australian history.

Some criticized Lindy for not showing more grief as a mother. Others claimed that the Seventh-day Adventist Church the Chamberlains belonged to was a cult that killed infants as part of bizarre religious ceremonies and that Azaria was taken to a remote desert location to be offered as a sacrifice. After all, Michael was, in fact, an ordained minister for that denomination. An alleged doctor of Azaria's even released an anonymous note stating that her name actually meant "sacrifice in the wilderness." In 1982, Lindy was found guilty of first-degree murder and sentenced to life in prison. Michael was convicted as an accessory after the fact and received an eighteen-month suspended sentence.

John Bryson, in his book *Evil Angels*, provided an in-depth look at the Chamberlain case, suggesting that they might have been wrongfully convicted.[35] In September 1988, the Northern Territory Court of Criminal Appeals unanimously overturned the convictions, exonerating Lindy and Michael on all charges. Two months later, the film *Evil Angels* (titled *A Cry in the Dark* outside of Australia and New Zealand) was released. Finally, on June 12, 2012, coroner Elizabeth Morris announced the cause of Azaria's death—she was killed by a dingo.

This is an example of how human justice can be faulty. But although humanity's justice may fail, God's never will. If you are the victim of unjust judgment, God will surely clear your case.

*M*ADISON COLLEGE

*"And these words which I command you today shall be in your heart. You shall
teach them diligently to your children, and shall talk of them when you sit in your
house, when you walk by the way, when you lie down, and when you rise up."*
—Deuteronomy 6:6, 7

Christian education means to make disciples who carry on Christ's model of redemptive service to humanity. This model should characterize each Adventist teacher and every Adventist educational institution. Few educational institutions developed the ideal of self-sacrificing service as effectively as the Nashville Agricultural and Normal School (renamed Madison College in 1937) in Madison, Tennessee.

Ellen White had a special burden for the work in the southern states of the United States. So, in 1904, following Mrs. White's advice, E. A. Sutherland and Percy T. Magan resigned their posts at Emmanuel Missionary College (now Andrews University) and moved to Nashville. They bought a four-hundred-acre farm to establish a self-supporting educational enterprise. In the **August 18, 1904**, issue of the *Advent Review and Sabbath Herald*, Mrs. White urged, "As these brethren go to the South to take hold of pioneer work in a difficult field, we ask our people to make their work as effective as possible by assisting them in the establishment of the new school near Nashville."[36]

The whole Madison educational system was based on self-sacrifice, a strict and persistent economy, one major study plan, and self-government, with the study of the Bible being a leading feature. As a large family-like community, teachers and students worked together and studied together. As stated in its Bulletin No. 1, the institution aimed to "train missionary teachers (using the word in its broadest sense) to be self-supporting."[37] The leaders wanted students to go out from Madison College and start their own smaller replicas of Madison. The training they received was so efficient and inspiring that graduates of Madison established some forty other small self-supporting schools in some of the poor communities of the southern United States.

Times have changed, and today many are more interested in their own rights and privileges than in sacrificing themselves for God's cause. Altruistic service is a universal Christian principle. What a difference we could make if we restored the spirit of simplicity and service that characterized the golden years of Madison College!

$\mathcal{P}$EOPLE OF THE $\mathcal{B}$OOK

I treasure your word in my heart, so that I may not sin against you.
—Psalm 119:11, NRSV

Seventh-day Adventists used to call themselves the "People of the Book." Many of them followed a one-year Bible reading plan and displayed their biblical understanding in doctrinal debates with other Christians. Adventists often performed well in major national and international Bible knowledge contests.

On **August 19, 1958**, the finals of the First International Bible Contest were held at the Hebrew University in Jerusalem. The contest was sponsored by the Israel Broadcasting Corporation to commemorate the nation's tenth anniversary. The finalists represented fifteen different countries and were from various Jewish and Christian backgrounds. Irene Santos, a thirty-nine-year-old Adventist schoolteacher from Brazil, won third prize.

At the Second International Bible Contest in Jerusalem in 1961, Yolanda da Silva, an Adventist schoolteacher and pastor's wife, also from Brazil, received the second prize. It was later upgraded to a gold medal. And Adventist pastor J. J. B. Combrinck, from South Africa, took fifth place. Graham Mitchell, an accountant at the Sanitarium Health Food Company in Australia, won the Third International Bible Contest in Jerusalem in 1964. Manuel Jara Calderon, an Adventist from Bolivia, scored fourth in the Fourth World Bible Contest held in 1969. In 1981, Francisco Alves de Pontes (nicknamed "Chico Bíblia"), another Brazilian Adventist, won second place. His prize was upgraded to a gold medal, as in the case of Mrs. da Silva.

These are only representatives of the many faithful Adventists who were and still are in love with God's Word. As Adventists, both families and individuals, we should revive the wonderful habit of memorizing portions of the Bible. But even more important than reciting Bible passages is understanding them correctly and living in conformity to their teachings. What a disaster it would be to end up having a big brain but an empty heart!

Christ prayed for His followers, "Sanctify them by the truth; your word is truth" (John 17:17, NIV). As good as it may be, our approach to memorizing the Bible and having an intellectual religion needs to be sanctified by the transforming power of God's Word. Let's put aside all human criticism and listen with humility and obedience to God's Word!

ᴘARADISE ᴙEGAINED

For as by one man's disobedience many were made sinners,
so also by one Man's obedience many will be made righteous.
—Romans 5:19

The first few pages of the Bible tell us the dramatic story of the original Paradise and how it was ruined by Adam and Eve's transgression (Genesis 2; 3). The last pages of the Bible portray the wonderful Paradise restored (Revelation 21; 22), the moment when God will "make all things new" (Revelation 21:5). In between these two contrasting scenes, we find the ongoing human drama in which each person decides his or her own destiny.

English poet John Milton (1608–1674) produced some of the most famous and epic poems on those scenes. Totally blind after 1652, Milton dictated his poems to transcribers and friends. He signed the contract to publish his book *Paradise Lost*, and four months later, on **August 20, 1667**, printer Samuel Simmons registered the work. Thomas Ellwood, who studied Latin with Milton, supposedly approached him with the following remarks, "Thou hast said much here of Paradise lost, but what hast thou to say of Paradise found?"

Milton reflected on that comment and sometime thereafter produced his follow-up work *Paradise Regained* (1671). This short book portrays a series of debates between Christ and Satan. Christ ultimately makes up for Adam and Eve's failure by victoriously resisting the temptations of the devil. As the Bible eloquently describes it: "For as by one man's [Adam's] disobedience many were made sinners, so also by one Man's [Christ's] obedience many will be made righteous" (Romans 5:19). Christ's amazing victory over Satan can deliver us now from the bondage of sin and ultimately take us to the restored Paradise.

The Great Controversy describes the moving moment in which Christ takes Adam back to the Paradise in which he used to live. Adam's "mind grasps the reality of the scene; he comprehends that this is indeed Eden restored, more lovely now than when he was banished from it. . . . He looks about him and beholds a multitude of his family redeemed, standing in the Paradise of God. Then he casts his glittering crown at the feet of Jesus and, falling upon His breast, embraces the Redeemer. He touches the golden harp, and the vaults of heaven echo the triumphant song: 'Worthy, worthy, worthy is the Lamb that was slain, and lives again!' "[38]

You and I must be there on that glorious occasion!

August 21

$\mathcal{A}$LWAYS $\mathcal{B}$EHOLDING $\mathcal{M}$E

The eyes of the LORD are everywhere, keeping watch on the wicked and the good.
—Proverbs 15:3, NIV

One of the most famous art thefts ever took place at the Musée du Louvre, in Paris, on **August 21, 1911**. None other than the *Mona Lisa*, by Leonardo da Vinci, was stolen by a museum employee and kept in his apartment for more than two years. It was a major disaster for that early sixteenth-century painting, considered "the best known, the most visited, the most written about, the most sung about, the most parodied work of art in the world."[39] It was returned to the Louvre in January 1914. People appreciate the smile of the woman in the *Mona Lisa* as well as the artistic effect that makes her eyes follow you wherever you go.

Perhaps the most famous and widely known Adventist painting is *The Christ of the Narrow Way* mural by Elfred Lee, on permanent display at the Ellen G. White Estate Visitor Center in Silver Spring, Maryland. Dedicated on October 22, 1991, the painting is a pictorial representation of Ellen White's first vision, enhanced with depictions of crucial and historic Seventh-day Adventist moments and several influential leaders. At the center of the mural is Christ standing with open arms. As with the *Mona Lisa*, His eyes also follow you wherever you go. I once asked Elfred Lee about the secret to achieving that effect. He told me that if the eyes are well painted, it happens naturally.

The ever-watching eyes in both the *Mona Lisa* and *The Christ of the Narrow Way* remind us that "the eyes of the LORD are everywhere, keeping watch on the wicked and the good" (Proverbs 15:3, NIV). There is a stark contrast between those who claim, "The LORD does not see us, the LORD has forsaken the land" (Ezekiel 8:12) and those who realize the futility of hiding.

Where can I go from Your Spirit?
Or where can I flee from Your presence?
If I ascend into heaven, You are there;
If I make my bed in hell, behold, You are there.
If I take the wings of the morning,
And dwell in the uttermost parts of the sea,
Even there Your hand shall lead me,
And Your right hand shall hold me (Psalm 139:7–10).

What would you change in your life if you were constantly aware that God is beholding you? Remember, you can hide from others, but not from yourself or God. Never lose sight of God's abiding presence.

$\mathcal{T}$HE $\mathcal{L}$IGHT OF THE $\mathcal{W}$ORLD

"I have come as a light into the world, that whoever
believes in Me should not abide in darkness."
—John 12:46

Light is a form of energy that travels in waves and allows us to see the things around us. We depend on light to discover the world and to explore what we can of the infinite universe. You can read this book because of the light shining on its pages and your eyes that can see. All that we know of the universe and its dimensions are due to the light of the stars that reach us and our understanding of the speed of light.

Until the seventeenth century, it was believed that light could travel any distance instantly, and there was no speed of light. Early attempts to measure it were made by the Dutch scientist Isaac Beeckman and Italian astronomer and physicist Galileo Galilei. Precise measurements were begun by the Danish astronomer Ole Rømer (1644–1710) at the Royal Observatory in Paris. Through his observation of the movement of planets themselves, Rømer estimated that light travels at about 136,701 miles per second (220,000 kilometers per second). On **August 22, 1676**, he announced some of his basic discoveries at the Royal Academy of Sciences in Paris. Later studies by other scientists helped determine the speed more accurately. In 1983, the seventeenth General Conference on Weights and Measures adopted 299,792,458 meters per second (186,282 miles per second) as the exact value for the speed of light in a vacuum.

It is remarkable that Jesus spoke of Himself as "the light of the world" (John 8:12). And He explained further, "I have come as a light into the world, that whoever believes in Me should not abide in darkness" (John 12:46). As physical darkness is the absence of light, spiritual darkness is the absence of Jesus from our lives. Conversely, when He comes into our lives, light shines and darkness is expelled.

As Christians, we must not only *receive* the light of Christ but also *reflect* it, like mirrors, to others. In the Sermon on the Mount, Jesus declared, "You are the light of the world. . . . Let your light so shine before men, that they may see your good works and glorify your Father in heaven" (Matthew 5:14–16). So, people should see the *direct* light of Christ *reflected* in us and through us, indicating the right way to the heavenly home.

$\mathcal{T}$HE $\mathcal{H}$UGUENOTS

"Then they will deliver you up to tribulation and kill you,
and you will be hated by all nations for My name's sake."

—Matthew 24:9

Every genuine Christian must pay the price for his or her faith. That price varies according to the circumstances in which one is immersed and his or her level of commitment to God's Word.

Few people have ever paid as high of a price for their faith as the Huguenots—French Calvinist Protestants. On the night of **August 23–24, 1572**, a huge wave of Catholic mob violence against the Huguenots began. It became known as the Saint Bartholomew's Day massacre. It started in Paris and extended outward to other urban centers and into the countryside. It lasted for several weeks. Modern estimates for the number of those who died across France vary widely, from five thousand to thirty thousand.

In 1598, King Henry IV of France signed the Edict of Nantes, granting the Huguenots significant religious tolerance. But in 1685, Louis XIV revoked the edict. Again, hostility against the Huguenots increased, and as many as four hundred thousand fled from France at risk of their lives.

In 1730, a nineteen-year-old Huguenot girl was arrested and taken to the Tour of Constance in the city of Aigues-Mortes in southern France. Her name was Marie Durand (1711–1776), and her crime was that of having a brother who was a Protestant minister. All she had to do to regain her freedom was say, "I recant." Instead, she engraved the French word *REÇISTER* (resist) on the rock of the prison wall. She spent the next thirty-eight years (1730–1768) in prison for her faith!

Would you be willing to pay such a high price for your faith? If you would, praise the Lord! At any rate, there is a huge contrast between the immovable conviction of the Christian martyrs and the flexible beliefs of modern pluralistic Christianity. The martyrs lived in a time of religious intolerance. For them, the truth was true, regardless of the circumstances and irrespective of what political and ecclesiastical authorities were endorsing.

Times have changed. In many countries of the world today, we have the blessing of religious freedom. Unfortunately, however, lack of commitment is often a by-product of that freedom. Many Christians today want to be politically correct. Let's enjoy the freedom we have but maintain our commitment to God's Word and our willingness to pay the price for our faith.

No Time to Escape

For when they say, "Peace and safety!" then sudden destruction comes upon them,
as labor pains upon a pregnant woman. And they shall not escape.
—1 Thessalonians 5:3

Pompeii was a thriving and sophisticated Roman city near the Bay of Naples, Italy. It attracted many wealthy tourists. With only about twelve thousand residents, the city had a pleasant Roman theater and a running water system with three streams—one to public fountains, another to public baths, and a third to the homes of wealthy residents. Archaeological excavations have revealed a town-wide system of prostitution and sexual immorality. There were at least six public Roman baths, the central Lupanare Grande (Purpose-Built Brothel) along with several other brothels, and 153 taverns. Walls decorated with pornographic pictures and graffiti were everywhere. Some believe that the city was the sexual capital of the Roman Empire, but modern historians suggest that it simply reflected the brutality and passion of ancient Roman society.

In AD 62, a strong earthquake damaged large sections of the city. This was a warning for the residents of Pompeii. Many left and never returned. Then, on the morning of **August 24, AD 79**, Mount Vesuvius erupted, propelling a tall mushroom cloud of superheated rock and gas into the air. Pompeii, being about five miles away, was not immediately hit by the volcanic lava. So, the inhabitants still could have escaped. But the next morning, a cloud of toxic gas poured into the city, suffocating all two thousand people who remained. Then a flood of volcanic ash completely buried the city, bringing its licentiousness to a dreadful end.

The Bible speaks of other immoral civilizations and cities that were punished by God for their brazen iniquity—the antediluvians (Genesis 6; 7), Sodom and Gomorrah (Genesis 19), and Babylon (Daniel 5). We could also add Pompeii and Herculaneum, the other city destroyed by the volcano's eruption. Our world today is rapidly becoming like it was in the days of Noah (Matthew 24:37–39) and Sodom and Gomorrah (Jude 7). What should we expect other than its impending destruction?

Yes, our world will soon be destroyed by God's intervening hand. But the same fire that will consume sin and all its expressions will also purify the earth, preparing it for God's new creation. Then there will be "new heavens and a new earth in which righteousness dwells" (2 Peter 3:13).

ꝗs God Ɗead?

The fool has said in his heart, "There is no God."

—Psalm 14:1

M any modern philosophers and scientists have denied the existence of God. But few became so derisive of God and the Christian value system as the German philosopher Friedrich Nietzsche. He was born on October 15, 1844, and died on **August 25, 1900**. He is widely known for his nihilistic philosophy, his notion that "God is dead," and his idea of the overman or superman that inspired the Nazi regime.

The notion that "God is dead" permeates much of Nietzsche's writings. For example, in his book *The Gay Science* (1882), he stated, "Gods too decompose. God is dead, God remains dead. And we have killed him."[40] In the famous work *Thus Spoke Zarathustra* (1883), he added, "Dead are all the Gods: now do we desire the Superman to live."[41] And in his *Ecce Homo* (1888), he mocked the biblical Creation-Fall account (Genesis 1–3), saying, "It was God himself who at the end of his great work, coiled himself up in the form of a serpent at the foot of the tree of knowledge. It was thus that he recovered from being a God. . . . The devil is simply God's moment of idleness, on that seventh day."[42]

When Nietzsche declared that "God is dead," he was not implying that God had once existed and later died in a literal sense. His point was that God never existed, and with the Enlightenment, all Christian absolute moral principles and values collapsed. In his view, life has no intrinsic meaning, purpose, or value—a notion that has played a major role in eroding the moral values of society.

In a time when many deny the existence of God, there are still sensible people who keep their confidence in Him. The story is told of Billy Graham being challenged by someone who said, "Billy, you talk very much about God as if He lives. He is dead. He has no more power in the affairs of men." Billy simply replied, "I do not know of His death. I spoke to Him this morning."

Can we *prove* the existence of God? No, we cannot prove *or disprove* it. But we have plenty of evidence for belief in Him. As testified by King David, "The heavens declare the glory of God; and the firmament shows His handiwork" (Psalm 19:1). And God Himself challenges us, "Lift up your eyes and look to the heavens: Who created all these?" (Isaiah 40:26, NIV). God is not dead; He is very alive and cares for each one of us, even those who deny His existence.

Rivers of Living Water

"He who believes in Me, as the Scripture has said,
out of his heart will flow rivers of living water."

—John 7:38

There are huge rivers in the world, but none of them can be compared to the enormous Amazon—the greatest of all rivers. With many Indigenous tribes already living along its banks, the Amazon was "discovered" in February 1542 by the Spanish explorer and conquistador Don Francisco de Orellana. Swept downriver by the current, his expedition arrived at the Atlantic Ocean on **August 26, 1542**. Since then, the Amazon has captivated the interest of many explorers, including Theodore Roosevelt and Jacques Cousteau.

With a basin of approximately eleven hundred tributaries, the Amazon discharges approximately 1,581 cubic miles (6,590 cubic kilometers) of water per year into the Atlantic Ocean. That's more than the seven next largest independent rivers combined! It represents close to 20 percent of the global riverine discharge. But that's not all.

On August 17, 2011, at the International Congress of the Brazilian Society of Geophysics in Rio de Janeiro, Valiya Hamza and Elizabeth Tavares Pimentel detailed the discovery of an underground river flowing miles beneath the mighty Amazon River. Scientific data suggests that this river is almost as long as the Amazon River but up to hundreds of times wider and much slower and that it discharges into the lower depths of the Atlantic Ocean.

The Amazon Basin is only part of the much larger water cycle of the world. In that cycle, "lake and ocean, river and water spring—each takes to give."[43] As gigantic as it may be, the Amazon River is what it is only because of the smaller rivers and even the tiny creeks that feed it. And it must empty its water into the ocean. But even the waters of the ocean do not remain there. A significant percentage evaporates and then returns to the earth in the form of rain, thus feeding the endless water cycle.

Whether you are a huge river or a little creek does not matter. What really matters is whether you are fulfilling your task in God's overall plan. You and I must share God's Word, being "the recipients and the channels of its life-giving energy."[44] What blessings would flow forth to the world if each of us were a recipient and channel of God's saving message!

ᏴIBLE CONFERENCES

*"You study the Scriptures diligently because you think that in them you
have eternal life. These are the very Scriptures that testify about me."*
—John 5:39, NIV

Seventh-day Adventists consider themselves an end-time prophetic movement raised by God for the final restoration of Bible truth. The great Millerite disappointment of October 1844 challenged the founders of the Seventh-day Adventist Church to further study the Scriptures. Ellen White explained, "There was diligent study of the Scriptures, point by point. Almost entire nights were devoted to earnest searching of the Word. We searched for the truth as for hidden treasures. The Lord revealed Himself to us. Light was shed on the prophecies, and we knew that we received divine instruction."[45]

By the end of 1846, the core group of early Sabbath-keeping Adventist leaders—Joseph Bates, James White, and Ellen White—were already essentially united on the distinctive doctrines of their emerging movement. Soon they began to share their newly discovered truths with other former Millerites. Crucial in that process were seven weekend Bible conferences held in 1848 in different locations in the northeastern United States. One of those occurred in Volney, New York, on August 18–19. About thirty-five people, holding all kinds of conflicting views, attended the meetings. According to Ellen White, hardly two of them agreed.

Another important conference was held on **August 27–28, 1848**, in Hiram Edson's barn in Port Gibson, New York. This was the same place where Edson, O. R. L. Crosier, and Franklin B. Hahn had studied the biblical basis of the sanctuary doctrine. During that conference, Ellen White had a vision about the importance of the brethren laying aside their differences and uniting in Bible truth. Indeed, the 1848 Bible conferences brought doctrinal unity among believers.

We inherited from our pioneers a well-established and consistent doctrinal system. But today, we should also manifest the same spirit of untiring commitment to prayer and the study of Scripture. Spending time with God and His Word is the strict condition for every true revival and reformation. So, rather than having only social-relational small groups, we should also establish study groups devoted to deepening our understanding of the Bible.

"*I* *Have a* *Dream*"

Brethren, I do not count myself to have apprehended; but one thing I do, forgetting those
things which are behind and reaching forward to those things which are ahead, I press
toward the goal for the prize of the upward call of God in Christ Jesus.
—Philippians 3:13, 14

One of the worst social problems in the world is racism, a form of social injustice in which people are judged not by what they are but rather by the color of their skin and their ethnic background. Conscious of how dangerous and threatening this problem is, many have joined anti-racist social and political movements.

On **August 28, 1963**, more than two hundred thousand people gathered in Washington, DC, for the March on Washington, a political rally for racial justice and equal opportunities for African Americans. The event culminated with Martin Luther King Jr.'s famous speech "I Have a Dream," in which he stated, "I have a dream that one day this nation will rise up, live out the true meaning of its creed: 'We hold these truths to be self-evident, that all men are created equal.' "[46]

But how can we truly overcome racism and other forms of discrimination? Should we hate those who hate us and discriminate against those who discriminate against us? If we do that, we end up adding more fuel to the fire, which can only generate an environment filled with even more hate. Dr. King also said, "Returning hate for hate multiplies hate, adding deeper darkness to a night already devoid of stars. Darkness cannot drive out darkness; only light can do that. Hate cannot drive out hate; only love can do that."[47] No wonder Jesus commanded, "Love your enemies, bless those who curse you" (Matthew 5:44). Love is the only oil that can effectively lubricate the rusty wheels of our society.

Geographical moves cannot transform our competitive, self-exalting instincts. Our own human efforts and best achievements cannot change our sinful nature. The task of overcoming our own selfishness—including the natural tendency to hate those who hate us and ignore those who ignore us—is a continuous process of being transformed more fully into Christ's image and likeness. As Paul said in Philippians 3:13, 14, we should forget our past failures and "press on" toward God's ideal for our lives. Only God's converting grace can give us a new, unselfish, and loving heart!

ℱLATTERING ℱRIENDS

A man who flatters his neighbor spreads a net for his feet.

—Proverbs 29:5

Our natural tendency is to appreciate those who applaud us and to avoid those who criticize us. Unquestionably, enemies can undermine our reputation and make our life quite difficult, as stated by David in some of his imprecatory psalms (e.g., Psalms 35; 58; 69; 109). Sometimes, however, our best friends can become our worst enemies. While our enemies point out our weaknesses and errors, our friends may end up just praising us and excusing our mistakes.

On **August 29, 1899**, Ellen White wrote a warning letter to John Harvey Kellogg from Australia. He was becoming increasingly self-sufficient and independent. She stated, "And why is it that I have written to you so often? Because there is none other whom you consider of sufficient authority to heed. This is the way the matter is represented to me. Your brethren and associates in the medical college and in the sanitarium are not the ones who can help you. You are your own authority. If the men connected with you were as true to you as they ought to be, you would hear words of counsel from them which you have not had."[48]

Two kings of Israel were notably misled because they followed the bad advice of their flattering friends. One was King Rehoboam (1 Kings 12:1–24), who rejected the advice of the elders and followed the suggestions of the young men who had grown up with him. Consequently, the whole nation of Israel was split into the kingdom of Israel to the north and the kingdom of Judah to the south. The other king was Ahab (2 Chronicles 18), who surrounded himself with four hundred flattering prophets to validate him, while he hated Micaiah, who rebuked him. Ahab's reckless attitude cost him his life.

A popular witticism warns, "Flattery will get you nowhere." It does not help the flatterer, who is dishonest with his or her own conscience and hypocritical with his or her supposed friend. And it deceives the person who is being flattered by creating a false assurance. As Christians, we must replace harsh criticism with sincere admonitions, and we must replace deceptive flattery with honest appreciation. Avoid offering "free advice" to those who do not want to be advised (Proverbs 9:7–9). Speaking the right word to the right person at the right time and place can make a positive impact in his or her life!

A Humble Marriage

Two are better than one,
because they have a good return for their labor:
If either of them falls down,
one can help the other up.
—Ecclesiastes 4:9, 10, NIV

Wedding ceremonies are special occasions on which brides become princesses wearing the dresses of their dreams. Some experts suggest that "selecting a wedding dress is more than just a fitting . . . it's a process—a memory in the making."[49] But not every couple can afford an ostentatious ceremony.

On Sunday, **August 30, 1846**, Elder "James Springer White and Miss Ellen Gould Harmon stood before Charles Harding, justice of the peace, in Portland, Maine, and were married."[50] There was no wedding ceremony, and Ellen did not wear a special wedding dress. Choosing not to burden others, James worked for a while hauling stone on the railroad without getting what he deserved for his labor. Later he began to chop cordwood from early morning until dark to earn about 50 cents a day. In mid-1848, he and two friends took a hundred acres of grass to mow at 87.5 cents per acre. He rejoiced, "Praise the Lord! I hope to get a few dollars here to use in the cause of God."[51]

After settling in Rochester, New York, in 1852, Ellen described her new home: "We have rented an old house for one hundred and seventy-five dollars a year. We have the press in the house. . . . You would smile could you look in upon us and see our furniture. We have bought two old bedsteads for twenty-five cents each. My husband brought me home six old chairs, no two of them alike, for which he paid one dollar, and soon he presented me with four more old chairs without any seating, for which he paid sixty-two cents. The frames are strong, and I have been seating them with drilling. Butter is so high that we do not purchase it, neither can we afford potatoes. We use sauce in the place of butter, and turnips for potatoes. Our first meals were taken on a fireboard placed upon two empty flour barrels. We are willing to endure privations if the work of God can be advanced."[52]

This was the spirit of self-sacrifice and commitment of the Adventist pioneers to spread the three angels' messages in the early days of our movement. Times have changed. But what can we do to continue the work and finish it in the same spirit?

CREATING OPPORTUNITIES

*"We must work the works of Him who sent Me as long
as it is day; night is coming when no one can work."*
—John 9:4, NASB

F amous people are still human, with their own feelings and spiritual needs. But conventional outreach methods might not always work with them as well as one would expect. One of the best methods is to discreetly care for them when they are facing an existential crisis.

Diana, Princess of Wales, was in much turmoil while the media was exposing her private life. In October 1994, she even went to Washington, DC, for a weekend with her close friend and "second mother," Lucia Martins Flecha de Lima, wife of the Brazilian ambassador to the United States. Concerned with the whole situation and owing to our own Brazilian citizenship, my wife and I sent a gift copy of Ellen White's book *The Desire of Ages* and a caring letter to Diana. A month later, Maureen A. Stevens, a clerk from the Prince of Wales's office, sent us a short letter expressing the Princess's gratitude for our letter and enclosure and extending "her best wishes."

The world was shocked when the news reported that Diana died in a terrible car accident in Paris, France, at around two o'clock in the morning on Sunday, **August 31, 1997**. We do not know whether she ever read the book we sent her. Maybe not. But we did our best at a time when she was more likely to be receptive to gestures of appreciation and care. According to Christ's own words, we should work "as long as it is day," for "night is coming when no one can work" (John 9:4, NASB).

In reality, "every year millions upon millions of human souls are passing into eternity unwarned and unsaved. From hour to hour in our varied life opportunities to reach and save souls are opened to us. These opportunities are continually coming and going. God desires us to make the most of them. Days, weeks, and months are passing; we have one day, one week, one month less in which to do our work."[53]

In proclaiming the everlasting gospel, we should not only take advantage of the opportunities that already exist but also create new opportunities to witness about our faith. The apostle Paul even requested an opportunity to preach to the Roman emperor (Acts 25:1–12). Like him, we should try to reach the most influential people in our society.

A Visit to Auschwitz

Then the LORD saw that the wickedness of man was great in the earth,
and that every intent of the thoughts of his heart was only evil continually.
—Genesis 6:5

Few places I have visited have disturbed me as much as the Auschwitz-Birkenau State Museum located in Oświęcim, Poland. On **September 1, 2004**, while I was lecturing at a Bible conference for Polish pastors, a friendly young man took me to see the horrific concentration camp that operated between 1940 and 1945. At the top of the main gate, one can still see the cruel German inscription, *Arbeit macht frei*—"Work sets you free." During my visit, I was filled with deep sorrow at seeing the tangible evidence of how brutal human beings can be to one another under the influence of the devil.

After arriving at Auschwitz, most prisoners were killed in the gas chambers, and their bodies were immediately incinerated. Then their ashes were used as fertilizer in the nearby fields. Initially, those spared were photographed for the sake of identification. But under a variety of ongoing tortures, including starvation and slave work, their appearances changed so much that they could no longer be recognized. So, the identification process had to be replaced with tattooing identification numbers on the prisoners. Some of the cruelest atrocities committed were the reproductive and genetic experiments on human beings. One of the main goals was to sterilize Slavic women and learn how to make Aryan women give birth to twins.

One wonders how such atrocities could be committed in the culturally developed Europe of the mid-twentieth century. Nazism includes a tragic blend of the nihilist philosophy of a dead God (taught by Friedrich Nietzsche) and the evolutionary theory of the survival of the fittest.

Nazism is one example of the practical expression of Satan's government, which he claimed was far better than God's. Undeniably, human beings are sinners by nature, and apart from God, they tend to destroy themselves. Only God can bring true stability to our world, to our social circles, and to our individual lives. Please do not leave God out of your plans!

OBERLIN COLLEGE

Train up a child in the way he should go,
And when he is old he will not depart from it.

—Proverbs 22:6

C hristian education should impart knowledge, develop thinking abilities, and perpetuate spiritual and moral values. On **September 2, 1833,** Oberlin Collegiate Institute (later known as Oberlin College) was founded as an independent, self-supporting college to educate students "thoroughly, and train them up in body, intellect and heart, for the service of the Lord."[1] By the early 1840s, students were being trained in manual labor; eating a vegetarian diet and avoiding tea, coffee, and strong condiments; adopting a modest dress code, eliminating tight dress and ornamental attire; using the Bible as their textbook; and being discouraged from reading novels.

There is no direct link between Oberlin College and the Seventh-day Adventist educational system. But following the inspired counsel of Ellen White, many Adventist boarding schools adopted similar educational and health standards. Early Adventist educator Edward A. Sutherland even commended Oberlin College as a model for Christian education. But, while many Adventist educational institutions still abide by those principles, Oberlin gave them up decades ago. This raises a crucial question: Why do educational institutions that were originally guided by solid biblical principles tend to reject those principles and be absorbed by their surrounding culture?

In his book *The Dying of the Light,* James T. Burtchaell examines how colleges and universities lost their original religious identity. He argues that, first, religion became an individual matter rather than the overall culture of the institution; and, second, the original doctrinal emphasis was replaced by a more subjective form of religion, opening the door to secularism and acculturation.[2] Long before Burtchaell wrote his book, Ellen White warned, "If a worldly influence is to bear sway in our school, then sell it out to worldlings and let them take the entire control."[3]

When we strengthen our Adventist educational system, we shape the future of our church. May that system remain faithful to the biblical principles on which it was originally built and that are the reason for its existence!

I'M INNOCENT

"Have nothing to do with a false charge and do not put an innocent
or honest person to death, for I will not acquit the guilty."
—Exodus 23:7, NIV

Sometimes a lack of conclusive evidence can lead to unfair verdicts. That was the case with Nicholas Yarris. After several months of anticipation, on July 1, 1982, he was convicted of murder, rape, and abduction and was sentenced to death. Yet, he continued to claim his innocence. Once forensic DNA testing became available, Yarris's case was reexamined, and on **September 3, 2003**, the court exonerated Yarris of the charges based on the conclusive results. After a few additional issues were cleared, he was finally freed from prison in 2004 after spending twenty-two years behind bars for a crime he did not commit.

As a death-row inmate, Yarris had every reason in the world to become angry and simply give up on life. For fourteen years, he was not allowed to hug another human being and experienced sensory deprivation. However, he was "made strong out of weakness" (Hebrews 11:34, ESV) and used his time to educate himself by reading thousands of books. He learned German and studied psychology to better understand himself and those around him. He has since shared his life-changing experience with many people around the world.

Four weeks after leaving prison, Yarris gave an insightful interview in which he stated, "The act of finding sanity in the house of insanity is humility. You have to let go of all the ego; it gets stripped away from you, and then you try and resurrect something from whatever you find, whatever you have left. You have to try and find that one good thing inside yourself that is everything to you, and try and build on that."[4] And more, "Despite everyone's expectations of bitterness and anger or the inability to let go of what happened to me, I am focusing on all the good things. I am a good man now and I want the world to know that people can be redeemed. People can change."[5]

In the book of Revelation, the souls of the martyrs are metaphorically calling for God's justice (Revelation 6:9, 10). Even if His vindication does not occur as quickly as we would like, by God's grace, we should complain less, do what we can to build our faith, and try to gain strength from even the most disastrous circumstances.

𝒯HE ℛOMAN 𝓔MPIRE

*"And the fourth kingdom shall be as strong as iron, inasmuch as iron
breaks in pieces and shatters everything; and like iron that crushes,
that kingdom will break in pieces and crush all the others."*

—Daniel 2:40

D aniel 2 symbolically presents a sequence of four major kingdoms: Babylon, Media-Persia, Greece, and Rome. Each nation would conquer the previous kingdom, and eventually, that nation would be defeated by another political power. The fourth kingdom was the Roman Empire, which formally became an empire when Augustus Caesar became the first emperor of Rome in 31 BC. At its height, the empire was the most extensive and powerful political and social structure in Western civilization. Nevertheless, the great Roman Empire fell on **September 4, AD 476,** when Romulus Augustus in the west was deposed by the Germanic king Flavius Odoacer. The eastern part of the empire survived as the Byzantine Empire until the fall of Constantinople to the Ottoman Turks in 1453.

What caused the decline and fall of the Roman Empire? That is a very complex issue, and many theories have been suggested. In 1776, Edward Gibbon suggested, "The decline of Rome was the natural and inevitable effect of immoderate greatness. Prosperity ripened the principle of decay; the causes of destruction multiplied with the extent of conquest; and as soon as time or accident had removed the artificial supports, the stupendous fabric yielded to the pressure of its own weight."[6]

From a human perspective, the fall of Rome was caused mainly by political, economic, and social factors. From a biblical perspective, we recognize that "the Most High rules in the kingdom of men, and gives it to whomever He chooses" (Daniel 4:32). Ellen White explains, "Every nation that has come upon the stage of action has been permitted to occupy its place on the earth, that it might be seen whether it would fulfill the purpose of 'the Watcher and the Holy One.' . . . Each had its period of test, each failed, its glory faded, its power departed, and its place was occupied by another."[7]

God is leading human history to its climax—the establishment of His own everlasting kingdom that "will never be destroyed, nor will it be left to another people" (Daniel 2:44, NIV).

CARING FOR HEALTH

"If you diligently heed the voice of the LORD your God and do what is right in His sight, give ear to His commandments and keep all His statutes, I will put none of the diseases on you which I have brought on the Egyptians. For I am the LORD who heals you."
—Exodus 15:26

Both the gift of life and the blessing of health are special treasures to be valued and preserved in the best condition possible. But many of us take action only when illnesses and diseases are threatening us. But we should take the proverb "Better safe than sorry" more seriously. After all, it is better to prevent disease than to cure it.

During the 1860s, Seventh-day Adventists began to actively promote health reform. An important part of that was Ellen White's extensive vision on June 5, 1863, in which she saw basic health reform principles. On December 25, 1865, God showed her that Seventh-day Adventists should establish their own health reform institution where they could apply those principles consistently. Finally, on **September 5, 1866**, the Western Health Reform Institute opened in Battle Creek, Michigan. It was eventually renamed Battle Creek Sanitarium. In 1875, Dr. John Harvey Kellogg joined the staff, and the following year he was appointed medical superintendent at age twenty-four. That institution became the forerunner of a worldwide system of health-care facilities operated by the church.

But why does the church carry on such an expensive health system? Would it not be far easier to perform healing miracles like many of the Pentecostal and charismatic preachers? Seventh-day Adventists believe that God still performs miracles today as He did in the past but less ostentatiously and with less publicity than those preachers want to receive (I'm reminded of Mark 1:40–45). Furthermore, many of those popular preachers perform their healing miracles without ever educating people to live a healthy lifestyle.

We know that diseases are not always the result of a sinful lifestyle (John 9:1–3). But there are many blessings that come from intentionally living a healthful lifestyle (Exodus 15:26). Let us not only teach our principles of healthful living to others but also practice them in our own lives. Our words need to be backed by our own example!

September 6

SUFFICIENT GRACE

And He said to me, "My grace is sufficient for you,
for My strength is made perfect in weakness."

—2 Corinthians 12:9

There is a human tendency to expect from God more than we have already received and to ask from Him more than we deserve. The reading for **September 6** in Max Lucado's *Grace for the Moment Daily Bible* is titled, "Is That All There Is?" He states that God's grace, as revealed at the cross, is sufficient for our salvation.

Maybe you've gone through the acts of religion and faith and yet found yourself more often than not at a dry well. Prayers seem empty. Goals seem unthinkable. Christianity becomes a warped record full of highs and lows and off-key notes.

Is that all there is? [Church] attendance. Pretty songs. Faithful tithings. Golden crosses. Three-piece suits. Big choirs. Leather Bibles. It is nice and all, but . . . where is the heart of it? . . .

Think about the words from Paul in I Corinthians 15:3. "I passed on to you what I received, of which this was most important: that Christ died for our sins, as the Scriptures say."

There it is. Almost too simple. Jesus was killed, buried, and resurrected. Surprised? The part that matters is the Cross. No more and no less.[8]

In our spiritual journey through this sinful and painful world, God provides us with His saving grace and even encourages us to ask for additional blessings (Matthew 7:7–11). The simple truth is that God has already provided everything we need to be saved, and we can know with certainty that "when I am weak, then I am strong" (2 Corinthians 12:10). Let's be thankful for His unlimited, saving grace every day of our lives.

THE FALL OF JERUSALEM

"But when you see Jerusalem surrounded by armies, then know that its desolation is near."
—Luke 21:20

One of the most tragic chapters in the history of Judaea was the conquest and destruction of Jerusalem by the Roman armies in AD 70, as predicted by Jesus in His eschatological sermon (see Matthew 24; Luke 21). In addition to Jesus' warnings, several strange events occurred as supernatural forewarnings of the impending calamities that would overthrow the city.

The Jewish historian Flavius Josephus mentions "a star resembling a sword . . . and a comet, that continued a whole year."[9] Then he says that "at the ninth hour of the night, so great a light shone round the altar and the holy house, that it appeared to be bright day time";[10] and "a heifer, as she was led by the high priest to be sacrificed, brought forth a lamb in the midst of the temple."[11] Moreover, the extremely heavy and securely locked eastern door of the temple opened by itself. Finally, he says, "Chariots and troops of soldiers in their armor were seen running about among the clouds."[12]

Four years before the war began, when the city was still enjoying peace and prosperity, a man called Jesus, the son of Ananus, began "to cry aloud, 'A voice from the east, a voice from the west, a voice from the four winds, a voice against Jerusalem and the holy house, a voice against the bridegrooms and the brides, and a voice against this whole people!' "[13] He continued to do so until a stone killed him during the siege of the city.

Jesus had warned His disciples that when they would "see Jerusalem surrounded by armies," they should know that its desolation would be near, and they should flee from Judaea to the mountains (Luke 21:20, 21). Another historian, Eusebius, explains that "Before the war began, members of the Jerusalem church were ordered by an oracle given by revelation to those worthy of it to leave the city and settle in a city of Perea called Pella."[14]

On **September 7,** AD **70,** Jerusalem was completely overtaken by the Romans. But all who followed Christ's warnings and left the city were saved! Just as Christ described signs of the fall of Jerusalem, He also outlined events that would indicate the nearness of His second coming and the end of the world. In His own words, "When these things begin to happen, look up and lift up your heads, because your redemption draws near" (Luke 21:28)!

September 8

BRIDGES OF HOPE

And how from infancy you have known the Holy Scriptures, which are
able to make you wise for salvation through faith in Christ Jesus.
—2 Timothy 3:15, NIV

Education is the master key that unlocks two major doors. The first is the door to access the past, revealing both the wisdom and mistakes of the previous generations. The second is the door to the future, providing hope for a better life. Kofi Annan, former United Nations secretary-general, stated that "literacy is a bridge from misery to hope."[15]

The Universal Declaration of Human Rights, Article 26, states that "everyone has the right to education"[16] and "elementary education shall be compulsory."[17] On November 17, 1965, with the purpose of encouraging nations and communities to reach this literacy goal, UNESCO designated **September 8** as International Literacy Day. But, as of 2013, there were "some 774 million adults who cannot read or write," and "two-thirds of these people are women."[18] In 2018, a UNESCO Institute for Statistics report showed that "about 258 million children and youth are out of school."[19]

Concerned over the issue, the Seventh-day Adventist Church, at its 1995 General Conference Session in Utrecht, the Netherlands, released an official statement on literacy. The document states that "the inability to read impacts every aspect of a person's life—earning power, career opportunities, access to health care information, and even the ability to raise a child properly. Without the skill of reading, few doors of opportunity can ever be opened."[20]

From a religious perspective, the document adds, "Adventists recognize a more vital reason to share the gift of reading. We believe that the ability to read God's Word—the good news of salvation—should not be reserved for the privileged few. We assert that every man, woman, and child should have access to the truths and uplifting power of the Bible."[21]

Are there illiterate people close to where you live and work? If so, perhaps you could mobilize your own community and establish a center of influence to teach illiterate people how to read. While developing their reading and writing skills, you could also show them the marvelous teachings of God's Word. In doing so, you will provide hope for the present and for eternity!

$\mathcal{A}$ $\mathcal{L}$EGACY FOR $\mathcal{L}$IFE

Do not repay anyone evil for evil. Be careful to do what is right in the eyes of everyone. If it is possible, as far as it depends on you, live at peace with everyone.
—Romans 12:17, 18, NIV

n 1927, Max Ehrmann (1872–1945) wrote his poem "Desiderata" (Latin for "Desired things"). He died on **September 9, 1945**, and those inspiring words remained widely unknown until the early 1970s. The text reads, in part, as follows:

Go placidly amidst the noise and haste,
and remember what peace there may be in silence.
As far as possible without surrender
be on good terms with all persons.
Speak [the] truth quietly and clearly;
and listen to others.

. . . .

. . . .
If you compare yourself with others,
you may become vain and bitter;
for always there will be greater and lesser persons than yourself. . . .
. . . .

. . . .
Nurture strength of spirit to shield you in sudden misfortune.
But do not distress yourself with dark imaginings.
Many fears are born of fatigue and loneliness.

. . . .

Therefore be at peace with God,
. . . .
and whatever your labors and aspirations,
in the noisy confusion of life keep peace with your soul.

. . . .
Be cheerful.
Strive to be happy.[22]

This advice can help us live a better life in a world that is growing increasingly chaotic.

September 10

CHEATING TO WIN

Do you not know that those who run in a race all run,
but one receives the prize? Run in such a way that you may obtain it.
—1 Corinthians 9:24

There was a time in the Western world when honesty and integrity were highly valued and intentionally cultivated. People used to say, "You have my word," and you knew they meant what they said. But our world is losing many basic moral values. Lying and cheating are too often considered normal.

The annual Berlin Marathon—with a length of 26 miles, 385 yards (42.2 kilometers)—is one of the largest and most popular road races in the world. On **September 10, 2000**, a group of thirty-three runners skipped some of the timekeeping stations. They started off running normally, but after some time, they disappeared only to reappear near the finish line. It turns out they decided to take a shortcut, riding the subway instead of running. But their plan did not work—they forgot about the computer chips they were wearing, which automatically recorded their time every 3 miles. All thirty-three runners were disqualified, and their times removed from the final race results.

Cheating has become a common practice in many cultures, and sometimes it's even perceived as cleverness. But as faithful Christians, we cannot accept cultural practices that undermine the universal principles of God's Word. Remember, "The integrity of the upright guides them, but the unfaithful are destroyed by their duplicity" (Proverbs 11:3, NIV).

God calls us to be honest in a dishonest society. We must not sell our souls at any price. Keep in mind Ellen White's words: "The greatest want of the world is the want of men—men who will not be bought or sold, men who in their inmost souls are true and honest, men who do not fear to call sin by its right name, men whose conscience is as true to duty as the needle to the pole, men who will stand for the right though the heavens fall."[23] May you and I be people of integrity and honor!

Selfless Love

"This is My commandment, that you love one another as I have loved you."
—John 15:12

After the horrific Al-Qaeda terrorist attacks of **September 11, 2001** (referred to as 9/11), many heartwarming stories began circulating. One such story is of sixty-two-year-old Rick Rescorla, a veteran of both the British and American armies and a hero on the battlefields of Vietnam. He was responsible for evacuating hundreds of people from the South Tower of the World Trade Center. And Rescorla calmed them by singing old songs from his native Cornwall, England. When one of his colleagues told Rescorla that he, too, had to evacuate the building, Rescorla replied, "You hear those screams? There's more people up there. I have to help get them out."[24]

Another story is told of twenty-four-year-old Welles Crowther, who came to be known as "the man in the red bandana." A group was trapped in the seventy-eighth-floor sky lobby. "A man with a red bandana covering his nose and mouth suddenly appeared from the wreckage and smoke. He spoke in a calm voice and guided them to a stairway, leading them to safety."[25] Crowther encouraged them to help others, and he made three trips up to the sky lobby before the tower collapsed. "As survivor Judy Wein, who was rescued by Crowther, notes, 'People can live 100 years and not have the compassion, the wherewithal to do what he did.' "[26]

In a world with so much cruelty and competition, what motivates people like Rescorla and Crowther to sacrifice their own lives for people they don't know? Would you be courageous enough to do the same? In James 1:17, we read, "Every good and perfect gift is from above, coming down from the Father of the heavenly lights, who does not change like shifting shadows" (NIV). Paul explains that the love of God is "poured out in our hearts by the Holy Spirit" (Romans 5:5), even in the hearts of non-Christians, who sometimes are more loving and thoughtful than many Christians.

As Christians, we should be first and foremost in demonstrating Christ's selfless love and compassion to the world. Christ's commandment for us today is to "love one another; as I have loved you, that you also love one another. By this all will know that you are My disciples, if you have love for one another" (John 13:34, 35). Let's choose to reflect the light of the Sun of Righteousness (Malachi 4:2) to all around us.

September 12

THE RACE OF FAITH

Therefore we also, since we are surrounded by so great a cloud of witnesses, let us lay aside every weight, and the sin which so easily ensnares us, and let us run with endurance the race that is set before us, looking unto Jesus, the author and finisher of our faith.
—Hebrews 12:1, 2

The modern marathon derives its name from the decisive battle at Marathon, Greece, where the Athenians repelled the Persian invasion on **September 12, 490 BC.**[27] Although outnumbered, the Greek soldiers defeated the Persians.[28] A popular legend about the event suggests that Pheidippides, a soldier, was sent ahead to Athens, a distance of about 25 miles, to announce the victory. Upon reaching the Acropolis, he exclaimed, "Nike! Nike! Nenikekiam" (Victory! Victory! Rejoice, we conquer!), and then collapsed dead from exhaustion.[29] The Pheidippides story inspired the organizers of the first modern Olympics in Athens (1896) to include a long-distance footrace in honor of his run.

Similarly, we must run the race of faith to announce Christ's victory over evil. In Hebrews 12:1, we are encouraged to "run with endurance." Even if we end up collapsing at the end of our journey, we should do so, exclaiming like the apostle Paul, "I have fought the good fight, I have finished the race, I have kept the faith. Finally, there is laid up for me the crown of righteousness, which the Lord, the righteous Judge, will give to me on that Day, and not to me only but also to all who have loved His appearing" (2 Timothy 4:7, 8).

But our task is not only to run the race of faith. We must also be courageous soldiers of the cross and heralds of the gospel. Indeed,

How beautiful on the mountains
    are the feet of those who bring good news,
who proclaim peace,
    who bring good tidings,
    who proclaim salvation,
who say to Zion,
    "Your God reigns!" (Isaiah 52:7, NIV).

$\mathcal{P}$REACHING $\mathcal{J}$ESUS

For I decided to know nothing among you except Jesus Christ, and him crucified.
—1 Corinthians 2:2, NRSV

Can you imagine someone who conducted more than four hundred evangelistic crusades and preached the Christian gospel to as many as 215 million people in live audiences in more than 185 countries on six continents?[30] And more, he met with the pope, the queen, several prime ministers and kings, and celebrities, and with every US president from Harry S. Truman to Donald Trump.[31] Speaking on many special occasions, he has been called "America's pastor."[32]

William Franklin Graham Jr. (1918–2018), popularly known as Billy Graham, was born on November 7, 1918, near Charlotte, North Carolina. On **September 13, 1947**, when he was only twenty-eight years old, Graham started his first citywide campaign in the Civic Auditorium in Grand Rapids, Michigan, "held under the banner of Youth for Christ."[33] His ministry team's goal of moral integrity was expressed in the "Modesto Manifesto" (1948). It pledged to uphold accurate reporting, financial honesty, sexual purity, and local clergy support. It was agreed that no man on their team would ever be alone with a woman other than his wife.[34]

Billy Graham saw his mission as leading people to repent from their sins and accept Jesus as their personal Savior. In his own words, "My one purpose in life is to help people find a personal relationship with God, which, I believe, comes through knowing Christ."[35] Furthermore, he wrote, "Sin is the second most powerful force in the universe, for it sent Jesus to the cross. Only one force is greater—the love of God."[36] Typically, Graham closed his powerful evangelistic sermons with an altar call for people to accept Christ while a choir solemnly sang the hymn "Just as I Am."[37]

Seventh-day Adventists have a unique prophetic message to proclaim to the world. It is summarized in the three angels' messages of Revelation 14:6–12. And, as Ellen White reminds us, "Christ is the center of all true doctrine."[38] And again, "Of all professing Christians, Seventh-day Adventists should be foremost in uplifting Christ before the world."[39] Christ cannot be known merely at the *doctrinal* level; He must be the *experiential* reality of our personal religion. Jesus Christ is at the heart of the Seventh-day Adventist message!

ℐNVESTING IN THE ℱUTURE

Do not merely listen to the word, and so deceive yourselves. Do what it says.
—James 1:22, NIV

The best investment that we as families and as a church can make is an investment in future generations. They will carry the torch of the everlasting gospel after our death. On Sabbath, **September 14, 1902**, Ellen White preached a stirring sermon at the East Los Angeles Campground[40] addressing the Christian responsibility to educate our children. She emphasized our duty to lead them to Christ and to teach them by precept and example how to practice our Adventist lifestyle.

For example, regarding how we should dress, she stated, "Have you linked right up with the Master? Has appetite and passion and all the enchantments of dress, the taste for dress, come in and cut off your connection with your heavenly Father? We do not ask you to be careless in dress. We ask you to dress simply, to dress your children simply, and to teach them how they can obtain the robe of Christ's righteousness that is without a spot or without a stain upon it."[41]

On eating meat, she affirmed, "We have no need to eat the flesh of dead animals at all. No, we will take the food at first; we will not wait to have it go through the animal, and then eat the dead flesh of the animal in order to get the food. We will take the food the first cooking. We will take the very best that we can get, and we will prepare it in the very best manner to give us strength."[42]

Mrs. White also emphasized the need for physical exercise: "God wants us to teach our children that they shall use every muscle and every nerve. What is the matter with us? Why, this machinery is all rusting out with inaction."[43] Crowning the whole sermon, she declared, "What we want is more of Christ and much less of self. Now, this is what fathers and mothers need in their homes. They need the softness of the Spirit of God to come right into their hearts."[44]

Our problem usually is a lack of balance and commitment. Many of us take some components of our Adventist lifestyle seriously and ignore others. Perhaps we need to follow Christ's advice: "These are the things you should have done without neglecting the others" (Matthew 23:23, NASB). Let's consistently live up to all the light that the Lord has given us!

ℱHE ℰVERLASTING GOSPEL

Then I saw another angel flying in the midst of heaven, having the everlasting gospel to preach to those who dwell on the earth—to every nation, tribe, tongue, and people.
—Revelation 14:6

Seventh-day Adventists understand the "everlasting gospel" of Revelation 14:6, 7, as a universal message to be preached "to every nation, tribe, tongue, and people." It is still the "gospel of the kingdom" (Matthew 24:14), but it is now proclaimed in the context of the end-time "hour of His judgment" (Revelation 14:7).

In 1858, Sabbath-keeping Adventists began to print their first pamphlets in Dutch, French, and German, some of which were eventually sent to Europe. But the church was quite reluctant to send missionaries overseas. That changed on **September 15, 1874,** when J. N. Andrews (a widower) and his two children, Charles and Mary, departed on the Cunard steamship *Atlas,* traveling from Boston to Liverpool on the way to Switzerland. Andrews was the first missionary officially sent overseas by the denomination. From then on, thousands of Seventh-day Adventist missionaries have carried the everlasting gospel around the globe.

The Adventist missionary spirit was well described by Booton Herndon, a non-Adventist author, in his book *The Seventh Day: The Story of the Seventh-day Adventists.* He stated,

Surely no other twenty-five words [those of Matthew 24:14] have had such a direct impact on so many of the world's peoples. For the Seventh-day Adventists accept this message literally. To them it means this: when every single living person in the world has been told the good news of the coming of Christ, then the world will end, Christ will come again, and the righteous shall live in happiness forever.

No human endeavor could have a more glorious goal, and to hasten that day when the last man on earth shall have been told the gospel, Seventh-day Adventists have gone forth into all the world.[45]

What a wonderful mission endeavor! Regardless of where you live or what you do, you must have this Adventist missionary passion and be part of this worldwide Adventist missionary movement. Remember that wherever there are people who do not yet know the everlasting gospel, there is a mission field for you to work in for the Lord.

$\mathcal{U}$NCHANGEABLE $\mathcal{T}$IME

There is a time for everything,
and a season for every activity under the heavens.

—Ecclesiastes 3:1, NIV

Perhaps the most used excuse is some form of, "I didn't have enough time to do it." On **September 16, 1909**, an article by Ellen White appeared in the *Advent Review and Sabbath Herald*, where she made an appeal for wholehearted service:

> The Lord claims the service of all who believe the truth for this time. They are to be laborers together with Christ in proclaiming the message of mercy to the world. God has committed to each talents to be used for his name's glory. . . .
>
> "Let your light so shine before men," the Saviour declared, "that they may see your good works, and glorify your Father which is in heaven." There is to be no limit to the places where the light should shine. It is to reach to the regions beyond. Tell it, urge upon all with earnest force, to give their service for those who are in the darkness of error. To teach the word of God to unbelievers, to unite our prayers for them, are duties that we owe to our Redeemer. . . .
>
> I would say to all our people, Place yourselves in the light, that you may reflect light, and that souls may be led to see the great and soul-saving truths of the Word of God. Every believer in Christ should be a laborer together with him in drawing souls from sin to righteousness. We are to keep in view the life that measures with the life of God. We are to watch for opportunities to bring the truths of the Word before those who do not see and understand. Christ is not now with us in person, but through the agency of the Holy Spirit, he is present to impart his power and grace and great salvation.[46]

Each day has twenty-four hours to spend in the best way possible. Some people accomplish much during those hours, and others very little. Let's strive to make the best use of our time in service to the kingdom of God.

You Are Not Forsaken

The Lord is near to those who have a broken heart,
And saves such as have a contrite spirit.

—Psalm 34:18

Tears and sorrows may blur your physical eyes, but God uses your pain to help you see Him more clearly. This is what happened to Radim Passer, a real estate developer in Prague, Czech Republic. On Friday, May 29, 1998, his wife, Jana, had their first baby, Little Max. At six weeks old, the baby had a neurosurgical operation. Afterward, the attending pediatrician announced, "I am sorry to have to tell you this, but Little Max has an inoperable tumor in his head. Unfortunately, he has no chance of survival. It's likely that he only has a few days left to live."

In despair, Jana and Radim prayed for healing, but on August 2, the doctor phoned with the sad news, "Mr. Passer, I am so sorry to tell you this, but at 3:45 A.M., Little Max passed away." In sorrow, Radim told his wife the news and added, "I'm not going to pray anymore." While they searched for answers to their sorrow, a friend lent them the five volumes of the Conflict of the Ages series by Ellen White. Radim and Jana took a vacation to the Austrian Alps and began reading the books. They also watched the worldwide satellite series NET '98—The Next Millennium, presented by Dwight Nelson. And on Friday, **September 17, 1999**, Radim and Jana, as well as Jana's mother, were baptized into the Seventh-day Adventist Church.

Sometimes, pain is the only way God can reach us. William O. Cushing expressed this concept in his beautiful song, "Hiding in Thee." Reflect on the first stanza and refrain:

O safe to the Rock that is higher than I,
My soul in its conflicts and sorrows would fly;
So sinful, so weary, Thine, Thine would I be;
Thou blest "Rock of Ages," I'm hiding in Thee.

Hiding in Thee, hiding in Thee,
Thou blest "Rock of Ages," I'm hiding in Thee.[47]

Remember, the Lord is with you, even when you are tempted, like Radim, not to pray anymore. You can trust that "the Lord is near to those who have a broken heart" (Psalm 34:18).

$\mathcal{F}$OLLOW THE $\mathcal{B}$IBLE

"So will My word be which goes forth from My mouth;
It will not return to Me empty,
Without accomplishing what I desire,
And without succeeding in the matter for which I sent it."

—Isaiah 55:11, NASB

D o you love the Bible? If so, how frequently do you read it? In April 2013, Religion News Service carried an insightful article entitled "Poll: Americans Love the Bible but Don't Read It Much."[48] Doug Birdsall, president of the American Bible Society, explained, "I see the problem as analogous to obesity in America. We have an awful lot of people who realize they're overweight, but they don't follow a diet. . . . People realize the Bible has values that would help us in our spiritual health, but they just don't read it."[49] This is a problem not only for the overall population but also for Christian denominations.

During the 2008 General Conference Annual Council in Manila, Philippines, the Follow the Bible rally was launched to promote both personal and collective study of God's Word. The ceremony included the dedication of a special Bible with each of its sixty-six books printed in a different language. From Manila, the Bible went on a twenty-month travel itinerary around the world as a visual appeal for people to spend more time studying the Bible. On **September 18, 2009**, the traveling Bible arrived in Tel Aviv, Israel, in the region where most of the Bible's events occurred and where many of its books were originally written. The Bible ended its journey at the 2010 General Conference Session in Atlanta, Georgia. Today, it is on permanent display at the General Conference headquarters in Silver Spring, Maryland.

Reading the Bible is vital, but is it enough to read the Bible in short devotional snippets? No, it is not. Superficiality is one of the greatest sins of our generation. In the parable of the sower, Jesus warned about the dangers of merely hearing God's word without understanding it and of not being deeply rooted in His Word (Matthew 13:19–21). Ellen White stated, "Every one should feel that there rests upon him an obligation to reach the height of intellectual greatness"[50] and that we should "become giants in the understanding of Bible doctrines and the practical lessons of Christ."[51] Let's take these inspired counsels more seriously and dig into the Bible!

$\mathcal{P}$RAYER AND $\mathcal{L}$ABOR

For if I preach the gospel, I have nothing to boast of, for I am
under compulsion; for woe is me if I do not preach the gospel.
—1 Corinthians 9:16, NASB

James Hudson Taylor (1832–1902) was born in Barnsley, England, on May 21, 1832, to Christian parents. As a teenager, he became skeptical about his faith and engaged in worldly activities. One day, his mother felt the urge to pray for him until she was convinced that her prayer was answered. That same day, Hudson had an amazing conversion experience, and eventually, he sensed God's call to become a missionary to China. He began to study Mandarin, as well as Greek, Hebrew, and Latin. Under the auspices of the Chinese Evangelization Society, he received medical training at a hospital in London. On **September 19, 1853**, at the age of twenty-one, Hudson left Liverpool on the vessel *Dumfries* and arrived in Shanghai, China, on March 1, 1854.

In 1865, Hudson Taylor founded the China Inland Mission (CIM). In his book, *China: Its Spiritual Need and Claims* (1865), Taylor stated,

Can the Christians of England sit still with folded arms while these multitudes are perishing—perishing for lack of knowledge—for lack of that knowledge which England possesses so richly, which has made England what England is, and has made us what we are? What does the MASTER teach us? Is it not that if one sheep out of a hundred be lost, we are to leave the ninety and nine and seek that one? But here the proportions are almost reversed, and we stay at home with the one sheep, and take no heed to the ninety and nine perishing ones![52]

Hudson Taylor dedicated fifty-one years of his life to being a missionary in China. There was a passion and an urgency in everything he did. It has been said that the sun never rose on China without finding Hudson Taylor on his knees. When he died, there were 205 CIM mission stations, 849 missionaries, and 125,000 Chinese Christians. Wherever we are serving the Lord, we should be filled with the same passion for souls and determination for mission that motivated Hudson Taylor.

ℱADING ℐOO SOON

But Jesus said, "Let the little children come to Me,
and do not forbid them; for of such is the kingdom of heaven."
—Matthew 19:14

J ust before I left for the airport, after some meetings with pastors and local church elders, a man approached me with a heavy burden on his heart. His wife was pregnant, and just a few days before, medical tests confirmed that the baby she was expecting had anencephaly (much of the brain and skull missing). Her physician advised her to have an abortion, but she wanted to have the baby. Months later, I learned that, by God's mercy, the baby was born and survived for two weeks, giving the mother some time with him. It is terrible to see miscarriages and little children suffering and dying so early in life!

On **September 20, 1860**, Ellen White had her fourth child, eventually called John Herbert. Later she stated,

> December 14 [Friday], I was called up. My babe was worse. I listened to his labored breathing, and felt his pulseless wrist. I knew that he must die. That was an hour of anguish for me. The icy hand of death was already upon him. We watched his feeble, gasping breath, until it ceased. . . . We followed our child to Oak Hill cemetery, there to rest until the Life-giver shall come, and break the fetters of the tomb, and call him forth immortal.
>
> After we returned from the funeral, my home seemed lonely. I felt reconciled to the will of God, yet despondency and gloom settled upon me.[53]

Many ask, "What about young children who die?" Ellen White offered some helpful insight on the subject. She explains that children of believing parents will be saved because the faith of those parents "covers the children, as when God sent His judgments upon the first-born of the Egyptians."[54] Yet, Ellen White adds, "Whether all the children of unbelieving parents will be saved we cannot tell, because God has not made known His purpose in regard to this matter."[55] Whatever God's purpose, it is a blessing to know that He loves and cares for our little ones!

*L*UTHER'S *B*IBLE

Your word is a lamp to my feet
And a light to my path.

—Psalm 119:105

The Bible is by far the most translated book in world history. Some sources say that today at least parts of the Bible are available in nearly thirty-five hundred different languages.[56] One of the most famous translations is Martin Luther's, but when his German Bible came off the press, there were already fourteen High German editions and four Low German versions in print. Why did his translation become so popular and influential? There were several contributing factors.

While staying at the Wartburg Castle, Luther translated the entire New Testament in less than three months—from mid-December 1521 to early March 1522. An amazing accomplishment! After some revisions, the German New Testament was published on **September 21, 1522.** From then on, Luther continued to revise it while translating the Old Testament. In 1534, the first edition of his complete German Bible was printed.

All previous German translations had been based on the Latin Vulgate, perpetuating some of its theological mistakes. But Luther's translation was translated from the original Greek, Hebrew, and Aramaic texts and better reflected the actual meaning of the original Bible text. It corrected some of the mistakes in the Vulgate.

Convinced that the Bible should be understood even by common people, Luther used simple and understandable language. He suggested, "We must inquire about this of the mother in the home, the children on the street, the common man in the marketplace. We must be guided by their language, the way they speak, and do our translating accordingly. That way they will understand it and recognize that we are speaking German to them."[57] No wonder Luther's Bible became the main driving force behind the modern High German language!

The Bible can be withheld from people either by denying them physical access or by employing a language too difficult to be understood. For the Bible to be a "lamp" to people's feet and a "light" to their path (Psalm 119:105), its message has to be translated and communicated in the most reliable and comprehensible way possible. Luther's Bible combined both characteristics.

GOD ℐS GOD

And that every tongue should confess that Jesus Christ is Lord, to the glory of God the Father.
—Philippians 2:11

C. S. Lewis (1898–1963) was born in Belfast, Ireland, on November 29, 1898. Although raised in a Christian home, Lewis became an atheist in 1929 and was paradoxically "angry with God for not existing."[58] One night, he had a long discussion with two Oxford colleagues who were Christians. The next day, **September 22, 1931**, he went with his brother, Warnie, to the zoo. Lewis recalled, "When we set out I did not believe that Jesus Christ is the Son of God, and when we reached the zoo I did."[59] So, he "gave in, and admitted that God was God."[60] Lewis became one of the most influential Christian thinkers ever.

Against evolutionism, he argued,

If the solar system was brought about by an accidental collision, then the appearance of organic life on this planet was also an accident, and the whole evolution of Man was an accident too. If so, then all our present thoughts are mere accidents—the accidental by-product of the movement of atoms. And this holds for the thoughts of the materialists and astronomers as well as for anyone else's. But if *their* thoughts— i.e. of materialism and astronomy—are merely accidental by-products, why should we believe them to be true? I see no reason for believing that one accident should be able to give me a correct account of all the other accidents. It's like expecting that the accidental shape taken by the splash when you upset a milkjug should give you a correct account of how the jug was made and why it was upset.[61]

About God, Lewis suggested, "There are only two kinds of people in the end: those who say to God, 'Thy will be done,' and those to whom God says, '*Thy* will be done.' "[62] Regarding the Christian hope, he declared, "If you read history you will find that the Christians who did most for the present world were just those who thought most of the next. . . . It is since Christians have largely ceased to think of the other world that they have become so ineffective in this."[63]

Keep praying for the atheists and unbelievers that you know, for they, too, can become friends of God!

$\mathcal{J}$EROME OF $\mathcal{P}$RAGUE

*And the Lord turned and looked at Peter. Then Peter remembered the
word of the Lord, how He had said to him, "Before the rooster crows,
you will deny Me three times." So Peter went out and wept bitterly.*
—Luke 22:61, 62

Peter, one of the Twelve Apostles, promised loyalty to Christ but then denied knowing Him after Jesus was arrested. Immediately after his denial, Peter wept in repentance and recommitted his life to following Jesus (Luke 22:31–33, 54–62). A similar experience also occurred with Jerome of Prague (ca. 1365–1416), the eloquent Bohemian reformer and close friend of Jan Hus.

While studying at Oxford, Jerome accepted John Wycliffe's teachings against papal supremacy. Jerome's new emphasis on the authority of Scripture and the headship of Christ generated strong opposition from the Roman Catholic clergy. In April 1415, he was arrested and brought before the Council of Constance. Under much pressure and physical exhaustion, on **September 23, 1415**, he signed a formal retraction from the so-called heretical teachings of John Wycliffe and Jan Hus. However, some of the clerics questioned the sincerity of his renunciation. So, his trial was resumed in 1416.

On May 26, Jerome publicly withdrew his earlier retraction. He even confessed to the council that no other sin had bothered him so much as having denied his own convictions. On May 30, the council condemned him as a relapsed heretic and sentenced him to be burned at the stake. When the executioners wished to start the fire behind his back, he said, "Come here and light the fire in front of me. If I had been afraid of it, I should never have come to this place." He died praying. His ashes, like those of Hus, were thrown into the Rhine River.

We may never have publicly denied our Lord and Savior like Peter and Jerome of Prague did, but perhaps our loyalty to Christ, our commitment to His Word, and our support for His church are not as strong as they used to be. Perhaps we even made promises to Him that we never fulfilled. If that is the case, we should follow the example of those two great Christians, rededicating our lives to Christ and His cause.

Golden Cords

"Enlarge the place of your tent,
And let them stretch out the curtains of your dwellings;
Do not spare;
Lengthen your cords,
And strengthen your stakes.
For you shall expand to the right and to the left,
And your descendants will inherit the nations,
And make the desolate cities inhabited.

—Isaiah 54:2, 3

Adventist education provides a learning environment for transmitting biblical knowledge and values that will last for eternity. Committed to that noble ideal, some schools have become models of training, inspiring missionaries to carry the Adventist message around the globe. One such school is Union College in Lincoln, Nebraska.

When Union College was dedicated on **September 24, 1891**, its first president, W. W. Prescott, stated that all its lines of education should center on Christ. The report in the *Advent Review and Sabbath Herald* ended with this insightful projection: "Union College will become a power in the cause, and aid in bringing many souls at last unto glory. So may it be."[64] And it has, indeed, been the case.

At the commencement exercises on Sunday evening, May 20, 1906, the graduating class of that year presented a large missionary map of the world to the school, which was accepted by President C. C. Lewis. It had a golden cord extending from Union College to each point in the world where a missionary from Union College had gone. The map was kept on the front wall of the college chapel, and cords were added as new graduates went to serve in foreign lands.

In 1936, at the hanging of the golden cords, President M. L. Andreasen proposed that the institution might be called the College of the Golden Cords. He also suggested that a piece of cord should be sent out to all their missionaries as a symbol that the college community continued to pray for their success and safety. The cords provided a sense of attachment and belonging to those serving in the hardship and loneliness of the mission fields.

Regardless of where you are right now, offer a prayer for the dedicated missionaries who are preaching the everlasting gospel around the globe. If you know some of them, you might even send a short note saying that you are praying for them. As simple as it may be, this gesture of care and support can make a great difference in their lives!

PASSION FOR OVERSEAS MISSIONS

But I do not account my life of any value nor as precious to myself,
if only I may accomplish my course and the ministry which I received
from the Lord Jesus, to testify to the gospel of the grace of God.
—Acts 20:24, RSV

On Sabbath evening, October 22, 2016, I participated in an inspiring program in the town of Tramelan, Switzerland, celebrating the 130-year anniversary of the dedication of the local Seventh-day Adventist meetinghouse. However, the Adventist presence in this beautiful country had begun many years earlier, on February 7, 1866, when Michael Czechowski baptized Louise Pigueron and Jean David Goymet in Lake Neuchâtel. It was the first Adventist baptism in Switzerland and perhaps the first (or at most the second) in all of Europe.

Michael Belina Czechowski was born in Poland on **September 25, 1818**. After becoming a Catholic priest, he went to Rome for an interview with Pope Gregory XVI. Disillusioned with the Roman Catholic Church, Czechowski gave up his vows and got married. In 1851, he and his wife moved to North America, where he worked as a Baptist evangelist. Then in 1856, he met a group of Sabbath-keeping Adventists and became a preacher in this newly forming movement.

As time went by, Czechowski felt a burden to preach the Adventist message in Europe. With the newly organized Seventh-day Adventist Church unable to support him, he convinced a group of Sunday-keeping Adventists to sponsor his missionary endeavor. So, on May 14, 1864, he with his wife and Annie Butler sailed to Europe and preached the Seventh-day Adventist message in Italy, Switzerland, Germany, France, Hungary, and Romania. Upon request of the Swiss Adventists, J. N. Andrews was sent ten years later to Europe as the first "official" Seventh-day Adventist overseas missionary.

Having planted the seeds of the Adventist message in Europe, Czechowski died on February 25, 1876, in Vienna, Austria. He left a legacy of dedicated service. Several of his converts and their descendants served as Adventist missionaries in different areas of the world. His efforts proved once again that small seeds could generate large harvests. Even as volunteers (without any official sponsorship), you and I have the privilege of being committed missionaries sharing the Adventist message.

𝒯HE 𝒫OST CRUCIAL 𝒟ECISION

He went a little farther and fell on His face, and prayed, saying, "O My Father, if it is possible, let this cup pass from Me; nevertheless, not as I will, but as You will."
—Matthew 26:39

It was early in the morning on Monday, **September 26, 1983**, in a small town near Moscow. The Soviet Union's early warning computer system detected an incoming missile, then a second, a third, a fourth, and a fifth, all launched from the United States. The Soviet military protocol was to retaliate against such threats with a nuclear attack. The officer on duty was Stanislav Petrov, who was responsible for communicating apparent enemy missile launches. The alert reliability level was "highest," and the command option was "launch." But instead of reporting the information to his superiors, he dismissed it as a false alarm. Many years later, he declared, "I had all the data. If I had sent my report up the chain of command, nobody would have said a word against it."[65] And most certainly, a nuclear war would have overspread the world.

A later investigation confirmed that "Soviet satellites had mistakenly identified sunlight reflecting on clouds as the engines of intercontinental ballistic missiles."[66] Petrov concluded that the alerts were false because he felt sure that any first strike made by the United States would be massive—not a meager five missiles. Additionally, the alarms came only from a newly installed launch detection system and were uncorroborated by ground radar. Far-reaching consequences were involved, and Petrov could have simply fulfilled his duty by passing on the information. But he took the responsibility on his own shoulders—and made the right decision at a crucial moment when the future of humanity was at risk.

An infinitely greater decision was made by Jesus Christ in the garden of Gethsemane. He confessed to three of His disciples, "My soul is exceedingly sorrowful, even to death" (Matthew 26:38). Then, while alone, He prayed, "O My Father, if it is possible, let this cup pass from Me; nevertheless, not as I will, but as You will" (verse 39). In that awful crisis, everything was at stake, and "the mysterious cup trembled in the hand of the sufferer."[67] But, thanks be to God, Jesus went on to the cross and paid the price for our salvation!

DECIPHERING THE SYMBOLS

Daniel answered in the presence of the king, and said, "The secret which the king has demanded, the wise men, the astrologers, the magicians, and the soothsayers cannot declare to the king. But there is a God in heaven who reveals secrets, and He has made known to King Nebuchadnezzar what will be in the latter days."
—Daniel 2:27, 28

It's challenging to function in an unfamiliar location—especially when you cannot even identify the characters of the local language! So it was with philologists—those who study the history of languages—who faced serious challenges trying to decipher ancient pictographic symbols.

For centuries, the ancient Egyptian hieroglyphic writing—with approximately one thousand different characters in the form of pictures—remained obscure and unreadable. But this began to change in 1799 when the famous Rosetta Stone was discovered, and philologists began deciphering its three parallel inscriptions. That process reached its conclusion on **September 27, 1822,** when Jean-François Champollion's report was read to the Académie des Inscriptions et Belles Lettres in Paris, France. The successful outcome revealed much of ancient Egyptian religious culture.

Remarkably, two major events in the late 1790s advanced crucial lines of biblical studies. One, as noted, was the discovery of the Rosetta Stone in 1799, opening the door for many subsequent archaeological discoveries that corroborate the historicity of the Bible record. Another event was the imprisonment of Pope Pius VI in 1798, sparking great interest in the prophetic element of Scripture. The sealed portion of the book of Daniel (Daniel 8:26; 12:4) was finally opened (Revelation 10), and many of its apocalyptic symbols and time periods were finally understood.

Apocalyptic symbols—as found in the books of Daniel and Revelation—present one of the most challenging aspects of biblical interpretation. Daniel explained that such symbols could not be truly understood by mere human wisdom (Daniel 2:27, 28). God's Word itself provides the key for the interpretation of those symbols. For example, John 1:29, which declares, "Behold! The Lamb of God," helps us understand who is represented by the Lamb in the book of Revelation. By allowing the Bible to interpret itself, we can avoid many false assumptions and biased views.

$\mathcal{T}$IME-SETTINGS

"But of that day and hour no one knows, not even the angels of heaven, but My Father only."
—Matthew 24:36

On September 18, 2015, *The Jim Bakker Show* aired from the United States, featuring Pastor Mark Biltz of El Shaddai Ministries. The program was about the final blood moon of **September 28, 2015**, imagined to be the last sign before Christ's return to establish His supposed millennial kingdom in Jerusalem. Jim Bakker even advertised his urgent survival kit—a bulk, basic eight-year food supply for $2,500; a trifold shovel for $20; a solar energy radio for $65; and a fuel-less generator for $2,500. This is just one example of many similar time-setting propositions throughout the ages. People who suggest the new date of Christ's return assume that all previous attempts were mistaken and that they have finally discovered the correct one.

In 1850, Ellen White warned, "Time has not been a test since 1844, and it will never again be a test."[68] Even so, some Adventists have presumed to set specific years for Christ's return. Some believed that the 40 years of Israel's pilgrimage in the wilderness represented the period from 1844 to 1884. Others argued that an end-time fulfillment of the 120 years of Noah's preaching would extend from 1844 to 1964. As the nineteenth century turned into the twentieth, some were encouraging Adventist couples to have and adopt as many children as possible so that the 144,000 would be reached and Christ would return. Still others speculated about a supposed end of the 6,000 years since Creation by 1996 or 1997.

Revivals based on time are like a comet that shines brightly for a short while and then disappears on the horizon. Much excitement precedes the proposed date, but frustration and spiritual lethargy follow. Those who set dates for Christ's return read into the Bible their own speculative views. Ellen White reminds us, "The more frequently a definite time is set for the second advent, and the more widely it is taught, the better it suits the purposes of Satan."[69]

Knowing our tendency to procrastinate, Christ identified the *signs* of His soon coming (Matthew 24; Luke 21) without revealing the *time* when the events would occur. Therefore, we must "watch" and "be ready" for His coming, for we do not know when He will come (Matthew 24:42, 44). Let's prepare to meet Him soon!

THE CULTURE OF COMPETITION

But Jesus called them to Himself and said to them, "You know that those who are considered rulers over the Gentiles lord it over them, and their great ones exercise authority over them. Yet it shall not be so among you; but whoever desires to become great among you shall be your servant. And whoever of you desires to be first shall be slave of all."

—Mark 10:42–44

On Friday, **September 29, 1916**, newspapers across the United States announced that John D. Rockefeller (1839–1937) had just become the world's first billionaire.[70] By the time he was twelve, Rockefeller had saved more than fifty dollars "from working for neighbors and raising some turkeys for his mother."[71] But, being a visionary, he dreamed of an oil company with distribution throughout the country. So, in 1870, his thriving Standard Oil Company was established in Cleveland, Ohio. It became the largest oil refinery in the world. To prevent competition, Rockefeller bought several other companies.

His success was due to his personal skills combined with aggressive business and marketing strategies. Unlike the medieval monastic ethic that considered the vow of poverty to be the ultimate goal, Rockefeller saw his wealth as an opportunity for philanthropy. Today, the Rockefeller Foundation continues to benefit a variety of humanitarian projects.

However, Rockefeller built his powerful oil empire by means of what has been called "social Darwinism." It means that the "fittest" people naturally rise to the top of society. For Rockefeller, "the growth of a large business is merely the survival of the fittest. . . . This is not an evil tendency in business. It is merely the working-out of the law of nature and a law of God."[72] But for him to win, many others had to lose! This competition—thriving at the expense of others—often appears in the world in which we live.

It's beneficial to ask the question, How does God's kingdom relate to the culture of competition? As citizens of that kingdom, we need to promote *internal* cooperation and *external* competition. Paul's analogy of the human body (1 Corinthians 12:12–31) suggests that we should *cooperate* with one another in building up God's kingdom. Paul's analogy of the Christian soldier (Ephesians 6:10–20) encourages us to *compete* in God's strength against the hosts of darkness and the sinful world. Our goal is to make all human beings winners in Christ.

September 30

$\mathcal{A}$ $\mathcal{R}$EPENTANT $\mathcal{H}$EART

Out of the depths I have cried to You, O LORD;
Lord, hear my voice!
Let Your ears be attentive
To the voice of my supplications.

—Psalm 130:1, 2

Captain Joseph Bates was sailing the ship *Empress* from New Bedford, Massachusetts, to Rio de Janeiro. When he went to choose a book to read, he discovered that his wife had put a copy of the New Testament on the top of the other books in his trunk. He began reading.

Tragically, a fellow sailor on the voyage, Christopher, got sick and died. On **September 30, 1824**, Bates read a prayer at his funeral service, and then, with a heavy bag of sand bound to his feet, Christopher's body was plunged into the sea. While the body of his friend sank in the cold waters, Bates repented of his sins and surrendered his life to God. A few days later, Bates penned "A Solemn Covenant With God," which reads,

Eternal and ever-blessed God: I desire to present myself before thee with the deepest humiliation and abasement of soul. Sensible how unworthy such a sinful worm is to appear before the Holy Majesty of Heaven, the King of kings and Lord of lords, . . . I come therefore acknowledging myself to have been a great offender. Smiting on my breast and saying with the humble publican, "God be merciful to me a sinner," . . . this day do I with the utmost solemnity surrender myself to thee. I renounce all former lords that have had dominion over me, and I consecrate to thee all that I am, and all that I have. . . . Use me, O Lord, I beseech thee, as an instrument of thy service; number me among thy peculiar people. Let me be washed in the blood of thy dear Son, to whom, with thee, O Father, be everlasting praises ascribed by all the millions who are thus saved by thee. Amen.[73]

Here, Bates (1) recognized God's holiness and majesty; (2) acknowledged his own insignificance and sinfulness; (3) fully repented of his sins; (4) surrendered his life to God; and (5) asked God to use him in His service. Let's join Bates in this covenantal prayer today and every day.

THE CHOOSING OF A NAME

A good name is to be chosen rather than great riches, loving favor rather than silver and gold.
—Proverbs 22:1

Names are far more meaningful than we usually realize. Dale Carnegie suggested that "a person's name is, to that person, the sweetest and most important sound in any language." But the fact of the matter is that some people like their names, but others do not like them and even try to change them. Thus, much care should be taken in choosing names for our children, a new company, and even a new church.

Early Sabbath-keeping Adventists were reluctant to choose a name for their new denomination. Up until 1860, they referred to themselves as the "little flock"[1] (Luke 12:32), the end-time "remnant"[2] (Revelation 12:17, KJV), the "Sabbath and shut door believers,"[3] "God's Peculiar People That Keep the Commandments of God, and the Faith of Jesus"[4] (Revelation 14:12), "God's covenant-keeping people,"[5] "the church of God who keep the Sabbath—the seal of the living God,"[6] and the "Philadelphia Church"[7] (Revelation 3:7–13). But there was no consensus about one specific name.

When Adventists decided to incorporate their publishing work under the laws of the state of Michigan, they had to choose an official name. On **October 1, 1860**, at the 1860 General Conference Session in Battle Creek, Michigan, the discussions on the subject revolved around the names Church of God and Seventh-day Adventists. Upon considering the first name to be too generic and presumptuous, the final decision was, "*Resolved,* That we call ourselves Seventh-day Adventists."[8]

In 1861, Ellen White declared, "The name Seventh-day Adventist carries the true features of our faith in front, and will convict the inquiring mind. Like an arrow from the Lord's quiver, it will wound the transgressors of God's law, and will lead to repentance toward God and faith in our Lord Jesus Christ."[9]

In many places around the world, Seventh-day Adventists are known as honest and trustworthy Christians. As members of this denomination, we are carrying its name too. So, what have we done to preserve the good reputation of this denomination among our neighbors, coworkers, schoolmates, and friends? Remember that many people will judge the whole denomination by our behavior.

CHRISTIAN LIFESTYLE

*"Let your light so shine before men, that they may see
your good works and glorify your Father in heaven."*

—Matthew 5:16

Mohandas Karamchand Gandhi (1869–1948), later known as Mahatma Gandhi, was born on **October 2, 1869**, in the town of Porbandar in Western India. "Employing nonviolent civil disobedience, Gandhi led India to independence [from the British Empire] and inspired movements for civil rights and freedom across the world."[10] Without denying his Hindu convictions, Gandhi claimed to believe "in the fundamental truth of all great religions of the world"[11] and had a special admiration for Jesus Christ and His teachings.

But Gandhi saw a major lifestyle contrast between Christ and Christianity. The great Hindu leader stated, "The message of Jesus as I understand it, is contained in the Sermon on the Mount unadulterated and taken as a whole. . . . If then I had to face only the Sermon on the Mount and my own interpretation of it, I should not hesitate to say, 'Oh, yes, I am a Christian.' . . . But . . . much of what passes as Christianity is a negation of the Sermon on the Mount."[12] And he added, "All of you Christians, missionaries and all, must begin to live more like Jesus Christ. . . . Practice your religion without adulterating it or toning it down."[13]

Regrettably, many professed Christians do not try to imitate Christ and live a Christian lifestyle. Some are conscious of their own weaknesses and even state, "Do as I say, not as I do." Others try to calm their consciences and justify their personal lifestyles saying, "It's not what's on the outside but what's on the inside that counts." Instead of helping others grow and mature, some people choose to affirm them at their low standard, saying, "You are who you are, and that's all you should ever want to be."

We should avoid judging people by the color of their skin, their physical appearance, their accent, or other superficial matters, for, as the saying goes, "no beauty shines brighter than that of a good heart." But this should never be used as an excuse for lowering our standards. We may have the best intentions, but people evaluate us—and the transforming power of our religion—by the way we dress, by what we eat and drink, and by our family and social behavior. So, Christ's appeal to us today is, "Let your light so shine before men, that they may see your good works and glorify your Father in heaven" (Matthew 5:16).

ＤOCTRINAL ＤISPUTES

Can two walk together, unless they are agreed?

—Amos 3:3

There is only one true God, and His Word is unified in all its expressions (Ephesians 4:4–6), but not all Christians interpret that Word similarly. Good Christians have disagreed on doctrinal matters, and sometimes their disputes have escalated into schisms.

The German reformer Martin Luther and the Swiss reformer Huldrych Zwingli could not agree on the meaning of the expressions "this is My body" (Luke 22:19) and "he who eats My flesh" (John 6:56) as they relate to the Lord's Supper. So, in 1529, the Marburg Colloquy was called to settle the dispute. On **October 3, 1529**, the Marburg Articles were signed by Luther, Zwingli, and eight other preachers. They reached a basic consensus on fourteen doctrinal points but did not agree on whether the true body and blood of Christ are corporally present in the bread and wine of Communion.

At the end of the discussion, Zwingli said, "I call upon you, Doctor Luther, to forgive my bitterness. I have always desired your friendship a great deal, and I want it still. There are no others in Italy and France whom I would rather see."

Luther replied, "Call upon God, that you may receive understanding."

Martin Bucer also approached Luther and said, "I ask you, you recognize me as a brother, or do you believe that I am in error?"

In his response, Luther stated, "It is apparent that we are not of the same spirit. For we cannot be of the same spirit when on the one side the word of Christ is believed in innocent faith and on the other this same faith is censured, contested, slandered, and violated with all sorts of outrageous blasphemy."[14] And those two large Reformation groups never reconciled.

How should we handle our own doctrinal differences? A classic statement (probably made by the Lutheran theologian Rupertus Meldenius [1582–1651]) suggests, "In essentials unity, in non-essentials liberty, in all things charity."[15] This is very helpful advice. The problem is how to distinguish between "essentials" and "non-essentials." This motto can easily be used to foster doctrinal pluralism. While recognizing the diversity of gifts and ministries (1 Corinthians 12), we should always seek doctrinal unity (1 Corinthians 1:10). Christ's prayer for us is "that they all may be one, . . . that the world may believe that You sent Me" (John 17:21).

October 4

$\mathcal{A}$FRAID OF THE $\mathcal{U}$NKNOWN

And when the disciples saw Him walking on the sea,
they were troubled, saying, "It is a ghost!" And they cried out of fear.
—Matthew 14:26

After the terrible atrocities of World War II ended, the world entered what became known as the Cold War. The Iron Curtain separated the Eastern Bloc (led by the Soviet Union) from the Western Bloc (led primarily by the United States). The wounds of the past remained unhealed, and there was still much anxiety and uncertainty about the future. As if this was not enough, on **October 4, 1957**, the Soviets shocked the world by launching Sputnik I, the world's first artificial satellite.

In the context of the two conflicting and competitive blocs, Sputnik stunned the Americans, who believed that their own country was the most advanced nation on the planet. From a higher philosophical perspective, many wondered about its whole meaning and purpose. Many asked, "What will happen now that artificial objects are orbiting above us? What if they fall on us? Could they be spy systems for invading our privacy?"

The negative global reactions to the launching of Sputnik confirmed once again that we, as human beings, tend to be overly afraid of the unknown. Any supposed threat to our well-being or survival can generate high levels of fear and anxiety. If not kept under control, fear can easily escalate into a psychological disorder, causing us to be fearful even of our own shadows.

Matthew 14:26, the Bible text for today, speaks of a collective fear that took over the disciples while they sailed the stormy waters of the Sea of Galilee. Seeing Jesus walking on the sea, they hastily concluded that He was a "ghost" and cried out in fear. But the inspired record tells us that when Jesus stepped into the boat, the wind ceased, and they worshiped Him (Mark 6:51; Matthew 14:33). The presence of Jesus made all the difference!

Remember that worries, concerns, and fears cannot solve problems; they only put us on alert. If you have uncontrollable fears, why not entrust them to the Lord? "Cast all your anxiety on him, because he cares for you" (1 Peter 5:7, NRSV). "And the peace of God, which surpasses all understanding, will guard your hearts and your minds in Christ Jesus" (Philippians 4:7, NRSV).

ᏢAYING ᎾUR ᎠEBT

For the wages of sin is death, but the gift of God is eternal life in Christ Jesus our Lord.
—Romans 6:23

The first US president, George Washington, once said, "It is better to offer no excuse than a bad one." Were he still alive in 2010, he would have had an opportunity to follow his own advice. On **October 5, 1789**, George Washington borrowed a copy of the book *The Law of Nations* (the English translation of 1760) by Emer de Vattel from the New York Society Library. Ten years later, he died without having returned the book. On April 16, 2010, a library archivist confirmed that the book was still missing.

Upon being made aware of the unreturned book, George Washington's Mount Vernon estate staff immediately began searching for "another copy of the same edition, which they found online for about $12,000." They purchased the book and, on May 18, 2010, ceremoniously returned it to the New York Society Library. After adjusting for inflation, the cumulative 221 years of late fees would be some $300,000. At the ceremony, Charles Berry, the New York Society Library's chairman of the board of trustees, declared, "I hereby absolve George Washington and his representatives for any overdue library fees incurred."[16]

As fallen human beings, we all have a huge debt of sin that must be repaid. The payment is death (Romans 6:23), for "without shedding of blood there is no remission" from sin (Hebrews 9:22). Being "dead in trespasses and sins" (Ephesians 2:1), we could never pay our own debts. But through His amazing love and grace, Jesus Christ paid the price at the cross on our behalf so that we can be forgiven of our sins. As stated by the apostle Paul, "By grace you have been saved through faith, and that not of yourselves; it is the gift of God" (verse 8).

As in the case of George Washington, someone else paid our debt. But in contrast, while Washington, being dead, could not take part in returning the book, we must decide whether to accept or reject God's provision for us. This is a personal matter that no one else can decide for us. God's appeal to us today is, "Seek the LORD while He may be found, call upon Him while He is near" (Isaiah 55:6). Why not offer a word of prayer right now, either accepting or confirming your previous acceptance of God's gracious payment for your sins?

$\mathcal{T}$HE $\mathcal{D}$ELAYED $\mathcal{L}$ETTER

Behold, how good and how pleasant it is for brothers to dwell together in unity!
—Psalm 133:1, NASB

The success of a family is often best measured in wins and losses. This applies to the family we are from and the family we establish. Often, pride, selfishness, competition, and miscommunication have divided families and separated family members from one another. And, sadly, sometimes our worst enemies are those closest to us.

In April 1880, Dr. John Harvey Kellogg (1852–1943) hired his younger brother Will Keith Kellogg (1860–1951) as his assistant at the Battle Creek Sanitarium. The two men disagreed on several matters, but especially over the institution's commercial production. As a physician, Dr. Kellogg was most concerned about providing healthy food—including granola, cereal flakes, and vegetarian meat alternatives—to former sanitarium patients. As a businessman, Will wanted to improve the taste of their products and sell them to the general population. The tension between the two brothers led to a split and the establishment of their own respective businesses through several lawsuits and court trials.

The two brothers were disfellowshiped from the Adventist Church in 1907: first, Will, who had not attended the church for the prior twenty-seven years; and a few months later, John Harvey, for not being in full accord with church beliefs and practices. On December 14, 1943, John Harvey died, having never settled his differences with his younger brother. But more than four years later, on June 22, 1948, Will was surprised to receive a seven-page reconciliation letter Dr. Kellogg had written a considerable time before his death. It turned out that the doctor's secretary thought his letter was too demeaning of himself and decided not to forward it. Perhaps if Will had received John Harvey's letter in time, the brothers could have reconciled. Sadly, there is no evidence of a renewed relationship between the brothers.

On **October 6, 1951**, Will Keith Kellogg, the "King of Cornflakes" and founder of the Kellogg Company, died. The story of the Kellogg brothers is a pointed reminder to settle disagreements sooner rather than later—the right time is now. Even if the other person involved does not want to forgive you, at least you can do your part and live at peace with God and your own conscience.

CHRONOLOGICAL CONJECTURES

But avoid foolish disputes, genealogies, contentions, and strivings about the law; for they are unprofitable and useless.

—Titus 3:9

M any have speculated about the end of the "six thousand years" of earth's history and the beginning of a seventh millennium of rest. In the ancient Jewish book of 2 Enoch, chapter 33, verses 1 and 2 suggest that each day of the Creation week represented a thousand years. Psalm 90:4—"A thousand years . . . are like yesterday"—and 2 Peter 3:8—"One day is as a thousand years"—have been quoted in support of this premise. Ellen White declared that for "nearly six thousand years," the great controversy has "continued upon the earth."[17] But some people push these and other similar statements too far, assuming that the period under consideration should be dated as precisely as the seventy weeks of Daniel 9:24–27 and the twenty-three hundred evenings and mornings of Daniel 8:14.

Without complicating the subject too much, let me just mention three interesting observations. Jews from the third century AD believed that God began to create this world on **October 7, 3761** BC. If they are correct, then the six thousand years should end about AD 2239. In his famous and influential work *The Annals of the World* (1658), the Archbishop of Ireland, James Usher, argued that the Creation week began on Sunday, October 23, 4004 BC. This theory led many to expect the end of the world around AD 1996 or 1997. By his time, William Miller believed that the world would end as early as AD 1843. Just from these three sources, we have 1843, 1996 or 1997, and even 2239 as alternative times for the end of the world.

Genealogies and chronologies are important sources of information; otherwise, Bible writers would not have included them. But, on the other hand, they can easily be twisted and carried too far in an attempt to prove personal speculations. Aware of this danger, Paul warned us against "fables and endless genealogies" (1 Timothy 1:4) and "unprofitable and useless" genealogical discussions (Titus 3:9).

The period of six thousand years can provide us with a general idea of the development of human history. But since it is not connected with any apocalyptic prophecies in Daniel or Revelation, it cannot be used to support the Adventist message. This message rests on a much stronger prophetic and historical basis!

THE THIEF OF TIME

Therefore, as the Holy Spirit says:
"Today, if you will hear His voice,
Do not harden your hearts as in the rebellion,
In the day of trial in the wilderness."

—Hebrews 3:7, 8

Some stolen objects can be recovered or at least replaced. But opportunities that are missed may not recur, and time, once spent, never returns. One of the greatest enemies of time is procrastination—postponing personal decisions and actions. The English poet and dramatist Edward Young (1683–1765) wrote, "Procrastination is the thief of time."[18] And an anonymous quote warns us, "Procrastinate now and panic later."[19]

The famous evangelist Dwight L. Moody (1837–1899) was conducting an evangelistic campaign in Chicago. On the night of Sunday, **October 8, 1871**, he preached a powerful sermon based on Matthew 27:22, "What then shall I do with Jesus who is called Christ?" At the end of his message, he asked the congregation to reflect on this text during the next week and return a week later with their decision on what to do with Jesus of Nazareth. Soon after he finished his sermon, the Great Chicago Fire broke out, killing many and destroying large portions of the city. Moody deeply regretted having given people a week to think about their personal decision for Christ. From then on, he always asked his audience to decide for Christ at the very meeting they were attending.

Procrastination is often an excuse to avoid responsibility. As a popular proverb says, "I'm very busy doing things I don't need to do in order to avoid doing anything I'm actually supposed to be doing." Unfortunately, many things we postpone "just for a while" we end up postponing forever. That was what happened with Felix, who told Paul, "Go away for now; when I have a convenient time I will call for you" (Acts 24:25). But that "convenient time" never came.

If you tend to procrastinate, then *today*—or, even better, *right now*—is a good time to improve your decision-making skills for your own benefit and for the sake of those who depend on you. If you have delayed making your decision for Christ, let me remind you that the Bible says the time of salvation is *today*. We can live only in the present, and today is another chance for you to make or reaffirm your commitment to Christ.

Winnekeag Camporee

"You shall dwell in booths for seven days. All who are native Israelites shall dwell in booths, that your generations may know that I made the children of Israel dwell in booths when I brought them out of the land of Egypt: I am the LORD your God."
—Leviticus 23:42, 43

A Pathfinder camporee is an unforgettable experience! If you have ever participated in one, you probably remember the months of planning and training, the arrival at the campground, the tents, the cooking, the program, the campfire stories, the new friends, and even the unexpected rain.

The first-ever Pathfinder camporee was sponsored by the Southern New England Conference at Camp Winnekeag, near Ashburnham, Massachusetts, on **October 9–11, 1953**. Fifty-five Pathfinders camped and slept on the ground in tents in units of six or eight. The weekend was full of activities. Friday evening, after sundown worship, one could see numerous little campfires burning on the beautiful shores of Winnekeag Lake. Elder H. F. Maxson was the storyteller at the campfire circle. On Sabbath afternoon, the secretary of the General Conference Young People's Missionary Volunteer Department, E. W. Dunbar, gave an inspirational message and told stories to the Pathfinders. At the end of the event, the Pathfinders, by unanimous vote, called for another camporee in June 1954. From this humble beginning, Pathfinder camporees have been organized in many places around the world in the decades since.

The whole Pathfinder concept was largely inspired by Ellen White's statement, "With such an army of workers as our youth, rightly trained, might furnish, how soon the message of a crucified, risen, and soon-coming Saviour might be carried to the whole world!"[20] And Pathfinder camporees resemble the social-spiritual gatherings of the Israelites during the Feast of Tabernacles (Leviticus 23:33–43), when they lived in tents like their forefathers in the wilderness.

According to Mrs. White, "Well would it be for the people of God at the present time to have a Feast of Tabernacles—a joyous commemoration of the blessings of God to them."[21] Early Adventists called their camp meetings feasts of tabernacles, and our modern Pathfinder camporees are very similar to them as well. Let us support the Pathfinders in our local congregations!

ℱREEDOM OF CHOICE

For this is good and acceptable in the sight of God our Savior,
who desires all men to be saved and to come to the knowledge of the truth.
—1 Timothy 2:3, 4

How would you react after finding out that God intentionally created you to be lost? This belief was essentially the position of the French Reformer John Calvin (1509–1564) and his followers. Calvin even stated, "By predestination we mean the eternal decree of God, by which he determined with himself whatever he wished to happen with regard to every man. All are not created on equal terms, but some are preordained to eternal life, others to eternal damnation; and, accordingly, as each has been created for one or other of these ends, we say that he has been predestinated to life or to death."[22]

This notion was challenged by the Dutch theologian Jacobus Arminius (1560–1609), who was born in Utrecht, Holland, on **October 10, 1560**. He was a theology professor at the University of Leiden and wrote many books and treatises. His views against Calvinist predestination were summarized in the Five Articles of Remonstrance (1610). In Article 2, we read, "Christ, the Saviour of the world, died for all men and for every man, and his grace is extended to all. His atoning sacrifice is in and of itself sufficient for the redemption of the whole world, and is intended for all by God the Father. But its inherent sufficiency does not necessarily imply its actual efficiency. The grace of God may be resisted, and only those who accept it by faith are actually saved. He who is lost, is lost by his own guilt (John iii:16; 1 John ii:2)."[23]

In his book *The Knowledge of the Holy*, A. W. Tozer explains, "Certain things have been decreed by the free determination of God, and one of these is the law of choice and consequences. God has decreed that all who willingly commit themselves to His Son Jesus Christ in the obedience of faith shall receive eternal life and become sons of God. He has also decreed that all who love darkness and continue in rebellion against the high authority of heaven shall remain in a state of spiritual alienation and suffer eternal death at last."[24]

There is no arbitrary decree of God choosing some to be saved and others to be lost. "The destiny of souls hangs upon the course they pursue and the decisions they make."[25]

REYKJAVIK SUMMIT

"Blessed are the peacemakers, for they shall be called sons of God."
—Matthew 5:9

In August 2016, I visited the Höfði House historic site in Reykjavik, Iceland. In the yard in front of the house, visitors can see a granite stone with the inscription, "In this historic house on **11–12 October 1986**, the Reykjavik Summit meeting of the Superpowers took place between Ronald Reagan, President of the United States of America, and Mikhail Sergeyevich Gorbachev, Secretary-General of the Central Committee of the Communist Party of the Soviet Union. This Summit meeting is regarded as heralding the beginning of the end of the Cold War."

Much of the discussion centered on proposals for both sides to eliminate ballistic missiles. But the talks collapsed at the last minute due to the lack of agreement on some of the details. Reagan asked Gorbachev if he would "turn down a historic opportunity because of a single word" in regard to laboratory testing.[26] Despite its apparent failure, that summit represented a breakthrough in the process that culminated in the Intermediate-Range Nuclear Forces Treaty, signed at the Washington Summit on December 8, 1987.

Many nations, tribes, and people still abide by the old Latin adage, "Si vis pacem, para bellum" (If you want peace, prepare for war). Unfortunately, this adage paved the way for World War I and perpetuated the Cold War. As Reagan and Gorbachev dialogued together in Reykjavik to end the Cold War, so we should be peacemakers helping end conflicts and tensions between nations, tribes, families, and friends. But to be a peacemaker, you need to be at peace with God and with yourself. Peace must become your lifestyle—thinking peaceful thoughts, saying peaceful words, and doing peaceful actions.

Your best efforts may fail, and your best intentions may be misunderstood, leaving you deeply frustrated. Nevertheless, a seemingly wasted seed of peace may end up germinating and producing unexpected fruit, as in the case of the Reykjavik Summit. If it doesn't happen, at least you are at peace with yourself and with your conscience, and, as Jesus said, you will be called a child of God (Matthew 5:9). "And the peace of God, which surpasses all understanding, will guard your hearts and minds through Christ Jesus" (Philippians 4:7).

*U*PLIFTING THE *B*IBLE

"Sanctify them by Your truth. Your word is truth."

—John 17:17

The Christ the Redeemer statue (Cristo Redentor), inaugurated on **October 12, 1931,** is a major landmark in Rio de Janeiro, Brazil. Exactly fifty-five years after the statue's inauguration, on **October 12, 1986,** the General Conference of Seventh-day Adventists voted to approve the document "Methods of Bible Study" at its Annual Council held in Rio. This official document provides basic guidelines for interpreting the Bible as the trustworthy Word of God and rejects all hermeneutics that undermine its divine origin and authority.

The document urges us "to avoid relying on the use of the presuppositions and the resultant deductions associated with the historical-critical method." Under the assumption that "human reason is subject to the Bible, not equal to or above it," the document states that "even a modified use" of the historical-critical method "that retains the principle of criticism which subordinates the Bible to human reason is unacceptable to Adventists."[27] This document helps the church maintain hermeneutical integrity.

Many theological tensions and controversies within Christianity have arisen because of human biases and faulty interpretations of the Bible. For instance, Lutheran theologian Gerhard Ebeling speaks of church history as "the history of the exposition of Scripture."[28] However, long before church history was thought of, a hermeneutical dispute occurred in the Garden of Eden between Eve and the serpent on how God's word should be understood (Genesis 2:15–17; 3:1–7). Almost all of Christ's debates were over the interpretation of Scripture or its fulfillment (Matthew 4:1–11; 15:1–20; 22:23–33; Luke 4:16–30; 10:25–37).

We know that in the final days of human history, there will be many hermeneutical storms, and every wind of false doctrine will blow (Ephesians 4:14; 2 Timothy 4:3, 4). At the same time, "God will have a people upon the earth to maintain the Bible, and the Bible only, as the standard of all doctrines and the basis of all reforms."[29] May we always be part of those faithful people who abide "by every word that proceeds from the mouth of God" (Matthew 4:4).

𝒯HE SABBATH ON A SPHERICAL 𝒲ORLD

It was Preparation Day, and the Sabbath was about to begin. . . .
But they rested on the Sabbath in obedience to the commandment.
—Luke 23:54–56, NIV

In a world with many different time zones, how can God's people properly keep the Sabbath from sunset Friday to sunset Saturday (Nehemiah 13:15–22; Luke 23:54; Leviticus 23:32)? Around the globe, some people are resting on the Sabbath, while in other places, they are still working!

Living on a spherical world has caused two major issues that humankind had to settle. One was to define the reference point from where time should be marked. After considering several options, on **October 13, 1884,** the International Meridian Conference in Washington, DC, defined the prime meridian as a straight vertical line from the North Pole to the South Pole, passing through the Royal Observatory of Greenwich, London. At longitude 0°, the prime meridian at Greenwich separates east from west in the same way that the equator separates north from south. So, Greenwich Mean Time became the reference point for our world's system of twenty-four different time zones.

Another decision that had to be made was where the transition from one day to another should occur. This was eventually resolved with the establishment of the international date line (IDL), a vertical but zigzagging line passing through the middle of the Pacific Ocean halfway around the world from the prime meridian. Much of it aligns with longitude 180°, but it occasionally deviates to avoid crossing through some small territories and island groups. Crossing the IDL going east, one must subtract a day; but crossing it going west, one must add a day. This imaginary line allows all the world's time zones to remain in their respective real times.

Some critics argue that the IDL is a conspiracy against Sabbath observance, but it affects all days of the week, including Sunday. God created a spherical world requiring different time zones, and we cannot treat it as if it were flat. The commandment to keep the seventh-day Sabbath holy does not require uniformity in time. We are to observe the Sabbath whenever it comes to us, regardless of the time zone in which we find ourselves. In all parts of our spherical world, we can enjoy God's blessings reserved for those who faithfully obey the Sabbath commandment, just as Christ's disciples did after His death on the cross (Luke 23:54–56).

October 14

ℰVANGELISTIC ℘RIORITY

And this gospel of the kingdom will be preached in all the world as a witness to all the nations, and then the end will come.

—Matthew 24:14

We are told that "the church is God's appointed agency for the salvation of men. It was organized for service, and its mission is to carry the gospel to the world."[30] But as time goes on, the church faces two serious temptations. One is *institutionalization*, which often leads to the church losing its missionary fervor and focusing only on itself. The other temptation is *secularism*, which means the church opens itself to the world so much that it becomes like the world.

To avoid these dangers, on **October 14, 1976**, the Annual Council of the General Conference of Seventh-day Adventists adopted a resolution entitled "Evangelism and Finishing God's Work." The document affirms that the Seventh-day Adventist Church's objective is "to proclaim to the whole world the everlasting gospel of Jesus Christ in the context of the Three Angels' Messages of Revelation 14, which, in addition to the cardinal doctrines of the Christian church, embodies the distinctive truths of the sanctuary and righteousness by faith."[31] The same document warns,

> There are many excellent programs and projects which are most advantageous to use in the pre-evangelistic context, such as those concerned with diet, smoking, welfare and other social benefits. But, worthy as they may be, if they do not lead to the new-birth experience in Christ and acceptance of the doctrinal tenets of God's remnant church, they consume time, attention and money of the church and its working force without achieving God's ultimate objective of saving a man for eternity. . . .
>
> Therefore, through administrative action, it must be made clear by precept and example that programs of the church shall be given attention and funding only as they aid in accomplishing the church's basic mission.[32]

Decades later, this mission must still be our goal. As Jesus prayed long ago, "I do not pray that You should take them out of the world, but that You should keep them from the evil one" (John 17:15).

Calendar Changes

"While the earth remains,
Seedtime and harvest,
Cold and heat,
Winter and summer,
And day and night
Shall not cease."

—Genesis 8:22

M any ancient civilizations developed their own calendars based on the seasons of the year. With so many different calendars and calendar changes, one may wonder, how do we know that the weekly cycle was never lost? How can we be sure that the Sabbath we keep today is the same one instituted at the end of the Creation week (Genesis 2:2, 3)? And how can Sunday keepers be sure that the Sunday they keep is the same as the original Sunday?

We should recognize first that there is no historical evidence that the week of seven days was ever lost. It is, in fact, Sabbath observance that has preserved the weekly cycle, keeping it unchanged throughout the ages. Jews worldwide have no uncertainty regarding when to keep the Shabbat. Even if the Sabbath had been lost in Old Testament times, Jesus could have corrected it. But He kept the same Sabbath the Jews of His time were keeping (Luke 4:16; 23:54–56). Undeniably, the Sabbath is too meaningful and holy for God to allow it to be lost.

During the Christian Era, the weekly cycle likewise remained unchanged. When the Gregorian calendar was first introduced in the late sixteenth century, the error accumulated during the thirteen centuries since the Council of Nicaea was corrected by a deletion of ten days. So, Thursday, October 4, 1582, of the old Julian calendar was followed by Friday, **October 15, 1582**, of the new Gregorian calendar. Some European countries didn't adopt the new calendar until later, but in every case, the weekly cycle remained unchanged. Even the Roman Catholic Church considers the Sunday it keeps to be the same day on which Jesus was raised from the dead—the first day of the week.

We can be certain that every seventh-day Sabbath arrives unchanged as God's sanctuary in time. The same day of the week God rested, blessed, and sanctified at the end of the Creation week (Genesis 2:2, 3) was kept by Jesus and His apostles (Luke 23:54–56; Acts 16:13). And we are encouraged to follow God's example by keeping the seventh-day Sabbath as a symbol of salvation by grace through faith (Hebrews 4:4, 9–11). In keeping it, we recognize God's sovereignty as our Creator and Redeemer and receive His blessing (Isaiah 58:13, 14).

ℒast ℳessage

When Moses finished reciting all these words to all Israel, he said to them,
"Take to heart all the words I have solemnly declared to you this day, so that
you may command your children to obey carefully all the words of this law."
—Deuteronomy 32:45, 46, NIV

E ventually, the time comes for leaders to turn over their positions and responsibilities to someone else. The farewell speeches that accompany this transition tend to highlight what the leader accomplished while in office and also offer the leader an opportunity to express his or her concerns about the future. This was precisely what Moses did at the end of his life, as recorded in the book of Deuteronomy. In a similar manner, on **October 16, 1978**, General Conference president Robert H. Pierson (1911–1989) announced his soon retirement due to health reasons and delivered his last presidential message to those attending the 1978 Annual Council.

In his message, Pierson referred to the cycle typically followed by a sect before it develops into a church. The first generation is generally poor, and it "arises as a protest against worldliness and formalism in a church." In the second generation, members tend to become prosperous, and growth generates "a need for organization and buildings." In the third generation, "organization develops, and institutions are established." In the fourth generation, "The movement seeks to become 'relevant' to contemporary society by becoming involved in popular causes. Services become formal. The group enjoys complete acceptance by the world."[33]

After reflecting on this cycle, Pierson appealed,

Brethren and sisters, this must never happen to the Seventh-day Adventist Church! This is not just another church—it is God's church! . . .

". . . There is only one way for us to face the future, and that is at the foot of the cross. A church with its eyes upon the Man of Calvary will never walk into apostasy.[34]

We have the prophetic assurance that the Adventist movement will triumph and that at the end of time, all uncommitted and formal members will be shaken out (Matthew 13:24–30, 36–43, 47–50). So, the crucial issue is not about the triumph of this movement but whether you and I will triumph with it. By God's grace, we must remain faithful to the Lord until His glorious return.

SHARING GOD'S LOVE

The Spirit of the Sovereign LORD is on me,
because the LORD has anointed me
to proclaim good news to the poor.
He has sent me to bind up the brokenhearted,
to proclaim freedom for the captives
and release from darkness for the prisoners.

—Isaiah 61:1, NIV

Few people in the twentieth century engraved their names on the walls of history like Mother Teresa of Calcutta. She was born Anjezë Gonxhe Bojaxhiu (1910–1997) in Üsküp, a town in the Ottoman Empire (now Skopje, Republic of Macedonia). In 1950, Teresa founded the Missionaries of Charity, a Roman Catholic religious order. When she received the Nobel Peace Prize in 1979, she said, "I am grateful and I am very happy to receive it in the name of the hungry, of the naked, of the homeless, of the crippled, of the blind, of the leprous, of all those people who feel unwanted, unloved, uncared, thrown away of the society, people who have become a burden to the society, and are ashamed by everybody."[35]

The congregation began as a small community with twelve members in Calcutta (now Kolkata), India, and grew significantly around the world. Mother Teresa was awarded the Nobel Peace Prize on **October 17, 1979**. In her Nobel lecture, delivered in Oslo on December 11, she stated that the unborn John the Baptist already "recognised the Prince of Peace, he recognised that Christ has come to bring the good news for you and for me. And as if that was not enough—it was not enough to become a man—he died on the cross to show that greater love, and he died for you and for me and for that leper and for that man dying of hunger and that naked person lying in the street not only of Calcutta, but of Africa, and New York, and London, and Oslo—and insisted that we love one another as he loves each one of us."[36]

Mother Teresa lived a life of service to the unloved and the unwanted. That is the ministry Jesus calls His followers to. He put it this way: "Inasmuch as you did it to one of the least of these My brethren, you did it to Me" (Matthew 25:40). Let's make a habit of living a life of service.

$\mathcal{T}$HE $\mathcal{M}$ASTER'S $\mathcal{H}$AND

Moved with compassion, Jesus stretched out His hand and touched him, and said to him,
"I am willing; be cleansed." Immediately the leprosy left him and he was cleansed.

—Mark 1:41, 42, NASB

In early 1921, Myra Brooks Welch (1877–1959) was inspired by the remarks of a speaker who mentioned that even ordinary things could become significant by the touch of a master's hand. Myra went home and, in a short time, wrote a beautiful poem titled "The Touch of the Master's Hand." The poem was printed anonymously in the *Gospel Messenger* (the official paper for the Church of the Brethren) on February 26, 1921. People enjoyed that piece, and it appeared in many other publications with the attribution "author unknown."

In 1936, another preacher read the "anonymous" poem at the end of his speech at the YMCA Conference in Hawaii. Dwight O. Welch stood and explained that the author of that poem was his own mother. The unknown author was finally known! The story of the poem was told by H. A. Brandt in his article "Remember the Singer as Well as the Song," published in the *Gospel Messenger* on **October 18, 1941**. The famous poem depicts an auction where an old violin was up for sale for an insignificant price. But after a master played the instrument, its value increased astronomically. The piece ends with a beautiful spiritual lesson:

> But the Master comes, and the foolish crowd
> Never can quite understand,
> The worth of a soul and the change that is wrought
> By the touch of the Master's hand.[37]

This is what happened to the leper described in Mark 1:40–45. As an unclean leper, he had to stay away from others, and no one was supposed to touch him (Leviticus 13:46). Ignoring the rule, Jesus touched the leper and cleansed him. Despite being instructed to say nothing to others, the healed man went out and proclaimed his healing freely (Mark 1:44, 45).

Regardless of your problems, all it takes for you to be made clean is the touch of the Master's hand. After His touch, your life will never be the same again. It will be virtually impossible for you to remain silent. You simply must tell others what Jesus did for you!

$\mathcal{B}$ROADCASTING THE $\mathcal{G}$OOD $\mathcal{N}$EWS

How beautiful upon the mountains
Are the feet of him who brings good news,
Who proclaims peace,
Who brings glad tidings of good things,
Who proclaims salvation,
Who says to Zion,
"Your God reigns!"

—Isaiah 52:7

Without hope for the future, life becomes meaningless. Paul says it this way: "If in this life only we have hope in Christ, we are of all men the most pitiable" (1 Corinthians 15:19).

One of the most outstanding preachers of hope of the twentieth century was the Seventh-day Adventist evangelist, radio speaker, and author H. M. S. Richards Sr. (1894–1985). Having experimented with radio announcements for his meetings, on **October 19, 1929**, on KNK (AM) in Los Angeles, California, Richards launched what is considered the first coast-to-coast regular religious radio program in the United States. His program was called *The Tabernacle of the Air* and later *The Voice of Prophecy*.

Shortly after the program began broadcasting, the Great Depression (1929–1933) hit the United States and the world. In contrast to many popular preachers who speculated about prophecies yet to be fulfilled, Richards placed his emphasis on prophecies that had already been fulfilled. In his own words, "A lot of the Bible prophecy is not given so we can predict what will happen, but so we can see what already happened, and get confirmation that the Bible is true. If it came true historically, then when Jesus gives his wonderful teachings, we ought to believe that, too."[38]

Christian hope is a three-dimensional assurance. It is rooted in the *past* historical scenario, in which many Bible prophecies were fulfilled. It is sustained in the *present* by being anchored "behind the veil" of the heavenly sanctuary, where Christ is patiently interceding for us (Hebrews 6:19, 20). And it generates strong anticipation for a glorious *future* when Christ, "the author and finisher of our faith" (Hebrews 12:2), will appear in the clouds of heaven to take us with Him to His heavenly home. As "prisoners of hope" (Zechariah 9:12), you and I should always be ready for His glorious appearing!

A Missionary Schooner

When Paul had finished speaking, he knelt down with all of them and prayed. They all wept as they embraced him and kissed him. What grieved them most was his statement that they would never see his face again. Then they accompanied him to the ship.

—Acts 20:36–38, NIV

Have you heard the story of how the inhabitants of the remote Pitcairn Island in the South Pacific accepted the Adventist message? In 1876, James White and John H. Loughborough sent a box of Seventh-day Adventist literature to Pitcairn Island. Ten years later, in 1886, John I. Tay paid his own way to Pitcairn Island to preach the Adventist message. All 110 inhabitants of the island accepted his message, and he requested that a minister come and organize a church.

At the 1889 General Conference Session, the church decided to build a missionary ship for the work among the islands in the South Pacific. Members of Sabbath Schools across the United States, including adults and children, contributed offerings to the project. The *Pitcairn* schooner was dedicated on September 25, 1890, and it departed from San Francisco, California, on **October 20, 1890**, with a group of Adventist missionaries aboard. After thirty-six days at sea, they finally arrived at Pitcairn Island. There they baptized eighty-two of the islanders and organized a church and Sabbath School. After several weeks on that island, the ship moved on to other islands.

The *Pitcairn* mission project started an era of great interest in and much support for foreign missions. In 1889, Ellen White urged, "My soul is stirred within me as the Macedonian cry comes from every direction, from the cities and villages of our own land, from across the Atlantic and the broad Pacific, and from the islands of the sea: 'Come over, . . . and help us.' Brethren and sisters, will you answer the cry? saying: 'We will do our best, both in sending you missionaries and money.' "[39]

As Seventh-day Adventists, our hearts should beat for the mission fields where people need to be reached by the Adventist message. Mission is the very reason for our existence as a church. With our prayers and finances, we should support not only our local church but also the global mission of the church.

$\mathcal{A}$ Simple Obituary

But by the grace of God I am what I am, and His grace toward me was not in vain; but I labored more abundantly than they all, yet not I, but the grace of God which was with me.
—1 Corinthians 15:10

Not many people have as sharp a mind for logic and reasoning as J. N. Andrews (1829–1883) had. Able to read in seven languages, he had extensive knowledge of secular and religious history. Once asked how much of the Bible he could quote from memory, he answered, "I would not presume to say that I could repeat all of the Old Testament, but I feel certain that if the New Testament was lost, I could reproduce it verbatim."[40] It is no surprise that, after he was sent as the first official Seventh-day Adventist missionary to Europe, Ellen White wrote to the "brethren in Switzerland," "We sent you the ablest man in all our ranks."[41]

After laboring for more than eight years in Europe, Andrews felt that his life was coming rapidly to an end. Plagued by tuberculosis, he wrote a letter on April 24, 1883, from Basel, Switzerland, to his close friend Uriah Smith, editor of the *Advent Review and Sabbath Herald*:

At the present time by reason of my great prostration I am brought to look death in the face. There is one thing that troubles me which I lay before you in the form of a petition. It will fall to your lot to mention my death in the *Review*. I beg you to make the simplest and briefest statement possible and I solemnly charge you to exclude any word of eulogy. One third of a column of the *Review* will suffice for all that should be said.

I make this request because I fear that your kind regard for me will constrain you to say what I do not merit and what ought not to be said. My best acts have had some trace of selfishness in them or have been lacking in love toward God and man. I beseech you therefore by all the affection which you bear me that you will regard this my earnest petition.[42]

On **October 21, 1883**, Andrews died, and his request was fully honored. The *Review and Herald* for October 30 came off the press with an obituary titled "The Death of Eld. Andrews." There was little eulogy for his accomplishments. How wonderful are the lives of those extremely skilled individuals who remain humble even when surrounded by success and words of praise.

𝒯HE GREAT ℰXPECTATION

And he said to me, "For two thousand three hundred days;
then the sanctuary shall be cleansed."

—Daniel 8:14

The year 1844 arrived with great expectations! William Miller never set a specific date for Christ's second coming. But from his early Bible studies, he had concluded that the twenty-three hundred symbolic days (twenty-three hundred literal years) of Daniel 8:14 would end around 1843, when he believed Christ would return. Later on, he suggested the spring of 1844 as the end of that time period. Meanwhile, Samuel S. Snow was convinced that the twenty-three hundred years extended from the autumn of 457 BC to the autumn of AD 1844, more precisely to **October 22, 1844**. He presented his exciting views at a Millerite camp meeting in Exeter, New Hampshire, in August of that year. From then on, Millerism gained a renewed fervor and a sense of urgency.

The Millerite hope made a great impact on both ministers and laypeople. It has been estimated that between 1,500 and 2,000 lecturers were proclaiming the advent message in the climactic phase of the movement. Despite the lack of exact numbers, we can estimate that between 50,000 and 100,000 people formally joined the movement. To those figures, W. R. Cross added "a million or more" skeptical expectants—an impressive number in a time when the American population was less than twenty million. The time was solemn, and many people prepared themselves to meet the Lord in the clouds of heaven.

When October 22 finally arrived, the Millerites were taken over by an indescribable solemn introspection and expectation. There was no room for wild excitement and public demonstrations. In the quietness of their homes, they patiently waited for the Lord's appearing. Joshua V. Himes went to the house of his close friend William Miller, where a few family members waited for the Lord on "Ascension Rock." They kept watching the eastern horizon, eager to behold Jesus as soon as the sign of His coming appeared.

Eventually, the sun went down, and night began to cover the earth with its usual darkness. But there was no reason for discouragement. After all, the parable of the wise and foolish virgins showed that "at midnight," the bridegroom would come (Matthew 25:6). The Millerites were at the very border of eternity.

ℬLESSED 𝒟ISAPPOINTMENT

Then I took the little book out of the angel's hand and ate it, and it was as sweet as honey in my mouth. But when I had eaten it, my stomach became bitter.
—Revelation 10:10

The Millerites eagerly expected Jesus to come on October 22, 1844, but their sweetest expectations gave way to the bitterest disappointment. Hiram Edson described his own experience as follows, "Our expectations were raised high, and thus we looked for our coming Lord until the clock tolled twelve at midnight. The day had then passed, and our disappointment had become a certainty. Our fondest hopes and expectations were blasted, and such a spirit of weeping came over us as I never experienced before. It seemed that the loss of all earthly friends could have been no comparison. We wept, and wept, till the day dawn."[43]

On the morning of **October 23, 1844**, after breakfast, Edson invited a friend (identified by J. N. Loughborough as O. R. L. Crosier) to accompany him and encourage some disappointed Millerite neighbors. In his own words, "We started, and while passing through a large field, I was stopped about midway of the field. Heaven seemed open to my view, and I saw distinctly and clearly that instead of our High Priest coming out of the most holy place of the heavenly sanctuary to this earth on the tenth day of the seventh month, at the end of the 2300 days, He, for the first time, entered on that day the second apartment of that sanctuary; and that He had a work to perform in the most holy place before coming to the earth."[44]

Critical historians have traditionally alluded to the 1844 disappointment in very negative terms. But more recent Adventist scholars have recognized its positive dimension. In reality, disappointments tend to lead people to break away from tradition and search for a new beginning. Restudying Scripture, the forefathers of Sabbath-keeping Adventism found biblical answers not only to the disappointment (see Revelation 10) but also to several other questions they hadn't even asked.

Out of the 1844 disappointment, God brought about the now worldwide Adventist movement to restore biblical truth in an end-time setting. Likewise, He can bring us out of our personal disappointments into a life of full victory. Let's trust His providential leadings today and always!

Beholding His Face

Beloved, now we are children of God; and it has not yet been revealed what we shall be,
but we know that when He is revealed, we shall be like Him, for we shall see Him as
He is. And everyone who has this hope in Him purifies himself, just as He is pure.

—1 John 3:2, 3

Airports tend to produce a variety of emotions in people. We find some people sad at saying goodbye to their loved ones. In contrast, we also observe people excitedly welcoming those they have been waiting for. Between departing and returning home, people communicate with devices and remember special memories by looking at pictures.

Jesus' first disciples contemplated with sadness His ascent to heaven (Acts 1:6–11). Having never seen His face, artists have portrayed Him in many different ways, according to their own imaginations. Of the paintings you have seen, which do you believe best portrays His coming? British artist John Sartain (1808–1897) was born in London on **October 24, 1808.** When he was twenty-two years old, Sartain immigrated to the United States, where he pioneered mezzotint engraving. His famous engraving *Our Saviour* (1865) was identified by Ellen White as the portrayal of Jesus that most resembled Him as she saw Him in vision.

But the day will come when we will no longer need to imagine what the face of Jesus looks like, for we will see Him face-to-face. In 1 John 3:2, 3, we are told that "when He is revealed, we shall be like Him, for we shall see Him as He is. And everyone who has this hope in Him purifies himself, just as He is pure." What an amazing privilege and blessed assurance for those who keep their eyes on Jesus now! (Hebrews 12:2).

Then our best portrayals of Jesus will lose their meaning, for we will see Him face-to-face. And even more, Jesus Himself promised us that we would see God the Father (Matthew 5:8)! Ellen White declared, "And what is the happiness of heaven but to see God? What greater joy could come to the sinner saved by the grace of Christ than to look upon the face of God and know Him as Father?"[45]

By God's grace, may you and I also be among those who will see both Jesus and God the Father face-to-face. Please, do not allow anything or anyone to distract you from this most glorious purpose.

ℒNFORGETTABLE ℳOMENTS

Moreover his mother used to make him a little robe, and bring it to him year by year when she came up with her husband to offer the yearly sacrifice.
—1 Samuel 2:19

E llen White wrote extensively about family life and child education. But her prophetic ministry required the heavy burden of putting God's cause above herself and her family. In 1848, when her firstborn son, Henry, was only one year old, she had to leave him with the Howland family. She wrote,

> Again I was called to deny self for the good of souls. We must sacrifice the company of our little Henry, and go forth to give ourselves unreservedly to the work. . . . I believed that the Lord had spared him to us when he was very sick, and that if I should let him hinder me from doing my duty, God would remove him from me. Alone before the Lord, with a sorrowful heart and many tears, I made the sacrifice, and gave up my only child to be cared for by another. . . .
> It was hard to part with my child. His sad little face, as I left him, was before me day and night; yet in the strength of the Lord I put him out of my mind, and sought to do others good.[46]

The original plan was that Henry would stay with the Howland family only for a short period of time, but it ended up lasting five years, with a few breaks in between. For instance, on Friday, **October 25, 1850**, the Howland family brought little Henry to Gorham, Maine, to spend the Sabbath with his parents and grandparents. Mrs. White declared, "We parted with them Sunday sorrowful, because we were obliged to part, but rejoicing that we were of one faith and that soon we should meet if faithful never more to part."[47] In early 1859, she rejoiced after returning from another trip, "Joyfully, we again met our family. . . . With gratitude to God I take my place in my family again. There is no place to be so dearly prized as home."[48]

As Adventist Christians, we are looking for that glorious day when we will be forever with our faithful beloved ones!

REWARDING ADDICTIONS

Do not be wise in your own eyes; fear the LORD and depart from evil.
—Proverbs 3:7

Most people like to be praised and rewarded for who they are and for what they do. But some are so addicted to praise that if nobody else praises them, they start praising themselves. It seems as if there were an invisible curriculum vitae hanging from their necks. Have you ever asked yourself, "Am I addicted to being praised and rewarded?"

Much of that addiction comes from our own sinful nature and the way our parents and teachers have educated us. On **October 26, 1993**, Alfie Kohn's book *Punished by Rewards: The Trouble With Gold Stars, Incentive Plans, A's, Praise, and Other Bribes* was released. The author maintained that the system of rewarding students and workers tends to bribe them and should be replaced by motivating them through collaboration (teamwork), content (meaningfulness), and choice (autonomy).[49]

Ellen White counseled, "Men are not [to] be exalted as great and wonderful. It is God who is to be magnified."[50] Also, "Praise should not be given or expected; for this will have a tendency to foster self-confidence rather than to increase humility, to corrupt rather than to purify."[51] Does this mean that we should be cold and indifferent to what others do? Not at all.

Appreciation is a key part of growth. About this importance, we are told, "There are many to whom life is a painful struggle; they feel their deficiencies and are miserable and unbelieving; they think they have nothing for which to be grateful. Kind words, looks of sympathy, expressions of appreciation, would be to many a struggling and lonely one as the cup of cold water to a thirsty soul."[52]

We can make a difference in the life of others. May the Lord give us the best attitude and the right words to encourage and inspire those around us. Remember that *inclusive* cooperation and appreciation can do much more than *selective* competition and reward.

*T*HE *B*EAUTY OF *N*ATURE

"Consider the lilies of the field, how they grow: they neither toil nor spin; and yet I say to you that even Solomon in all his glory was not arrayed like one of these. Now if God so clothes the grass of the field, which today is, and tomorrow is thrown into the oven, will He not much more clothe you, O you of little faith?"

—Matthew 6:28–30

In my living room at home, we have a beautiful orchid that blooms occasionally. Whenever it is not blooming, my wife creatively sticks an artificial orchid on it that resembles the real one. Even then, people are impressed by its beauty! As nice as they can be, artificial flowers only imitate real ones. Artificial flowers are not alive and, consequently, do not go through the mysterious growing process. More importantly, artificial flowers do not carry God's fingerprints!

In the *Advent Review and Sabbath Herald* of **October 27, 1885**, Ellen White stated,

Christ sought to draw the attention of his disciples away from the artificial to the natural: "If God so clothe the grass of the field, which to-day is, and to-morrow is cast into the oven, shall he not much more clothe you, O ye of little faith!" Why did not our heavenly Father carpet the earth with brown or gray? He chose the color that was most restful, the most acceptable to the senses. How it cheers the heart and refreshes the weary spirit to look upon the earth, clad in its garments of living green! Without this covering the air would be filled with dust, and the earth would appear like a desert. Every spire of grass, every opening bud and blooming flower is a token of God's love, and should teach us a lesson of faith and trust in him. Christ calls our attention to their natural loveliness, and assures us that the most gorgeous array of the greatest king that ever wielded an earthly scepter was not equal to that worn by the humblest flower. You who are sighing for the artificial splendor which wealth alone can purchase, for costly paintings, furniture, and dress, listen to the voice of the divine Teacher. He points you to the flower of the field, the simple design of which cannot be equaled by human skill."[53]

God gave us the Sabbath as a special day for us to contemplate the beauty of His creation (Genesis 2:1–3; Exodus 20:8–11). May the message of nature bring us closer to Him!

$\mathcal{A}$ Global Community

Then they all wept freely, and fell on Paul's neck and kissed him,
sorrowing most of all for the words which he spoke, that they would
see his face no more. And they accompanied him to the ship.

—Acts 20:37, 38

When my great-grandparents left the north of Germany and immigrated to the south of Brazil in the early 1870s, they said goodbye to their parents and other relatives, never to see them again. Since then, communication and transportation have improved significantly, and they have become more affordable. And the cyber revolution completely changed the way we connect with others.

On **October 28, 2003**, Harvard University student Mark E. Zuckerberg, with the help of three of his classmates, released a new website called Facemash. Zuckerberg hacked into Harvard's security network and copied student ID images used by dormitories and posted them two by two, allowing visitors to choose who of the two was "hot" and who was "not."

Then on February 4, 2004, at Harvard, Zuckerberg launched the Facebook social network. The next month, it expanded to Stanford, Columbia, and Yale and, eventually, to the whole world. On January 28, 2015, Timothy Stenovec wrote the headline, "Facebook Is Now Bigger Than the Largest Country on Earth."[54] At that time, the network had 1.39 billion people logging in each month

to scroll their News Feeds, communicate with friends and look at photos.
That's more than the entire population of China . . . which [is] estimated to have 1.36 billion people.[55]

Our modern world has become a huge global community. Some of the loneliness caused by geographic distance and physical separation has decreased due to social media. Instead of saying goodbye forever to family and friends, as Paul did in Acts 20:37, 38, we can suggest, "Let's keep in touch while I'm gone." Through Facebook and other social networks, we may even find old friends and reconnect with them.

As Adventist Christians who believe in Christ's soon return, we can use social media to share Jesus as we socialize. I suggest we develop creative ways of shortening the distance between our friends and our Savior, Jesus Christ. Think about how you could do it!

PLANNED OBSOLESCENCE

"Do not lay up for yourselves treasures on earth, where moth and rust destroy and where thieves break in and steal; but lay up for yourselves treasures in heaven, where neither moth nor rust destroys and where thieves do not break in and steal."
—Matthew 6:19, 20

Everything that is continuously used eventually wears out. But this process has been accelerated by the modern ideology of always wanting the newest option. During the 1920s, the US stock market experienced rapid expansion, and there was much financial speculation. But stock prices began to decline, and on **October 29, 1929**, known as Black Tuesday, the stock market crashed, leading to the Great Depression (1929–1939), "the deepest and longest-lasting economic downturn in the history of the Western industrialized world."[56] "By 1933, nearly half of America's banks had failed, and unemployment was approaching 15 million people."[57]

With factories closing, some creative minds developed new production and marketing strategies. Bernard London is credited with having coined in 1932 the expression *planned obsolescence*, a manufacturing and marketing principle that forces people to buy new models of products they already have. Giles Slade's insightful book *Made to Break: Technology and Obsolescence in America*[58] describes how "repetitive consumption"[59] came into existence through innovations in paper production, the development of plastic industries, and "the annual model change"[60] and is being kept alive by a consumer culture willing to replace old products with new ones.

Planned obsolescence helped nourish the transient-and-disposable ideology. The desire to have something "new" can lead people to reject anything of a lasting nature, including marriage, family, and friends. This ideology goes something like this, "You are important to me as long as I can take advantage of you; when I no longer can, I will replace you with someone else!"

In contrast to this ideology, the Bible emphasizes commitment; for example, the sacred duty to honor our parents (Ephesians 6:1–3), loving "the wife of your youth" (Proverbs 5:18), and respecting our children (Ephesians 6:4). Truly, people are much more important than possessions! This means that, as Christians, we cannot allow the obsession with *new things* to destroy our *old relationships*, which are intended to last throughout this life and beyond.

UNFINISHED SYMPHONY

*Being confident of this very thing, that He who has begun a good
work in you will complete it until the day of Jesus Christ.*

—Philippians 1:6

There are many unfinished works in the world. Some were never completed due to lack of funds, others for political reasons, and still others because the author of the project died. In music, one of the most famous incomplete pieces is Schubert's *Unfinished Symphony.*

Franz Schubert (1797–1828) was a brilliant and prolific Austrian composer who has been described as the first "poet of music." After looking at some of Schubert's works, Beethoven is said to have exclaimed, "Truly, there is a divine spark in this Schubert."[61]

On **October 30, 1822**, Schubert began composing his famous Symphony no. 8 in B Minor. He wrote two movements but didn't finish. Then, nearly a year later, Schubert gave the score to a friend, who kept it for thirty years.[62] Not until several decades after Schubert's death did the world discover the greatness of this symphony. It became known as the *Unfinished Symphony.* It premiered in Vienna on December 17, 1865.

Why did Schubert leave this masterpiece unfinished? Some say that he put it aside to concentrate on another work. Others argue that the symphony was already perfect, and there was nothing to add. The truth is, we don't know why the piece was never finished.

Sometimes unfinished projects don't have serious consequences. However, in spiritual matters, there is no such thing as almost saved or partially saved. Either you are saved, or you are completely lost. But praise the Lord; if you surrender yourself completely to God, He will not leave your salvation unfinished! Paul affirms, "He who has begun a good work in you will complete it until the day of Jesus Christ" (Philippians 1:6). Although growing in Christ is a life-long endeavor (Philippians 3:12–16), through Christ's perfect righteousness, you can be completely saved right now. May this be your experience and mine as well!

ƁY ƑAITH ＡLONE

For in it the righteousness of God is revealed from faith
to faith; as it is written, "The just shall live by faith."

—Romans 1:17

Imagine that today is **October 31, 1517**, and we are visiting the town of Wittenberg, Germany. Many others are arriving in expectation of All Saint's Day (November 1) and the opportunity to see the collection of sacred relics belonging to Frederick the Wise, the elector of Saxony. In his book, *Here I Stand: A Life of Martin Luther*, Roland H. Bainton tells us that the collection allegedly included teeth belonging to various saints; garment pieces and four hairs belonging to the Virgin Mary; thirteen pieces of Jesus' swaddling cloth, a wisp of straw from Jesus' manger, one strand of hair from His beard, one piece of the bread eaten at the Last Supper, a thorn from His crown, and one of the nails driven into His hands; and there was even one twig of Moses' burning bush. "By 1520 the collection had 19,013 holy bones. Those who viewed these relics . . . and made the stipulated contributions might receive . . . indulgences for the reduction of purgatory, either for themselves or others, to the extent of 1,902,202 years and 270 days."[63]

Meanwhile, Johann Tetzel had been selling indulgences in surrounding regions, leading people to believe that they no longer needed to repent of their sins. Disgusted with the whole business, Martin Luther crafted ninety-five theses against the sale of indulgences and displayed them on the door of the Wittenberg Castle Church. Theses 21 and 22 stated, in essence, that "an indulgence will not save a man" and "a dead soul cannot be saved by an indulgence." Theses 56–58 added that the relics were not, in fact, relics of Christ but were instead an evil notion.[64]

Luther wrote his theses in Latin, anticipating an academic debate. But they were soon translated into German and eventually into other languages. As a result, many people began questioning Roman Catholic teachings on the merits of the saints, the sacred relics, and the sale of indulgences. It is no wonder that October 31, 1517, is considered the beginning of the great Protestant Reformation!

When Luther displayed his ninety-five theses on the Wittenberg Castle Church door, he could not have envisioned the far-reaching consequences of his action. Those ninety-five theses lit the fire of the Reformation that continues to burn in many Christian circles and that will continue until the end of time.

$\mathcal{A}$nd the $\mathcal{E}$arth $\mathcal{T}$rembled

I looked when He opened the sixth seal, and behold, there was a great earthquake.

—Revelation 6:12

The world has experienced many severe natural disasters throughout its history. When speaking to His disciples, Jesus warned that as we approach the time of the end, earthquakes would occur "in various places" (Matthew 24:7). Later on, Revelation 6:12 foretells "a great earthquake" at the opening of the sixth seal. Seventh-day Adventists see this prediction fulfilled by the terrible earthquake that hit Lisbon on Saturday morning, **November 1, 1755.**

According to Otto Friedrich, several people were claiming beforehand to have received supernatural revelations that Lisbon, "the Queen of the Sea," would soon be punished for its wickedness. Just the night before the earthquake, Father Manuel Portal of the Oratory "dreamed that Lisbon was being ravaged by two successive earthquakes."[1]

Whatever the origin of those revelations, on that tragic morning, shortly after 9:30 A.M., while many were attending the early Mass, Lisbon was severely shaken for ten minutes by three successive seismic disasters, followed by a huge tidal wave and a devastating fire that lasted for a week. Between thirty thousand and forty thousand people were killed in Lisbon and ten thousand more elsewhere.

No other earthquake has ever had such a weighty philosophical, cultural, and religious impact. Voltaire referred to it as "a terrible argument against optimism."[2] Harry Fielding Reid qualified it as "the most notable earthquake in history."[3] T. H. Kendrick affirmed that the Lisbon earthquake shocked "Western civilization more than any other event since the fall of Rome in the fifth century."[4] The title of Edward Paice's outstanding book, *Wrath of God: The Great Lisbon Earthquake of 1755*, aptly expresses the deep religious significance of the catastrophe.

The Lisbon earthquake can be considered the first major sign in the great earthquake-sun-moon-stars sequence described in Revelation 6:12, 13. Many people were convinced that the time of God's judgment had then arrived. Today we are far closer to the end than they were. May our prayer be, "Lord, open our eyes to see the signs of Your soon coming and make us ready for that glorious event."

My Mother

Her children rise up and call her blessed;
Her husband also, and he praises her.

—Proverbs 31:28

A loving and faithful mother is irreplaceable! Today marks the birthday of my dear mother, Frieda Conrad Timm, who was born in São Lourenço do Sul, Brazil, on **November 2, 1917.** She passed away in 2004, but her memory will remain in my heart forever. When I was a child, she was our children's Sabbath School teacher at church. And at home, she would read the junior one-year Bible reading plan to me before I learned how to read. Time passed, and as a teenager, I continued my studies in another city. Just before my departure, she hugged me, kissed me, and said, "Always be faithful!" Those simple words still echo in my mind today.

Ellen White honors mothers with these words:

There is a God above, and the light and glory from His throne rests upon the faithful mother as she tries to educate her children to resist the influence of evil. No other work can equal hers in importance. She has not, like the artist, to paint a form of beauty upon canvas, nor, like the sculptor, to chisel it from marble. She has not, like the author, to embody a noble thought in words of power, nor, like the musician, to express a beautiful sentiment in melody. It is hers, with the help of God, to develop in a human soul the likeness of the divine.[5]

And we can add that a loving Christian mother brings heaven close to her family and leads her children into the heavenly courts. "When the judgment shall sit, and the books shall be opened; when the 'well done' of the great Judge is pronounced, and the crown of immortal glory is placed upon the brow of the victor, many will raise their crowns in sight of the assembled universe and, pointing to their mother, say, 'She made me all I am through the grace of God. Her instruction, her prayers, have been blessed to my eternal salvation.' "[6]

Our Christian mothers would like to see our families become sacred units "where life begins and love never ends," as the anonymous saying goes. May the bonds of love that unite us in this life continue uniting us for all eternity.

THE PUREST GOSPEL

Therefore there is now no condemnation for those who are in Christ Jesus. For the law of the Spirit of life in Christ Jesus has set you free from the law of sin and of death.
—Romans 8:1, 2, NASB

The gospel is God's amazing strategy to justify sinners while condemning sin, deliver them from the power of Satan, and convey them into the kingdom of Christ (Colossians 1:13). One of the clearest expositions of the gospel is provided by Paul in his Epistle to the Romans.

Martin Luther learned the gospel by studying Romans. Early in his career, he presented a series of lectures on the epistle. The series began on **November 3, 1515**, and continued until September 7, 1516. In September 1522, his German translation of the New Testament came off the press with a preface to the Epistle to the Romans (the work was revised in 1546). Several people, including John Wesley, better understood the gospel through reading that preface.

Luther believed, "This Epistle is really the chief part of the New Testament and the very purest Gospel, and is worthy not only that every Christian should know it word for word, by heart, but occupy himself with it every day, as the daily bread of the soul. It can never be read or pondered too much, and the more it is dealt with the more precious it becomes, and the better it tastes."[7]

Summarizing the epistle, Luther pointed out that to keep the law outwardly does not change our hearts, which continue to hate the law and are unable to keep it in its spiritual dimension. But "faith alone makes righteous and fulfills the law; for out of Christ's merit, it brings the Spirit, and the Spirit makes the heart glad and free, as the law requires that it shall be."[8] Grace "makes the law dear to us, and then sin is no more there, and the law is no longer against us, but with us."[9]

Those who are in Christ are not *partially* saved—they are *completely* saved. According to Luther, "Grace does so much that we are accounted wholly righteous before God. For His grace is not divided or broken up, as are the gifts, but it takes us entirely into favor."[10] But the most amazing aspect of all is that, through the merits of "Christ, our Intercessor and Mediator,"[11] God's saving grace can be ours right *here* and right *now*! As we finish our devotional time today, we can leave the place where we are right now as new creatures in Christ Jesus.

November 4

SPELLING AND BIBLE BEES

I have thought much about your words, and stored them
in my heart so that they would hold me back from sin.

—Psalm 119:11, TLB

People who practice good memorization strategies improve their overall memory too. Memorizing words and their respective meanings and spellings is crucial for any effective human communication. So, since 1925, children across America have participated in spelling bees in schools and at local and regional levels, always hoping to make it to the National Spelling Bee held in Washington, DC. Some eleven million students every year are involved in this literacy project. The project helps them learn grammar, enhance their vocabulary, compete in a supportive environment, develop an interest in the origin and etymology of words, develop a range of cognitive skills (including the ability to handle pressure), and develop the confidence to speak in public and accept their mistakes. If memorizing spelling words is so crucial, shouldn't the memorization of God's Word receive at least as much attention?

On **November 4–6, 2009**, three hundred contestants—children and youth from seven to eighteen years old—gathered in Washington, DC, for the first annual National Bible Bee sponsored by the Shelby Kennedy Foundation. The competition calls young people back to the lost discipline of Scripture memorization, as well as asks them to learn, speak, and live out their Christian faith. Each contestant ends up having a unique experience with God's Word!

There is no such thing as an empty mind. If we do not fill our minds with God's Word, other secular and perhaps even vulgar thoughts will occupy them. Memorizing Bible passages is not just a matter of building up knowledge; it can shield us against sin, strengthening our spiritual life. In Psalm 119:11, we read, "I have thought much about your words, and stored them in my heart so that they would hold me back from sin" (TLB).

When you are asked to recite a Bible passage, how many different ones come to your mind? Why not challenge yourself—and those around you—to memorize a new Bible text every day? It can be a passage basic to the Adventist message, a Bible promise, or any other verse of your choosing. No matter what you select, this habit will align your mind more closely with God's Word and put you more in tune with His will for your life.

313

ON ENCHANTED GROUND

*Then the serpent said to the woman, "You will not surely die. For God knows that in the day
you eat of it your eyes will be opened, and you will be like God, knowing good and evil."*
—Genesis 3:4, 5

What do you do when the word of Satan seems to be more logical, up-to-date, and relevant than the Word of God? This was precisely the dilemma of Eve in the Garden of Eden (Genesis 2:15–17; 3:1–6) and continues to be the problem of many today who allow human reason to have the final word.

Moses Hull (1836–1907) accepted the Adventist message in July 1857 and was ordained to the gospel ministry the next year. He became an eloquent preacher, a good writer, and a skillful apologist in public debates, especially in opposition to Spiritualists. But James and Ellen White warned him about his penchant for these debates and the danger of exposing himself to Satan's influence. Initially, he appeared to be faithful. In the *Advent Review and Sabbath Herald* of March 25, 1862, he called Spiritualism "the worst form of infidelity."[12] However, in October 1862, in Paw Paw, Michigan, he debated a Spiritualist named W. F. Jamieson, and from then on, his life was no longer the same.

On **November 5, 1862**, Ellen White received a vision revealing Moses Hull's dangerous condition. She warned him, "You have parleyed with Satan, and reasoned with him, and tarried upon forbidden ground,"[13] but he was still fully "asleep to his danger."[14] And she added, "He was presented to me as standing upon the brink of an awful gulf, ready to leap. If he takes the leap, it will be final; his eternal destiny will be fixed. He is doing work and making decisions for eternity."[15]

Many rejoiced when Hull returned to the Adventist Church and rejoined the ministry, but sadly, his recommitment did not last very long. On September 20, 1863, in Manchester, New Hampshire, he preached his last sermon as an Adventist pastor. Later he became an influential Spiritualist lecturer and author, and he remained so until his death in 1907. Ultimately, he leaped onto the forbidden ground, and Satan triumphed.

Satan's enchanted ground is too attractive, and his arguments are too persuasive. We must stay away from them!

MISSIONARY CHURCHES

So shall My word be that goes forth from My mouth;
It shall not return to Me void,
But it shall accomplish what I please,
And it shall prosper in the thing for which I sent it.

—Isaiah 55:11

I s it possible to revitalize a church that has forsaken its "first love" (Revelation 2:4)? Such a church needs to be *revived* through a living relationship with Christ, *reformed* according to God's Word, and *transformed* into a missionary training school for all its members. According to Ellen White, "Every church should be a training school for Christian workers. Its members should be taught how to give Bible readings, how to conduct and teach Sabbath-school classes, how best to help the poor and to care for the sick, how to work for the unconverted."[16]

No other early Adventist missionary strategy was so effective in transforming local congregations into missionary agencies as the Tract and Missionary Societies. On **November 6, 1870**, the first of those societies was organized by Stephen N. Haskell for the newly formed New England Conference. Its threefold purpose was to visit people, circulate books and tracts, and obtain subscribers for Adventist periodicals. Any Adventist could join the society by contributing a dollar. Each member kept a record of his or her labor and gave a report at the quarterly meetings. In 1873, the General Conference asked Haskell to travel to each of the other conferences to promote tract and missionary work. And in 1874, the International Tract and Missionary Society was formed.

Our world today is very different. Many of the good outreach methods of the past might not work as successfully today. They may need to be either updated or replaced. But imagine your local church becoming an effective "training school for Christian workers." Remember, "the church must be a working church if it would be a living church."[17]

As important as it might be to ask what the *church* should be doing, it is far more effective to ask and then act upon the more crucial question, What am *I* doing to revitalize my local church? Allow God to use your talents and skills to help transform your local church into a powerful missionary agency.

$\mathcal{A}$BSOLUTE $\mathcal{R}$ELATIVITY

There is one body and one Spirit, just as you were called to one
hope when you were called; one Lord, one faith, one baptism.
—Ephesians 4:4, 5, NIV

M any people claim that, according to Albert Einstein, everything is relative. But there is no evidence that he ever suggested such a generic notion of reality. However, the French philosopher Auguste Comte stressed "the purely relative nature of all our knowledge."[18] And the Marxist revolutionary and theorist Leon Trotsky suggested, "Everything is relative in this world, where change alone endures."[19] But should we question how absolute the notion is that "everything is relative"? As asserted by Albert Einstein himself, "Philosophers play with the word [*relativity*], like a child with a doll. . . . It does not mean that everything in life is relative."[20]

On **November 7, 1919**, the leading British newspaper *The Times* came off the press with the headline, "Revolution in Science—New Theory of the Universe—Newtonian Ideas Overthrown." But what did Einstein have in mind when he proposed his *special* and *general* theories of relativity in 1905 and 1916, respectively? To explain concisely, his *special* theory was based on the theory that the speed of light is constant for all observers and that observers moving at constant speeds should be subject to the same physical laws. The *general* theory proposed that matter causes space to curve. Thus, light from another star could be bent by the sun's gravity.

In a world with so many gods and so many conflicting expressions of truth, religion has become subjective and is seen as largely a matter of personal taste. There is a general tendency to consider whatever one likes as absolute truth, while anything one does not like is viewed as relative truth. But in Ephesians 4:4, 5, we read, "There is one body and one Spirit, just as you were called to one hope when you were called; one Lord, one faith, one baptism" (NIV). This implies that instead of *opening* our minds to an ever-increasing variety of human theories and ideologies, we should, indeed, *refocus* our scattered minds on the "one Lord, one faith."

Remember, God is God, and He knows what is best for us. He gave His Word to us not to be questioned but to be obeyed.

*U*NERRING *A*CCURACY

O LORD, You have searched me and known me.

—Psalm 139:1

Have you ever had an X-ray that revealed a broken bone? Wilhelm Conrad Röntgen (1845–1923) was a German mechanical engineer and physicist. On **November 8, 1895**, while he was studying the phenomena of an electric current passing through an extremely low-pressure gas, he discovered a new kind of ray. Those rays became known as Röntgen rays, but he called them X-rays, a previously unknown type of radiation. He was the first recipient of the Nobel Prize in Physics, awarded to him in 1901. X-rays remind us that God knows our innermost lives. He sees what others around us can't. Ellen White explains,

Sin may be concealed, denied, covered up from father, mother, wife, children, and associates; no one but the guilty actors may cherish the least suspicion of the wrong; but it is laid bare before the intelligences of heaven. The darkness of the darkest night, the secrecy of all deceptive arts, is not sufficient to veil one thought from the knowledge of the Eternal. . . .

How solemn is the thought! Day after day, passing into eternity, bears its burden of records for the books of heaven. Words once spoken, deeds once done, can never be recalled. Angels have registered both the good and the evil. The mightiest conqueror upon the earth cannot call back the record of even a single day. . . .

As the features of the countenance are reproduced with unerring accuracy on the polished plate of the artist, so the character is faithfully delineated in the books above. Yet how little solicitude is felt concerning that record which is to meet the gaze of heavenly beings. Could the veil which separates the visible from the invisible world be swept back, and the children of men behold an angel recording every word and deed, which they must meet again in the judgment, how many words that are daily uttered would remain unspoken, how many deeds would remain undone.[21]

The fact that God knows us in every detail should worry those with hidden agendas and relieve those who are in Christ.

*T*HE *B*ERLIN *W*ALL

So the wall was finished on the twenty-fifth day of Elul, in fifty-two days. And it happened,
when all our enemies heard of it, . . . they perceived that this work was done by our God.
—Nehemiah 6:15, 16

I am writing our reflection for today while traveling through Berlin, Germany, and I was reminded of several historical facts related to this city. For instance, in 1871, Otto von Bismarck integrated the German States into a powerful German Empire under Prussian leadership, with its capital in Berlin. Less than a century later, World War II split the country in two—into West Germany and East Germany—and divided Berlin into two sections. In 1961, construction began on the Berlin Wall to create a permanent divide between the eastern and the western sections of the city. But on **November 9, 1989**, the wall was demolished to show that the Cold War with the Soviet Union was at an end.

Although the Berlin Wall divided the city of Berlin, restricting travel between the two sections, the wall of Jerusalem surrounded the city of Jerusalem, protecting its inhabitants from invaders. As stated, the Berlin Wall was *demolished* at the end of the Cold War, and Berlin was reunited as one city. But at the end of the Babylonian captivity, the wall of Jerusalem, as well as the city and temple, were *rebuilt*. The fall of the Berlin Wall had major historical significance. The rebuilding of Jerusalem, however, had major prophetic meaning.

The book of Daniel identifies "the going forth" of the decree to restore and rebuild Jerusalem as the starting point for both the 70 prophetic weeks (Daniel 9:24–27) and the 2,300 prophetic evenings and mornings (Daniel 8:14). That starting point was the autumn of 457 BC, when Artaxerxes's decree was issued in the seventh year of his reign (Ezra 7:7). Reliable studies indicate that these time periods represent 490 years and 2,300 years, taking us respectively to AD 34, ending the time allotted to the Jewish people—3½ years after the Messiah was "cut off," or crucified (Daniel 9:26)—and to 1844, when He would begin to cleanse the heavenly sanctuary (Daniel 8:14; cf. Hebrews 9:23).

The fulfillment of these and many other Bible prophecies confirms that God is in control of human history, patiently guiding it toward its glorious climax: the second coming of Christ!

ＨUMAN ＲEASON

But the natural man does not receive the things of the Spirit of God, for they are
foolishness to him; nor can he know them, because they are spiritually discerned.
—1 Corinthians 2:14

Many people confuse faith with credulity and place reason above faith. Perhaps no other movement in history emphasized the role of reason and perceived liberty as did the French Revolution (1789–1799). With a strong anti-Christian agenda, the revolution even transformed many French churches into Temples of Reason. On **November 10, 1793**, the huge, licentious Feast of Reason and Liberty was celebrated in Paris, in which a woman was carried into the Notre Dame Cathedral and enshrined as the Goddess of Reason. According to the *New Monthly Magazine* (1868), the republican activist Madame Momoro (Sophie Momoro) was proclaimed Goddess of Reason, and the actress Mademoiselle Maillard (Marie-Thérèse Davoux) was named Representative of Beauty and Nature.

Additionally, the Enlightenment prompted a skeptical reading and interpretation of Scripture called the historical-critical method. Denying the Bible's divine origin and inspiration, critical scholars regarded it as a mere expression of the milieu in which it was produced. Its miracles were either denied or reinterpreted as having been produced by natural causes. Bible prophecies were categorized as *vaticinium ex eventu*—prophecy after the event had occurred. Thus, human reason sat in judgment of Scripture, undermining its transformative power.

In 1 Corinthians 2:14, Paul contrasts *natural* reason with *sanctified* reason. Speaking of sanctified reason, Martin Luther acknowledged that "when illuminated by the Holy Spirit, reason helps to interpret the Holy Scriptures."[22] Regarding natural reason, the Reformer warned, "For reason is the greatest enemy that faith has: it never comes to the aid of spiritual things, but—more frequently than not—struggles against the Divine Word, treating with contempt all that emanates from God."[23]

Saving faith is a gift from God that goes beyond reason and takes us into spiritual and heavenly realities (Hebrews 11:1). As Jesus said to Martha, "If you believe, you will see the glory of God" (John 11:40, NASB). So, allow true faith to enhance your capacity to reason.

GREAT THINGS FOR GOD

"Enlarge the place of your tent,
And let them stretch out the curtains of your dwellings;
Do not spare;
Lengthen your cords,
And strengthen your stakes.
For you shall expand to the right and to the left,
And your descendants will inherit the nations,
And make the desolate cities inhabited."

—Isaiah 54:2, 3

The great Christian preachers and missionaries who impacted the world have been men and women completely dedicated to God and unconditionally committed to His mission. Such was the case for William Carey (1761–1834), the "father of modern missions." While working as a shoemaker in Hackleton, in southern England, Carey made a world map and hung it by his workbench to raise his awareness of worldwide mission. On Wednesday, May 31, 1792, Carey preached a sermon based on Isaiah 54:2, 3, in which he repeatedly said, "Expect great things from God; attempt great things for God." Sadly, the congregation did not respond as he expected, and Carey turned to a friend and said, "Oh, let us do something in answer to God's call."

When he shared with a group of pastors the duty of all Christians to spread the gospel throughout the world, one of them said, "Young man, sit down; when God pleases to convert the heathen, he will do it without your aid or mine." Initially, Carey's wife was unwilling to go to the mission field, but finally, she accepted the challenge. On **November 11, 1792**, they landed in Calcutta, India, where Carey and his team translated the Bible into Bengali, Sanskrit, and other major languages and dialects.

Carey could not resist the great commission of Matthew 28:18–20. To a friend he confessed, "I never could say—no. I began to preach at Moulton, because I could not say—no. I went to Leicester, because I could not say—no. I became a missionary, because I could not say—no."[24] Indeed, the divine and the human elements must work together in perfect harmony. Ellen White wrote, "When divine power is combined with human effort, the work will spread like fire in the stubble."[25] To what extent are you willing to become a modern William Carey, surrendering your life to God and allowing Him to use you in His mission?

*T*HE *U*NREAD *T*ESTIMONY

Jehoshaphat stood and said, "Hear me, O Judah and you inhabitants of Jerusalem: Believe in the LORD your God, and you shall be established; believe His prophets, and you shall prosper."
—2 Chronicles 20:20

In the autumn of 1851, the Sabbath-keeping community in Washington, New Hampshire, was in much turmoil, so James and Ellen White went there for a weekend conference. On Sabbath, November 1, Mrs. White received a vision about the various problems of that congregation, including the extremely critical and aggressive spirit of Stephen Smith (1806–1889). Several members repented and confessed their sins, but not Smith. So, that Sunday afternoon, the church voted to withdraw his membership.

On **November 12, 1851,** Ellen White described in a letter the challenges they faced at those meetings and how on Monday, November 3, they "held another meeting and it was the best meeting of the whole; sweet union and love prevailed in the meeting."[26] From then on, the life of Stephen Smith was full of ups and downs. At times he even supported offshoot movements. "At some point in the 1850s . . . , Ellen White wrote him a testimony [describing] what his life would be if he persisted in the course he was following." But Smith kept the letter "in a trunk, . . . unopened and unread."[27]

In 1885, while revival meetings were being held in the little Washington church, Stephen Smith publicly confessed,

I received a testimony myself twenty-eight years ago. I took it home and locked it up in my trunk, and I never read it till last Thursday. . . .

Brethren, every word of the testimony for me is true, and I accept it. And I have come to that place where I finally believe they [the testimonies] all are of God, and if I had heeded the one God sent to me as well as the rest, it would have changed the whole course of my life, and I should have been a very different man.[28]

May the Lord help us read and apply His counsels and warnings to our daily lives. The promise for us today is, "Believe His prophets, and you shall prosper" (2 Chronicles 20:20).

$\mathcal{T}$HE $\mathcal{F}$ALLING OF THE $\mathcal{S}$TARS

"Immediately after the tribulation of those days the sun will be
darkened, and the moon will not give its light; the stars will fall
from heaven, and the powers of the heavens will be shaken."
—Matthew 24:29

Perhaps no other celestial phenomenon has stirred more excitement and fear than the famous Leonid meteor storm of **November 13, 1833**. Seen throughout North America, this phenomenon was caused by the earth passing through the orbital path of the comet Tempel-Tuttle. Small meteor showers can be observed every year in November, but more intense meteor storms usually occur every thirty-three years. No meteor storm has exceeded the intensity nor the meaning of the 1833 display, which is said to have produced more than one hundred thousand meteors per hour.

Frederick Douglass stated, "I witnessed this gorgeous spectacle, and was awe-struck. The air seemed filled with bright descending messengers from the sky. It was about daybreak when I saw this sublime scene. I was not without the suggestion, at that moment that it might be the harbinger of the coming of the Son of Man; and in my then state of mind I was prepared to hail Him as my friend and deliverer. I had read that the 'stars shall fall from heaven;' and they were now falling."[29]

Two years earlier, on the east coast of the United States, William Miller had begun to preach the coming of Christ and the end of the world, anticipating it to happen around 1843. The meteor storm of 1833 appeared unexpectedly, lighting up the entire night sky in that same region, convincing many that Judgment Day was at hand. Although Christ did not return at the time Miller taught, the meteor storm of 1833 remains a landmark in prophetic interpretation (Revelation 6:13).

Some question the prophetic significance of "signs" that have natural causes or scientific explanations. From a human perspective, the great Lisbon earthquake of 1755 was just another shaking and vibration of the earth's crust due to the movements of tectonic plates. Likewise, the Leonid meteor storm of 1833 was simply caused by the earth passing through the comet Tempel-Tuttle's trail. But from a biblical perspective, natural events are often used by God to awaken people and serve as forerunners of His intervention in human history. Regardless of their cause, let's allow the Bible to interpret the meaning of those signs.

ℬLESSED ℒOSSES

Then God said, "Take your son, your only son, whom you love—Isaac—and go to the region of Moriah. Sacrifice him there as a burnt offering on a mountain I will show you."
—Genesis 22:2, NIV

What image comes to your mind when you hear the word *idolatry*? We usually envision ancient physical idols crafted out of stone, metal, or wood (Isaiah 44:9–20). But idols and gods can take many forms and are often very difficult to recognize. Even good things or beloved people can become gods for us.

On **November 14, 2007**, I arrived in the town of Canela, in southern Brazil, for the meetings of AFAM (Ministerial Spouses Association) of the South Brazil Union Conference. My task was to translate the presentations of Sharon Cress, who was from the General Conference. One of her talks was about God asking Abraham to sacrifice his beloved son Isaac (Genesis 22). She explained that the reason for God's command was that Abraham might easily make his beloved son Isaac his idol that could take the place of God in his life.

Mrs. Cress added that God might do the same with us today. He may remove something or someone we love more than Him. He acts as a loving mother who sees her little boy happily playing with a sharp knife in his hand. She gently opens his fist and removes the knife, knowing that a little frustration now can prevent a much bigger tragedy later.

This thought-provoking analogy should lead us to some very personal reflections: What or who are the idols in your life? How can you recognize and get rid of them? An idol is anything or anyone to whom we devote our most precious time and our deepest feelings. It can be a spouse, a child, or a friend. One way to discover it in our day is to look through your computer's browser history. In his book *Gods at War*, Kyle Idleman states, "What you are searching for and chasing after reveals the god that is winning the war in your heart."[30]

Today can be a new beginning in our lives. We can clean what needs to be cleaned, give up what needs to be given up, and refocus our priorities. So, let's surrender everything we have and everything we do to God. In other words, let's allow God to be God in our lives!

$\mathcal{M}$Y $\mathcal{P}$ERSONAL SALVATION

But I discipline my body and make it my slave, so that,
after I have preached to others, I myself will not be disqualified.
—1 Corinthians 9:27, NASB

Oswald Chambers was a Scottish evangelist and teacher in the early 1900s. While serving as a chaplain for the British Commonwealth troops in Egypt during World War I, he was stricken with appendicitis and shortly thereafter suffered a pulmonary hemorrhage that took his life on **November 15, 1917**, when he was just forty-three years old. In 1924, his widow, Biddy,[31] began editing hundreds of pages of shorthand she had recorded whenever Oswald preached. Those notes became the basis for daily devotions, collectively published as *My Utmost for His Highest.*[32]

In the January 18 entry of Chambers's devotional, we read, "Beware of anything that competes with your loyalty to Jesus Christ. The greatest competitor of true devotion to Jesus is the service we do for Him. It is easier to serve than to pour out our lives completely for Him. The goal of the call of God is His satisfaction, not simply that we should do something *for* Him. We are not sent to do battle for God, but to be used by God in His battles. Are we more devoted to service than we are to Jesus Christ Himself?"[33]

Much earlier—in 1898 to be exact—Ellen G. White warned,

As activity increases and men become successful in doing any work for God, there is danger of trusting to human plans and methods. There is a tendency to pray less, and to have less faith. Like the disciples, we are in danger of losing sight of our dependence on God, and seeking to make a savior of our activity. We need to look constantly to Jesus, realizing that it is His power which does the work. While we are to labor earnestly for the salvation of the lost, we must also take time for meditation, for prayer, and for the study of the word of God.[34]

Paul's concern in 1 Corinthians 9:27 is captured perfectly in the two preceding quotations. In reality, each of us has only one life to live, during which we should work out our own "salvation with fear and trembling" (Philippians 2:12). But in this process, we should never forget that *yesterday* has already passed, and *tomorrow* may never arrive. God entrusts us with *today* to live for Him and with Him. Let's live today as if it were the last day of our life.

A Christian Theocracy

The dragon gave him his power, his throne, and great authority.
—Revelation 13:2

Jesus established a church without secular authority and without soldiers to defend it (John 18:36). So, how did the Roman Church become so powerful in secular issues, with its authority culminating in the union of church and state? From the fourth to the sixth century, several important steps were taken in that process.

During the time of Constantine, Christianity became the official religion of the state. The emperors that succeeded Constantine proceeded to make Christianity the exclusive religion of the state. After the sacking of Rome by the Visigoths in 410, Augustine wrote his famous work *The City of God*, in which he outlined the idea of a universal church in control of a universal state. His ideal was implemented with the support of both the Western Roman Empire and the Byzantine Empire in the east.

The conversion of Clovis, king of the Franks, was a significant event leading to the unification of Western Europe in support of the papacy during the first part of the Middle Ages. Clovis's war against the Visigoths and his victory over them in 508 represented another important step by providing an effective army to the Roman Catholic Church for punishing so-called heretics.

On **November 16, 534**, Justinian, emperor of the Byzantine Empire, sent a letter to Pope John II recognizing him as "the head of all the Holy Churches" and promising "to increase the honor and authority" of his Holy See. But it was not until 538 that the city of Rome became free from the domination of any "heretical tribes" and the Roman Catholic Church could effectively develop its ecclesiastical supremacy.

There was a radical change from the early *persecuted* church of the first century to the later *persecuting* church of the Middle Ages, which killed thousands through the Christian Crusades and the Inquisition. Undoubtedly, New Testament Christianity can remain truly Christian only by following Christ's principle: "My kingdom is not of this world" (John 18:36). The theocratic model of the Old Testament must never be imposed on it. And "in everything, therefore, treat people the same way you want them to treat you" (Matthew 7:12, NASB), especially when it comes to religious freedom.

"LOVE YOUR ENEMIES"

"But I say to you, love your enemies, bless those who curse you, do good to those
who hate you, and pray for those who spitefully use you and persecute you."
—Matthew 5:44

One of the most challenging components of practical religion is Christ's radical commandment to love our enemies, as recorded in Matthew 5:43–48. In this passage, Christ recognized that our natural human tendency is to love those who love us and to hate those who hate us. But this kind of behavior can have disastrous consequences. If we do not love our enemies, we will most certainly end up hating them; and in hating them, we end up poisoning ourselves.

Martin Luther King Jr. warned of this danger in his famous sermon "Loving Your Enemies," delivered at Dexter Avenue Baptist Church in Montgomery, Alabama, on **November 17, 1957**. In King's words, "Hate destroys the very structure of the personality of the hater. . . . Hate at any point is a cancer that gnaws away at the very vital center of your life and your existence. It is like eroding acid that eats away the best and the objective center of your life. So Jesus says love, because hate destroys the hater as well as the hated."[35]

We live in a sinful world where "all who desire to live godly in Christ Jesus will suffer persecution" (2 Timothy 3:12). Your worst enemy could be in the outside world (John 15:18–25), or very close to you, living under the same roof (Matthew 10:34–36) or perhaps even sleeping in the same bed with you. The question is not so much who the person is, where he or she lives, or how he or she has harmed you. The real question is, How have you handled the situation? Have you responded with poisonous hate or with healing love?

In hating others, you confirm that you are a victim of their maltreatment. By loving them, you demonstrate that you control your circumstances. Choosing to love your enemies is choosing to love not only them but also yourself (Matthew 22:39), proving that you are a son or daughter of your heavenly Father (Matthew 5:44, 45). How different would our world be—including our workplaces, our classrooms, our social circles, our homes, and even our own marriages—if we would forgive more and accuse less, love more and expect less gratification. You can make the world a better place by sowing seeds of love around you!

MOVING BY FAITH

"But you shall receive power when the Holy Spirit has come upon you; and you shall be witnesses to Me in Jerusalem, and in all Judea and Samaria, and to the end of the earth."

—Acts 1:8

After the Great Disappointment of October 22, 1844, early Sabbath-keeping Adventists were still convinced that Jesus would come back soon; indeed, at any moment. In 1848, they held several Bible conferences to share the biblical doctrines they discovered from their careful study of Scripture with other former Millerites. On **November 18, 1848**, at a conference held in Dorchester, Massachusetts, Ellen White received a short but very significant vision. "After coming out of vision, [she] said to [her] husband: 'I have a message for you. You must begin to print a little paper and send it out to the people. Let it be small at first; but as the people read, they will send you means with which to print, and it will be a success from the first. From this small beginning it was shown to me to be like streams of light that went clear round the world.' "[36]

But how could the instructions described in this vision be implemented? James White had no financial resources to print even the first issue of the paper. Furthermore, if Jesus was coming back soon, there was not enough time for the paper to go "clear round the world."[37] Nevertheless, by the following summer, James had determined to overcome the financial barrier by taking a job mowing a field of grass. But before he started, Ellen had another vision in which she saw that if he did so, he would be cut down by sickness because God wanted him to "write, write, write, and walk out by faith."[38]

Finally, one July day, James brought home a thousand copies of the first paper from Middletown, Connecticut. They were laid on the floor, and a little group of people knelt around them and prayed, asking God's blessings on the tracts that would soon be mailed out to interested people. Donations began coming in to support the new publishing endeavor, which eventually encircled the whole globe.

The Adventist publishing work began because James White chose to trust God when the road ahead of him seemed quite uncertain. Remember, following God's leading may not make things easier for you, but faith in Him makes all things possible.

"*The King of Soccer*"

Whatever your hand finds to do, do it with all your might.
—Ecclesiastes 9:10, NIV

There were high expectations in the Maracaná Stadium in Rio de Janeiro on **November 19, 1969**. Hundreds of photographers and cameramen huddled behind the goal area where Pelé would attempt a free penalty kick. As expected, he scored his famous one-thousandth goal in official soccer games. On January 13, 2014, Pelé was greeted with loud applause during the FIFA Ballon d'Or Prix d'Honneur. Why was he receiving this honor thirty-six years after having retired from professional sports in 1977? It was simply for what he accomplished—on the soccer field as the King of Soccer and off the field as the "global ambassador for soccer."

Edson Arantes do Nascimento, popularly known as Pelé, was born in Três Corações, Brazil. Growing up in poverty, he worked as a tea-shop server in Bauru, São Paulo State. Without money to buy a soccer ball, he often played with a sock stuffed with newspaper and tied together with string. Even as a young boy, his skills caught the attention of those who saw him play. In 1956, he joined Santos Futebol Clube and began his extremely successful professional career.

Pelé is the only player to have won three soccer World Cups. He retired with 1,281 goals in 1,363 games. Sir Bobby Charlton once said, "I sometimes feel as though football was invented for this magical player."[39] Soccer player Tostão declared, "Pelé was the greatest—he was simply flawless. And off the field, he is always smiling and upbeat. You never see him bad-tempered. He loves being Pelé."[40] Indeed, he set the standard that later soccer players would measure themselves against.

What is the secret to a successful career? Different people may answer this question in different ways. But humanly speaking, a recipe for success includes at least four basic ingredients: skills, dedication, opportunities, and relationships. An adequate blend of these four ingredients can make a huge difference.

Pelé and many others have done their best to play and promote soccer around the globe. You and I should demonstrate the same passion and determination for God's cause. How would you rate your commitment to Him? Those who are striving for "an imperishable crown" should be no less committed than those who are seeking a perishable one (1 Corinthians 9:25)!

Spiritual Lethargy

"I counsel you to buy from Me gold refined in the fire, that you may be rich; and white garments, that you may be clothed, that the shame of your nakedness may not be revealed; and anoint your eyes with eye salve, that you may see."

—Revelation 3:18

Early Sabbath-keeping Adventists identified themselves with the faithful Philadelphia church (Revelation 3:7–13). They regarded Sunday-keeping Adventists as the lukewarm Laodicea church (Revelation 3:14–22) and non-Adventists as the dead Sardis church (Revelation 3:1–6). By the mid-1850s, Sabbath keepers concluded that they were Laodiceans, not Philadelphians.

On **November 20, 1855**, Ellen White received a vision portraying the prevailing spiritual lethargy of the church at that time. The content of the vision was published in *Testimonies for the Church*, where she sadly stated, "I saw that the Spirit of the Lord has been dying away from the church."[41] Among the reasons for such a deplorable condition, she listed (1) trust in human reasoning instead of a firm reliance upon God; (2) a spirit of self-exaltation and independence rather than humility and unity; (3) greed in accumulating personal property, instead of financially supporting God's cause; (4) needless indulgence merely to gratify the feelings, the taste, the appetite, and the eyes; and (5) loss of the spirit of self-denial and sacrifice.

Time and context have changed significantly. The church is far more stable and prosperous today than in the early days of the Advent movement. But how are we in spiritual terms? Are we more committed today than the Adventist pioneers were? Is it possible that some of the same causes for their spiritual lethargy are prevalent in our midst as well?

When we blame others for the prevailing spiritual lukewarmness in our midst, we are attempting to justify ourselves. If we really want to overcome our Laodicean, lukewarm condition, each of us must stop blaming the "church" for the condition and humbly ask ourselves, "What part of the message to Laodicea applies to me directly?" Remember, true revival and reformation is a deeply personal matter. It radically changes the focus of our spiritual lives from self-centered *pride* to Christ-centered *humility*.

"More Truth and Light"

"I still have many things to say to you, but you cannot bear them now. However, when He, the Spirit of truth, has come, He will guide you into all truth."
—John 16:12, 13

One of the most remarkable voyages of the seventeenth century was that of the Pilgrim Fathers, who traveled from England to Holland and then from Holland to the New World. After more than two months spent crossing the Atlantic Ocean, the *Mayflower* finally dropped anchor on **November 21, 1620**, on the tip of Cape Cod, which is now Provincetown, Massachusetts. These hearty voyagers arrived in the New World seeking religious freedom for themselves and hoping to establish a nation according to the will of God.

While still in Leiden, Holland, the Pilgrims' beloved pastor, John Robinson, had planned to join them on their voyage. But he had to stay behind. Nevertheless, he delivered a meaningful farewell address. He began, "We are now ere long to part asunder, and the Lord knoweth whether ever he should live to see our faces again. But whether the Lord had appointed it or not, he charges us before God and his blessed angels, to follow him no further than he have followed Christ; and if God should reveal any thing to us by any other instrument of his, to be as ready to receive it as ever we were to receive any truth by his ministry; for he was very confident that the Lord had more truth and light yet to break forth out of his holy word."[42]

Robinson then called the attention of the Pilgrims to the stagnant condition of the Reformed Churches. While the Lutherans "could not be drawn to go beyond what Luther saw," the Calvinists "stick where he [Calvin] left them." In contrast, the Pilgrim Fathers were encouraged to remain open to new understandings of biblical truth under the guidance of the Holy Spirit.[43] It is evident from his speech that Robinson was closely in tune with the famous motto, "The reformed church, always being reformed according to the Word of God."[44]

A never-ending passion for a deeper understanding of biblical truth also inspired the founders of Seventh-day Adventism. A good example is J. N. Andrews, who said in 1849, "I would exchange a thousand errors for one truth."[45] May the Lord give us the same passion as we search the exhaustless mine of truth.

𝒯HE SANCTUARY SYSTEM

Then the temple of God was opened in heaven,
and the ark of His covenant was seen in His temple.
—Revelation 11:19

Seventh-day Adventism has two basic characteristics. The first, easily seen, is the strong biblical foundation for each of its doctrines. The second, less obvious trait is how all those doctrines are blended into one coherent doctrinal system by the sanctuary message. This is the beauty and strength of the Adventist message!

In 1877, Uriah Smith illustrated the unifying function of the sanctuary with the analogy of a wagon wheel, having a central hub and an exterior rim connected by spokes. He suggested, "In the great wheel of truth, the sanctuary occupies this central position. In it, the great truths of revelation find their focal point. From it, in every direction, they radiate. It unites the two great dispensations, the Mosaic and the Christian, and shows their relation to each other. It divides with no other subject the high honor of explaining the position and work of our Lord Jesus Christ."[46]

The **November 22, 1881**, issue of the *Advent Review and Sabbath Herald* carried an article in which Uriah Smith spoke of the sanctuary as the "great central subject of that system of truth which belongs to this time."[47] He listed ten different doctrinal components directly linked to the sanctuary, including the pre-Advent investigative judgment, free will, Christ's atoning sacrifice and priestly ministry, the seventh-day Sabbath, Christ's second coming, and the state of the dead. Six years later, in 1887, he enlarged his list to thirteen.

The sanctuary message gives the Adventist doctrinal system a Christ-centered emphasis not found in other theological systems. In 1893, Ellen White stated, "Christ, His character and work, is the center and circumference of all truth. He is the chain upon which the jewels of doctrine are linked. In Him is found the complete system of truth."[48] We should study this message thoroughly and pray like King David,

That I may dwell in the house of the LORD
All the days of my life,
To behold the beauty of the LORD,
And to inquire in His temple (Psalm 27:4).

DEAD SEA SCROLLS

The words of the LORD are pure words,
Like silver tried in a furnace of earth,
Purified seven times.
You shall keep them, O LORD,
You shall preserve them from this generation forever.

—Psalm 12:6, 7

On **November 23, 1947**, E. L. Sukenik, the distinguished archaeologist of the Hebrew University in Jerusalem, received a message from his Armenian friend Faidi Salahi, a dealer in antiquities. The next morning, the two met, and Salahi showed Sukenik a scrap of leather with old Hebrew characters like those on early Jewish funeral ossuaries. The documents had been discovered by chance the preceding winter (1946–1947) by two Bedouin shepherds near Qumran. The scrolls date to sometime between 200 BC and AD 70. They confirm that the original reading of the Old Testament has been accurately preserved throughout the ages.

Some might question why, if the Bible is God's Word, He didn't preserve its autographs—the original documents written by the biblical prophets. If He had, we would not need to rely on textual criticism to confirm the original reading of the biblical text. True, having the originals could expedite the whole process, but it might also generate other problems. Siegfried J. Schwantes saw the non-survival of the original documents as providential. Given the human tendency toward idolatry, many would undoubtedly end up worshiping the documents rather than seeking the truth they contain. Whatever the reason, we know that God cannot err.

What really counts is that the Bible text we have today is reliable. Critics challenge its trustworthiness. For example, the Mormon prophet Joseph Smith Jr. claimed that "many important points touching the salvation of men, had been taken from the Bible, or lost before it was compiled."[49] If this were the case, then the Bible could no longer be trusted, and its transforming power would be lost. But praise the Lord; He not only inspired the Bible text itself but also preserved the reliability of its original Hebrew, Aramaic, and Greek texts.

Ellen White says, "Brethren, cling to your Bible, as it reads, and stop your criticisms in regard to its validity, and obey the Word, and not one of you will be lost."[50] Let us respect the Bible and be faithful to its message!

NEW ANCESTORS?

Then God said, "Let the earth bring forth the living creature according to its kind: cattle and creeping thing and beast of the earth, each according to its kind"; and it was so.

—Genesis 1:24

Charles Darwin (1809–1882) was studying at Cambridge to become an Anglican priest. But he was increasingly fascinated with natural theology and natural philosophy, which explain the laws of nature exclusively through observation. In 1831, he joined a worldwide exploratory voyage on the HMS *Beagle*. The adventure was supposed to last two years but ended up lasting almost five. As a naturalist, Darwin was much impressed with the different species he found in South America, especially the exotic ones in the Galapagos archipelago. During the voyage, Darwin collected 1,529 specimens preserved in alcohol and 3,907 dried specimens.

On **November 24, 1859**, the renowned publisher John Murray released Darwin's famous book *On the Origin of Species by Means of Natural Selection, or the Preservation of Favoured Races in the Struggle for Life* (usually known simply as *The Origin of Species*). In Darwin's view, the general law in "the war of nature," leading to the advancement of all organic beings, is "multiply, vary, let the strongest live and the weakest die."[51] His theory of natural selection implied that a Creator could have breathed the life energy "into a few forms or into one," but from then on, "this planet has gone cycling," and life evolved into "endless forms most beautiful and most wonderful."[52]

The real issue is who actually holds creative power. According to the biblical *creationist* model, God is the only source and sustainer of life in all its uncountable expressions. The Darwinian *evolutionary* theory empties God of His creating and sustaining power and transfers it to the creatures themselves. Atheistic evolutionists go a step further and erase God completely from the scenario. So creation is deified, and God is made void. Instead of having a noble ancestry that leads back to God, humanity is seen as nothing more than an evolving expression of primitive forms of animal life.

Only the Eternal God who "made the universe" (Hebrews 1:2, NIV) can explain its origin to us. To Him alone be the glory today and forever. Amen.

ᴍEATLESS ᴅAY

The righteous care for the needs of their animals,
but the kindest acts of the wicked are cruel.

—Proverbs 12:10, NIV

Life is a gift from God that was originally intended to last forever. However, the sin of Adam and Eve brought death into the world, "for the wages of sin is death" (Romans 6:23). As Christians, we are forbidden by God to murder human beings (Exodus 20:13) and we are encouraged to care for the lives and needs of animals (Proverbs 12:10; Psalm 104:10–27). We are told Jesus cared not only for human beings but also for animals. "The little creatures of the groves, the patient beasts of burden,—all were happier for His presence. He whose word of power upheld the worlds would stoop to relieve a wounded bird."[53]

An anonymous statement (often attributed to Jeremy Bentham) points out that "man is the only animal that can remain on friendly terms with the victims he intends to eat until he eats them." In contrast, the Seventh-day Adventist Church has encouraged members to become vegetarians. As early as February 1843, Joseph Bates "resolved to eat no more meat."[54] Ellen White, after her 1863 health reform vision, continued to eat meat sporadically. But while in Australia, she wrote, "Since the camp meeting at Brighton (January, 1894), I have absolutely banished meat from my table. It is an understanding that whether I am at home or abroad, nothing of this kind is to be used in my family, or come upon my table. I have had much representation before my mind in the night season on this subject."[55]

Many Seventh-day Adventists are vegetarians for health reasons. Scientific studies conducted by Loma Linda University and many other universities around the world have confirmed the benefits of a vegetarian diet as proposed by Ellen White. However, an increasing number of people today follow a meatless diet out of value and care for animals. It is good to remember that **November 25** is International Meatless Day and Animal Rights Day. On this day, people are encouraged not to eat meat.

American actor Denis Leary stated, "Not eating meat is a decision. Eating meat is an instinct."[56] Perhaps you could care for animals, too, by turning a meatless day into a meatless life!

A Modern Prophet

*Surely the Sovereign L*ORD *does nothing without
revealing his plan to his servants the prophets.*

—Amos 3:7, NIV

William F. Albright (1891–1971) was a renowned American archaeologist, biblical scholar, and philologist who received twenty-five honorary doctorates. In the second edition of his book *From the Stone Age to Christianity* (1957), he refers to Ellen White as a true modern prophet. In 2005, the Barna Group released a nationwide US survey among Protestant pastors. Unlike many older pastors, those under forty listed Ellen White as one of their favorite authors.[57] As Seventh-day Adventists, we know she is more than just an *inspiring* author; she is, in fact, an *inspired* prophet.

Born in Gorham, Maine, on **November 26, 1827**, Ellen G. Harmon (later White) received her first prophetic vision in December 1844. She had just turned seventeen. During her prophetic ministry, she received some two thousand prophetic dreams and visions. She wrote about a hundred thousand pages and became one of the most translated authors of all time. But many still ask, "If all we need to be saved is found in the Bible, why do we still need a modern prophet?"

Amos 3:7 declares, "The Sovereign LORD does nothing without revealing his plan to his servants the prophets" (NIV). God has provided special prophetic assistance throughout history, especially when major struggles between truth and error have occurred and truth needed to be restored. For example, when the world was to be destroyed by the Flood, God called Noah to be a prophet and "preacher of righteousness" (Genesis 6–8; 2 Peter 2:5). When God intended to liberate the Israelites from Egypt, He chose Moses as a prophet and leader (Exodus 3; 4; Hosea 12:13). When God's people turned away from Him and engaged in idolatry, He sent prophet after prophet to warn them (2 Chronicles 36:15, 16). When the time had come for Christ to begin His ministry on earth, God sent John the Baptist to prepare the way for the Messiah (Matthew 3).

Amid the challenges of the last days (2 Timothy 3:1–5; 4:3, 4), God sent another prophet—Ellen White—to assist in the final restoration of biblical truth (Daniel 8:9–14; Revelation 14:6–12). As valuable as her writings are, they are relevant only to those who systematically read and study them in connection with the Bible. So, make a Bible-reading plan today, and then gain added insight from the modern prophet.

$\mathcal{N}$OBEL $\mathcal{P}$RIZES

"To the one who is victorious, I will give the right to sit with me on my throne,
just as I was victorious and sat down with my Father on his throne."
—Revelation 3:21, NIV

A prize is an award given to the winner of a competition or as a reward for an outstanding performance or contribution. Among the most prestigious awards are Nobel Prizes. Alfred Nobel (1833–1896) was a Swedish chemist, engineer, inventor, businessman, and philanthropist. He held 355 different patents but became best known as the inventor of dynamite. Criticized for developing the explosive, Nobel was concerned with how he would be remembered. Since he had never married and had no children, he decided to do something to benefit humanity.

"On **November 27, 1895**, at the Swedish-Norwegian Club in Paris, Nobel signed his last will and testament, setting aside the bulk of his . . . estate . . . to establish Nobel Prizes, to be awarded annually,"[58] without distinction of nationality, for outstanding contributions to humanity. The first of those prizes was awarded in 1901. The annual prize ceremonies for chemistry, economics, literature, physics, and physiology or medicine are held in Stockholm, Sweden, and the ceremony for the peace prize is held in Oslo, Norway.

Each recipient, or laureate, receives a gold medal, a diploma, and a significant sum of money. The award ceremonies are followed by special banquets attended in Stockholm by the Swedish royal family and in Oslo by the king and queen of Norway. The list of recipients includes such names as Marie Curie, Albert Einstein, Albert Schweitzer, Ernest Hemingway, Jean-Paul Sartre, Martin Luther King Jr., Mother Teresa, and Nelson Mandela.

The book of Revelation tells of the awards that will be given to those who overcome the forces of evil. The awards are far more than just a gold medal, a diploma, and some money to spend. They include eternal life (Revelation 2:11), a record of the person's name in the book of life (Revelation 3:5), the right to abide in God's temple, the honor of carrying His name (verse 12), and the joy of sitting with Christ on His glorious throne (verse 21). None of the Nobel Prizes can be compared to the heavenly ones.

How are you planning your future? Are the awards of this world more attractive to you than the everlasting rewards? Remember that all human prizes will soon vanish, and only heavenly ones shall last!

NOT ENOUGH FUEL

"Ten bridesmaids took their lamps and went to meet the bridegroom.
Five of them were foolish, and five were wise. When the foolish took their lamps,
they took no oil with them; but the wise took flasks of oil with their lamps."
—Matthew 25:1–4, NRSV

There was much excitement—for the first time, the Chapecoense soccer team, from a small city in southern Brazil, would play the two-match Copa Sudamericana final. The opponent was Atletico Nacional of Medellin, Colombia, where the first match would occur. On their trip to Colombia, the Chapecoense first took a commercial flight to Bolivia, and from there, an Avro RJ85 charter operated by LaMia, a Bolivian-based airline.

On Monday, **November 28, 2016**, around ten o'clock at night local time, the plane ran out of fuel and crashed just a few miles from Medellin's international airport. Of the seventy-seven people aboard (including nine crew and sixty-eight passengers), only six survived. Official sources confirmed that the pilot was warned before taking off from the airport in Bolivia that he might not have enough fuel. Even so, he thought he could make it. The tragic result was seventy-one people died, including the pilot.

Newspapers around the globe covered the heartbreaking story, and soccer games around the world began with a minute of silence. The Atletico Nacional team asked the South American Football Confederation to grant the 2016 Copa Sudamericana Championship to the Chapecoense, and the team was given the award posthumously. But no award or honor could bring back those who died in the plane crash.

This disastrous incident reminds us of the foolish bridesmaids who, not having enough oil with them, were barred from the wedding banquet (Matthew 25:1–13). We are told that "the class represented by the foolish virgins are not hypocrites. They have a regard for the truth, they have advocated the truth, they are attracted to those who believe the truth; but they have not yielded themselves to the Holy Spirit's working."[59]

While the LaMia flight accident generated much earthly sorrow, the spiritual ramifications of being unprepared are irreversible eternal consequences. Please do not risk your spiritual life as the pilot did on this disastrous flight. The price is too high.

God Cares for Us

And the Lord said: "I have surely seen the oppression of My people who are in Egypt, and have heard their cry because of their taskmasters, for I know their sorrows."
—Exodus 3:7

Sometimes life has unpleasant surprises! When Valdecir Simões Lima had finished his BA in theology at Southwestern Adventist College, he planned to stay a little longer in the United States before returning home. But his father greatly missed him and asked him to return to Brazil as soon as possible. So Valdecir visited his family, and less than a week later, after lunch on Sunday, November 11, 1984, his father had a heart attack and died. It was a heartbreaking experience for the whole family.

On **November 29, 1984**, still grieving the tragic loss, Valdecir sat at his father's desk and penned the original Portuguese lyrics of the touching hymn "Deus Sabe, Deus Ouve, Deus Vê" (God knows, God hears, God sees). The chorus can be translated as follows,

God knows what goes on inside your soul,
God hears the pleading prayer,
God sees your anguish and calms you,
God makes a giant out of you.
God knows what goes on inside your soul,
God hears the pleading prayer,
God sees your anguish and calms you;
God knows, God hears, God sees.

During life's violent storms, we may find ourselves asking, "Is God already done with me? Why has He forsaken me?" Remember, God knows what you are going through, and He will never forsake you. He cares about you and has a perfect plan for your life. Just surrender your life to Him and trust in Him!

A Man of Prayer

Now when Daniel knew that the writing was signed, he went home. And in his upper room,
with his windows open toward Jerusalem, he knelt down on his knees three times that day,
and prayed and gave thanks before his God, as was his custom since early days.
—Daniel 6:10

Spiritual revival and religious reformation come only through fervent and unceasing prayer. A classic example is Martin Luther, who not only wrote about prayer but also lived a life of powerful prayer. After kneeling in humility before God, he could boldly stand before anyone.

Luther realized that only through prayer can we be effectively shielded against the powers of evil, the temptations of the world, and our own sinful nature. In his *Large Catechism*, published in 1529, he warned, "The devil with all his power, together with the world and our own flesh, resists our efforts [to keep the Ten Commandments]. Therefore, nothing is more necessary than that we should continually turn towards God's ear, call upon Him, and pray to Him."[60]

In his table talk of **November 30, 1531**, Luther reflected on his own prayer life: "Whenever I happen to be prevented by the press of duties from observing my hour of prayer, the entire day is bad for me. Prayer helps us very much and gives us a cheerful heart, not on account of any merit in the work [of praying], but because we have spoken with God and found everything to be in order."[61]

Helpful, practical advice on prayer is also found in his book *A Simple Way to Pray* (published in 1535). There he recommends that prayer "be the first business of the morning and the last at night. Diligently guard against those false, deluding ideas which tell you, 'Wait a little while. I will pray in an hour; first I must attend to this or that.' Such thoughts get you away from prayer into other affairs which so hold your attention and involve you that nothing comes of prayer for that day."[62]

All great men and women of God have one characteristic in common: they have always been people of prayer! To live a life of prayer, we do not need great displays of rhetorical flourish or a multitude of unnecessary words. Our public prayers should be short and succinct. And our private prayers are the most precious opportunities for us to open our hearts to God and speak to Him as our Best Friend.

PEACE IN THE STORM

And the peace of God, which surpasses all understanding,
will guard your hearts and minds through Christ Jesus.

—Philippians 4:7

Horatio G. Spafford (1828–1888) was a prosperous lawyer in Chicago who invested heavily in real estate. When the Great Chicago Fire of 1871 destroyed much of the city, Spafford lost many properties. In 1873, Horatio Spafford, his wife, Anna, and their four daughters planned to sail to Europe for vacation. Due to a business emergency, Spafford had to postpone his own travel, but he sent his family ahead aboard the French steamship *Ville du Havre*. "At about 2 o'clock am on 22 November 1873, in the eastern North Atlantic, the *Ville du Havre* collided with the British iron clipper *Loch Earn*. The *Ville du Havre* sank in a mere 12 minutes,"[1] and of the 316 passengers and crew, only 90 survived, including Anna, but not her daughters.

On **December 1, 1873**, the survivors finally reached Cardiff, Wales. There Anna Spafford cabled her husband saying, " 'Saved alone. What shall I do.' Horatio Spafford took the next available ship to join his wife."[2] During the voyage, "the captain of the ship . . . called him to the bridge. 'A careful reckoning has been made,' he said, 'and I believe we are now passing the place where the *Ville du Havre* was wrecked. The water is three miles deep.' "[3] In that tragic context, Horatio Spafford wrote the lyrics of the great hymn "It Is Well With My Soul,"

When peace, like a river, attendeth my way,
When sorrows like sea billows roll—
Whatever my lot, Thou has taught me to say,
"It is well, it is well with my soul."[4]

Some sources say that Horatio Spafford wrote this hymn the very same day he passed close to the place where his four daughters drowned; others suggest that it was sometime later. Whatever the case, the fact of the matter is that this wonderful hymn reflects the peace that God gave him in that most dreadful moment of his life. Remember, that same peace can sustain you during the stormy days of your own life.

TALENT IS NOT ENOUGH

"I know your works, your labor, your patience, and that you cannot bear those who are evil. . . . Nevertheless I have this against you, that you have left your first love."

—Revelation 2:2–4

One of the most skilled and prolific Adventist songwriters was Franklin E. Belden (1858–1945), who was the son of Ellen White's older sister Sarah. Frank, as he was usually called, could write both lyrics and accompaniment on a sermon topic while it was still being preached. At the end of the service, he and his wife would perform the newly created song and then give a copy of the manuscript to the preacher.

The *Seventh-day Adventist Hymnal* contains several of his inspiring songs. For example, "Wholly Thine" is a hymn of full surrender. Its first stanza reads, "I would be, dear Savior, wholly Thine," and "I would do Thy will, O Lord, not mine."[5] The last stanza of "Cover With His Life" is

Reconciled by His death for my sin,
Justified by His life pure and clean,
Sanctified by obeying His word,
Glorified when returneth my Lord.[6]

Many people have found comfort and assurance in the message of "A Shelter in the Time of Storm."[7] The solemnity of God's judgment is addressed in "The Judgment Has Set."[8] The hymn "We Know Not the Hour" emphasizes the need to "watch and be ready" for Christ's second coming.[9] And "Joy By and By" speaks of the joy that will be "when the work is done" and "when the workers gather home."[10]

Belden died on **December 2, 1945**, leaving a rich legacy of spiritual songs. But unfortunately, his personal life did not fully reflect the spiritual tone of his hymns. Already in 1895, Ellen White wrote to him from Australia, "Men may labor in connection with the work of God as did Noah's carpenters, and yet resist the divine influences."[11] In 1897, she added, "Frank, what can I say to you? From the light I have received from God, I know that you have a prayerless home. The time of your sojourning here is short. You think that you have surrendered yourself to God, but you have never yet fully given up your bitter feelings against others."[12]

If a true prophet sent you a personal letter, what do you think would be its tenor? Reflect on this question today, and change what needs to be changed.

$\mathcal{A}$ $\mathcal{N}$EW $\mathcal{H}$EART

*"I will give you a new heart and put a new spirit in you; I will
remove from you your heart of stone and give you a heart of flesh."*
—Ezekiel 36:26, NIV

On **December 3, 1967**, the South African cardiac surgeon Dr. Christiaan N. Barnard (1922–2001) performed the world's first human-to-human heart transplant and the second-ever heart transplant at Groote Schuur Hospital in Cape Town. The patient was Louis Washkansky, who lived only eighteen days with the new heart. With the development of more powerful antirejection drugs and additional experience, heart transplant operations have become a standard procedure around the world.

In the spiritual realm, all human beings need a heart transplant. The Lord promised that He Himself would do the procedure. In Ezekiel 36:26, He says, "I will give you a new heart and put a new spirit in you; I will remove from you your heart of stone and give you a heart of flesh" (NIV). Verse 27 presents the purpose of the transplant: "And I will put my Spirit in you and move you to follow my decrees and be careful to keep my laws" (NIV). And Jeremiah 31:33 adds,

"I will put my law in their minds,
and write it on their hearts.
I will be their God,
and they will be my people" (NIV).

In reality, "Our hearts are evil, and we cannot change them. . . . Education, culture, the exercise of the will, human effort, all have their proper sphere, but here they are powerless. They may produce an outward correctness of behavior, but they cannot change the heart; they cannot purify the springs of life. There must be a power working from within, a new life from above, before men can be changed from sin to holiness. That power is Christ. His grace alone can quicken the lifeless faculties of the soul, and attract it to God, to holiness."[13]

As in the days of Jesus, many good Christians today have only an outward religion without a genuine conversion experience (Matthew 23:1–36). Could this be true of us as well? Why not surrender completely to the Lord now, and ask Him for a new heart?

ℒIFE 𝒲ITHOUT ℒIMITS

I can do all things through Christ who strengthens me.

—Philippians 4:13

As a midwife and pediatric nurse in Melbourne, Australia, Dushka had participated in hundreds of deliveries and cared for the newborn babies. Now, at the age of twenty-five, she would have her own baby—she was so excited! The doctors and two ultrasounds had confirmed that everything was going well and that she would have a boy.

On **December 4, 1982,** Nicholas (or "Nick") was born, but the doctor carried him away without allowing Dushka to see him. Concerned about the whole situation, she asked the doctor if the baby was all right. The doctor responded simply, "Phocomelia," and the young mother was absolutely devastated. Dushka and her husband, Boris, could not understand why God allowed their own child to be born without arms or legs.

It took quite some time for Dushka and Boris to accept what had happened to their child. It took even more time for Nick to accept it himself. But eventually, they realized that God had a plan for Nick's life. With amazing determination, Nick went to school, began to practice some sports, and even became a powerful Christian evangelist and motivational speaker. On February 12, 2012, he married Kanae Miyahara, and they have four children.

In his book *Life Without Limits*, Nick Vujicic states,

> You can't always control what happens to you. There are some occurrences in life that are not your fault or within your power to stop. . . .
> . . . You see, I don't think we are ever given more than we can handle. I promise you that for every *disability* you have, you are blessed with more than enough *abilities* to overcome your challenges.[14]

Sometimes the best way to stop our own complaining and overcome our own self-pity is to meet someone in a worse situation than our own. An old proverb says, "I complained that I had no shoes until I met someone who had no feet." When you are tempted to complain about your difficulties, keep in mind that you are not the first to suffer from shortcomings and weaknesses. When you are tempted to give up, remember that God wants to strengthen you and use you as He did Nick.

COMPELLING LOVE

"How God anointed Jesus of Nazareth with the Holy Spirit
and power, and how he went around doing good and healing all
who were under the power of the devil, because God was with him."

—Acts 10:38, NIV

David Livingstone (1813–1873), the famous missionary to Africa, is credited with having said, "God had only one Son, and He made that Son a missionary." Yes, the Bible affirms that God "gave His only begotten Son" (John 3:16); but Christ Himself explained further, "I lay down my life voluntarily" (John 10:18, TLB). This means that Christ was the greatest volunteer missionary that ever existed. At the appointed time, He left the heavenly courts and came to this world to accomplish His amazing volunteer mission of doing good to those in need, and at last, gave His own life for humanity.

Following Christ's example of volunteer mission, many Seventh-day Adventist volunteers have gone around the globe to serve in different capacities. The 1968 General Conference Autumn Council established the Adventist Volunteer Service Corps and tasked it with sending volunteers to serve overseas in self-sustaining mission work. This entity was eventually reorganized and renamed Adventist Volunteer Service. It identifies the official Adventist short-term and long-term mission projects around the world and coordinates sending volunteers to carry on those projects.

Volunteers make the world a better place to live. Aware of this, the United Nations General Assembly, at its plenary meeting on December 17, 1985, established **December 5** as International Volunteer Day for Economic and Social Development. It urged governments "to take measures to heighten awareness of the important contribution of volunteer service, thereby stimulating more people in all walks of life to offer their services as volunteers, both at home and abroad."[15]

Acts 10:38 says that Christ "went about doing good and healing all who were oppressed by the devil, for God was with Him." Following Christ's example, we can make December 5 a special day to encourage volunteer service in our own local communities. And every day, we should represent Christ to the world and share His love with those around us. Spend some time today creating a strategy that can make a difference in the lives of others.

ℱIRST 𝒲EEK OF 𝒫RAYER

Now it came to pass, as He was praying in a certain place, when He ceased, that one of His disciples said to Him, "Lord, teach us to pray, as John also taught his disciples."
—Luke 11:1

D o you remember a Week of Prayer that became a turning point in your life? Modern Weeks of Prayer are often periods of spiritual revival, with the purpose of strengthening people's relationships with God. However, the first Adventist Weeks of Prayer were intended both to deepen conversion and to encourage generosity. They could even be called Weeks of Stewardship.

By the mid-1880s, the Adventist Church was growing significantly, but members were not generous enough to financially support the expanding church's mission. Many local conferences had debts; the urban missionary work lacked resources and workers; the International Missionary and Treaties [*sic*] Society was without funds; foreign missions were heavily indebted to the Review and Herald, and all Adventist schools were in deficit but also needed larger facilities. How could this challenging condition be reversed?

On Sunday, **December 6, 1885**, the General Conference assembly set aside the period of December 25, 1885, to January 2, 1886, to be the first Adventist Week of Prayer. The delegates of that session called for all conference presidents and pastors to give immediate and faithful attention to this matter so that every church—and, as much as possible, every individual—would receive information as to the nature and the purpose of this Week of Prayer. In addition, the Week of Prayer was to encourage everyone to join in humiliation before God, begging for a deeper conversion, so that their blessing would remain upon the initiated work, that it might open the hearts of those who had resources to use the talent the Lord had given them to take the message to the nations of the earth, gathering from them a people for His name.

Often our prayers become very self-centered, preoccupied only with our own needs and afflictions. We even pray for the needs of others, but we do not help them. We can intercede for the preaching of the gospel around the world, but do we support it with our resources? In addition to asking for this and many other projects, we must also sustain the mission of the church with our personal influence and our possessions.[16]

STARVING FOR GOD'S WORD

"Behold, the days are coming," says the Lord GOD,
"That I will send a famine on the land,
Not a famine of bread,
Nor a thirst for water,
But of hearing the words of the LORD.*"*

—Amos 8:11

The Bible is the most loved and the most hated book. As stated by H. L. Hastings, "The hammers of infidels have been pecking away at this book for ages, but the hammers are worn out, and the anvil still endures."[17] On the other hand, many people have sacrificed their lives to study and distribute the Bible, as the Waldensians did in the Middle Ages, and as Christians are still doing in some hostile regions of the world today.

Love for the Bible was ably demonstrated by a Welsh girl named Mary Jones (1784–1864). She had a strong desire to have a Welsh Bible of her own, but in those days, Bibles were quite rare and expensive. When she was nine years old, Mary began saving money to buy a copy. Six years later, in 1800, she walked barefoot the 26 miles (42 kilometers) to Bala, Wales, to see Rev. Thomas Charles, the only individual with Bibles for sale in the area. He sold her three Bibles for the price of one, and her story became the talk of all the churches.

There was a great need for low-cost Bibles in Wales. On **December 7, 1802**, Rev. Joseph Hughes, inspired by Mary's story, put a bold question to the Religious Tract Society leaders: "If for Wales, why not for the kingdom? And if for the kingdom, why not for the world?"[18] This question continued to reverberate in the minds of those leaders. And on March 7, 1804, the British and Foreign Bible Society was formed, paving the way for the formation of several other Bible societies around the globe.

Today the Bible is available in some six hundred languages and at least one of its books in close to twenty-four hundred more. Sadly, that doesn't necessarily mean that the more the Bible becomes available, the more people read it. Never before in history have so many means of distraction taken over the time that should be spent with God's Word. It is a tragic reality. Today is a good opportunity to reconsider our priorities so that God and His Word can occupy the highest place in our daily activities. This would make our lives much better.

"*I* Shall *M*eet *Y*ou in *H*eaven"

As for me, I am already being poured out as a libation,
and the time of my departure has come.
—2 Timothy 4:6, NRSV

James and Ellen White planned to visit Adventist believers in the states of New Hampshire, Vermont, and New York. So, they left their three boys—Henry, Edson, and Willie—with the Howland family in Topsham, Maine. But while James and Ellen were traveling, James had a dream that not everything was well with their sons. Returning to Topsham, the parents found that their oldest son, Henry, who was sixteen, had a severe cold. Four days after their arrival, the cold turned into pneumonia, and his condition grew worse.

Realizing that he might not live much longer, Henry had some very touching conversations with his parents and two brothers. As his mother attended him, he asked her, "Promise me, mother, that if I die, I may be taken to Battle Creek, and laid by the side of my little brother, John Herbert [who had died at three months of age], that we may come up together in the morning of the resurrection."[19]

Two days before Henry died, he asked for his brothers to come to his side. To Edson, he said, "Eddie, I shall not be a brother to you anymore; never give up trying to do right; a death-bed is a poor place for repentance." And to Willie, he added, "Willie, be a good boy, obey your parents, and meet me in heaven. Don't mourn after I am dead." Henry then called his father and said, "Father, you are losing your son. You will miss me, but don't mourn. It is better for me. I shall escape being drafted [during the American Civil War], and shall not witness the seven last plagues. To die so happy is a privilege."[20]

On **December 8, 1863**, the dying son told his mother, "Mother, I shall meet you in heaven in the morning of the resurrection, for I know you will be there." Then he "beckoned to his brothers, parents, and friends, and gave them all a parting kiss, after which he pointed upward and whispered, 'heaven is sweet.' "[21] He died at 1:30 P.M.

Two days earlier, he had dictated a special message to the youth, in which he stated, "I would appeal to all my young friends, not to let the pleasures or accomplishments of the world eclipse the loveliness of the saviour. . . . Spend the best of your days in serving the Lord. Farewell."[22] Let us all reflect on that message!

December 9

RESUMING THE MINISTRY

And there he went into a cave, and spent the night in that place; and behold, the word of the LORD came to him, and He said to him, "What are you doing here, Elijah?"

—1 Kings 19:9

iscouragement undermines God's plans for our lives. On **December 9, 1856**, while in Round Grove, Illinois, Ellen White had a vision about the critical spiritual condition of some Sabbath-keeping Adventist families who had moved from the east coast of the United States to Waukon, Iowa.[23] The weather was terrible—a mixture of snow and rain—and at one point on the journey, Ellen reported, "I never witnessed such cold weather."[24] James White was hesitant to make the long journey to Waukon, but Ellen said, "We shall go."[25]

It was early winter, and, to reach Iowa, they had to cross the great Mississippi River. There was no bridge, and boats were unable to sail through the ice-covered waters. To safely cross, they needed firm, thick ice. When they came to the river in the sleigh, Josiah Hart turned to Ellen and said, "We have come to the Red Sea; shall we cross?" Mrs. White replied, "Go forward, trusting in Israel's God." By faith, they crossed the dangerous river—arriving safely on the other side.[26] Eventually, they reached Waukon, where they encouraged the Adventist believers. They also kept two powerful Adventist preachers from backsliding.

While in Waukon, James and Ellen White were taken to a store building where Hosea Mead, an Adventist from Washington, New Hampshire, and J. N. Loughborough, a former Adventist preacher, were working as carpenters. James and Ellen remained in the sleigh, and when Loughborough reached the sleigh, Mrs. White asked him, "What *doest* thou here, Elijah?" Astonished, he answered, "I am working with Brother Mead at carpenter work." Then she asked a second time, "What doest *thou* here, Elijah?" And then a third time, "*What* doest thou here, Elijah?"[27]

Due to James and Ellen White's visit to Waukon, Loughborough gave up the carpentry work, and J. N. Andrews stopped farming. Both resumed their ministries and became influential preachers and writers. If you have taken some "vacation" time from the mission the Lord has entrusted to you, this is the right time to resume it. Please do not delay your decision!

RELIGIOUS LIBERTY

"And if it seems evil to you to serve the LORD, choose for yourselves this day whom you will serve, whether the gods which your fathers served that were on the other side of the River, or the gods of the Amorites, in whose land you dwell. But as for me and my house, we will serve the LORD."

—Joshua 24:15

Freedom is a human right we seem to value only when we lose it. Shortly after World War II (1939–1945) ended, important measures were taken in an effort to avoid the reoccurrence of such a catastrophe in the future. The United Nations (UN) was created on October 24, 1945, as an intergovernmental organization promoting international cooperation. On **December 10, 1948**, the UN General Assembly, convened in Paris, adopted the thirty-article "Universal Declaration of Human Rights," recognizing the dignity and worth inherent in the human person and affirming his or her human rights and fundamental freedoms.

In regard to freedom of religion, Article 18 of the declaration affirms: "Everyone has the right to freedom of thought, conscience and religion; this right includes freedom to change his religion or belief, and freedom, either alone or in community with others and in public or private, to manifest his religion or belief in teaching, practice, worship and observance."[28] Disregarding the content of this article, some fundamentalist religious groups still levy the death penalty on adherents who leave their ranks and on those who encouraged them to leave.

Deeply concerned with manifestations of religious intolerance, the Seventh-day Adventist Church has traditionally promoted religious liberty and, more recently, organized several large festivals of religious freedom around the world. Freedom of conscience and religion must be granted to all, not only to those in power. Joshua fully committed to "serve the LORD" and encouraged others to do the same. Yet, he also acknowledged that God has given humans free choice, and we may choose to follow our own path, despite negative consequences (Joshua 24:15).

We should be extremely thankful to the Lord and those who have paved the way for the religious liberty that is enjoyed today in many regions of the world. But now that the banner of religious liberty is in our hands, let us pray and work to help those regions of the world without such freedom.

ADVENTIST FOREBEAR

Now after Jesus was born in Bethlehem of Judea in the days of Herod the king, behold, wise men from the East came to Jerusalem, saying, "Where is He who has been born King of the Jews? For we have seen His star in the East and have come to worship Him."
—Matthew 2:1, 2

The Gospel of Matthew speaks of wise men from the East who came to worship the newborn King Jesus Christ. They did not formally belong to God's people, but we are told that they studied the Hebrew Scriptures and realized that the time had come for the Messiah to appear. The mysterious star eventually led them to Bethlehem, where they found Jesus. Likewise, other people have discovered meaningful biblical teachings by studying Scripture for themselves.

Francisco Hermógenes Ramos Mexía (1773–1828) was born in Buenos Aires, Argentina, on **December 11, 1773**.[29] He became a wealthy and prominent landowner in the province of Buenos Aires and a defender of the native Indians. With a Roman Catholic background, he was devoted to the study of Scripture. His interest in Bible prophecy was influenced by Manuel Lacunza (1731–1801), the Chilean Jesuit, but Ramos Mexía went much further than Lacunza in his understanding of Bible teachings.

Ramos Mexía emphasized the Bible as the only source of faith and doctrine, regarded Jesus Christ and the apostles as the only true foundation of the Christian church, kept the seventh-day Sabbath, and even closed his estate for business on that day. He believed in a literal and imminent second coming of Jesus, understood the state of the dead as waiting in the grave for the resurrection at the second coming of Jesus, highlighted salvation by faith in Christ alone, and acknowledged baptism by immersion. He also rejected transubstantiation, accepted the universal priesthood of all believers, and opposed image worship.

Ramos Mexía faced strong opposition from his contemporaries—both religious and political—but he never gave up. Sometimes referred to as the first modern Seventh-day Adventist, he advocated those Bible teachings though he was a lone voice for truth. Like Ramos Mexía, let your faith shine like a star regardless of the circumstances.

$\mathcal{P}$ASSIONATE $\mathcal{P}$HILANTHROPIST

*May the Lord make your love increase and overflow for each other
and for everyone else, just as ours does for you.*
—1 Thessalonians 3:12, NIV

Not everyone can go out and change the world, but everyone can make a difference in the life of someone who lives nearby. This notion is well expressed by the motto of ADRA—the Adventist Development and Relief Agency—which says, "Changing the world, one life at a time." Much depends on how we use our resources. What do we spend on ourselves, and what should we use for the sake of humanity and God's cause?

Milton S. Afonso was born on **December 12, 1921**, in the little town of Nova Lima, Minas Gerais, Brazil. From humble origins, he worked hard and became an extremely successful businessman. One of Afonso's major enterprises, Golden Cross, became the fourth largest health insurance company in Brazil. Nevertheless, he continued to show loving care for needy children, and he enthusiastically shared the Adventist message that he had embraced as a teenager. As a philanthropist, Afonso helped improve the infrastructure of many schools and colleges, sponsored several thousand students annually, and ran a chain of orphanages. He helped build and maintain the largest Adventist radio and television network in the South American Division.

Speaking of his philanthropic motives, Afonso said, "The Bible teaches that we should develop our talents and prosper. . . . However, I have never thought of making money just for my own gratification. The most important thing for me is to help needy people, provide homes for orphans and abandoned children, and support the preaching of the good news of salvation. This gives me great personal satisfaction. At times people criticize me for being a philanthropist, accusing me of giving money just to show off. But that is not true. I can honestly affirm that I have never boasted about helping someone."[30]

The record of the earthly ministry of Jesus Christ is the most powerful appeal for philanthropy to our own neighbors. But "who is my neighbor" today? (See Luke 10:29.) According to Ellen White, "Any human being who needs our sympathy and our kind offices is our neighbor. The suffering and destitute of all classes are our neighbors; and when their wants are brought to our knowledge, it is our duty to relieve them as far as possible."[31]

ᏀHE ᎠRESS OF ᏀHOUGHT

"For the mouth speaks what the heart is full of."
—Matthew 12:34, NIV

People usually associate the words *dress* and *dressing* with fashion and clothing. But the famous English writer and lexicographer Samuel Johnson (1709–1784), who died on **December 13, 1784**, insightfully suggested that "language is the dress of thought."[32] The author seems to imply that language is a form of decoration—the way our thoughts are adorned. Just as there is an endless variety of clothes, so there are countless ways of expressing our thoughts, some more attractive and accurate than others.

As a general rule, language is an effective way to express oneself. When Jesus declared that "the mouth speaks what the heart is full of" (Matthew 12:34, NIV), He suggested that what we say and the way we speak end up communicating to others much of what we are. It reflects many of our inner feelings and emotions, our priorities and desires.

But too often, language is used to cover up and distort reality. In Matthew 23, Jesus contrasted the flowery speeches of the scribes and Pharisees with their own hidden immorality. According to a famous quote (usually attributed to the German chancellor Otto von Bismarck), "People never lie so much as after a hunt, during a war, or before an election."[33] Certainly, our world would be improved if leaders carefully weighed their words and the promises they make!

The repetition of lies exercises a negative influence on others, but especially on the liars themselves. We are warned that "words are more than an indication of character; they have power to react on the character. Men are influenced by their own words. . . . Having once expressed an opinion or decision, they are often too proud to retract it, and try to prove themselves in the right, until they come to believe that they are."[34]

What a blessing it would be if we were more concerned about what we say of others than about what others say of us! As well stated in a popular quote on the internet, "Judging others does not define who they are. It defines who you are." We need to remember that our words have the power to destroy people or to save them, to undermine their reputation or uplift it.

Lord, help me speak to others with the same kindness with which I would like them to address me!

$\mathcal{A}$STROLOGICAL $\mathcal{P}$REDICTIONS

Beloved, do not believe every spirit, but test the spirits, whether they are of God; because many false prophets have gone out into the world.
—1 John 4:1

Our postmodern, somewhat mystical era has fabricated many alleged prophets. One of the most famous is the French astrologer Michel de Nostradamus (1503–1566). Born on **December 14, 1503**, in St-Rémy, France, Nostradamus worked first as an apothecary—researching herbal remedies—and then moved toward occultism. He wrote many almanacs, which, altogether, supposedly contain more than six thousand prophecies. But his most famous work is *Les Prophéties* of 1555, written in a poetic style and published in English as *Prophecies* in 1672.

Followers of Nostradamus argue that he predicted many historical events, including the two world wars and the attack on 9/11, the rises of Napoleon and Adolf Hitler, and even Donald Trump's presidency. We may ask, "How much do people read the present into those alleged predictions?" In Nostradamus's *Prophecies* X.72, he stated:

In the year 1999 and seven months,
From the skies shall come an alarming powerful king,
To raise again the great King of the Jacquerie,
Before and after, Mars shall reign at will.[35]

We're past 1999, and this prophecy wasn't fulfilled!
Then, in *Prophecies* I.48, Nostradamus astrologically predicted,

Twenty years of the reign of the moon having passed,
Seven thousand years another shall hold his monarchy,
When the sun shall resume his days past,
Then is fulfilled and ends my prophecy.[36]

When should one expect these "seven thousand years" to begin? Bible eschatology does not provide room for such a long time prophecy!

Regardless of their alleged fulfillment, all astrological predictions and enchantments are strictly forbidden by the Bible (Isaiah 47:12–15). We are also warned against false prophets and their unfulfilled predictions (Deuteronomy 18:21, 22; Jeremiah 28:8, 9). While true prophets describe future events in a concrete way, false prophets speak in general terms and use ambiguous language—allowing for the explanation that the prophecy was wrongly interpreted.

The world is coming to its end, and the number of false prophets will significantly increase. We should be well grounded in the Bible and prepared to face those challenges.

$\mathcal{F}$IRST $\mathcal{A}$MENDMENT

*Jesus answered, "My kingdom is not of this world. If My kingdom
were of this world, My servants would fight, so that I should not
be delivered to the Jews; but now My kingdom is not from here."*

—John 18:36

Much of the religious intolerance around the world is due to the union of religious and secular powers. History has confirmed the danger of allowing secular governments to legislate on religious matters or for religious leaders to hold secular power. In many of these instances, those who do not observe the official religion are persecuted for their faith.

The founding fathers of the United States of America understood the value of separation of church and state and expressed it very well in the First Amendment of the Constitution. The amendment was ratified on **December 15, 1791**, and it reads as follows: "Congress shall make no law respecting an establishment of religion, or prohibiting the free exercise thereof; or abridging the freedom of speech, or of the press; or the right of the people peaceably to assemble, and to petition the Government for a redress of grievances."[37] This amendment has assured ample freedom for people of all faiths and religious convictions to live peacefully together in the same country.

But in the end-time crisis, the United States Congress will legislate on religious matters and restrict religious freedom. Ellen White warns, "When our nation, in its legislative councils, shall enact laws to bind the consciences of men in regard to their religious privileges, enforcing Sunday observance, and bringing oppressive power to bear against those who keep the seventh-day Sabbath, the law of God will, to all intents and purposes, be made void in our land, and national apostasy will be followed by national ruin."[38]

Christ established His church as a religious entity without secular power, declaring, "My kingdom is not of this world" (John 18:36). And He added, "Give back to Caesar what is Caesar's, and to God what is God's" (Matthew 22:21, NIV). The separation of church and state is truly a New Testament principle that must be uplifted and promoted by all those who want to remain faithful to Christ's teachings.

$\mathcal{T}$HE $\mathcal{O}$PENING IN $\mathcal{O}$RION

Then I, John, saw the holy city, New Jerusalem, coming down out
of heaven from God, prepared as a bride adorned for her husband.
—Revelation 21:2

M any Evangelical Christians center their eschatological hope on the political state of Israel and the ancient city of Jerusalem. But instead of the man-made earthly Jerusalem, we await the God-made New Jerusalem, which will come down out of heaven (Revelation 21:2).

On **December 16, 1848,** Ellen White had a vision about the shaking of the powers of the heavens:

The powers of heaven will be shaken at the voice of God. Then the sun, moon, and stars will be moved out of their places. They will not pass away, but be shaken by the voice of God.

Dark, heavy clouds came up and clashed against each other. The atmosphere parted and rolled back; then we could look up through the open space in Orion, whence came the voice of God. The Holy City will come down through that open space.[39]

This statement has caused much speculation. Some critics reject its relevance, saying that there is no "open space in Orion." In contrast, others point out similarities between telescopic images of the intriguing Orion Nebula and portraits of Christ's second coming. Whether there is already an opening in Orion or not doesn't really matter. What Ellen White is saying is that by God's powerful word, "the sun, moon, and stars will be moved out of their places," and *then* "the Holy City will come down through that open space."

We should understand *how* final events will take place so we can avoid speculative theories and distortions of the inspired text (Revelation 22:18, 19). But what is more important than merely understanding future events is our need to *be ready now* to live in the presence of God and His holy angels for all eternity (Psalm 24:3, 4; 1 John 3:1–3). All the mysteries of the universe will then be opened for us to explore. Nothing in this sinful world can be compared with heaven! I plan to be there, and I hope you do too!

ℋARMONY OF SCRIPTURE

*Now these were more noble-minded than those in Thessalonica, for they received the word
with great eagerness, examining the Scriptures daily to see whether these things were so.*
—Acts 17:11, NASB

One section of the Bible that is most difficult to synchronize is the chronology of Hebrew kings found in 1–2 Kings and 1–2 Chronicles. After centuries of exhaustive studies, the scholarly community has concluded that some discrepancies were simply mistakes in the Bible record. For instance, how could 2 Kings 9:29 say that Ahaziah of Judah began to reign in the eleventh year of Joram of Israel when 2 Kings 8:25 states that it was in the twelfth year?

As a student at the Oriental Institute of the University of Chicago, Edwin R. Thiele attempted to write his master's thesis on the topic of biblical discrepancies, but his adviser, W. A. Irwin, did not want such an "unsolvable" subject revisited. Eventually, however, Irwin allowed Thiele to write his doctoral dissertation on the controversial topic. Beginning with the assumption that the Bible does not contradict itself, Thiele attempted to synchronize the troublesome chronologies.

Thiele took into consideration co-regencies and overlapping reigns and, whenever possible, also the month of the year a ruler began his regnal year. Deeper in his investigation, Thiele discovered that many apparent discrepancies were attributable to "dual dating"—sometimes, the first year of a king's reign was considered his accession year, and other times it was recorded as the first year of his reign.

On **December 17, 1943**, Edwin Thiele was awarded a PhD degree from the University of Chicago, and his dissertation became a standard work for biblical chronology. The findings of this renowned Adventist scholar were first published as an article in the *Journal of Near Eastern Studies*[40] and then in the book *The Mysterious Numbers of the Hebrew Kings*.[41]

Truly, "the difficulties of Scripture have been urged by skeptics as an argument against the Bible; but so far from this, they constitute a strong evidence of its divine inspiration."[42] Many times the problem is not so much with the Bible itself but with our own lack of understanding. By digging a little deeper, our problems may be solved, and our doubts may disappear.

THE POWER OF WORDS

Out of the same mouth come praise and cursing. My brothers and sisters, this should not be.
—James 3:10, NIV

William McKendree Carleton (popularly known as Will Carleton) was an American poet who died on **December 18, 1912**, leaving a rich literary legacy. In his famous poem "The First Settler's Story," he narrates the story of an intrepid man who moved west into the unsettled rural territory, taking his lovely young wife with him. In that lonely life, the young wife willingly used her strength to help him and transformed their humble cabin into a pleasant place to live. Time passed, and the man became very stressed by isolation, bad weather, failed crops, and poverty.

One night he came back from work and did not see the cows on their usual feeding ground. For half a minute, he accused his lovely wife of not taking good care of the cows and for just lying around, letting him do all the work. No word of reply. She remained silent, yet she was completely devastated. The next afternoon, sensing an oncoming storm, he left work early and hurried home. There, on the table, he found a penciled note from his wife, explaining that the cows had escaped again, despite all her care, and asking him not to scold her, for she decided to go out one more time to find the cows. She ended the note pleading, "Darling, piece out with love the strength I lack, and have kind words for me when I get back."[43]

He finished reading her note, and then the thunder sounded and the storm began. Frantically rushing out with his dog, he spent all night searching for his beloved wife. Three times he went home expecting to find her there but in vain. Early in the morning, when the sun started to shine again, he came home. The cows were there, exactly where they should be. Yes, she succeeded at getting them back! He then hurried into the cabin, and there was his wife lying exhausted and lifeless on the cold floor. His "house had lost its soul," and his mind continued to echo her written words, "I've tried to do my best—I have indeed!"[44]

Words. Only words. But how devastating they can be! Will Carleton added to his poem, *"Boys flying kites haul in their white-winged birds; you can't do that when you're flying words."*[45]

Dear Lord, may my words always be a source of blessing to others, especially my beloved ones. Amen.

$\mathcal{A}$N $\mathcal{I}$NSPIRING $\mathcal{L}$EADER

Rejoice in the Lord always. Again I will say, rejoice!
Let your gentleness be known to all men. The Lord is at hand.

—Philippians 4:4, 5

Too often, leadership generates pride and inaccessibility. But some very successful leaders have been able to combine efficiency and humility in a truly inspiring way. One such leader was William A. Spicer (1865–1952), who was born **December 19, 1865**, in Freeborn, Minnesota. With a deep passion for the mission fields, he went as a missionary to England and India. He also served as secretary of the church's Mission Board (1901–1903), secretary of the General Conference (1903–1922), and president of the General Conference (1922–1930).

Recognized as a man of the people, Spicer was well known and much loved. He lived a frugal lifestyle, saving as much as he could by searching for the least expensive train tickets and hotel rooms. When his family and friends asked him to choose better and safer places to stay, he answered, "It is good enough. I have a bed. The Lord will take care of me." About food, he once said, "A bag of peanuts can last me all day."[46] Spicer had few clothes, and he even used to do his own laundry in the bathroom sink of the hotels where he stayed. To him, every dollar he saved could help advance the mission of the church.

A later General Conference president, J. L. McElhany, referred to Spicer as a man of clear and definite convictions, without ever being proud of his own opinions. "He never assumed an attitude of officialism, self-importance, or arbitrary authority. . . . He was as ready to lay down any office or official position as he was to take it up. . . . His attitude toward his successors has always been that of a benign and helpful counselor, always ready to render any service within his power." As a preacher and writer, he had a great ability to inspire courage in the hearts of believers. "His unwavering faith in the triumph of the Advent Movement was prominent in all his labors."

It does not matter so much what leadership role has been entrusted to you. Remember that all of us end up influencing people in one way or another. What really counts is how we exercise our influence in our workplace, academic setting, church, and other social and home circles. Wherever you are and whatever you do or say, "Let your gentleness be known to all men" (Philippians 4:5)!

$\mathcal{K}$eep $\mathcal{Y}$our $\mathcal{C}$rown

"I am coming soon. Hold on to what you have, so that no one will take your crown."
—Revelation 3:11, NIV

Many believers in Christ's second coming went to the grave expecting that glorious event to occur during their own lifetimes. One inspiring example is William Miller (1782–1849), whose hope was severely tested when Christ did not return at the time he expected. From his own studies of Scripture, he was convinced that Christ would return about 1843. Later on, he agreed with the generally accepted date of October 22, 1844. After the passing of those dates, Miller was heavily criticized and mocked for having caused unfounded expectations. Even so, he did not give up his faith and hope.

On November 10, 1844, Miller wrote to his close friend Joshua V. Himes:

I have been waiting and looking for the blessed hope, and in expectation of realizing the glorious things which God has spoken of Zion. Yes, and although I have been twice disappointed, I am not yet cast down or discouraged. God has been with me in Spirit, and has comforted me. I have now much more evidence that I do believe in God's word; and although surrounded with enemies and scoffers, yet my mind is perfectly calm, and my hope in the coming of Christ is as strong as ever. . . .

Brethren, hold fast; let no man take your crown. I have fixed my mind upon another time, and here I mean to stand until God gives me more light—and that is To-day, TO-DAY, and T O - D A Y, until He comes, and I see HIM for whom my soul yearns.[47]

This continued to be Miller's conviction for the rest of his life. On December 3, 1844, he wrote to Joshua Himes and Sylvester Bliss: "I cannot sit down to write without the reflection that this letter may never reach its destination. Yet I believe in occupying until Christ shall come."[48]

In September 1848, now completely blind, Miller stated in a letter to Himes: "It would, indeed, be a sad and melancholy time with me were it not for the 'blessed hope' of soon seeing Jesus. . . . And although my natural vision is dark, yet my mind's vision is lit up with a bright and glorious prospect of the future."[49]

Miller died peacefully on **December 20, 1849**, leaving us with a compelling example of unconditional commitment to the Adventist hope. May the Lord help us live and, if necessary, die for this very same hope.

GOD STILL CARES

For He shall give His angels charge over you,
To keep you in all your ways.

—Psalm 91:11

Michael Hasel had been studying three months at college in Europe when his father, Gerhard F. Hasel, called him from Michigan with a very tempting offer. Michael should fly back to the United States and join his family in Florida for the Christmas break. Before making a final decision, Michael decided to pray about it with a few friends.

Three hours later, Gerhard called his son again. "Michael, guess what?" his father announced enthusiastically. "I was able to book you on one of the last flights available. You will be flying from Frankfurt via London to New York and then to Miami. We can pick you up there!"[50] Somewhat confused but sensing peace, Michael decided to stay and spend the break with his uncle and other relatives in southern Germany. His father respected his decision.

On Christmas Eve, Michael and his extended family read the Gospel account of Christ's birth and then sat around the Christmas tree to open presents. The telephone rang. It was Michael's family calling from the United States. After Michael had talked with his mother and two sisters, his father got on the phone. "Michael, there's something I have to tell you. I'm glad you didn't come to Florida this year. You made the right decision. The flight that I had you booked on was Pan Am Flight 103 that crashed in Lockerbie, Scotland, last week."[51]

"On **December 21, 1988**, Pan Am Flight 103 from London to New York [exploded] in midair over Lockerbie, Scotland," an hour after its departure. "A bomb hidden inside an audio cassette player detonated in the cargo area."[52] All 259 passengers perished, plus 11 residents of Lockerbie who were killed by falling debris from the plane.

Why did God allow 270 people to die while sparing Michael? We still live in a sinful world, living in the midst of the great controversy between good and evil, and we are too limited in our knowledge to answer that question. But we can trust that "God never leads His children otherwise than they would choose to be led, if they could see the end from the beginning, and discern the glory of the purpose which they are fulfilling as co-workers with Him."[53]

$\mathcal{M}$ODERN $\mathcal{M}$ARTYRS

"Remember the word that I said to you, 'A servant is not greater than his master.' If they persecuted Me, they will also persecute you."

—John 15:20

Many popular preachers suggest that those who accept Christ are shielded from all of life's problems, which is certainly not the case. Some Christians are called to witness for Christ through persecution and death. One such modern example was the DePaiva missionary family. Originally from Brazil, the family spent some years at Andrews University before going as missionaries to the archipelago of Palau, Micronesia, in August 2002. Ruimar DePaiva was pastor of the Koror Seventh-day Adventist Church, and his wife, Margareth, served as a teacher in the local church school.

Everything went quite well until the early morning of **December 22, 2003,** when a stranger broke into their home. The intruder killed Ruimar, Margareth, and Larisson (their eleven-year-old son). He then assaulted their daughter, Melissa, who was ten years old at the time. Believing her to be dead, early the next morning, the killer dumped her body on an empty road. Providentially, a couple passing by found her and took her to the hospital. At a special memorial service on the island, Ruimar's mother, Ruth DePaiva, publicly forgave the attacker. Her act of grace shocked the population of the island.

But why did the Lord allow such a tragedy to happen? Several years later, Melissa stated, "Looking back, I can see that my parents and brother accomplished much more in death than in life, and many blessings came out of what seemed to be the end of everything. I learned to be a much stronger person, and my relationship with the Lord flourished. Numerous opportunities came that would never have come had things not happened the way they did. . . . Before leaving Palau, I told the people that I would be back someday as a missionary."[54]

The disciple John wrote in his Gospel that Peter's martyrdom "would glorify God" (John 21:19). In his famous *Apology,* Tertullian argued, "The oftener we are mown down by you, the more in number we grow; the blood of Christians is seed."[55] In reality, some children of God are called to witness for Him in good health, others in sickness, and still others through their death. Let us trust that He knows what is best for us and for His cause.

Sustaining Grace

Cast your burden on the Lord,
And He shall sustain you;
He shall never permit the righteous to be moved.

—Psalm 55:22

P erhaps you and someone you love are facing difficult times. It might be a broken relationship, a severe health issue, or financial difficulty. Whatever the problem, remember that God's grace is always able to sustain us. Soon after arriving in Australia, Ellen White faced what she described as "the most terrible suffering of my whole life."[56] Even so, on **December 23, 1892**, she penned an inspiring letter to the brethren of the General Conference. She declared,

> All through my long affliction I have been most signally blessed of God. In the most severe conflicts with intense pain, I realized the assurance, 'My grace is sufficient for you.' At times when it seemed that I could not endure the pain, when unable to sleep, I looked to Jesus by faith, and His presence was with me, every shade of darkness rolled away, a hallowed light enshrouded me, the very room was filled with the light of His divine presence.
>
> I have felt that I could welcome suffering if this precious grace was to accompany it. I know the Lord is good and gracious and full of mercy and compassion and tender, pitying love. In my helplessness and suffering, His praise has filled my soul and has been upon my lips. My meditation has been so comforting and so strengthening as I have thought how much worse condition I should be in without the sustaining grace of God. My eyesight is continued to me, my memory has been preserved, and my mind has never been more clear and active in seeing the beauty and preciousness of truth.[57]

We tend to allow the absence of one expected "blessing" to overshadow the blessings we receive from God every day. We must develop a spirit of thankfulness even during challenging circumstances. Not all things happen as we would like, but there are two very important blessings God always grants to His faithful children—grace and hope!

CHRISTMAS CELEBRATION

So it was, that while they were there, the days were completed for her to be
delivered. And she brought forth her firstborn Son, and wrapped Him in swaddling
cloths, and laid Him in a manger, because there was no room for them in the inn.
—Luke 2:6, 7

Christmas Eve, or **December 24,** is a time of many memories! For some, it means the city with many lights, well-decorated houses, Christmas trees, family reunions, and children eagerly waiting for their gifts. For others, it's another empty table with scarce food. And some think it is an ancient, pagan festival that shouldn't be celebrated by Christians. But what is the real origin and meaning of Christmas?

There is no biblical or historical evidence that Christ was born on December 25. That was winter, and the shepherds would not have been in the fields at night taking care of their flocks (Luke 2:8–20). This traditional date came from ancient Persian Mithraism, a prominent sect of Zoroastrianism. Mithraists honored the Sun (Mithra) every Sunday and celebrated his birthday on December 25. Roman soldiers who fought in Persia brought those festivals back to Rome. In AD 270, Emperor Aurelian established the worship of the Sol Invictus (the invincible sun) as the first universal religion of the Greco-Roman Empire. Correlating the Sol Invictus with Christ as the "Sun of Righteousness" (Malachi 4:2), many Christians began keeping Sunday instead of Saturday and celebrating Christmas on December 25.

With all of that said, we should not be inhibited from celebrating Christmas as a symbol and a remembrance of Christ's incarnation. The problem lies in keeping or venerating it as a holy day. In her book *The Adventist Home*, Ellen White explains that God "has concealed the precise day of Christ's birth, that the day should not receive the honor that should be given to Christ as the Redeemer of the world."[58] She explains that there is nothing wrong with commemorating Christmas and having a Christmas tree. However, instead of expecting to receive presents, children should be taught to give useful presents to one another and offerings to the poor.

Remember, Christmas is our greatest opportunity to replace our selfish expectations with altruistic benevolence for others!

$\mathcal{A}$ Christmas Story

And the Word became flesh and dwelt among us, and we beheld His glory,
the glory as of the only begotten of the Father, full of grace and truth.

—John 1:14

P aul Harvey Aurandt (1918–2009), popularly known as Paul Harvey, was an American radio broadcaster for the ABC Radio Network. Each **December 25** at noon, he would repeat his modern Christmas parable of "The Man and the Birds." It tells of a man who did not believe in the mystery of Jesus' incarnation, often referred to during the Christmas season. Not wanting to act like a hypocrite, he would stay home on Christmas Eve while his family went to church.

One Christmas Eve, shortly after the family left, snow began to fall. While reading his newspaper, the man heard several thudding sounds. At first, he thought someone was throwing snowballs against his living room window. But then, he saw birds flying desperately against the window, searching for shelter. In an attempt to provide a warm shelter for the birds, the man opened the barn doors wide and turned on a light. But the birds did not come in. So, he hurried back to the house, fetched bread crumbs, and sprinkled them on the snow, making a trail to the lighted stable. Then he tried catching the birds, but that did not work either.

Finally, he realized that instead of attracting the birds, he was frightening and confusing them. He thought to himself, "If only I could be a bird and mingle with them and speak their language. Then I could tell them not to be afraid. Then I could show them the way to the safe, warm barn. But I would have to be one of them so they could see and hear and understand."[59] At that moment, the church bells began to ring, pealing the glad tidings of Christmas. And at last, he understood the mystery of Christ's incarnation—that "the Word became flesh and dwelt among us" for our salvation (John 1:14).

The mystery of incarnation means far more than just Christ becoming a man! In giving up His Son, God "has poured out to us all heaven in one gift. The Saviour's life and death and intercession, the ministry of angels, the pleading of the Spirit, the Father working above and through all, the unceasing interest of heavenly beings—all are enlisted in behalf of man's redemption."[60] If God gave us all heaven in one gift, why should we not give Him our whole life!

WAITING FOR HIS ARRIVAL

For the vision is yet for an appointed time;
But at the end it will speak, and it will not lie.
Though it tarries, wait for it;
Because it will surely come,
It will not tarry.

—Habakkuk 2:3

On December 26, 1944, Hiroo Onoda was sent to Lubang Island in the Philippines to serve the Japanese Sugi Brigade. Before leaving, his division's commanding officer, Major Yoshimi Taniguchi, ordered, "You are absolutely forbidden to die by your own hand. It may take three years, it may take five, but whatever happens, we'll come back for you. Until then, so long as you have one soldier, you are to continue to lead him. You may have to live on coconuts. If that's the case, live on coconuts! Under no circumstances are you [to] give up your life voluntarily."[61]

In October 1945, Onoda and his three remaining companions saw a leaflet announcing, "The war ended on August 15. Come down from the mountains!" But they didn't trust the information. Later, other leaflets with pictures were dropped by air, which they also disregarded. In 1949, one of his companions walked away; in 1954, another one was shot to death; and in 1972, the third was killed. Onoda was now alone. In February 1974, a Japanese explorer found him, but Onoda still refused to surrender, saying that he was still waiting for orders from his superior officer. Arrangements were made, and Major Yoshimi Taniguchi flew to Lubang. On March 9, 1974, he met Onoda and released him from his duty. Thus, twenty-nine years later, the promise was fulfilled, "Whatever happens, we'll come back for you."

World War II ended a long time ago, but the great controversy is still going on. Soon it will be over, and Jesus will come back to take home His faithful soldiers (Ephesians 6:10–20). We do not know when He will come. But since He has fulfilled all His previous promises, we can be sure that He will fulfill this one too. As Habakkuk 2:3 says, "Though it tarries, wait for it; because it will surely come." Instead of complaining about the *delay* of His arrival, we should *watch* for His coming, which could happen at any moment (Matthew 24:36–51). Never give up! His word is trustworthy, and His coming is sure.

THE DEAD WILL BE RAISED

For the trumpet will sound, and the dead will
be raised incorruptible, and we shall be changed.

—1 Corinthians 15:52

F riday, **December 27, 1985**, was a day of much sorrow for our family. After four days in a coma, my sister Eleda passed away, and the day of her funeral had arrived. Prior to the funeral service, we went to the house where she used to live. Arriving there, I met Henrique, her little three-and-a-half-year-old son, who was innocently playing as if nothing had happened. Soon he approached me and asked, "Uncle Ronald, do you know that my mother died?"

Surprised by his question, I replied, "Is it true? And where is your mother now?"

"My mother is in the church!" he stated.

"And what will happen to her?" I asked him.

His touching answer was, "My mother will remain at the church cemetery, but when Jesus returns, she will be raised from the dead."

Henrique's words reflected the explanation given to him about what was going on. But his words were loaded with unquestioning hope: "But *when* Jesus returns"! In fact, that hope has been cherished by Christians throughout the centuries and has been one of the prevailing themes of Adventist preaching. The dense clouds of pain, sorrow, and despair seem to vanish when we hear hymns full of hope, such as "Jesus Is Coming Again," "When We All Get to Heaven," and "We Have This Hope."

The expectation of Christ's second coming and the resurrection of the dead are not fantasies or merely "life vests" for moments of existential crisis. They are predominant themes in the New Testament, with a solid prophetic foundation, an obvious Christocentric motif, and profound existential relevance. This hope comes to us as a valuable legacy with ever-increasing value.

Christ's second coming is much nearer now that when Henrique spoke those touching words. So, let's take Paul's counsel seriously: "And do this, understanding the present time: The hour has already come for you to wake up from your slumber, because our salvation is nearer now than when we first believed. The night is nearly over; the day is almost here. So let us put aside the deeds of darkness and put on the armor of light" (Romans 13:11, 12, NIV). Soon our hope will be fulfilled!

Westminster Abbey

And you shall know the truth, and the truth shall make you free.

—John 8:32

I n November 2005, I was speaking at a Week of Prayer in London, England, and I took some time to visit the famous Westminster Abbey. This remarkable church was originally built in honor of Saint Peter the apostle and consecrated on **December 28, 1065**. There I saw the graves of George F. Handel, Sir Isaac Newton, Charles Darwin, David Livingstone, and many others. But there was one specific tombstone I wanted to see. Some years earlier, I had purchased an inspirational print entitled "Start With Yourself," with the following quotation,

When I was young and free and my imagination had no limits, I dreamed of changing the world. As I grew older and wiser, I discovered the world would not change, so I shortened my sights somewhat and decided to change only my country. But it, too, seemed immovable.

As I grew into my twilight years, in one last desperate attempt, I settled for changing only my family, those closest to me, but alas, they would have none of it.

And now as I lie on my deathbed, I suddenly realize: If I had only changed myself first, then by example I would have changed my family. From their inspiration and encouragement, I would then have been able to better my country and, who knows, I may have even changed the world.

Below the quotation, it read, "These words are found inscribed on the tomb of an 11th century Anglican Bishop at Westminster Abbey." So, while there, I wanted to see the inscription for myself. I asked the tour guides, and one suggested I go upstairs and talk with the Abbey librarian. Upon posing the same question to the librarian, he replied, "This statement does not exist." And then, he explained, "The statement was published and popularized in the book *Chicken Soup for the Soul*, volume 1. But there is no tombstone here with such an inscription."

The aforementioned quotation is very meaningful, but it reminds me that all that glitters is not gold. Many quotations have been erroneously attributed to the Bible. It is important that we search Scripture for ourselves to know what is true.

When the Show Is Over

And it happened, when the sun arose, that God prepared a vehement east wind; and the sun beat on Jonah's head, so that he grew faint. Then he wished death for himself, and said, "It is better for me to die than to live."

—Jonah 4:8

Racers and players, actors and artists may have their names and performances immortalized, but they are still human. Winners climb a platform, receive their trophy, and shortly afterward, step down. Every outstanding performance comes to an end—the applause ends, the curtains are closed, the actors and players leave the stage, and the lights are turned off. Then people turn back to real life.

The German race car driver Michael Schumacher was born on January 3, 1969. He became a seven-time Formula One World Champion (1994, 1995, 2000, 2001, 2002, 2003, 2004) and is widely regarded as one of the greatest drivers of all time. After surviving all those very dangerous car races, Schumacher's life radically changed while he was on vacation. On **December 29, 2013,** he suffered a terrible accident. While skiing with his fourteen-year-old son, Mick, in Méribel in the French Alps, Schumacher fell and hit his head on a rock, sustaining a traumatic brain injury despite wearing a ski helmet. For some time, he was put into a medically induced coma, and sadly, he never wholly recovered physically or mentally from that trauma.

Ellen White warns us that "the most signal victories and the most fearful defeats have been on the turn of minutes."[62] What a contrast between the Schumacher who climbed the Formula One podium and the Schumacher whose health was so severely damaged on that ski slope! Removed from the podiums and the applause of the thrilled crowds, he had to cope with isolation and loneliness.

People have a natural tendency to enjoy being celebrated only to become depressed afterward. Both the prophet Elijah and the prophet Jonah were affected by post-success depression (1 Kings 19:1–18; Jonah 4). It is important to ask yourself, "How do I feel when no one praises me, or when someone who replaced me is now receiving all the honor that I used to receive?" Remember, only God can bring true stability to your life when the human applause ceases and you are alone with yourself.

REJECTED BY HIS OWN

He came to what was his own, and his own people did not accept him.
—John 1:11, NRSV

Dr. Adolf Lorenz (1854–1946), from the University of Vienna, was one of the most famous orthopedic surgeons of his time. Due to his noninvasive techniques, he became known as the bloodless surgeon of Vienna. In October 1902, he was invited by the American meatpacking magnate J. Ogden Armour and his wife, Lola, to come to Chicago and perform surgery on their daughter, also named Lola (or "Lolita"), who had been crippled since birth. The surgery took place on October 13 and was a complete success.

Many other parents sent the doctor letters begging for an interview, but he could care for only a few of them. Among the letters was one from a wealthy lady in east Chicago, willing to pay any price to heal her child. After sending the letter, she told her pastor that she and her friends were holding daily prayer meetings asking God to send Dr. Lorenz to her. She was sure that her prayers would be answered.

Dr. Lorenz used to walk after lunch every day. On the afternoon of **December 30, 1902**, while he was walking, it began to rain, and he went to a nearby house for shelter. Taking off his hat, he asked the lady in his foreign accent, "Madam, may I sit on your porch until the rain stops?"[63] She coldly pointed him to a chair and then went inside and shut the door and the windows. After a while, a car stopped outside and picked him up. But she had no interest.

The next day the local newspaper carried a picture of Dr. Lorenz and the information that, after three months, he was leaving from Chicago to New York on his way back to Europe. The woman who gave him such an aloof reception recognized in the picture the very same man who had asked her for shelter. Desperately, she cried, "Oh, had I only known him. God sent him to me in answer to my prayer, and I did not receive him!"[64]

The Gospel says that Jesus came to His people, and they did not accept Him (John 1:11). They ignored and rejected Him because He did not come according to their expectations. Times have changed, but the problem remains the same. Jesus has come to us, too, and we have often ignored Him and His teachings because they don't always match our preferences and personal tastes.

Lord, open our eyes so that we can always recognize You and be always faithful to You!

REMAIN IN CHRIST

Finally, brethren, farewell. . . .
The grace of the Lord Jesus Christ, and the love of God,
and the communion of the Holy Spirit be with you all. Amen.
—2 Corinthians 13:11–14

December 31: We have arrived at the end of another year! As we reflect on the events of the year, let us take some time to express our gratitude to God for our blessings and determine our spiritual goals for the new year.

In 1890, Ellen White wrote an extensive letter to a couple who were losing their spiritual fervor. Let's read the following portion as if it were written to us:

There is hope for you both; you may have a transformation of character, if you will. You may have it now; it is not too late to make your calling and election sure. There is a fountain open for Judah in Jerusalem. Here you may wash and be clean. Jesus will cleanse you from every sin if you sincerely repent. Oh, if you would only see and feel the necessity of keeping step with the leader, Jesus Christ. Lift the cross, deny self, humble your hearts before God, and you can now recover yourselves out of the snare of Satan.

Bring a new meaning into your life and work. Represent Jesus in character. You both need this transformation before you are fitted for the work of God. If you will make the most of your God-given capabilities, and walk and work in the Spirit of the Master, your life may even now be made a glorious success. The Lord would have you and your family if you work with a purpose now, and you may receive the crown of glory that fadeth not away, reserved in heaven for all those that love His appearing.[65]

Perhaps you spent too much time this year with things that do not count for eternity. Please do not let the final hours of this year expire without surrendering yourself unconditionally to our beloved Lord and Savior, Jesus Christ. As you know, there is a marvelous heaven and a glorious crown waiting for you. "Hold fast what you have, that no one may take your crown" (Revelation 3:11). Let's remain faithful until the blessed day on which our hope becomes a reality and we are united with the heavenly family. God bless and keep you until then!

ENDNOTES

A WORD TO THE READER

1. George Santayana, *The Life of Reason: Introduction and Reason in Common Sense*, Common-Sense-ebook.pdf, 172, https://santayana.iupui.edu/wp-content/uploads/2019/01/Common-Sense-ebook.pdf.

2. Ellen G. White, "The Light of the World," *Signs of the Times*, October 20, 1887.

JANUARY

1. Ansel Adams, "1948 Introduction to Portfolio One," in *Photographers on Photography* (Englewood Cliffs, NJ: Prentice-Hall, 1966), 32.

2. Ellen G. White, *The Great Controversy* (Mountain View, CA: Pacific Press®, 1911), 602; emphasis added.

3. Ellen G. White, *The Publishing Ministry* (Hagerstown, MD: Review and Herald®, 1983), 33–35.

4. Ellen G. White, *Colporteur Ministry* (Mountain View, CA: Pacific Press®, 1953), 5.

5. "Newton to Hooke, 5 February 1675/6," in *The Correspondence of Isaac Newton*, vol. 1, 1661–1675, ed. H. W. Turnbull (Cambridge: University Press, 1959), 416.

6. David Brewster, *The Life of Sir Isaac Newton* (New York: J & J Harper, 1833), 301.

7. Isaac Newton, *The Mathematical Principles of Natural Philosophy* (London: Benjamin Motte, 1729), 388.

8. Samuel Horsley, *Isaaci Newtoni* (London: Excudebat Joannes Nichols, 1782), 436, 437.

9. David Brewster, *Memoirs of the Life, Writings, and Discoveries of Sir Isaac Newton*, vol. 2 (Cambridge: Macmillan, 1860), 347.

10. Eva Moore, *The Story of George Washington Carver* (New York: Scholastic Book Services, n.d.), 87, 88.

11. Dennis Abrams, *George Washington Carver: Scientist and Educator, Black Americans of Achievement Legacy Edition* (New York: Chelsea House, 2008), 68, 69.

12. Michael Rougier, "The Little Boy Who Wouldn't Smile," *Life* magazine, July 23, 1951, 91.

13. Rougier, 92.

14. Rougier, 92.

15. Rougier, 92.

16. Halis Gözpinar, "The Role of Proverbs in Forming Intercultural Awareness (on the Basis of Teaching English, Georgian and Turkish Languages)" (PhD diss., Ivane Javakhishvili Tbilisi Sate University, 2014), 28.

17. Marissa Newhall, "Top 11 Things You Didn't Know About Nikola Tesla," Energy.gov, November 18, 2013, https://www.energy.gov/articles/top-11-things-you-didnt-know-about-nikola-tesla.

18. "Examining the Theological Status of Geocentrism and Heliocentrism and the Devastating Problems This Creates for Baptism of Desire Arguments," VaticanCatholic.com, June 6, 2007, https://vaticancatholic.com/geocentrism-heliocentrism-galileo/.

19. Ellen G. White, "To the Students at Battle Creek College," *Advent Review and Sabbath Herald*, January 9, 1894, 2.

20. Ellen G. White, Manuscript 40, 1895.

21. William Arthur Ward, comp. and ed., *For This One Hour* (Anderson, SC: Droke House, 1969), 5.

22. *101 Objects That Changed the World* (Takoma Park, MD: JWM Productions, 2013).

23. Augustine, Kevin Knight, ed., "The Confessions, book VI," New Advent, from, *Nicene and Post-Nicene Fathers*, vol. 1, ed. Philip Schaf, trans. J. G. Pilkington (Buffalo, NY: Christian Literature, 1887), accessed June 12, 2022, https://www.newadvent.org/fathers/110106.htm.

24. Ellen G. White, *Messages to Young People* (Washington, DC: Review and Herald®, 1930), 30.

25. *Encyclopaedia Britannica Online*, s.v. "total war," accessed May 11, 2022, https://www.britannica.com/topic/total-war.

26. Ellen G. White, *Prophets and Kings*, (Mountain View, CA: Pacific Press®, 1917), 175.

27. Ellen G. White, *Great Controversy*, 530.

28. Ellen G. White, *Fundamentals of Christian Education* (Nashville, TN: Southern Publishing Association, 1923), 537.

29. Ellen G. White, *Great Controversy*, 560.

30. James Brooke, " 'Le Schweitzer' Still Inspires Deep Loyalty," *New York Times*, March 1, 1988, https://www.nytimes.com/1988/03/01/science/le-schweitzer-still-inspires-deep-loyalty.html.

31. Albert Schweitzer, *Out of My Life and Thought: An Autobiography* (Baltimore, MD: Johns Hopkins University Press, 1998), 2.

32. Ara Paul Barsam, *Reverence for Life: Albert Schweitzer's Great Contribution to Ethical Thought* (New York: Oxford University Press, 2008), 141.

33. Albert Schweitzer, *Reverence for Life*, trans. by Reginald H Fuller (New York: Harper & Row, 1969), 85.

34. Albert Schweitzer, *Thoughts for Our Times*, edited by Erica Anderson (New York: Pilgrim Press, 1975), 49.

35. Schwitzer *Reverence for Life*, 51.

36. Rick Newman, "How Sullenberger Really Saved US Airways Flight 1549," *US News and World Report*, February 3, 2009, https://money.usnews.com/money/blogs/flowchart/2009/02/03/how-sullenberger-really-saved-us-airways-flight-1549.

37. Joe Dorsey, " The Miracle on the Hudson—The Incredible Story of Captain 'Sully' and US Airways Flight 1549," Travel Thru History, February 6, 2014, http://www.travelthruhistory.tv/miracle-hudson/.

38. "US Airways Flight 1549 Crew Receive Prestigious Guild of Air Pilots and Air Navigators Award," *Guild News*, January 22, 2009, https://www.yumpu.com/en/document/view/3709270/us-airways-flight-1549-crew-receive-prestigious-guild-of-air-pilots-.

39. Ellen G. White, *Great Controversy*, 648.

40. Ittai Gradel, *Emperor Worship and Roman Religion*

(New York: Oxford University Press, 2002), 148.

41. *Bulletin of the Atomic Scientists. Records*, Hanna Holborn Gray Special Collections Research Center, University of Chicago Library abstract, University of Chicago Library, accessed May 11, 2022, https://www.lib.uchicago.edu/e/scrc/findingaids/view.php?eadid=ICU.SPCL.BULLETIN.

42. "FAQ: What Is the Doomsday Clock?" *Bulletin of the Atomic Scientists*, accessed April 18, 2022, https://thebulletin.org/doomsday-clock/faq/.

43. *Bulletin of the Atomic Scientists*, October 1949, cover.

44. Ellen G. White, *Testimonies for the Church*, vol. 5 (Mountain View, CA: Pacific Press®, 1948), 88.

45. E.g., "God Bless Our Home," Courier-Journal, December 2, 1970, 18-A. https://www.nyshistoricnewspapers.org/lccn/np00020004/1970-12-02/ed-1/seq-18.pdf.

46. Ellen G. White, *Testimonies for the Church*, vol. 6 (Mountain View, CA: Pacific Press®, 1948), 99; emphasis added.

47. Ellen G. White, "Disease and Its Causes," *Adventist Review and Sabbath Herald*, January 23, 1900.

48. Reuters Staff, "British Explorer Dies on Record Antarctica Solo Trip," Reuters, https://www.reuters.com/article/britain-explorer/british-explorer-dies-on-record-antarctica-solo-trip-idINKCN0V31ES.

49. Ellen G. White, *Great Controversy*, 160.

50. Ellen G. White, *The Ministry of Healing* (Mountain View, CA: Pacific Press®, 1905), 503; emphasis added.

51. Karl Barth, *Wolfgang Amadeus Mozart*, trans. Theologischer Verlag Zurich (Eugene OR: Wipf and Stock, 2003), 23.

52. Ellen G. White, *Messages to Young People*, 143.

53. Ellen G. White, *Testimonies for the Church*, vol. 1 (Mountain View, CA: Pacific Press®, 1948), 504.

54. Adolph Hitler, speech before the Nazi Reichstag, January 30, 1939, The History Place, https://www.historyplace.com/worldwar2/holocaust/h-threat.htm.

55. William Shakespeare, *Winter's Tale*, act 2, scene 3.

56. Wikipedia, s.v. "Waldensians," last modified May 4, 2022, 1:20 (UTC), https://en.wikipedia.org/wiki/Waldensians.

57. Ellen G. White, "Duties and Dangers of Ministers," *Advent Review and Sabbath Herald*s February 12, 1880, 1.

ℱEBRUARY

1. Julia Ward Howe, "Battle Hymn of the Republic," 1862, public domain.

2. Quoted in Benjamin Woolley, *Virtual Worlds: A Journey in Hyper and Hyperreality* (London: Penguine Books, 1993), Kindle loc. 2655.

3. Kaushik Patowary, "Franz Reichelt's Fatal Jump," December 15, 2020, https://www.amusingplanet.com/2020/12/franz-reichelts-fatal-jump.html.

4. Stephanie A. Sarkis, "25 Quotes on Excellence," Psychology Today, November 19, 2012, https://www.psychologytoday.com/us/blog/here-there-and-everywhere/201211/25-quotes-excellence.

5. D. T. Bourdeau, "Geology and the Bible," *Advent Review and Sabbath Herald*, February 5, 1867, 98.

6. George McCready Price quoted in Harold W. Clark, *Crusader for Creation: The Life and Writings of George McCready Price* (Mountain View, CA: Pacific Press, 1966), 82.

7. Ellen G. White, Letter 8, 1896.

8. Ellen G. White, *The Desire of Ages* (Oakland, CA: Pacific Press®, 1898), 671.

9. G. C. T., "To Correspondents," *Advent Review and Sabbath Herald*, June 9, 1896, 10.

10. Ellen G. White, *Desire of Ages*, 88, 131.

11. Ellen G. White, *Selected Messages*, book 1 (Washington, DC: Review and Herald®, 1958), 37.

12. Arthur L. White, *The Later Elmshaven Years: 1905–1915* , Ellen G. White Biography, vol. 6, (Hagerstown, MD: Review and Herald®, 1982), 455.

13. "Global Positioning System," National Aeronautics and Space Administration Wiki, accessed May 11, 2022, https://nasa.fandom.com/wiki/Global_Positioning_System.

14. Malachi Martin, *The Keys of This Blood: The Struggle for World Domination between Pope John Paul II, Mikhail Gorbachev, and the Capitalist West* (New York: Simon and Schuster, 1990).

15. "Decree on Ecumenism: *Unitatis Redintegratio*," par. 1, Documents of the Second Vatican Council, *La Santa Sede*, November 21, 1964, https://www.vatican.va/archive/hist_councils/ii_vatican_council/documents/vat-ii_decree_19641121_unitatis-redintegratio_en.html.

16. *"Dominus Iesus:* Declaration on the Unicity and Salvific Universality of Jesus Christ and the Church," Congregation for the Doctrine of the Faith, Boston College, August 6, 2000, par. 17, https://www.bc.edu/content/dam/files/research_sites/cjl/texts/cjrelations/resources/documents/catholic/cdf_dominusiesus.htm.

17. Fanny Crosby, *Fanny Crosby's Life-story* (New York: Every Where, 1903), 27.

18. "Fanny Crosby: Prolific and Blind Hymn Writer," *Christianity Today*, accessed July 18, 2022, https://www.christianitytoday.com/history/people/poets/fanny-crosby.html.

19. Fanny J. Crosby, "Blessed Assurance," 1873, public domain.

20. Ellen G. White, *Education* (Oakland, CA: Pacific Press®, 1903), 168.

21. Ellen G. White, Letter 4, 1867.

22. "Why Did the Egyptians Mummify Their Dead," DailyHistory.org, last modified January 4, 2018, https://dailyhistory.org/Why_did_the_Egyptians_Mummify_their_Dead.

23. Daniel Belvedere, sermon, Brazil Adventist College, São Paulo, Brazil, in the 1980s.

24. Ellen G. White, *Selected Messages*, book 2 (Washington, DC: Review and Herald®, 1958), 162, 166, 167.

25. Ellen G. White, *Testimonies for the Church*, vol. 1 (Mountain View, CA: Pacific Press®, 1948), 145.

26. Arthur L. White, *Ellen White: Woman of Vision* (Hagerstown, MD: Review and Herald®, 2000), 417.

27. Ellen G. White, *Testimonies for the Church*, vol. 8 (Mountain View, CA: Pacific Press®, 1948), 96.

28. Ellen G. White, *Testimonies*, vol. 8, 97.

29. Ernest R. Sandeen, "John Humphrey Noyes as the New Adam," Church History 40, no. 1 (March 1971): 82, 83. https://doi.org/10.2307/3163109.

30. Letter published in " 'The Battle Axe Letter,' " *The Witness* 1, no 7 (January 23, 1839), 49.

31. Ellen G. White, *Desire of Ages*, 189.

32. Ellen G. White, Letter 61, 1891.

33. Ellen White quotes from Charles Beecher's sermon in *The Great Controversy* (Mountain View, CA: Pacific Press®, 1911), 444, 445.

34. Charles Beecher, *The Bible a Sufficient Creed: Being Two Discourses Delivered at the Dedication of the Second Presbyterian Church*. Fort Wayne, Iowa, February 22, 1846 (Boston: Christian World, 1846), 7; emphasis in the original.

35. Beecher, 8–18.

36. Beecher, 13.

37. Beecher, 17.

38. W. W. Prescott, "Report of the Educational Secretary," *Daily Bulletin of the General Conference*, February 23, 1893, 350.

39. William Warren Prescott, *Victory in Christ* (Washington, DC: Review and Herald®, n.d.), 5, 6.

40. The authorship of the famous "Peace Prayer of St. Francis of Assisi," traditionally credited to Francis of Assisi, is currently being questioned. According to French scholar Christian Renoux, this prayer first appeared in 1912 in the religious magazine *La Clochette*.

41. S. N. Haskell, *The Cross and Its Shadow* (⁥ caster, MA: Bible Training School, 1914), 5.

42. Martin Hengel, *Crucifixion* (London: SC 1977).

43. Ellen G. White, *Desire of Ages*, 83.

44. William Miller, "Lecture on the Great Sabbː Xx.12," in *View of the Prophecies and Prophetic Chː* Miller's Works, vol. 1, (Boston: Joshua V. Himes, 162.

45. Thomas Motherwell Preble, *A Tract, Showing ⁊ Seventh Day Should Be Observed as the Sabbath, Inst the First Day According to the Commandment* (Nashua, Murray and Kimball, 1845), 3.

46. Preble, 9, 10; emphasis in the original.

47. Preble, 9, 10.

48. Preble, 3.

49. Preble, 11.

MARCH

1. "Yellowstone National Park," UNESCO, World Heritage Convention, accessed May 12, 2022, https://whc.unesco.org/en/list/28.

2. Annie Leibovitz, quoted in Mark DiOrio, "2017 in Pictures: Our Photographer Selects His Favorites," Colgate University, December 30, 2017, https://www.colgate.edu/news/stories/2017-pictures-our-photographer-selects-his-favorites.

3. Academic Dictionaries and Encyclopedias, s.v. "geyser," accessed July 18, 2022, https://etymology.en-academic.com/16808/geyser.

4. Suraj Radhakrishnan, "Old Faithful's Plumbing Revealed for the First Time: Sesimograph Shows Geyser's Interior," *International Business Times*, October 9, 2017, https://www.ibtimes.com/old-faithfuls-plumbing-revealed-first-time-seismograph-shows-geysers-interior-2598901.

5. "Yellowstone National Park," slide 17 of 17, *Christian Science Monitor*, accessed May 12, 2022, https://www.csmonitor.com/Photo-Galleries/In-Pictures/Yellowstone-National-Park/(photo)/239070.

6. Greg Laurie, Let God Change Your Life: How to Know and Follow Jesus (Colorado Springs, CO: David C. Cook, 2,012), 156.

7. Ellen G. White, *The Acts of the Apostles* (Mountain View, CA: Pacific Press®, 1911), 510.

8. Martin Buber, *I and Thou*, trans. Charles Scribner's Sons (New York: Charles Scribner's Sons, 1970), 56.

9. Emil Brunner, *Eternal Hope*, trans. Harold Knight (Philadelphia: Westminster Press, 1954), 7.

10. Ellen G. White, *Testimonies for the Church*, vol. 5 (Mountain View, CA: Pacific Press®, 1948), 512.

11. White, 512.

12. White, 512.

13. *The Works of Ralph Emerson: Representative Men* (Boston and New York: Fireside Edition, 1909), 186.

14. Ellen G. White, *The Great Controversy* (Mountain View, CA: Pacific Press®, 1911), vi.

15. Billy Graham quoted in Debbi Bryson, The One Year Wisdom for Women Devotional: 365 Devotion Through the Proverbs (Carol Stream, IL: Tyndale, 2013), 349.

16. Ellen G. White, *An Appeal to the Youth* (Battle, Creek, MI: Seventh-day Adventist Publishing Association, 1864), 76, 77.

17. White, 77.

18. The disputed authorship of this quote is settled in Garson O'Toole, "The Only Thing Necessary for the Triumph of Evil Is That Good Men Do Nothing," Quot Investigator, accessed July 18, 2022, https://quoteinvestigato.com/2010/12/04/good-m en-do/

19. United States Holocaust Memorial Museum, "Martin Niemöller: 'First They Came for the Socialists,' " Holocaust Encyclopedia, last edited March 30, 2012, https://encyclopedia.ushmm.org/content/en/article/martin-niemoeller-first-they-came-for-the-socialists.

20. Ellen G. White, *Christ's Object Lessons* (Battle Creek, MI: Review and Herald®, 1900), 362, 363.

21. Philip Schaff, *History of the Christian Church*, vol. 3: *Nicene and Post-Nicene Christianity, ad 311–600*, n693, Christians Classics Ethereal Library, accessed May 12, 2022, https://www.ccel.org/ccel/schaff/hcc3.iii.x.ii.html.

22. *Hachi: A Dog's Tale*, directed by Lass Hallström (Culver City, CA: Affirm Films et al., 2009).

23. Ellen G. White, *Testimonies*, vol. 5, 459.

24. Adam Clarke, *The Preacher's Manual* (n.p.: G. Lane & P. P. Stanford, 1842), 11.

25. Vladimir Lenin, "Socialism and Religion," Marxists Internet Archive, https://www.marxists.org/archive/lenin/works/1905/dec/03.htm.

26. J. R. Spangler, "Thousands Turn from Communism to Christ," *Adventist Review*, June 4, 1992, 27.

27. Ellen G. White, *Prophets and Kings* (Mountain View, CA: Pacific Press®, 1917), 631.

28. Jonathan Aitken, *John Newton: From Disgrace to Amazing Grace* (Wheaton, IL: Crossway Books, 2007), 72–76.

29. John Newton, "Amazing Grace," 1799, public domain.

30. Ellen G. White, *Spiritual Gifts*, vol. 1 (Battle Creek, MI: James White, 1858).

31. Ellen G. White, *Early Writings* (Battle Creek, MI: Seventh-day Adventist Publishing Association, 1882).

32. Ellen G. White, *Testimonies for the Church*, vol. 8 (Mountain View, CA: Pacific Press®, 1948), 27.

33. Gail Giorgio, *Footprints in the Sand: The Life Story of Mary Stevenson, Author of the Immortal Poem* (Gold Leaf Press, 1995), 38–39.

34. Wikipedia, s.v. "Intelligent Design," last modified April 6, 2022, https://en.wikipedia.org/wiki/Intelligent_design.

35. Ellen G. White, Letter 63, [March 17], 1893.

36. Ellen G. White, *Testimonies for the Church*, vol. 6 (Mountain View, CA: Pacific Press®, 1948), 53, 54.

.th Lan-

A Press,

h. Eze.
nology,
842),

at the
id of
VH:

monies to Ministers and Gospel
A: Pacific Press®, 1923), 155.

stimonies for the Church, vol. 7
fic Press®, 1948), 46.

Lectures to My Students: A Selection
to the Students of the Pastors' College,
(New York: Sheldon, 1875), 112;
al.

, 128.

te, The Ministry of Healing (Mountain
ess®, 1905), 481.

utler, ed., John Wesley (New York: Ox-
ess, 1964), 72; italics in the original.

ers of John Wesley: 1777," Wesley Center
://wesley.nnu.edu/john-wesley/the-letters-of
esleys-letters-1777/

oughborough, The Great Second Advent Move-
and Progress (Washington, DC: Review and
)), 141, 142.

G. White, The Adventist Home (Washington,
w and Herald®, 1952), 487.

lobal Tree Search," Botanic Gardens Conservation
onal, accessed May 12, 2022, https://www.bgci.org
es/bgci-databases/globaltreesearch/.

John Donne, Devotions Upon Emergent Occasions and
ll Steps in My Sicknes—Meditation XVII, 1624.

. Jean Zurcher, « L'homme, sa nature et sa destinée.
i sur le problème de l'union de l'âme et du corps »

(Neuchatel: Delachaux & Niestlé, 1953).

49. Jean Zurcher, The Nature and Destiny of Man: Essay on the Problem of the Union of the Soul and the Body in Relation to the Christian Views of Man, trans. Mabel R. Bartlett (New York: Philosophical Library, 1969).

50. Zurcher, Nature and Destiny, 168, 169.

51. "The Vulture and the Little Girl," Rare Historical Photos, last modified November 18, 2021, https://rarehistoricalphotos.com/vulture-little-girl/.

52. "The Vulture and the Little Girl."

53. "The Vulture and the Little Girl."

54. "The Vulture and the Little Girl."

55. "The Vulture and the Little Girl."

56. Some helpful principles and guidelines on this matter are found in sections 2–7 of Ellen G. White, The Adventist Home, 491–530.

57. "20 Forbidden Places You Can Never Visit," Travelden, accessed May 12, 2022, https://www.travelden.co.uk/20-forbidden-destinations-you-can-never-visit/5.

58. Regina Brett, "Regina Brett's Forty-Five Life Lessons and Five to Grow On," Cleveland.com, May 28, 2006, https://www.cleveland.com/brett/blog/2006/05/regina_bretts_45_life_lessons.html.

59. Ellen G. White, Testimonies, vol. 5, 645.

60. Ellen G. White, The Desire of Ages (Oakland, CA: Pacific Press®, 1898), 746.

61. Ellen G. White, Early Writings, 59, 60, 87–92, 262–266.

APRIL

1. "World's Biggest Liar Championship," BBC, https://www.bbc.com/storyworks/a-year-of-great-events/worlds-biggest-liar-championship

2. Gerhard F. Hasel, "Foreword," in Hans K. LaRondelle, Chariots of Salvation: The Biblical Drama of Armageddon (Washington, DC: Review and Herald, 1987), 7.

3. Edward Heppenstall, The Man Who Is God (Washington, DC: Review and Herald®, 1977), 133.

4. Ellen G. White, The Desire of Ages (Oakland, CA: Pacific Press®, 1898), 329.

5. Dietrich Bonhoeffer, The Cost of Discipleship, trans. R. H. Fuller with some revision by Irmgard Booth (New York: Simon and Schuster, 1995), 43–45.

6. Bonhoeffer, 45; emphasis in the original.

7. "Constitution," World Health Organization, accessed May 3, 2022, https://www.who.int/about/governance/constitution.

8. Ellen G. White, The Ministry of Healing (Mountain View, CA: Pacific Press®, 1905), 128.

9. White, 127.

10. "The Path to Transform Your Health Begins Today," NEWSTART, accessed July 18, 2022, https://www.newstart.com/.

11. "Our Story," About Us, International Society for Human Rights," accessed May 12, 2022, https://ishr.org/about/.

12. "At a Glance," About Us, International Society for Human Rights, accessed May 12, 2022, https://ishr.org/about/ishr-at-a-glance/.

13. John L. Allen Jr., "The War on Christians," Spectator, October 5, 2013, https://www.spectator.co.uk/article/the-war-on-christians.

14. Ellen G. White, The Acts of the Apostles (Mountain View, CA: Pacific Press®, 1911), 49.

15. J. Evan Smith, Booth the Beloved: Personal Recollections of William Booth, Founder of the Salvation Army (Melbourne: Geoffrey Cumberlege, 1949), 123, 124.

16. June Knop, "Welcome," Mission and Ministry on Fire (Australia) 17, no. 7 (August 2016), 3. https://issuu.com/salvos/docs/onfire-aug-2016.

17. Ellen G. White, Ministry to the Cities (Hagerstown, MD: Review and Herald®, 2012), 137–139.

18. Leonard Mlodinow, "Psychology Today: On the Power of Appearance," LeonardMlodinow.com, accessed May 3, 2022, https://leonardmlodinow.com/leonard-mlodinow-article/psychology-today-on-the-power-of-appearance/.

19. Ellen G. White, The Great Controversy (Mountain View, CA: Pacific Press®, 1911), 666, 667.

20. Ellen G. White, Testimonies for the Church, vol. 1 (Mountain View, CA: Pacific Press®, 1948), 123.

21. Ellen G. White, Sons and Daughters of God (Washington, DC: Review and Herald®, 1955), 349.

22. "Human Brain Project: Ethics and Society," Linnaeus University, updated November 24, 2020, https://lnu.se/en/research/searchresearch/human-brain-project/.

23. "The Human Brain Is the Most Complex Structure in the Universe. Let's Do All We Can to Unravel Its Mysteries," Independent, April 2, 2014, https://www.independent.co.uk/voices/editorials/the-human-brain-is-the-most-complex-structure-in-the-universe-let-s-do-all-we-can-to-unravel-its-mysteries-9233125.html.

24. Ellen G. White, Testimonies for the Church, vol. 6 (Mountain View, CA: Pacific Press®, 1948), 380.

25. Encyclopaedia Britannica Online, s.v. "Demosthenes," by James J. Murphy, accessed May 12, 2022, https://www.britannica.com/biography/Demosthenes-Greek-statesman-and-orator.

26. Ellen G. White, Selected Messages, book 1 (Washing-

ton, DC: Review and Herald®, 1958), 122.

27. Ellen G. White, *Steps to Christ* (Oakland, CA: Pacific Press®, 1892), 91.

28. Ellen G. White, *Testimonies*, vol. 1, 504.

29. Ellen G. White, *Daughters of God* (Hagerstown, MD: Review and Herald®, 1998), 160.

30. Roland H. Bainton, *Here I Stand: A Life of Martin Luther* (New York: Meridian, 1995), 181–185.

31. Howard E. Gardner, *Frames of Mind: The Theory of Multiple Intelligences* (New York: Basic Books, 1983).

32. Ellen G. White, *Testimonies*, vol. 1, 124.

33. Jerry L. Walls, *The Problem of Pluralism: Recovering United Methodist Identity* (Wilmore, KY: Good News Books, 1986).

34. "The History of Earth Day," Earth Day, accessed May 12, 2022, https://www.earthday.org/history/.

35. "History of Earth Day."

36. "Stewardship of the Environment," Seventh-day Adventist Church, October 1996, https://www.adventist .org/official-statements/stewardship-of-the-environment/.

37. Thomas Edison quoted in J. L. Elkhorne, "Edison— the Fabulous Drone," *Amateur Radio* 73, no. 3 (March 1967), 52.

38. "The Man in the Arena," Theodore Roosevelt Center, accessed May 3, 2022, https://www.theodorerooseveltcenter .org/Learn-About-TR/TR-Encyclopedia/Culture-and-Society /Man-in-the-Arena.aspx.

39. Ellen G. White, *Patriarchs and Prophets* (Mountain

View, CA: Pacific Press®, 1917), 509.

40. Ellen G. White, *Great Controversy*, 677, 678.

41. "Fundamental Beliefs of Seventh-day Adventists," *Seventh-day Adventist Church Manual*, 19th ed. (Hagerstown, MD: Review and Herald®, 2016), 162.

42. Oscar Cullman, "Immortality of the Soul and Resurrection of the Dead: The Witness of the New Testament" *Harvard Divinity School Bulletin* 21 (1955–1956).

43. Justin Martyr, Kevin Knight, ed. "Dialogue With Trypho: The Opinion of Justin With Regard to the Reign of a Thousand Years. Several Catholics Reject It," New Advent, from *Ante-Nicene Fathers*, vol 1, eds. Alexander Roberts, et al., trans. Marcus Dods and George Reith (Buffalo, NY: Christian Literature, 1885), accessed June 12, 2022, https:// www.newadvent.org/fathers/01286.htm.

44. Ellen G. White, *Ministry of Healing*, 376, 377.

45. Immanuel Kant, *Critique of Practical Reason*, trans. Mary Gregor (Cambridge: Cambridge University Press, 2015), 129.

46. Ellen G. White, *Early Writings* (Battle Creek, MI: Seventh-day Adventist Publishing Association, 1882), 16.

47. "Wedding Dress of Catherine Middleton," British Royal Family Wiki, accessed May 12, 2022, https://british royalfamily.fandom.com/wiki/Wedding_Dress_of_Catherine _Middleton.

48. Ellen G. White, *Christ's Object Lessons* (Battle Creek, MI: Review and Herald®, 1900), 309, 310.

MAY

1. *Encyclopaedia Britannica Online*, s.v. "David Livingstone," by George Albert Shepperson, last modified April 27, 2022, https://www.britannica.com/biography/David -Livingstone.

2. *Encyclopaedia Britannica Online*, s.v. "David Livingstone."

3. *Encyclopaedia Britannica Online*, s.v. "David Livingstone."

4. William Garden Blaikie, *The Personal Life of David Livingstone, LLD, DCL: Chiefly From His Unpublished Journals and Correspondence in the Possession of His Family* (London: John Murray, 1880), 143.

5. *Dr. Livingston's Cambridge Lectures*, ed. by William Monk (London: Bell and Dalby, 1858), 23.

6. Roland H. Bainton, *Here I Stand: A Life of Martin Luther* (New York: Abingdon-Cokesbury, 1950), 185.

7. Bainton, 197.

8. Booton Herndon, *The Unlikeliest Hero* (Mountain View, CA: Pacific Press®, 1967). Frances M. Doss, *Desmond Doss: Conscientious Objector* (Nampa, ID: Pacific Press, 2005).

9. Sigmund Freud, "The Future of an Illusion" (1927), in *The Standard Edition of the Complete Psychological Works of Sigmund Freud*, vol. 21, trans. by James Strachey (London: Hogarth, 1961), 53.

10. Tony Campolo, "Religion After Freud," May 25, 2011, https://www.huffpost.com/entry/religion -after-freud_b_4007.

11. Henry van Dyke, "Joyful, Joyful, We Adore Thee," 1907, public domain.

12. Wikipedia, "The Prince and the Pauper (1937 film)," last modified June 23, 2022, https://en.wikipedia.org/wiki /The_Prince_and_the_Pauper_(1937_film).

13. Wikipedia, "The Prince and the Pauper."

14. Ellen G. White, *Early Writings* (Battle Creek, MI:

Seventh-day Adventist Publishing Association, 1882), 179.

15. Ellen G. White, *In Heavenly Places* (Washington, DC: Review and Herald®, 1967), 78.

16. Ellen G. White, Manscript 6, 1900.

17. Ellen G. White, Manscript 76, 1903.

18. Ellen G. White, Counsels to Parents, Teachers, and Students, (Mountain View, CA: Pacific Press®, 1943), 267.

19. Edward Cook, *The Life of Florence Nightingale*, 2 vols. (London: MacMillan, 1914), 1:506; italics in the original.

20. Cook, 2:406.

21. Cook, 2:257; italics in the original.

22. Catechism of the Catholic Church, 2nd ed. (Vatican City: Libreria Editrice Vaticana, 1997), 252.

23. Jean M. Heimann, *Fatima: The Apparition that Changed the World* (Charlotte, NC: TAN Books, 2017), 30.

24. Michael Burlingame, *Abraham Lincoln: A Life*, online edition, 206n, https://www.knox.edu/documents/Lincoln Studies/BurlingameVol1Chap1.pdf.

25. "May 9, 1914, President Wilson Declares National Mother's Day," President Wilson House, November 13, 2020, https://www.woodrowwilsonhouse.org/wilson-mothers-day/

26. Ellen G. White, *Patriarchs and Prophets* (Battle Creek, MI: Seventh-day Adventist Publishing Association, 1890), 243, 244.

27. Will Durant, *The Story of Philosophy*, rev. ed. (Garden City, NY: Garden City Publishing Co., 1933), 87.

28. Emma Crichton-Miller, "Why Violin Makers' Choice of Wood Is the Key to Perfection" *Financial Times*, May 12, 2017, https://www.ft.com/content/73fb8ed0 -3013-11e7-9555-23ef563ecf9a.

29. J. N. A., "The Tithing System," *Advent Review and Sabbath Herald*, May 18, 1869, 168.

30. Ellen G. White, *Testimonies for the Church*, vol. 2 (Mountain View, CA: Pacific Press®, 1948), 518.

31. Ellen G. White, *Testimonies for the Church*, vol. 9, (Mountain View, CA: Pacific Press, 1948), 247, 250.

32. Ellen G. White, *The Great Controversy* (Mountain View, CA: Pacific Press®, 1911), 306–309.

33. Jaroslav Pelikan and Valerie Hotchkiss, eds., *Creeds and Confessions of Faith in the Christian Tradition*, 3 vols. (New Haven: Yale University Press, 2003), 1:159.

34. Pelikan and Hotchkiss, 1:159.

35. Pelikan and Hotchkiss, 2:609.

36. Ellen G. White, *The Desire of Ages* (Oakland, CA: Pacific Press®, 1898), 530.

37. J. N. Loughborough, *The Church, Its Organization, Order and Discipline* (Washington, DC: Review and Herald®, 1907), 87; emphasis in original.

38. Ellen G. White, "Communication From Sister White: Organization," *Advent Review and Sabbath Herald*, August 27, 1861, 101.

39. Ellen G. White, *Testimonies to Ministers and Gospel Workers* (Mountain View, CA: Pacific Press®, 1923), 27, 28.

40. "Archives: Five Bulls of Pope Gregory XI Against Wycliffe," Christian History Institute, accessed July 19, 2022, https://christianhistoryinstitute.org/magazine/article/archives-five-bulls-of-pope-gregory-xi-against-wycliffe.

41. "Five Bulls of Pope Gregory XI."

42. William Antliff, *The Protestant Reformers and the Reformation* (London: Thomas Holliday, 1853), 15.

43. Thomas Fuller, *The Church History of Britain* (Oxford: Oxford University Press, 1845), 2:424.

44. Ellen G. White, *Sons and Daughters of God* (Washington, DC: Review and Herald®, 1955), 356.

45. Charles Wesley, *The Journal of the Rev. Charles Wesley, M.A.*, 2 vols. (London: Wesleyan Methodist Book-Room, n.d.), 1:92.

46. Wesley., 94.

47. Charles Wesley, "And Can It Be, That I Should Gain?" 1738, public domain.

48. Roger Steer, *George Müller: Delight in God!* (Wheaton, IL: Harold Shaw, 1975), 243.

49. Nicolaus Zinzendorf, *Sixteen Discourses on the Redemption of Man by the Death of Christ: Preached at Berlin* (London: James Hutton, 1711), 119.

50. John Calvin, *Commentary on the Book of Psalms*, 5 vols. (Edinburgh: Calvin Translation Society, 1849), 5:178.

51. Mark Dever, "The Church Is the Gospel Made Visible (Session 1)" Together for the Gospel, 2010, video, 1:01:29, https://t4g.org/resources/mark-dever/the-church-is-the-gospel-made-visible-session-i-3/.

52. Patch Adams, *Gesundheit! Bringing Good Health to You, the Medical System, and Society through Physician Service, Complementary Therapies, Humor, and Joy* (Rochester, VT: Healing Arts Press, 1998), 82, 83.

53. Adams, 132.

54. Birmingham Live, "Tributes Pour in for Sir Edmund Hillary," *Birmingham Mail*, January 11, 2008, https://www.birminghammail.co.uk/news/local-news/tributes-pour-in-for-sir-edmund-hillary-56287.

55. "Symposium of Foreign National Representatives," General Conference Report—No. 5, *Advent Review and Sabbath Herald*, June 2, 1936, 106.

56. "Symposium of Foreign National Representatives," 107.

57. "Symposium of Foreign National Representatives," 107.

58. Ellen G. White, *Testimonies to Ministers and Gospel Workers*, 18.

JUNE

1. Marilyn Monroe, *Fragments: Poems, Intimate Notes, Letters*, eds. Stanley Buchthal and Bernard Comment (New York: Farrar, Straus and Giroux, 2010), 34, 35.

2. Raimundo Correia, "Secret Evil," trans. Carlos Alberto Santos, accessed June 16, 2022, http://interlingua.wikia.com/wiki/Mal_secrete_en.

3. Ellen G. White, *The Desire of Ages* (Oakland, CA: Pacific Press®, 1898), 17.

4. Ellen G. White, *Messages to Young People* (Washington, DC: Review and Herald®, 1930), 432.

5. Ellen G. White, *The Great Controversy* (Mountain View, CA: Pacific Press®, 1911), 509.

6. Ellen G. White, "Gethsemane," *Signs of the Times*, June 3, 1897, 4, 5.

7. William Adams Simonds, *Henry Ford: His Life, His Work, His Genius*, rev. ed. (Los Angeles, CA: Floyd, Clymer, 1946), 321.

8. "A Talk with Henry Ford," *The Guardian*, November 16, 1940, 8.

9. Ellen G. White, *Counsels on Diet and Foods* (Washington, DC: Review and Herald®, 1938), 481.

10. Ellen G. White, *Selected Messages*, book 3 (Hagerstown, MD: Review and Herald®, 1930), 279, 280.

11. Ellen G. White, *Testimonies for the Church*, vol. 2 (Mountain View, CA: Pacific Press®, 1948), 371.

12. Ellen G. White, Manuscript 49, 1909.

13. Arthur L. White, *The Later Elmshaven Years 1905–1915*, Ellen G. White Biography, vol. 6, (Washington, DC: Review and Herald®, 1982), 197.

14. "Spurgeon's Sermons," vol. 31 (1885), 59, 60, http://mis.kp.ac.rw/admin/admin_panel/kp_lms/files/digital/SelectiveBooks/Theology/Spurgeons%20Sermons%20Volume%2031%201885.pdf.

15. J. Edwin Hartill, quoted by Douglas S. Huffman, "What Is the Christian Life About?" in *Christian Contours: How a Biblical Worldview Shapes the Mind and Heart*, ed. Douglas S. Huffman (Grand Rapids, MI: Kregal Academic & Professional, 2011), 144.

16. Aristotle, *Politics*, trans. by Ernest Baker, Oxford World's Classics (Oxford: Oxford University Press, 1995), 10 (1252b).

17. Xenophanes of Colophon, *Fragments*, trans. J. H. Lesher (Toronto: University of Toronto Press, 1992), Fragments 15, 16.

18. Karen Armstrong, *A History of God: The 4000-Year Quest of Judaism, Christianity and Islam* (New York: Ballantine Books, 1993), 397.

19. Robert Wright, *The Evolution of God* (New York: Little, Brown and Company, 2009), 11.

20. Ellen G. White, *The Acts of the Apostles* (Mountain View, CA: Pacific Press®, 1911), 492–513.

21. White, 507.

22. *Diodorus of Sicily*, 12 vols., trans. C. Bradford Welles (London: William Heinemann, 1963), 8:465, 467.

23. Ellen G. White, *Counsels on Health* (Mountain View, CA: Pacific Press®, 1923), 588.

24. Ellen G. White, Letter 20, 1883.

25. Walter Isaacson, Steve Jobs (London: Abacus, 2011), xx.

26. " 'You've Got to Find What You Love,' Jobs Says," *Stanford News*, June 14, 2005 https://news.stanford.edu/2005/06/14/jobs-061505/

27. " 'You've Got to Find What You Love.' "

28. Ellen G. White, *Testimonies for the Church*, vol. 5 (Mountain View, CA: Pacific Press®, 1948), 200.

29. Samuele Bacchiocchi, *From Sabbath to Sunday* (Rome: Pontifical Gregorian University Press, 1977), 2.

30. Ellen G. White, *Great Controversy*, 509.

31. Artur Weiser, "πιστεύω κτλ.," in Gerhard Friedrich, ed., Theological Dictionary of the New Testament, trans. by Geoffrey W. Bromiley (Grand Rapids, MI: Eerdmans, 1968), 6:182.

32. Ellen G. White, *Patriarchs and Prophets* (Oakland, CA: Pacific Press®, 1890), 431.

33. Martin Luther, *Luther's Works*, vol. 54, *Table Talk*, ed. and trans. Theodore G. Tappert (Philadelphia: Fortress, 1967), 359, 360.

34. "Distribution of Labor," *Advent Review and Sabbath Herald*, June 17, 1909, 24.

35. Ferdinand Anthony Stahl, *In the Land of the Incas* (Mountain View, CA: Pacific Press®, 1920), 198.

36. Stahl, 198.

37. Stahl, 198.

38. Stahl, 231.

39. F. A. Stahl, "Bolivia," *Advent Review and Sabbath Herald*, January 20, 1910, 17.

40. Michel Quoist, *Prayers of Life*, trans. Anne Marie de Commaile and Agnes Mitchell Forsyth (Dublin: Gill and Macmillan, 1963), 17.

41. Ellen G. White, *The Adventist Home* (Washington, DC: Review and Herald®, 1952), 179.

42. Ellen G. White, "Brethren Who Shall Assemble in General Conference," Letter 20, 1888.

43. Ellen G. White, Manuscript 5, 1889.

44. Arthur L. White, *Later Elmshaven Years* 18.

45. Ellen G. White, Letter 27, 1906.

46. Ellen G. White, *Medical Ministry* (Washington, DC: Review and Herald®, 1932), 57.

47. Ellen G. White, "Dear Brethren and Sisters," *Present Truth*, November 1850, 87.

48. Ellen G. White, *Selected Messages*, book 1 (Washington, DC: Review and Herald®, 1958), 188.

49. Pope Bl. Pius IX, "*Ineffabilis Deus*: The Immaculate Conception," Papal Encyclicals Online, 1854, https://www.papalencyclicals.net/pius09/p9ineff.htm.

50. Pope Leo XIII, "*Octobri Mense:* On the Rosary," Papal Encyclicals Online, 1894, https://www.papalencyclicals.net/leo13/l13ro5.htm.

51. James Harvey Robinson, "The Newer Ways of Historians," American Historical Review 35, no. 2 (January 1930): 254. https://doi.org/10.2307/1837436.

52. Charles Haddon Spurgeon, *Men With Two Faces* (Philadelphia: Henry Altemus, 1896), 164.

53. Spurgeon, 171.

54. History.com Editors, "Formula One Champ Kidnapped," History, November 13, 2009, https://www.history.com/this-day-in-history/formula-one-champ-kidnapped.

55. Gerald Donaldson, *Fangio: The Life Behind the Legend* (Kindle ed.).

56. Chris Carter, "Lionel Messi: The world's most expensive football player who'd play for nothing," Money Week, January 7, 2015, https://moneyweek.com/372024/lionel-messi-the-worlds-most-expensive-football-player-whod-play-for-nothing.

57. Ellen G. White, *Medical Ministry*, 168.

58. Ellen G. White, *Desire of Ages*, 523.

59. "Cancer," World Health Organization Africa, accessed May 22, 2022, https://www.afro.who.int/health-topics/cancer.

60. Billy Graham, *How to Be Born Again* (Nashville, TN: Thomas Nelson, 1989), 78.

61. Helen Keller, *Optimism: An Essay* (New York: T. Y. Crowell & Co., 1903), 17.

62. Helen Keller's Journal, 1936–1937 (Garden City, NY: Doubleday, Doran & Co., 1938), 60.

63. Helen Keller, *We Bereaved* (New York: Leslie Fulenwider, 1929), 23.

64. Keller, Optimism, 18.

65. Helen Keller, *The Story of My Life* (New York: Doubleday, Doran & Co., 1903), 203.

66. "Clothing & Fashion," Victorian Age, November 18, 2014, https://victorian-age.weebly.com/victorian-clothing-fashion.html.

67. Alison Lurie, *The Language of Clothes* (United Kingdom: Vintage Press, 1983), 3.

68. General Conference of Seventh-day Adventist Administrative Committee (ADCOM), "Religious Liberty, Evangelism, and Proselytism," Seventh-day Adventist Church, June/July 2000.

69. ADCOM, "Religious Liberty."

70. C. Mervyn Maxwell, *Tell It to the World* (Mountain View, CA: Pacific Press®, 1977), 113, 114.

71. This statement is usually attributed to Sir Isaac Newton, but is unconfirmed.

72. Ellen G. White, *Education* (Oakland, CA: Pacific Press®, 1903), 80.

73. Ellen G. White, *Testimonies for the Church*, vol. 9 (Mountain View, CA: Pacific Press®, 1948), 189.

$\mathcal{J}$ULY

1. Susi Hasel Mundy, *A Thousand Shall Fall* (Hagerstown, MD: Review and Herald®, 2001).

2. Mundy, back cover.

3. Mundy, *Thousand Shall Fall*, 52.

4. *D. Martin Luthers Werke: Tischreden* (Weimar: Hermann Böhlaus Nachfolger, 1916), 4:440 (par. 4707).

5. Neale Donald Walsch, *On Abundance and Right Livelihood* (Charlottesville, VA: Hampton Roads, 1999), 116.

6. Hal Lindsey, *The Late Great Planet Earth* (Grand Rapids, MI: Zondervan, 1970), 48–54.

7. Ellen G. White, *The Great Controversy* (Mountain View, CA: Pacific Press®, 1911), 595.

8. "The Life of Dolly," The University of Edinburgh, accessed July 19, 2022, https://dolly.roslin.ed.ac.uk/facts/the-life-of-dolly/.

9. William J. Clinton, "President's Letter to Congress: Cloning Prohibition Act," The White House, June 9, 1997, https://clintonwhitehouse5.archives.gov/New/Remarks/Mon/19970609-15987.html.

10. "Universal Declaration on the Human Genome and Human Rights," Article 11, United Nations, November 11, 1997, https://www.ohchr.org/en/instruments-mechanisms/instruments/universal-declaration-human-genome-and-human-rights.

11. "European Ban on Human Cloning," BBC, January 12, 1998, http://news.bbc.co.uk/2/hi/uk_news/46862.stm.

12. Jonathan Edwards, "Sinners in the Hands of an Angry God," Blue Letter Bible, accessed May 12, 2022, https://www.blueletterbible.org/Comm/edwards_jonathan/Sermons/Sinners.cfm.

13. John Furniss, *The Sight of Hell* (Dublin: James Duffy and Co., 1874), 24.

14. Ellen G. White, *Life Sketches of Ellen G. White* (Mountain View, CA: Pacific Press®, 1915), 29–31, 48–50.

15. Ellen G. White, *Great Controversy*, 543.

16. "Chapter and Verse Divisions Keep You From Understanding Many of Words of the Bible," *BHC Bible Studies* (blog), June 17, 2020, https://bhcbiblestudies.blogspot.com/2020/06/.

17. Ellen G. White, *Fundamentals of Christian Education* (Nashville, TN: Southern Publishing Association, 1923), 195.

18. Ellen G. White, *Counsels to Parents, Teachers, and Students* (Mountain View, CA: Pacific Press®, 1913), 484.

19. G. B. Thompson, "The Sabbath-School and Young People's Convention," *Advent Review and Sabbath Herald*, August 8, 1907, 6.

20. Ellen G. White, *Gospel Workers* (Washington, DC: Review and Herald®, 1915), 67.

21. Ellen G. White, *Daughters of God* (Hagerstown, MD: Review and Herald®, 1998), 189.

22. Ellen G. White, *The Ministry of Healing* (Mountain View, CA: Pacific Press®, 1905), 397.

23. Ellen G. White, Manuscript 34, 1892.

24. Ellen G. White, Letter 40, 1892.

25. Olivier Vergnault, "Friday the 13th Superstitions and Legends Explained by Experts at the Museum of Witchcraft and Magic," CornwallLive, April 13, 2018, https://www.cornwalllive.com/whats-on/family-kids/friday-13th-superstition-witchcraft-museum-588243.

26. Nicole Pelletiere, " 'Forgotten Baby Syndrome': A Parent's Nightmare of Hot Car Death," ABC News, July 14, 2016, https://abcnews.go.com/Lifestyle/forgotten-baby-syndrome-parents-nightmare-hot-car-death/story?id=40431117.

27. Ellen G. White, *Ministry of Healing*, 229.

28. Martin Hengel, *Crucifixion in the Ancient World and the Folly of the Message of the Cross*, trans. John Bowden (Philadelphia: Fortress Press, 1977).

29. Ellen G. White, *Selected Messages*, book 1 (Washington, DC: Review and Herald®, 1958), 55.

30. Ellen G. White, *Our Father Cares* (Hagerstown, MD: Review and Herald®, 1991), 296.

31. Isaac Watts, "Never Part Again," 1707, public domain.

32. "Genesis 2:21–25," *Matthew Henry's Commentary*, Bible Gateway, accessed July 19, 2022, https://www.biblegateway.com/resources/matthew-henry/Gen.2.21-Gen.2.25.

33. *Report of the Woman's Convention: Held at Seneca Falls, N. Y., July 19th and 20th, 1848* (Rochester, NY: John Dick, 1848), 5, 8.

34. John F. Kennedy, "Special Message to the Congress on Urgent National Needs," NASA.gov, May 25, 1961, https://www.nasa.gov/pdf/59595main_jfk.speech.pdf.

35. Natalie Wolchover, " 'One Small Step for Man': Was Neil Armstrong Misquoted?," Space.com, August 27, 2012, https://www.space.com/17307-neil-armstrong-one-small-step-quote.html.

36. Richard Nixon, "7.24.1969—Apollo 11 Astronauts Return From the Moon," Richard Nixon Foundation, July 24, 2011, https://www.nixonfoundation.org/2011/07/7-24-1969-apollo-11-astronauts-return-from-the-moon/.

37. Oscar Wilde, "Lady Windermere's Fan," Act 1, in *Complete Works of Oscar Wilde*, ed. Robert Ross (Boston, MA: Wyman-Fogg Co., n.d.), 15.

38. Mae West, in the film *My Little Chickadee*, directed by Edward F. Cline (Universal Pictures, 1940), 57:14. https://archive.org/details/mylittlechickadee1940minhadengosamonpetitpoussincheri.

39. Ellen G. White, *Sermons and Talks*, vol. 1 (Silver Spring, MD: Ellen G. White Estate, 1990), 154.

40. Ellen G. White, *Spiritual Gifts*, vol. 2 (Battle Creek, MI: James White, 1860), 277.

41. Randy Alcom, *The Purity Principle* (Colorado Springs, CO: Multnomah Books, 2003), 55, italics in the original.

42. Ellen G. White, *Education* (Oakland, CA: Pacific Press®, 1903), 166.

43. J. W., "The Cause," *Advent Review and Sabbath Herald*, July 23, 1857, 93.

44. Ellen G. White, *Testimonies for the Church*, vol. 1 (Mountain View, CA: Pacific Press®, 1948), 504.

45. Ellen G. White, *Christian Service* (Washington, DC: Review and Herald®, 1925), 40.

46. Ellen G. White, Letter 1, 1855.

47. "Ellen G. White Notes" on Colossians 1:15, in Francis D. Nichol, ed., *Seventh-day Adventist Bible Commentary*, vol. 7 (Washington, DC: Review and Herald, 1957), 906.

48. Thomas à Kempis, *The Imitation of Christ* (Milwaukee: Bruce, 1940), 2.

49. Kempis, 27.

50. Kempis, 6.

51. Wayne Hooper, "We Have This Hope," (Wayne Hooper, 1962, 1995).

52. Ellen G. White, *Testimonies for the Church*, vol. 9 (Mountain View, CA: Pacific Press®, 1948), 27.

53. Leo B. Halliwell, *Light Bearer to the Amazon* (Nashville, TN: Southern Publishing Association, 1945), 159.

54. B. M. Preston, "Brazil Honors the Halliwells," *Advent Review and Sabbath Herald*, January 21, 1960, 21, 22.

55. Ellen G. White, *Testimonies for the Church*, vol. 3 (Mountain View, CA: Pacific Press®, 1948), 542.

56. "International Day of Friendship: July 30," https://www.un.org/en/observances/friendship-day.

57. Ellen G. White, *Great Controversy*, 482.

58. Clark B. McCall, "Why Not Use the Net Too?," *Ministry*, (December 1977): 2, 3.

59. Ellen G. White, *Testimonies*, vol. 9, 189.

60. Ellen G. White, *Ministry of Healing*, 143.

61. Ruth E. Van Reken, *Letters Never Sent* (Indianapolis, IN: "Letters," 1988), 1.

August

1. Aldus Manutius, quoted in "Effects of Excessive Work on Health," Mirror Review, accessed July 19, 2022, https://www.mirrorreview.com/excessive-work-injurious-health/.

2. Ellen G. White, *Testimonies for the Church*, vol. 1 (Mountain View, CA: Pacific Press®, 1948), 103.

3. White, 106.

4. White, 109, 110.

5. Ellen G. White, *Selected Messages*, book 1 (Washington, DC: Review and Herald®, 1958), 104, 105.

6. Ellen G. White, *Testimonies*, vol. 1, 105.

7. Francis A. Schaeffer, *Letters of Francis A. Schaeffer* (Westchester, IL: Crossway Books, 1985), 170, 171.

8. Viktor E. Frankl, *Man's Search for Meaning* (New York: Simon and Schuster, 1984), 105.

9. David Hewitt, "From Bro. Hewitt," *Advent Review and Sabbath Herald*, August 4, 1853, 47.

10. J. N. Loughborough, *The Great Second Advent Movement: Its Rise and Progress*, (Washington, DC: Review and Herald®, 1992), 548, 549.

11. Ellen G. White, *The Desire of Ages* (Oakland, CA: Pacific Press®, 1898), 195.

12. Biblical Archaeology Society Staff, "The Tel Dan Inscription: The First Historical Evidence of King David From the Bible," Biblical Archaeology Society, June 11, 2021, https://www.biblicalarchaeology.org/daily/biblical-artifacts /the-tel-dan-inscription-the-first-historical-evidence-of-the -king-david-bible-story/.

13. Ellen G. White, *Education* (Oakland, CA: Pacific Press®, 1903), 173.

14. Frederick M. Lehman, "The Love of God," 1917, public domain.

15. Ellen G. White, *Testimonies for the Church*, vol. 5 (Mountain View, CA: Pacific Press®, 1948), 740.

16. Alvin Toffler, *The Adaptive Corporation* (Toronto: Bantam Books, 1985), xi. s.

17. Ellen G. White, Letter 24, 1892.

18. *Seventh-day Adventist Encyclopedia*, 2nd rev. ed. (Hagerstown, MD: Review and Herald, 1996), s.v. "Jones, Alonzo T."

19. Ellen G. White, *Desire of Ages*, 189.

20. Ellen G. White, Letter 123, 1893.

21. Ellen G. White, Letter 20, 1868.

22. White.

23. White.

24. White.

25. White.

26. "*Quelle / Rede vom* 14, September 1935 (Adolf Hitler)," Metapedia, last modified November 23, 2015, https://de.metapedia.org/wiki/Quelle_/_Rede_vom_14 ._September_1935_(Adolf_Hitler). The last sentence of Hitler's speech reads, "Ihr seid die Zukunft der Nation, die Zukunft des Deutsches Reiches!"

27. Adolf Hitler, *Mein Kampf*, complete and unabridged fully annotated (New York: Reynal & Hitchcock, 1941), 30.

28. "World Programme of Action for Youth," United Nations, December 18, 2007, 2, https://www.un.org/esa /socdev/unyin/documents/wpay_text_final.pdf.

29. Ellen G. White, *Education*, 271.

30. Associated Press, "Evangelist Billy Graham Who Reached Millions, Dies at 99," Snopes, February 21, 2018, https://www.snopes.com/ap/2018/02/21/evangelist -billy-graham-reached-millions-dies-99/.

31. Ted Olsen, "Ruth Graham 'Close to Going Home to Heaven,' " *Christianity Today*, June 13, 2007, https://www .christianitytoday.com/news/2007/june/ruth-graham-close -to-going-home-to-heaven.html.

32. "Maximilian Kolbe—Biography," Society of Saint Pius X, March 16, 2015, https://fsspx.asia/en/news-events /news/maximilian-kolbe-biography.

33. Courtney Mares, "80 Years Ago St. Maximilian Kolbe Gave His Life in Auschwitz to Save a Father of a Family," Catholic News Agency, August 14, 2021, https:// www.catholicnewsagency.com/news/248688/80-years-ago -st-maximilian-kolbe-gave-his-life-in-auschwitz-to-save -a-father-of-a-family.

34. Ellen G. White, "The Principles of Righteousness Revealed in the Life," *Advent Review and Sabbath Herald*, March 21, 1893, 177.

35. John Bryson, *Evil Angels: The Case of Lindy Chamberlain* (New York: Open Road Media, 1985).

36. Ellen G. White, "A Visit to the South—No. 2," *Advent Review and Sabbath Herald*, August 18, 1904, 7, 8.

37. Bulletin No. 1 of the Nashville Agricultural and Normal School, Madison, Tennessee, Near Nashville: Announcement (Nashville, TN: Southern Publishing Association, 1904), 5.

38. Ellen G. White, *The Great Controversy* (Mountain View, CA: Pacific Press®, 1911), 648.

39. John Lichfield, "The Moving of the Mona Lisa", *The Independent*, April 2, 2005.

40. Friedrich Nietzsche, *The Gay Science*, trans. by Thomas Common (Mineola, NY: Dover Publications, 2006), 90, 91 (par. 125).

41. Friedrich Nietzsche, *Thus Spake Zarathustra*, trans. by Thomas Common (New York: Modern Library, [1917]), 83.

42. Friedrich Nietzsche, *Ecce Homo* (Portland, ME: Smith & Sale, Printers, 1911), 35.

43. Ellen G. White, *Education*, 103.

44. White, 192.

45. Ellen G. White, *Selected Messages*, book 2 (Washington, DC: Review and Herald®, 1958), 109.

46. Martin Luther King Jr., "I Have a Dream," (1963), https://www.cbsd.org/cms/lib010/PA01916442/Centricity /Domain/2773/dream-speech.pdf.

47. Martin Luther King Jr., *Strength to Love* (Philadelphia: Fortress Press, 1981), 53.

48. Ellen G. White, Letter 135, 1899.

49. Tessa Harvey, "25 Wedding Dress Captions That'll Make You Stand Out From Every Other Bride," May 21 2018, https://www.elitedaily.com/p/25-captions-for -wedding-dress-pictures-thatll-make-you-stand-out-from -every-other-bride-9136276.

50. Arthur L. White, *The Early Years: 1827–1862*, Ellen G. White Biography, vol. 1, (Hagerstown, MD: Review and Herald, 1985), 112.

51. Ellen G. White, *Life Sketches of Ellen G. White* (Mountain View, CA: Pacific Press, 1915), 109.

52. White, 142.

53. Ellen G. White, *Christ's Object Lessons* (Battle Creek, MI: Review and Herald®, 1900), 202.

September

1. "Covenant of the Oberlin Colony," accessed April 20, 2022, https://www2.oberlin.edu/external/EOG /Documents/Oberlin_Covenant.html.

2. James T. Burtchaell, *The Dying of the Light: The Disengagement of Colleges and Universities From Their Christian Churches* (Grand Rapids, MI: Eerdmans, 1998).

3. Ellen G. White, *Testimonies for the Church*, vol. 5 (Mountain View, CA: Pacific Press®, 1948), 25.

4. Catherine Wise, "Free—After 22 Years on Death Row," *Beliefnet*, accessed April 20, 2022, https://www.beliefnet.com/inspiration/2004/04/free-after-22-years-on-death-row.aspx.

5. Wise, "Free."

6. Edward Gibbon, *The History of the Decline and Fall of the Roman Empire*, vol. 2 (New York: Harper's Edition, 1831), 442.

7. Ellen G. White, *Education* (Oakland, CA: Pacific Press®, 1903), 176, 177.

8. Max Lucado, *Grace for the Moment Daily Bible* (Nashville, TN: Nelson Bibles, 2006), 858.

9. Flavius Josephus, *War of the Jews*, 6.5.3, accessed April 21, 2022, https://www.biblestudytools.com/history/flavius-josephus/war-of-the-jews/book-6/chapter-5.html.

10. Josephus, 6.5.3.

11. Josephus, 6.5.3.

12. Josephus, 6.5.3.

13. Josephus, 6.5.3.

14. Paul L. Maier, *Eusebius—The Church History* (Grand Rapids, MI: Kregel Publications, 2007), 82.

15. United Nations, "Secretary-General Stresses Need for Political Will and Resources to Meet Challenge of Fight Against Illiteracy," press release SG/SM/6316 OBV/9, September 4, 1997, https://press.un.org/en/1997/19970904.SGSM6316.html.

16. United Nations General Assembly, "Universal Declaration of Human Rights," United Nations, accessed April 19, 2022, https://www.un.org/en/about-us/universal-declaration-of-human-rights.

17. United Nations General Assembly, "Universal Declaration."

18. Sue Williams, "Literacy for All Remains an Elusive Goal, New UNESCO Data Shows," UNESCO, accessed April 21, 2022, https://en.unesco.org/news/literacy-all-remains-elusive-goal-new-unesco-data-shows.

19. "Out-of-School Children and Youth," UNESCO Institute for Statistics, accessed April 21, 2022, http://uis.unesco.org/en/topic/out-school-children-and-youth.

20. General Conference of Seventh-day Adventists Administrative Committee (ADCOM), "Literacy," Seventh-day Adventist Church, accessed April 21, 2022, https://www.adventist.org/official-statements/literacy-1/.

21. General Conference of Seventh-day Adventists ADCOM, "Literacy."

22. Max Ehrmann, "Desiderata," All Poetry, accessed April 21, 2022, https://allpoetry.com/desiderata---words-for-life.

23. Ellen G. White, *Education*, 57.

24. Richard Sisk, "The Story of Rick Rescorla, Vietnam Vet and 9/11 Hero," Military.com, September 13, 2019, https://www.military.com/daily-news/2019/09/13/story-rick-rescorla-vietnam-vet-and-9-11-hero.html.

25. 9/11 Memorial Staff, "Remembering the 'Man in the Red Bandana,' " *9/11 Memorial & Museum* (blog), accessed April 21, 2022, https://www.911memorial.org/connect/blog/remembering-man-red-bandana.

26. 9/11 Memorial Staff, " 'Man in the Red Bandana.' "

27. This date is disputed, but for the purposes of this book, I've chosen to use the September 12, 490 BC, date.

28. History.com Editors, "Battle of Marathon," History, October 8, 2019, https://www.history.com/topics/ancient-history/battle-of-marathon.

29. Dean Karnazes, "The Real Pheidippides Story," *Runner's World*, December 6, 2016, https://www.runnersworld.com/runners-stories/a20836761/the-real-pheidippides-story/.

30. BGEA, "Official Obituary: Billy Graham 1918–2018," Billy Graham Evangelistic Association, February 21, 2018, https://memorial.billygraham.org/official-obituary/.

31. BGEA, "Billy Graham: Pastor to the Presidents," Billy Graham Evangelistic Association, February 21, 2022, https://billygraham.org/gallery/billy-graham-pastor-to-the-presidents/.

32. BGEA, "Families Come From Across the Region to Honor 'America's Pastor,' " Billy Graham Evangelistic Association, February 26, 2018, https://billygraham.org/gallery/families-come-from-across-region-to-honor-americas-pastor-billy-graham/.

33. "Billy Graham's First City-Wide Campaign Begins," *This Date in History* (blog), The Billy Graham Library, , September 13, 2012, https://billygrahamlibrary.org/billy-grahams-first-city-wide-campaign-begins/.

34. Billy Graham, "What's 'the Billy Graham Rule'?" Billy Graham Evangelistic Association, July 23, 2019, https://billygraham.org/story/the-modesto-manifesto-a-declaration-of-biblical-integrity/.

35. Billy Graham, "About: Biographies," Billy Graham Evangelistic Association, accessed April 21, 2022, https://billygraham.org/about/biographies/.

36. Billy Graham, *Hope for Each Day* (Nashville, TN: HarperCollins Publishers, 2017), 108.

37. Charlotte Elliott, "Just As I Am," 1835, public domain.

38. Ellen G. White, *Counsels to Parents, Teachers, and Students* (Mountain View, CA: Pacific Press®, 1913), 453.

39. Ellen G. White, *Gospel Workers* (Washington, DC: Review and Herald®, 1915), 156.

40. Ellen G. White, "Sermon: Becoming Like Little Children," Manuscript 230, September 14, 1902, *Letters and Manuscripts—Volume 17 (1902)*.

41. White.

42. White.

43. White.

44. White.

45. Booton Herndon, *The Seventh Day: The Story of the Seventh-day Adventists* (New York: McGraw-Hill, 1960), 23.

46. Ellen G. White, "An Appeal for Self-Sacrificing Effort," *Advent Review and Sabbath Herald*, September 16, 1909, 8.

47. William O. Cushing, "Hiding in Thee," 1876, public domain.

48. Caleb K. Bell, "Poll: Americans Love the Bible But Don't Read It Much," RNS—Religion News Service, April 4, 2013, https://religionnews.com/2013/04/04/poll-americans-love-the-bible-but-dont-read-it-much/.

49. Bell, "Americans Love the Bible."

50. Ellen G. White, *Gospel Workers*, 279.

51. White, 281.

52. J. Hudson Taylor, *China's Spiritual Need and Claims* (London: Morgan & Scott, 1887), 12.

53. Ellen G. White, *Spiritual Gifts*, vol. 2 (Battle Creek, MI: James White, 1860), 296.

54. Ellen G. White, *Selected Messages*, book 3 (Washington, DC: Review and Herald®, 1980), 313.

55. White, 315.

56. "2021 Scripture Access Statistics," Wycliffe Global Alliance, September 1, 2021, https://www.wycliffe.net/resources/statistics/.

57. Martin Luther, *Luther's Works*, vol. 35 (Philadelphia: Muhlenberg, 1960), 189.

58. Harvey E. Solganick, "The Hard Knock at the Door

of Christianity," C. S. Lewis, August 5, 2008, https://www.cslewis.com/the-hard-knock-at-the-door-of-christianity/.

59. A. N. Wilson, *C. S. Lewis: A Biography* (New York: W. W. Norton, 1990), 127.

60. Wilson, 110.

61. C. S. Lewis, *The Business of Heaven* (New York: HarperCollins, 1984), 97.

62. C. S. Lewis, *The Great Divorce* (New York: HarperOne, 2009), 90.

63. C. S. Lewis, *Mere Christianity* (San Francisco: Harper SanFrancisco, 2001), 134.

64. "Dedication of Union College," *Advent Review and Sabbath Herald*, October 6, 1891, 614, 615.

65. Pavel Aksenov, "Stanislav Petrov: The Man Who May Have Saved the World," BBC News, September 26, 2013, https://www.bbc.com/news/world-europe-24280831.

66. "Stanislav Petrov, Who Averted Possible Nuclear War, Dies at 77," BBC News, September 18, 2017, https://www.bbc.com/news/world-europe-41314948.

67. Ellen G. White, *The Desire of Ages* (Oakland, CA: Pacific Press®, 1898), 693.

68. Ellen G. White, *Early Writings* (Battle Creek, MI: Seventh-day Adventist Publishing Association, 1882), 75.

69. Ellen G. White, *The Great Controversy* (Mountain View, CA: Pacific Press®, 1911), 457.

70. Greg Daugherty, "Who Was Really the First American Billionaire?" *Time,* September 26, 2016, https://time.com/4480022/first-american-billionaire-dispute/.

71. Keith Poole, "Biography: John D. Rockefeller, Senior," PBS, accessed April 25, 2022, https://www.pbs.org/wgbh/americanexperience/features/rockefellers-john/.

72. Peter Baida, "The Business of America: Beasts in the Jungle," *American Heritage* 37, no. 3, (April/May 1986), https://www.americanheritage.com/beasts-jungle.

73. James White, *The Early Life and Later Experience and Labors of Elder Joseph Bates* (Battle Creek, MI: Steam Press Seventh-day Adventist Publishing Association, 1877), 184–190.

OCTOBER

1. On April 1, 1850, the *Present Truth* contained a letter on page 71 from Ellen G. White, addressed "To the 'Little Flock.' "

2. Ellen G. White, *A Sketch of the Christian Experience and Views of Ellen G. White* (Saratoga Springs, NY: James White, 1851), 54.

3. Joseph Bates, *A Vindication of the Seventh-day Sabbath and the Commandments of God* (New Bedford, MA: Benjamin Lindsey, 1848), 86.

4. This was part of the name of a hymnbook published in 1849, *Hymns for God's Peculiar People That Keep the Commandments of God, and the Faith of Jesus.*

5. Arthur L. White, *The Early Years: 1827–1862*, Ellen G. White Biography, vol. 1, (Hagerstown, MD: Review and Herald®, 1985), 170.

6. Hiram Edson, "An Appeal to the Laodicean Church," *Advent Review Extra*, September 1850, 4.

7. Ellen G. White, "Our Duty in View of the Time of Trouble," Manuscript 3, 1849, published in The Ellen G. White Letters & Manuscripts With Annotations, Vol. 1 (Hagerstown, MD: Review and Herald, 2014), 146.

8. Joseph Bates, "The Laodicean Church," *Second Advent Review, and Sabbath Herald*, November 1850, 7, 8.

9. "Business Proceedings of B. C. Conference (Concluded)," *Advent Review, and Sabbath Herald*, October 23, 1860, 179; emphasis in the original.

10. Ellen G. White, *Testimonies for the Church*, vol. 1 (Mountain View, CA: Pacific Press®, 1948), 224.

11. "Mahatma Gandhi," Short Biography, October 2, 2021, https://short-biography.com/mahatma-gandhi.htm.

12. Mahatma Gandhi, " 'T'awards the Brotherhood of Man," *Harijan*, February 16, 1934, 5.

13. *The Collected Works of Mahatma Gandhi*, vol. 35 (New Delhi: Publications Division, Ministry of Information and Broadcasting, Government of India, n.d.), vi-vii.

14. E. Stanley Jones, *Mahatma Gandhi: An Interpretation* (New York: Abingdon-Cokesbury Press, 1948), 51.

15. Donald J. Ziegler, ed., *Great Debates of the Reformation* (New York: Random House, 1969), 105, 106.

16. A helpful discussion of the authorship of this saying is provided from Steve Perisho, "A Common Quotation from 'Augustine' ?" Georgetown.edu, https://faculty.georgetown.edu/jod/augustine/quote.html.

17. Christina Boyle, "Book That George Washington Borrowed From New York Library Is Returned—221 Years Later," *Daily News*, May 19, 2010, https://www.nydailynews.com/new-york/book-george-washington-borrowed-new-york-library-returned-221-years-article-1.448238.

18. Ellen G. White, *The Great Controversy* (Mountain View, CA: Pacific Press®, 1911), 552.

19. Edward Young, *Night Thoughts* (London: C. Whittingham, 1798), 13 (line 393).

20. "100 Procrastination Quotes to Get You Through the Day", *Vantage Circle* (blog), last updated July 12, 2022, https://blog.vantagecircle.com/procrastination-quotes/.

21. Ellen G. White, *Education* (Oakland, CA: Pacific Press®, 1903), 271.

22. Ellen G. White, *Patriarchs and Prophets* (Battle Creek, MI: Seventh-day Adventist Publishing Association, 1890), 540.

23. John Calvin, *Institutes* 3.21.5, Christian Classics Ethereal Library, accessed May 25, 2022, https://ccel.org/ccel/calvin/institutes.v.xxii.html.

24. "66. The Remonstrance," *Creeds of Christendom*, vol. 1, Christian Classics Ethereal Library, accessed May 22, 2022, https://www.ccel.org/ccel/schaff/creeds1.ix.iii.v.html.

25. A. W. Tozer, *The Knowledge of the Holy: The Attributes of God Their Meaning in the Christian Life* (Cambridge: Lutterworth Press, 2022), 102.

26. Ellen G. White, Testimonies, vol. 1, 471.

27. Jack F. Matlock Jr., *Reagan and Gorbachev: How the Cold War Ended* (New York: Random House, 2004), 235.

28. General Conference Committee Annual Council, "Methods of Bible Study," October 12, 1986, https://www.adventistbiblicalresearch.org/materials/methods-of-bible-study/.

29. Gerhard Ebeling, *The Word of God and Tradition* (Philadelphia: Fortress, 1968), 11–31.

30. Ellen G. White, *Great Controversy*, 595.

31. Ellen G. White, *The Acts of the Apostles* (Mountain View, CA: Pacific Press®, 1911), 9.

32. "Evangelism and Finishing God's Work," Annual Council, October 14, 1976, 76-266.

33. "Evangelism and Finishing God's Work," 76-271, 76-272.

34. Robert H. Pierson, "An Earnest Appeal," *Adventist*

World, February 28, 2021, https://www.adventistworld.org/an-earnest-appeal/.

35. Pierson, "An Earnest Appeal."

36. "Mother Teresa Acceptance Speech," The Nobel Prize, accessed April 13, 2022, https://www.nobelprize.org/prizes/peace/1979/teresa/acceptance-speech/.

37. Mother Teresa, "Nobel Lecture, Dec. 11, 1979," Iowa State University Archives of Women's Political Communication, accessed April 13, 2022, https://awpc.cattcenter.iastate.edu/2017/03/21/nobel-lecture-dec-11-1979/.

38. Myra Brooks Welch, "The Touch of the Master's Hand," *Gospel Messenger*, February 26, 1921, 130.

39. H. M. S. Richards quoted in Laurinda Keys, "Religion . . . In the News," *Ludington Daily News*, June 13, 1980, 6.

40. Ellen G. White, *Testimonies for the Church*, vol. 5 (Mountain View, CA: Pacific Press®, 1948), 732.

41. J. N. Andrews quoted in J. O. Corliss, "The Experiences of Former Days — No. 8," *Adventist Review and Sabbath Herald*, September 15, 1904, 9.

42. Ellen G. White to "Dear Brethren in Switzerland," Letter 2a (August 29), 1878.

43. J. N. Andrews to Uriah Smith, April 24, 1883, in James R. Nix, " 'Faithful to His Service' : J. N. Andrews (1829–1883): Adventism's First Official Missionary," in Alberto R. Timm and James R. Nix, eds., *Lessons From Battle Creek* (Silver Spring, MD: Review and Herald, 2018), 213.

44. Ellen G. White, *Christ in His Sanctuary* (Mountain View, CA: Pacific Press®, 1969), 6.

45. White, 7.

46. Ellen G. White, *Testimonies for the Church*, vol. 8 (Mountain View, CA: Pacific Press®, 1948), 267.

47. Ellen G. White, *Life Sketches of Ellen G. White* (Mountain View, CA: Pacific Press®, 1915), 120.

48. Ellen G. White, *Manuscript Releases*, vol. 15 (Silver Spring, MD: Ellen G. White Estate, 1990), 210.

49. Ellen G. White, Manuscript 5, *Letters and Manuscripts*, vol. 1, , 1859.

50. Alfie Kohn, *Punished by Rewards* (Boston: Houghton Mifflin, 1993).

51. Ellen G. White, *Medical Ministry* (Mountain View, CA: Pacific Press®, 1932), 168.

52. Ellen G. White, *Testimonies for the Church*, vol. 3 (Mountain View, CA: Pacific Press®, 1948), 474.

53. Ellen G. White, *Thoughts From the Mount of Blessing* (Oakland, CA: Pacific Press®, 1896), 23.

54. Ellen G. White, "Seek First the Kingdom of God," *Advent Review and Sabbath Herald*, October 27, 1885, 1.

55. Timothy Stenovec, "Facebook Is Now Bigger Than the Largest Country on Earth," *HuffPost*, updated December 6, 2017, https://www.huffpost.com/entry/facebook-biggest-country_n_6565428.

56. Stenovec, "Facebook Is Now Bigger."

57. History.com Editors, "Stock Market Crash of 1929," *History*, April 21, 2021, https://www.history.com/topics/great-depression/1929-stock-market-crash.

58. History.com Editors, "Stock Market Crash."

59. Giles Slade, *Made to Break: Technology and Obsolescence in America* (Cambridge, MA: Harvard University Press, 2006).

60. Slade, 9.

61. Slade, 29.

62. Peter Clive, *Schubert and His World: A Biographical Dictionary* (Oxford: Clarendon Press, 1997), 11.

63. Phillip Huscher, "The Mystery of Schubert's 'Unfinished' Symphony,' " *Experience*, October 6, 2021, https://cso.org/experience/article/7349/the-mystery-of-schuberts-unfinished-symphony.

64. Roland Bainton, *Here I Stand: A Life of Martin Luther* (Nashville: Abingdon Press, 1978), 57.

65. Joshua J. Mark, "Martin Luther's 95 Theses," *World History Encyclopedia*, December 1, 2021, https://www.worldhistory.org/article/1891/martin-luthers-95-theses/.

𝒩OVEMBER

1. Otto Friedrich, *The End of the World: A History* (Madison, WI: Fromm International, 1986), 179.

2. Voltaire quoted in James Parton, *Life of Voltaire* (Boston: Houghton, Mifflin and Co., 1881), 209.

3. Harry Fielding Reid, "The Lisbon Earthquake of November 1, 1755," *Bulletin of the Seismological Society of America* 4, no. 2 (June 1914): 80.

4. T. D. Kendrick, *The Lisbon Earthquake* (Philadelphia: J. B. Lippincott Co., n.d.), 185.

5. Ellen G. White, *The Ministry of Healing* (Mountain View, CA: Pacific Press®, 1905), 377.

6. Ellen G. White, *Child Guidance* (Washington, DC: Review and Herald®, 1954), 564.

7. Bryan Wolfmueller, "Martin Luther's Preface to Romans," *World Wide Wolfmueller* (blog), May 30, 2019, https://wolfmueller.co/martin-luthers-preface-to-romans/.

8. Wolfmueller, "Preface to Romans."

9. Wolfmueller, "Preface to Romans."

10. Wolfmueller, "Preface to Romans."

11. Wolfmueller, "Preface to Romans."

12. Moses Hull, "The Mission of Spiritualism," *Advent Review and Sabbath Herald*, March 25, 1862, 131.

13. Ellen G. White, *Testimonies for the Church*, vol. 1 (Mountain View, CA: Pacific Press®, 1948), 428.

14. White, 426.

15. White, 427.

16. Ellen G. White, *Ministry of Healing*, 149.

17. Ellen G. White, *Christian Service* (Hagerstown, MD: Review and Herald®, 2002), 83.

18. Auguste Comte, *The Essential Comte*, trans. Margaret Clarke (New York: Barnes & Noble Books, 1974), 211.

19. Leon Trotsky, *The Revolution Betrayed: What Is the Soviet Union and Where Is It Going?* trans. Max Eastman (London: Faber and Faber, n.d.), 103, 104.

20. Albert Einstein quoted in David Bodanis, *E=mc2: A Biography of the World's Most Famous Equation* (London: Macmillan, 2000), 258, 259.

21. Ellen G. White, *The Great Controversy* (Nampa, ID: Pacific Press®, 2005), 486, 487.

22. Martin Luther, "No. 439," *Luther's Works*, vol. 54, Table Talk, ed. and trans. Theodore G. Tappert (Philadelphia: Fortress, 1967), 71.

23. Luther, no. 353.

24. Eustace Carey, *Memoir of William Carey, D.D.* (Hartford: Canfield and Robins, 1837), 467.

25. Ellen G. White, *Selected Messages*, book 1 (Washington, DC: Review and Herald®, 1958), 118.

26. Ellen G. White, *Letters and Manuscripts*, vol. 1 (1844–1868), Letter 8, 1851.

27. Arthur L. White, *The Early Years: 1827–1862*, Ellen

G. White Biography, vol. 1, (Hagerstown, MD: Review and Herald®, 1985), 491.

28. White, 492.

29. Frederick Douglass, *My Bondage and My Freedom* (New York: Miller, Orton & Mulligan, 1855), 186.

30. Kyle Idleman, *Gods at War* (Grand Rapids, MI: Zondervan, 2013), 34.

31. Born Gertrude Annie Hobbs, she went by Gert or Biddy.

32. Oswald Chambers, *My Utmost for His Highest* (London: Marshall, Morgan and Scott, 1927).

33. Chambers, January 18; emphasis in the original.

34. Ellen G. White, *The Desire of Ages* (Oakland, CA: Pacific Press®, 1898), 362.

35. " 'Loving Your Enemies,' Sermon Delivered at Dexter Avenue Baptist Church," The Martin Luther King Jr. Research and Education Institute, Stanford University, accessed July 20, 2022, https://kinginstitute.stanford.edu /king-papers/documents/loving-your-enemies-sermon -delivered-dexter-avenue-baptist-church.

36. Ellen G. White, *Life Sketches of Ellen G. White* (Mountain View, CA: Pacific Press®, 1915), 125.

37. White, 125.

38. White, 125.

39. Bonny Charlton quoted in David McDonnell, "Sir Bobby Charlton, Denis Law and Trevor Francis Pay Tribute to Pele on His 80th Birthday," Mirror, October 23, 2020, https://www.mirror.co.uk/sport/football/news/sir-bobby -charlton-denis-law-22891743.

40. Wasi Manazir, "The Best Quotes on Pele," Footie Central, March 7, 2016, https://www.footiecentral .com/20160307/best-quotes-on-pele/.

41. Ellen G. White, *Testimonies for the Church*, vol. 1 (Mountain View, CA: Pacific Press®, 1948), 113.

42. Alexander Young, *Chronicles of the Pilgrim Fathers of the Colony of Plymouth from 1602 to 1625* (Boston: Charles C. Little and James Brown, 1841), 396, 397.

43. Young, 397.

44. This motto appears in Edward A. Dowey, "Always to Be Reformed," in John C. Purdy, *Always Being Reformed: The Future of Church Education* (Philadelphia, PA: Geneva Press, 1985), 9, 10.

45. J. N. Andrews quoted in Ellen G. White, *Spiritual Gifts*, vol. 2 (Battle Creek, MI: James White, 1860), 117.

46. Uriah Smith, *The 2300 Days and the Sanctuary: Advent and Sabbath Tracts, No. 5* (Rochester, NY: Advent Review Office, 1854?), 10, 11.

47. "The Great Central Subject," *Advent Review and Sabbath Herald*, November 22, 1881, 328.

48. Ellen G. White, *Our High Calling* (Washington, DC: Review and Herald®, 1961), 16.

49. Joseph Fielding Smith, comp., "Scriptural Teachings of the Prophet Joseph Smith," Brigham Young University, 10, https://scriptures.byu.edu/tpjs/STPJS.pdf.

50. Ellen G. White, *Selected Messages*, book 1, 18.

51. Charles Darwin, *On the Origin of Species by Means of Natural Selection, or the Preservation of Favored Races in the Struggle for Life* (London: John Murray, 1859), 79, 244.

52. Darwin, 490.

53. Ellen G. White, *Desire of Ages*, 74.

54. *The Autobiography of Elder Joseph Bates* (Battle Creek, MI: Steam Press of the Seventh-day Adventist Publishing Association, 1868), 314.

55. Ellen G. White, *Counsels on Diet and Foods* (Washington, DC: Review and Herald®, 1938), 488.

56. Denis Leary, "Meat," Last.fm, accessed July 20, 2022, https://www.last.fm/music/Denis+Leary/_/Meat/+lyrics.

57. The Barna Group, "Survey Reveals the Books and Authors That Have Most Influenced Pastors," Barna, May 30, 2005, https://www.barna.com/research/survey-reveals-the -books-and-authors-that-have-most-influenced-pastors/.

58. Ken Makovsky, "Nobel: How He Built His Reputation," *Forbes*, November 7, 2011, https://www.forbes.com /sites/kenmakovsky/2011/11/07/nobel-how-he-built-his -reputation/?sh=1ebbd49b2d36.

59. Ellen G. White, *Christ's Object Lessons* (Battle Creek, MI: Review and Herald®, 1900), 411.

60. Martin Luther, "Large Catechism," in *Concordia: The Lutheran Confessions*, 2nd ed. (Saint Louis, MO: Concordia Publishing House, 2006), 408.

61. Martin Luther, *Luther's Works*, vol. 54, Table Talk edition, trans. Theodore G. Tappert (Philadelphia: Fortress, 1967), no. 17.

62. Mary Jane Haemig and Eric Lund, *Little Prayer Book, 1522 and A Simple Way to Pray, 1535*, Annotated Luther Study edition, (Minneapolis: Fortress, 2017), 257.

DECEMBER

1. Lin Van Buren, "Horatio Spafford," RootsWeb, accessed May 26, 2022, https://sites.rootsweb.com/~nyrensse /bio220.htm

2. Chris Field, "Horatio Gates Spafford Turns Tragedy Into Song," *Chris Field* (blog), October 20, 2008, https:// chrisfieldblog.com/2008/10/20/horatio-gates-spafford -turns-tragedy-into-song.

3. Lin Van Buren, "Horaio Spafford."

4. Horatio Gates Spafford, "It Is Well With My Soul," 1873, public domain.

5. F. E. Belden, "Wholly Thine," (1886) in *The Seventh -day Adventist Hymnal*, 308.

6. F. E. Belden, "Cover With His Life," (1899) in *The Seventh-day Adventist Hymnal*, 412.

7. Vernon J. Charlesworth, "A Shelter in the Time of Storm," (1880) in *The Seventh-day Adventist Hymnal*, 528.

8. F. E. Belden, "The Judgment Has Set" (1886) in *The Seventh-day Adventist Hymnal*, 604.

9. F. E. Belden, "We Know Not the Hour," (1886) in *The Seventh-day Adventist Hymnal*, 604.

10. F. E. Belden, "Joy By and By," (1886) in *The Seventh -day Adventist Hymnal*, 430.

11. Ellen G. White, Letter 15, 1895.

12. Ellen G. White, Letter 29, 1897.

13. Ellen G. White, *Steps to Christ* (Oakland, CA: Pacific Press®, 1892), 18.

14. Nick Vujicic, *Life Without Limits* (New York: Doubleday, 2010), 12; emphasis in original.

15. "International Volunteer Day 5 December," United Nations, accessed May 23, 2022, https://www.un.org/en /observances/volunteer-day/background.

16. "The First Adventist Week of Prayer—Stewardship," Stewardship Ministries, accessed May 26, 2022, https:// stewardship.adventist.org/the-first-adventist-week-of -prayer%E2%80%94stewardship.

17. H. L. Hastings, quoted in John W. Lea, *The Book of Books and Its Wonderful Story* (Philadelphia, PA: John W. Lea, 1922), 19.

18. Alison Ford, "Open the Book: Past, Present and Future," Diocese of St. Davids, accessed July 20, 2022, https://stdavids.churchinwales.org.uk/en/pobl-dewi/open-the-book-past-present-and-future/.

19. Ellen G. White, *Life Sketches of James White and Ellen G. White* (Battle Creek, MI: Seventh-day Adventist Publishing Association, 1888), 346.

20. White, 347, 348.

21. White, 349.

22. White, 347.

23. Arthur L. White, *The Early Years: 1827–1862,* Ellen G. White Biography, vol. 1, (Hagerstown, MD: Review and Herald®, 1985), 345.

24. White, 347.

25. White, 346.

26. Ellen G. White, *Life Sketches*, 330.

27. Arthur L. White, *Early Years*, 348, 349; emphasis in original.

28. United Nations General Assembly, "Universal Declaration of Human Rights," United Nations, accessed April 19, 2022, https://www.un.org/en/about-us/universal-declaration-of-human-rights.

29. There is some question whether Francisco Hermógenes Ramos Mexía was born on November 20 or December 11 in 1773. For the purposes of this book, I've chosen to use the December 11 date.

30. Milton S. Afonso, in Manuel Vásquez, *Milton Afonso: Vida e Obra,* trans. Beth Vollmer Chagas (Tatuí, SP, Brazil: Casa Publicadora Brasileira, 2004), 89.

31. Ellen G. White, *Testimonies for the Church*, vol. 4 (Mountain View, CA: Pacific Press®, 1948), 226, 227.

32. Samuel Johnson, *The Lives of the English Poets*, vol. 1 (Leipzig: Bernhard Tauchnitz, 1858), 42.

33. German original: "*Es wird niemals so viel gelogen wie vor des Wahl, während des Krieges und nach der Jagd.*" For the authenticity of this statement, see Otto von Bismarck, Quotes of Famous People, accessed July 20, 2022, https://quotepark.com/quotes/1766970-otto-von-bismarck-at-no-time-there-is-more-lying-than-before-the-ele/.

34. Ellen G. White, *The Desire of Ages* (Oakland, CA: Pacific Press®, 1898), 323.

35. Henry C. Roberts, trans. and ed., *The Complete Prophecies of Nostradamus* (New York: Crown Publishers, 1947), 336.

36. Roberts, 25.

37. Joint Resolution of Congress, "The Bill of Rights: A Transcription," *National Archives*, accessed April 19, 2022, https://www.archives.gov/founding-docs/bill-of-rights-transcript.

38. Ellen G. White, *Last Day Events* (Nampa, ID: Pacific Press®, 1992), 133.

39. Ellen G. White, *Early Writings* (Battle Creek, MI: Seventh-day Adventist Publishing Association, 1882), 41.

40. Edwin R. Thiele, "The Chronology of the Kings of Judah and Israel," *Journal of Near Eastern Studies* 3, no. 3 (July 1944): 137–186.

41. Edwin R. Thiele, *The Mysterious Numbers of the Hebrew Kings* (Chicago: University of Chicago Press, 1951). Revised in 1966 and 1994.

42. Ellen G. White, *Steps to Christ*, 107.

43. Joe Wheeler, "Will Carleton's 'The First Settler's Story,' " *Wednesdays With Dr. Joe*, July 24, 2013, https://joewheeler.wordpress.com/2013/07/24/will-carletons-the-first-settlers-story/.

44. Wheeler.

45. Wheeler; emphasis in the original.

46. William A Spicer quoted in Daniel A. Ochs and Grace Lillian Ochs, *The Past and the Presidents* (Nashville, TN: Southern Publishing Association, 1974), 143, 144.

47. James White, *Sketches of the Christian Life and Public Labors of William Miller* (Battle Creek, MI: Steam Press, 1875), 300–304.

48. White, 315.

49. White, 394.

50. Michael G. Hasel, "The Power of Prayer," *Adventist Review*, North American Division edition, April 1997, 9.

51. Hasel, 9.

52. History.com Editors, "Pan Am Flight 103 Explodes Over Scotland—1989," History, accessed May 26, 2022, https://www.history.com/this-day-in-history/pan-am-flight-103-explodes-over-scotland.

53. Ellen G. White, *Desire of Ages*, 224.

54. Melissa DePaiva, "God Helped Me Forgive," *Southwestern Union Record*, March 2012, 11.

55. Tertullian, Kevin Knight, ed., "Apology," trans. S. Thelwall, from *Ante-Nicene Fathers*, vol. 3, ed. Alexander Roberts, James Donaldson, and A. Cleveland Coxe (Buffalo, NY: Christian Literature Publishing, 1885), http://www.newadvent.org/fathers/0301.htm.

56. Ellen G. White, *Experiences in Australia* (1891), 10, accessed April 19, 2022, http://text.egwwritings.org/book/b12670.

57. Ellen G. White, *Life Sketches of Ellen G. White* (Mountain View, CA: Pacific Press®, 1915), 338, 339.

58. Ellen G. White, *The Adventist Home* (Washington, DC: Review and Herald®, 1952), 477.

59. Louis Cassels, "The Parable of the Birds" (United Press International, 1959).

60. Ellen G. White, *Steps to Christ*, 21.

61. Jennifer Rosenberg, "World War II Japanese Soldier Lt. Hiroo Onoda," ThoughtCo., updated February 24, 2019, https://www.thoughtco.com/war-is-over-please-come-out-1779995.

62. Ellen G. White, *Testimonies for the Church*, vol. 3 (Mountain View, CA: Pacific Press®, 1948), 497.

63. Herman Bauman, *I Am Saved and, Yes, I Am Perfect* (n.p.: Xlibris, 2011), 227; Robert W. Jackson and Fabian E. Pollo, "The legacy of Professor Adolf Lorenz, the 'bloodless surgeon of Vienna' " January 17, 2004, doi: 10.1080/08998280.2004.11927952.

64. Bauman, 228.

65. Ellen G. White, Letter 23, 1890.